THE PROMISE OF PUBLIC SERVICE

In the United States, new government employees begin their careers by pledging their allegiance to the Constitution and by committing to conscientious service dedicated to solving public problems. But what do public servants get in return? For many, a chance to serve provides public servants with a higher purpose as well as professional and personal meaning in their lives and careers. In *The Promise of Public Service: Ideas and Examples for Effective Service*, Michael M. Stahl, a 40-year veteran in the executive and legislative branches of state and federal service, explores what makes public servants effective by offering useful ideas and examining the accomplishments of public servants throughout American history. The book blends practical ideas and illustrative profiles as Stahl reflects seriously on theoretical frameworks, skillfully synthesizing practical experience with rigorous theoretical and conceptual analysis. Undergraduate- and graduate-level courses will benefit from *The Promise of Public Service* as a resource, and practitioners of public service in all its forms will benefit from these ideas and examples at any stage of their careers.

Michael M. Stahl is a 40-year veteran of public service in the legislative and executive branches in state and federal government in the United States. He led organizations ranging from 10 to 3,100 people, managing programs to provide grants and loans to schools for asbestos abatement, ensuring compliance with all environmental laws, and working with international partners to solve environmental problems in other countries and regions of the world. He taught for almost 20 years as an Adjunct Faculty member in the Master of Public Administration (MPA) Program at George Mason University in Fairfax, Virginia. He was awarded both the Meritorious Presidential Rank Award and the Distinguished Presidential Rank Award by the U.S. government, and the Distinguished Career Service Award by the U.S. Environmental Protection Agency. He has authored several articles on public administration, including, most recently, *Sustaining the Public Service Mentality*, and *New Imperatives for Public Managers*. He holds an MPA from the University of Missouri, a Leadership Coaching Certificate from Georgetown University, and is the CEO of Stahl Strategic, LLC, a coaching and consulting firm in Staunton, Virginia.

THE PROMISE OF PUBLIC SERVICE

Ideas and Examples for Effective Service

Michael M. Stahl

NEW YORK AND LONDON

Cover image: Getty Images

First published 2023
by Routledge
605 Third Avenue, New York, NY 10158

and by Routledge
4 Park Square, Milton Park, Abingdon, Oxon, OX14 4RN

Routledge is an imprint of the Taylor & Francis Group, an informa business

Library of Congress Cataloging-in-Publication Data
Names: Stahl, Michael M., author.
Title: The promise of public service: ideas and examples
for effective service/Michael M. Stahl.
Identifiers: LCCN 2021062657 (print) | LCCN 2021062658 (ebook) |
ISBN 9781032209883 (Hardback) | ISBN 9781032209876 (Paperback) |
ISBN 9781003266235 (eBook)
Subjects: LCSH: Civil service–United States. |
United States–Officials and employees.
Classification: LCC JK692 .S72 2022 (print) | LCC JK692 (ebook) |
DDC 352.6/30973–dc23/eng/20220308
LC record available at https://lccn.loc.gov/2021062657
LC ebook record available at https://lccn.loc.gov/2021062658

ISBN: 9781032209883 (hbk)
ISBN: 9781032209876 (pbk)
ISBN: 9781003266235 (ebk)

DOI: 10.4324/9781003266235

Typeset in Bembo
by Newgen Publishing UK

My father, Albert "Bud" Stahl and my mother Ann Mary Stahl, who shaped me and whose presence I still feel in my life today, and my brother John who pointed me toward the path to public service.

My wife, Ann Pontius, who ended my long search for my life's partner when I met her at the U.S. EPA. Her help in proofreading, editing, and keeping me focused on finishing the book was indispensable.

The surgeons, cardiologists, other physicians, nurses, and staff of the Pauley Heart Center at the Virginia Commonwealth University Medical Center, for their skill, caring, and professionalism in steering me through two surgeries, one to implant an artificial heart and the second for the actual heart transplant. (And to my donor family, who remain anonymous to this day.)

The teachers and mentors at the Riverview Gardens School District in St. Louis County, Missouri, the University of Missouri – St. Louis, the University of Missouri – Columbia, and in federal service at the U.S. Consumer Product Safety Commission and the U.S. Environmental Protection Agency.

The men and women, who served with me and are currently serving at the U.S. Environmental Protection Agency, are always faithful to their mission of "protecting human health and the environment."

The St. Louis Cardinals baseball team, the sustained excellence of which over the years has been an inspiration to me since the day I walked into Busch Stadium in St. Louis for the 1964 World Series.

CONTENTS

A BLESSING FOR PUBLIC SERVANTS

As you enter public service, be aware you are joining a profession with a noble legacy. Although not everyone in public service can "bend the arc of history," you can contribute to the American democratic project by being conscientious about your duty, developing new and improved ways of delivering services, and increasing the fairness and integrity of the organizations of which you are a part.

May you be able to work on public issues or problems that you find endlessly fascinating and rewarding, full of opportunities to use yourself for the good of others.

May you be fortunate enough to work for effective leaders for whom you feel willing to spend yourself in pursuit of their goals and aspirations for the nation and the world.

May you work with and for people you like and respect, learning and teaching as you travel your journey with them, seeing them learn to achieve together and be recognized for what they create.

May you listen with patience and empathy to those you serve, using what power you have to help them achieve what they seek, whether it is to be granted simple respect, or some benefit which you may be able to bestow.

May you supervise people with a fair and just hand, putting the people you work with in the best position to succeed, keeping them focused on the importance of the mission, and stirring them to keep sight of the nobility of public service.

May you reach the conclusion of your public service career without "commitments undefined, convictions unexpressed, and service unfulfilled." May you have the satisfaction of knowing that your energy was spent solving public problems, collaborating with colleagues, making government more transparent, accessible, and effective.

FOREWORD

This book is focused on the important work that career public servants perform for the nation, and it will attempt to serve several purposes:

To **reaffirm** the choice of thousands of Americans currently serving in local, state, and federal governments, and associated organizations, to continue their careers in public service;

To **encourage** undergraduate and graduate students in public affairs/administration who are preparing themselves to be practitioners in government agencies, interest groups, non-profit organizations, and private sector contractors, consultants, and co-producers to continue to pursue careers in public service;

To **support** in-service professionals aspiring to management positions or those who are newly serving managers in their organizations;

To **advise** faculty members of public affairs/administration degree programs about what is important for students to know, based on the author's 40 years of experience in public service at the federal and state levels;

To **provide a booster shot** to in-service professionals who have reached a point in their careers where they need to refresh themselves about the purposes they wanted to serve and the accomplishments they had hoped to achieve;

To **contribute** to the ongoing dialogue about leadership in the management of public programs.

In achieving these purposes, this book can serve as a field guide or source book for people contemplating or pursuing careers in public service, or already serving as managers or leaders in public agencies or public interest groups.

THE OUTLINE OF THIS BOOK

Chapter 1 describes the target audiences for this book, the sense of purpose public service careers can provide, and the covenant individuals enter into when they take their oath and get the opportunity to serve the public. Chapter 2 explores the attitude to which public servants should aspire, a blend of idealism, altruism, pragmatism, receptivity, moral courage, perseverance, and resilience. Chapter 2 also encourages a career-long openness to learning and new ideas, by maintaining a student's orientation to public affairs/administration. Finally, Chapter 2 also describes the value of having mentors and the benefits of serving as a mentor in the middle and later stages of a career. Chapter 3 offers ideas for leading public organizations, based on the concepts of public management developed by Mark H. Moore and Malcolm K. Sparrow of Harvard University's Kennedy School of Government. Chapter 4 describes the challenges of implementing public policy and using networks of organizations and individuals to carry out public policies. Chapter 5 explores the issues surrounding government performance, and why measuring the performance of government programs requires critical skills for public managers/leaders now and for the foreseeable future. Chapter 6 describes and celebrates government's greatest achievements over the previous 50 years. Chapter 7 suggests qualities public servants will need in order to be effective and to ensure the nation's continued progress. The end of each chapter provides a "key concepts" summary and reference notes will appear at the conclusion of each chapter.

Part II of this book provides a set of Profiles of Heroes in Public Service (e.g., Harry Truman, Robert Kennedy, Rachel Carson, and Frances Perkins, among others). These are all persons who provide a model of public service, who exhibit qualities worth emulating, and who have inspired me by their example. This is followed by an Epilogue section describing the lessons learned from the public service heroes. The Appendix ("Ripples of Hope") offers a set of uplifting quotations that can be used as inspiration and a reminder to public servants of the purposes that brought them into public service.

AUTHOR'S LIFE IN PUBLIC SERVICE

I started in public service as a state probation and parole officer managing a case-load of 120 adult felons on probation or parole, after earning a bachelor's degree in Administration of Justice at the University of Missouri – St. Louis in 1975. After working for three years as an officer, I then pursued a master's degree in Public Administration at the University of Missouri, while simultaneously working as a Research Assistant to the Majority Floor Leader of the Missouri Senate. Upon graduating from "Mizzou," I was accepted into the U.S. government's Presidential Management Intern Program (in its current iteration, the program is now the Presidential Management Fellows Program).

I went to work at the U.S. Consumer Safety Commission (CPSC) in Washington, DC, working in program evaluation, Congressional Affairs, and as a Special Assistant to the Executive Director. After three years, I moved to the U.S. Environmental Protection Agency (EPA) in the wake of Administrator Anne Gorsuch's tenure, starting in the Office of Administration (including personnel, contracts, and grants). I then moved to EPA's Office of Toxic Substances, where I was one of three managers in the asbestos-in-schools program. I implemented two Acts of Congress to distribute $50 million per year in loans and grants to schools for asbestos abatement, and a second law ordering EPA to write regulations requiring schools to inspect and abate asbestos hazards. (EPA chose to use a negotiated rulemaking process that involved all stakeholders.)

After six years at the EPA, I was appointed to positions in the Senior Executive Service (SES – the Federal government's highest level for career civil servants), including the Director of Compliance Monitoring for the pesticides and toxics substances program, and then six years as a Deputy Assistant Administrator for the Agency's newly organized compliance and enforcement program for all environmental laws.

I then served for nine years as the Director of the Office of Compliance where I developed a slate of performance measures to assess and guide the national program for compliance and enforcement programs. I served as a featured practitioner at Harvard University's executive education course entitled *Strategic Management of Regulatory and Enforcement Agencies* in October 2010 and October 2011. I served as a guest instructor at the Bren School of Environmental Management at the University of California – Santa Barbara, teaching a four-day workshop entitled *Implementing Environmental Laws and Programs* in February 2008 and February 2010. I also conducted many training programs in other nations (12 countries in Africa, Asia, Europe, and Latin America) to help them develop environmental compliance and enforcement programs. I then moved to EPA's Office of International Affairs, where I ultimately became Deputy Assistant Administrator, managing bilateral relationships with other countries to work cooperatively on environmental problems.

During my 20-plus years in the Senior Executive Service, I also held an Adjunct Faculty appointment in the Master of Public Administration program at George Mason University in Fairfax, Virginia, teaching graduate students in courses on program planning and implementation.

During my career in federal service, I earned two EPA Gold Medals for my work in the asbestos program (1986) and my contribution to the reorganization of the Agency's compliance and enforcement program (1995), and I was twice awarded the Senior Executive Service's highest awards for my achievements, first for Meritorious Executive in 2002, and then for Distinguished Executive in 2008. As I retired, I was awarded EPA's Distinguished Career Service Award for my efforts to "identify, define, produce, and measure public value in domestic and international environmental programs."

After 40 years in public service, and after returning to work from receiving a heart transplant at Virginia Commonwealth University Medical Center in Richmond, Virginia, in June 2014, I retired in January 2015. I have formed an LLC (Stahl Strategic) that serves as a platform from which I do leadership coaching, organizational consulting, management training, and public affairs courses for life-long learning programs.

My career experience offers a rich vein of ideas that can be helpful to current and future public servants. I was fortunate to serve simultaneously as an academician and a practitioner, staying abreast of evolving ideas in public affairs/administration literature, and as a practitioner who could apply the latest thinking to operating programs. This book is an attempt to pass those ideas to others who will benefit from them.

EXPLANATION OF NOTES

The Notes sections of this book provide the customary reference information about resources quoted in each section of the text.

In addition, the Notes sections provide information from my own experience in public service, which will illuminate or further explain concepts or assertions in the text. These notes, taken together, provide a memoir-like aspect for the book and are intended to bolster the text with doses of my own experience.

The Bibliography includes works cited in the text, and works consulted in connection with specific sections of the text.

PART I

Ideas for Effective Public Service

1

INTRODUCTION

The Oath and the Opportunity

"I [state name] do solemnly swear or affirm that I will faithfully support and defend the Constitution of the United States against all enemies foreign and domestic; that I will bear true faith and allegiance to the same; that I take this obligation freely without any mental reservation or purpose of evasion; and that I will well and faithfully discharge the duties of the office on which I am about to enter. So help me God."

With these words, brand new federal employees begin their careers working for the federal government. They pledge their allegiance to the Constitution, and they pledge to faithfully discharge their duties. Public servants enter a covenant: they pledge to faithfully discharge their duties and, in turn, receive the opportunity to serve, to achieve things for the greater good, and to derive meaning from their lives.

Elements of the New Public Service[1]

Public servants include more than just those who serve in federal, state, and local governments. Succeeding generations of public servants increasingly are moving across sectors including government agencies, to interest groups and NGOs (nongovernment organizations), to contracting and consulting firms, all with a stake in public policy and issues.

Who are the members of the new public service? The definition of public service has transformed and expanded as young people have looked to begin careers in public service, and as the number of positions in government has been reduced.

DOI: 10.4324/9781003266235-2

Public service no longer only means service in government agencies, but broader service in multiple sectors.

Similarly, public service is no longer about only "government," it is about serving a role in "governance," much of which takes place outside of government. The academic programs (i.e., institutes, schools, and departments of public administration, public affairs, or public policy) that have previously prepared students for jobs in government now see value in preparing students for jobs in various destinations. The National Association of Schools of Public Affairs and Administration describes master's degrees in Public Administration and master's degrees in Public Policy as "the credential for work in ... legislative advocacy ... nonprofit associations ... charitable foundations ... international affairs... service organizations ... agency management ... and every level of government imaginable."

Those preparing for roles in public service are destined for jobs in the government sector, the nonprofit sector, or the private sector, and over the course of a career are likely to serve in any or all of these sectors.

The government sector on which this book focuses includes those positions in federal, state, and local governments in executive, legislative, and judicial branches. This book is addressed primarily to those in unelected career-service positions selected through merit systems and political appointments, and though the primary focus of this book is not on elected officials, it contains many ideas that can be useful to such officials.

The nonprofit sector on which this book focuses includes those positions in advocacy or interest groups. These groups lobby legislative bodies about pending legislation, represent particular viewpoints about regulatory provisions and their implementation in front of executive agencies, and speak out publicly about how pending regulations will affect their interests.

The aspect of the private sector on which this book is focused includes the following: (1) contractors who are co-producing government services or products, (2) consultants who work with the government to produce studies about key aspects of government policy and help regulated entities ensure their compliance with government requirements, and (3) the community of regulated entities who can help suggest adjustments to regulatory policies after an initial period of implementation.

The people in these three sectors are the primary focus of this book, and the advice and ideas in the book are for their benefit. These are the people who, in recent times, have been referred to derisively as the "deep state" or the "unelected bureaucrats," or more charitably as the "steady state."[2] They are also the people who have pledged their careers to the nation, will serve honorably in difficult times, and ensure that the idea of America survives and advances.

Seeking Their Purpose

The commitment that public servants make when they take their oath of office is to serve, to the best of their ability, mankind's greatest experiment: sustaining democracy in the form of the United States of America. But these public servants get something very valuable in return. Simply put, *they receive an opportunity to partake of a higher purpose that will aid their search for what they personally find meaningful in their lives*. In return, citizens receive a commitment for conscientious service dedicated to solving public problems.

Though there is no equivalent English word, in ancient Greece, the word *arete* (pronounce ahr-i-tey) referred to excellence of any kind, reaching one's full potential, and moral virtue. The *arete* of something is the highest quality stage it can achieve. The meaning of the word changes depending on what is being described, as everything has its own particular *arete*. For Aristotle, something is excellent when it manifests its own unique purpose, and he felt that human excellence involves the correct use of reason in connection with moral choice. Lance Morrow, in his article "George Marshall, The Last Great American," for the *Smithsonian* magazine, said "The Greeks ... would have assigned George Washington and Marshall to the realm of *arete* or virtue – the self-fulfilled in noble accomplishments for the state."

Viktor E. Frankel, the Viennese psychiatrist, Holocaust survivor, and founder of the *logotherapy* school of psychiatry, has written in his groundbreaking book, *Man's Search for Meaning*, that "striving to find meaning in one's life is the primary motivational force in man ... he needs ... the call of a potential meaning waiting to be fulfilled by him."[3] For many public servants, this gift of meaningfulness in their lives is the principal reason for pursuing a career in public service, in spite of the many soul-crushing aspects of life in a bureaucracy or working in an administration or for a leader with whom they disagree.

The call to public service may be different for every person who hears it. Whether inspired by heroic words from a leader (for example, John Fitzgerald Kennedy's words from his inaugural speech to "ask not what your country can do for you, ask what you can do for your country"); heroic deeds from a leader, an activist, or a citizen; a public problem that needs a dedicated effort to find a solution; or the unique circumstances of an individual's life; all these and more can lead to answering the call for public service.

As Gregg Levoy writes in his book *Callings, Finding and Following an Authentic Life*,[4] calls may be to *do* something, or to *be* something. They may be calls toward something or away from something, calls to change something, review our commitment to it, or come back to it in an entirely new way. Levoy quotes writer P.L. Travers who points out that calls and the questions they raise may provide "a spark of instructive fire."[5]

John Kennedy said that "one person can make a difference, and everyone should try." But even those who are committed, dedicated, and motivated can feel overwhelmed by the gravity and intractable nature of the world's problems and challenges, such as climate change, income inequality, and poverty. Facing these problems with only our gridlocked legislative bodies, sclerotic institutions, and divided politics gives rise to a kind of "doom loop," as former U.S. Ambassador to the United Nations (UN) and now Director of the Agency for International

Development Samantha Power describes it.[6] Individuals considering careers in public service and looking at the scope of these problems and the tools available to address them realize they cannot single-handedly fix them and too often see their role as futile or opt to do nothing.

But big problems are most often addressed by a sequence of small steps and solutions, sometimes over weeks, and sometimes over decades. Power describes an approach she used in her days at the UN, in which she would urge her staff to "shrink the change" they wanted to achieve, realizing that even if they could not solve the whole problem, there must be something they could do.[7] Making even incremental progress, the prospect of **contributing to improvement** in some way, in our own sphere of influence, using the tools we can provide or which are available to us can become our way of making a difference.

Robert F. Kennedy, in a speech delivered on June 6, 1966, to students at the University of Cape Town in South Africa for their Day of Affirmation celebration, eloquently described a way in which public servants can view their work:

> Few will have the greatness to bend history itself, but each of us can work to change a small portion of events, and in the total of all those acts will be written the history of this generation. **It is from numberless diverse acts of courage and belief that human history is shaped. Each time a man stands up for an ideal, or acts to improve the lot of others, he sends forth a tiny ripple of hope, and crossing each other from a million different centers of energy and daring, those ripples can build a current that can sweep down the mightiest walls of oppression and resistance.**[8]

Taking the oath to faithfully execute your duties as a public servant earns the opportunity to serve others, be dedicated to a cause larger than yourself, and work on a public problem(s) that needs solving. Making contributions to improve myriad conditions and ensure the well-being of others are worthy purposes of a career in public service. **Every contribution to improvement can be seen as a "ripple of hope" sent forth to make things better for individuals, the nation, and the world.**

Key Concepts

1. By taking the oath of office to faithfully discharge the duties of their office, public servants also earn the opportunity to serve the public and make contributions to the welfare of the nation. This is "the promise of public service."

2. Public servants include people serving in federal, state, and local institutions (i.e., legislative bodies, courts, executive agencies), and people serving in advocacy or interest groups (nongovernment agencies or NGOs), and private

sector actors in contracting and consulting firms. All are part of the field of "governance."

3. The call to public service may come from any number of different sources, but it is a call that offers the chance for meaning in a person's life. It may be a call to **do** something or to **be** something.

4. The call to public service opens up opportunities to **contribute to improvement**, and in Robert Kennedy's words, to **"send forth tiny ripples of hope"** that can make things better for individuals, the nation, and the world.

Notes

1 A definitive discussion of the changing shape of the public service can be found in *The New Public Service*, by Paul Light (Brookings Institution Press, Washington, DC, 1999). Also see *The New Public Service, Serving Not Steering*, by Janet V. Denhardt and Robert B. Denhardt (M.E. Sharpe, Armonk, NY, 2003).

2 "Deep State" is the term popularized by Steve Bannon, formerly Chief Strategist of the White House staff. "Steady State" is the phrase used by Anonymous, the noted Trump Administration official (and author of *A Warning*, Hachette Book Group, New York, NY, November 2019), to refer more benignly to career civil servants, though the use of the term "steady" has, in my opinion, too much of the connotation of "inert." Based on my 40 years working closely with these public servants, I believe the more accurate terms for these dedicated individuals is the "responsible state" or the "competent state." This more accurately reflects their primary contributions to public service: their conscientious approach, their willingness to be held accountable for their work, and their expertise in their areas of public policy. (Furthermore, these terms more precisely distinguish them from the Trump administration crop of politically appointed executive branch officials.)

3 Viktor E. Frankel, *Man's Search for Meaning* (Beacon Press, Boston, MA, 2006). Frankel is seen as the father of an approach to psychiatry known as logotherapy. "Logos" is the Greek word for "meaning," and patients undergoing logotherapy embark on a search for what is meaningful in their lives.

4 Gregg Levoy, *Callings, Finding and Following an Authentic Life* (Three Rivers Press, New York, NY, 1997).

5 In my own case, the "spark of instructive fire" came to me while running for Student Council president at my high school in St. Louis County, Missouri in 1970. At a particular point in my campaign, I became distinctly aware that my candidacy would have ramifications for the path I would choose for the rest of my life, whether or not I won the election. It affirmed my interest in politics and public affairs and it set before me a life-long desire to serve.

6 Samantha Power, *The Education of an Idealist, a Memoir* (HarperCollins, New York, NY, 2019).

7 Chip and Dan Heath, *Switch: How to Change Things When Change Is Hard* (Currency/ Penguin Random House, New York, NY, 2010).

8 I discovered this quote from Robert F. Kennedy's Day of Affirmation Speech at the University of Cape Town, South Africa, when I was in graduate school in public administration at the University of Missouri. I immediately had it printed and mounted in a frame, which hung in every one of my offices in my 40 years career in public service. It served as a daily reminder of my purpose. I have come to think of it as my own public service creed.

Bibliography

Anonymous. *A Warning.* New York, NY: Hachette Book Group, 2019.

Denhardt, Janet V. and Robert Denhardt. *The New Public Service: Shaping Not Steering.* Armonk, NY: M.E. Sharpe, 2003.

Frankel, Victor E. *Man's Search for Meaning.* Boston, MA: Beacon Press, 2006.

Heath, Chip and Dan Heath. *Switch: How to Change Things When Change Is Hard.* New York, NY: Crown Business, 2010.

Kennedy, Robert. Town, South Africa, MPEG-4, 33:52, 1966. www.jfklibrary.org/asset-viewer/day-of-affirmation-address june6-1966.

Kennedy, Robert F. "Day of Affirmation Address." June 6, 1966. Cape.

Levoy, Gregg. *Callings: Finding and Following an Authentic Life.* New York, NY: Three Rivers Press, 1997.

Light, Paul. *The New Public Service.* Washington, DC: Brookings Institute Press, 1999.

Power, Samantha. *The Education of an Idealist: A Memoir.* New York, NY: HarperCollins, 2019.

2

THE ATTITUDE OF A PUBLIC SERVANT[1]

Each one in public service has his or her own story, and motives. But I believe … you will find that those who serve – no matter how outwardly tough or jaded or egotistical – are in their heart of hearts, romantics and idealists. And optimists. We actually believe we can make the lives of others better, that we can make a positive difference in the life of the greatest country in the history of the world

Former U.S. Secretary of Defense Robert Gates, from a
speech at Texas A&M University, 2007

Public servants need to consider the attitude they will use as they approach the challenges of working to develop and implement solutions to public problems. They need an approach that helps them identify and work toward the best outcomes for the public, but which is tempered by an understanding of the practical implications of their actions. Put another way, public servants need to select aspirational goals, while simultaneously remaining realistic about what can be accomplished.

We must deal with the world as it is. We must get things done. But idealism, high aspirations, and deep convictions are not incompatible with the most practical and efficient of programs. There is no basic inconsistency between ideals and realistic possibilities. There is no separation between the deepest desires of the heart and mind and the rational application of human effort to solve human problems … **The future does not belong to those who are content with today, apathetic towards common problems and their fellow man alike, timid and fearful in the face of new ideas**

DOI: 10.4324/9781003266235-3

and bold projects. Rather, it will belong to those who can blend passion, reason, and courage in a personal commitment to the ideals and great enterprises of American society.

Robert F. Kennedy[2]

Necessary Elements

The attitude of a public servant needs to combine several elements into a mixture that can be called upon as needed over the course of a career. Among the elements that need to be present in the attitude of a public servant are idealism, altruism, pragmatism, receptivity, moral courage, perseverance, and resilience.

Idealism

Some men see things as they are, and ask why? I dream things that never were and say, why not?

George Bernard Shaw, used by Robert F Kennedy in his 1968 presidential campaign[3]

Ideals offer a standard of perfection or excellence that can serve as an ultimate objective or aim of an endeavor. Ideals are aspirational, often viewed (sometimes prematurely or unfairly) as impractical or beyond our reach. President John F. Kennedy used to describe himself as "an idealist without illusions."

But ideals have value in public policy and in public discourse, serving as important benchmarks for achievement of public goals or outcomes. They need to be considered in the process of developing mission statements, goals, and objectives for public organizations and programs.

Altruism

Altruism is the principle and moral practice of concern for the welfare and happiness of other human beings. Altruists exhibit an unselfish regard for or devotion to the welfare of others. Altruism can be thought of as a primary motivator of those seeking careers in public service, a way of giving expression to their compassion or empathy.

These feelings of altruism can be an antidote to the bureaucratic hazard of defining and operating an organization or program as an end unto itself. Altruism is a vehicle for staying focused on who the organization or program is truly designed to serve.

Pragmatism

Public servants need an attitude that is grounded in practical possibilities. While they should never lose sight of the idealistic and altruistic possibilities or options that might be available to them, they need to be aware of: (1) the limits of the organization's fiscal and human resources, (2) the authority available to address a public problem, and (3) the capacity of their organization to engage a particular problem. These limitations should also be shared in initial briefings with newly arrived political appointees who need to understand the full scope of their responsibilities and their organization's capacity to meet those responsibilities.[4]

Receptivity

The ability to be open-minded and take in and consider new ideas, weigh their implications, and be willing to implement those that represent improvements over the status quo, is crucial to making progress inside bureaucracies. When public servants become leaders of organizations, they should operate their organizations as a **"marketplace of ideas"** in which there is receptivity to new ideas and the best ideas can be adopted.

Moral Courage

Robert F. Kennedy, in his famous Day of Affirmation Speech at the University of Cape Town in South Africa in June 1966, said that "moral courage is a rarer commodity than bravery in battle or great intelligence, yet is the one essential vital quality for those who seek to change a world which yields most painfully to change."[5]

Moral courage involves the bravery to take action for moral reasons despite the risk of adverse consequences. Courage is required to take action when one has doubts or fears about the consequences, and moral courage, therefore, requires deliberation and careful thought.

Perseverance

Energy and persistence conquer all things.

Benjamin Franklin

During a public service career, there will be many instances when obstacles will block efforts to change or improve the performance of individuals or organizations. Public servants need to be aware of these obstacles, understand their causes, adapt and learn to work with them, overcome them, or to move them so they no longer obstruct progress.

This will require public servants to develop the ability to resolutely persist in a position or organization in spite of counter influences, opposition, or discouragement. It will often be the case that personal or organizational goals that require our attention will take long periods of time to come to fruition.

Perseverance also can lead to incremental progress – taking an increment of improvement now with the intention of returning to the same project again to push for more progress later.[6] The concept of "shrinking the change" (discussed previously in Chapter 1, cited by Samantha Power) is a way of persevering in the face of opposition or obstacles.

Resilience

> human beings are not born once and for all on the day their mothers give birth to them, but ... life obliges them over and over again to give birth to themselves.
>
> *Gabriel Garcia Marquez, Love in the Time of Cholera*

In their book *Resilience/Why Things Bounce Back*, authors Andrew Zolli and Ann Marie Healy point out that in defining resilience, different fields use the term to mean slightly different things. In engineering, resilience generally refers to the degree to which a structure or building can return to a baseline state after being disturbed. In ecology, it connotes an ecosystem's ability to resist being irrevocably degraded. In psychology, it signifies the capacity of an individual to deal effectively with trauma. In business, it is used to mean putting in place backups (e.g. of data and resources) to ensure continuous operations in the face of disaster. The authors point out that these definitions have two essential aspects: continuity and recovery in the face of change. They offer their own definition of resilience as *the capacity of a system, enterprise, or person to maintain its core purpose and integrity in the face of dramatically changed circumstances.*[7]

In summary, resilience is the ability to bounce back. People who are resilient are capable of functioning with a sense of core purpose, meaning, and forward momentum in the face of trauma. Developmental psychologists have helped define a quality they call *ego-resiliency*, that is, the capacity to overcome, steer through, or bounce back from adversity. This is a very useful trait for public servants.

Using the Elements to Serve the Public

These qualities – idealism, altruism, pragmatism, receptivity, moral courage, perseverance, and resilience – can be called forth in response to particular situations and the interplay of them is, in many ways, the principal challenge of serving the public.

When engaged in strategic planning exercises in which public servants are developing organizational statements of mission, goals, and objectives, turn to **idealism** to think broadly about organizational purposes and outcomes.

When developing processes to deliver specific services, turn to **altruism** to help determine the most effective means to deliver these services, and to **pragmatism** and **perseverance** to set up the most efficient way to get these services to their intended beneficiaries.

When confronted with a request or directive that is clearly inappropriate, or even illegal, turn to **moral courage** to take action or resist in spite of doubts or fears about the consequences. Moral courage is also needed when there is fierce opposition to a proposed action: first, it is needed to listen to and consider opposing views; and second, it is needed to proceed with the proposed action or a modified form of it.

When presented with a new idea or, more radically, a paradigm shift that will change organizational structures and practices, turn to **receptivity** and open-mindedness as a way of taking in and considering new approaches. Public servants need to evaluate whether these ideas are a net improvement over current practice. They need to have an openness to new ideas that allows those ideas to have standing in the marketplace of ideas they are willing to consider.

When Congressional budget proposals call for a program or agency to be reduced by significant amounts leading to reductions in existing staff or dollars, or when Congress fails to pass a budget proposal into law and forces most or all agencies of government to shut down for indefinite periods, **resilience** becomes a necessity. The ability to discontinue temporarily all planned activities for a shutdown and then breathe life back into those plans at the conclusion of the shutdown will test the patience and perseverance of most public servants during the course of their careers.

In the last analysis, public servants need to carry an attitude throughout their career that balances the idealistic and altruistic with the pragmatic and possible. They need to be smart about when to call forth each of these elements.

Public servants need to persevere against all manner of obstacles – insufficient authority, resource shortages, lack of expertise and capacity, and incompetent or corrupt political leadership. These challenges add to the difficulty of doing their important and vital work. But if they are willing to persevere, they can use their time and talent toward improving the nation and the world.

Maintaining the Student Mindset

> Leadership and learning are indispensable to each other.
>
> *John F. Kennedy*

Remaining open to new ideas throughout a public service career is important to being an effective leader. It is very useful to have a foot in two camps – one as a practitioner and another as a student of public affairs. Making the effort to stay connected to the academic side of public affairs can pay dividends since it can be a source for new ideas and approaches to solving public problems and managing public organizations.[8]

Being a lifelong learner is a wise course for public servants. There are many circumstances in our lives where we find ourselves in the role of a student. When we take on a new job, a new assignment, a new role in an organization, or any new challenges we often realize that we don't know all we need to know to succeed. These situations force us to study, learn new skills, and grow to match the challenges confronting us.

The writer, teacher, and activist Parker J. Palmer[9] describes "beginner's mind,"

> which includes the idea of being open to learning new things. Palmer says that, "clinging to what you already know is the path to an unlived life. So cultivate beginner's mind, walk straight into your not-knowing, and take the risk of failing and falling, again and again – then getting up to learn again and again."

Thomas Jefferson is known to have kept a journal known as a "commonplace book." "Commonplacing," as it was known at the time, was a widespread practice among scholars. It meant keeping a notebook with lines from various writers, poets, and playwrights that had resonance for the journalist. Jefferson said he copied these passages into his journal "at a time of life when I was bold in the pursuit of knowledge, never fearing to follow truth and reason."

The physical act of copying down these quotations helped to focus his own understanding of the world around him and his place in it. Public servants would be well-served by the practice of keeping such a journal as they go through their careers.[10]

Having and Being a Mentor

Careers can be greatly aided by securing a mentor. Ideally, a mentor should be senior (in terms of position and time in the organization) to those he or she is mentoring and should have a base of experiences from which they can extract and communicate lessons. They should be able to advise on everyday workplace dilemmas to help mentees through a difficult time or situation. Mentors should be called on to help shape a career trajectory. They should be able to help identify what skills or traits need to be developed through training or work projects or assignments. They should be able to explain current or future priorities of the agency or its constituent offices or divisions, and should be able to open the door to a network of agency colleagues that will help advise their mentees.

Stepping up to serve as a mentor should be a welcome obligation for veteran public servants. Parker Palmer states,

> Age and experience have taught me that mentoring is not a one-way street. It's a mutuality in which two people evoke the potentials in each other ... Mentoring is a gift exchange in which we elders receive at least as much as we give, often more.[11]

For the mentor, serving in that role provides the opportunity to become a "reflective practitioner." Being a mentor offers a chance to reflect deeply on your career, assessing the contribution specific people made to your success, reviewing the situations or projects that were instrumental in your development and growth, and examining the factors that have accounted for your upward career trajectory. As a mentor you can provide a model worth emulating,[12] and you will get the satisfaction of seeing your mentees progress and even excel. You can also develop an aptitude for coaching that may give you an excellent way to contribute after your retirement from public service.[13]

Epilogue

In the last analysis, public servants need to carry an attitude throughout their career that balances the idealistic and altruistic with the pragmatic and the possible. Public servants need to persevere against all manner of obstacles – insufficient authority, resource shortages, lack of expertise and capacity, and incompetent or corrupt political leadership. These challenges add to the difficulty of doing their important and vital work.

But if they are willing to persevere, if they are willing to give their energy and their persistence, they can use their time and talent to contribute to improving the nation and the world.

> What really counts is not the immediate act of courage or valor, but those who bear the struggle day in and day out – not the sunshine patriots but those who are willing to stand for a long period of time.
>
> *John F. Kennedy*

Key Concepts

1. Public servants are best served by developing and using an attitude throughout their careers which has elements such as: **idealism, altruism, pragmatism, receptivity, moral courage, perseverance, and resilience.** Understanding how to blend these elements under the right circumstances to be most effective is an important skill for public servants.
2. Public servants would be wise to maintain the mindset of the student as they progress through their careers in public service. Being open to learning at all points in a career is a wise course. Maintaining a "commonplace book" of useful thoughts, quotes and writings, as Thomas Jefferson did, can provide a useful resource to anyone in public service.
3. Finally, having mentors in the early and middle stages of a public service career can be of enormous value, and serving as a mentor to younger employees can provide the opportunity to deeply reflect on your own career and evaluate what persons and experiences were critical to your own development.

Notes

1 The chapter title, *The Attitude of a Public Servant*, is an homage to the best speech I ever heard. Called *The Attitude of An Athlete*, it was not a political speech, but a talk delivered by "Easy Ed" Macauley, the former NBA basketball player (for the old St. Louis Hawks and Boston Celtics) at his summer basketball camps in the Midwest and Southern United States. Each summer between my high school years, I attended his camp in Martin, Tennessee at a branch of the University of Tennessee, in furtherance of my ill-fated dream of becoming a college basketball player.

   At his camp sessions Mr. Macauley would deliver a speech called "The Attitude of An Athlete." Mr. Macauley would invoke the life of his son Patrick, who was afflicted from birth with a horrible condition which left him helpless, unable to take care of himself, and robbed of his potential and ability to do anything. Mr. Macauley would talk about the gifts we had been given to do anything we wanted, the tragedy of wasting that potential, and the failure to give our utmost to any pursuit we chose. The speech left me deeply moved. This was not a mere sports pep talk. It was the eloquent and very personal sharing of a life lesson, and recalling it many times in my life caused me to rise to many challenges and find resilience throughout my life.

2 These words are combined from two speeches delivered by Robert F. Kennedy. Beginning with the words, "The future does not belong …" is from his famous Day of Affirmation speech at the University of Cape Town, South Africa, on June 6, 1966.

3 This is a quote from George Bernard Shaw, which Robert F. Kennedy adopted as the closing words of his stump speech in his 1968 presidential campaign. In addition, when Robert Kennedy was assassinated, his brother Ted's very moving eulogy closed with these words.

4 During my career, there were many occasions when I had to conduct initial "program briefings" for incoming political appointees, either because I was the office director in charge of a program in their portfolio or because I was serving as their deputy. We always took a pragmatic approach to these briefings, and there were several things that needed to be achieved during these initial discussions with a new leader. *First*, we needed to make clear what **responsibilities and authorities** our program had. This might include acquainting the appointee of the need to get our authorities bolstered or changed. *Second*, we would describe who our **clients** were and the state of our relationships with them. (This would include a frank discussion of the state of our relationships with our own Regional offices.). *Third*, we also took the opportunity to **describe some recent or upcoming accomplishments.** We might also include any **upcoming needs** with which he or she might be able to help us. *Fourth*, we needed to alert the appointee of any **short-fuse items** that the appointee was going to have to decide or otherwise deal with in the near-term. We did not want him or her to be surprised by anything we needed them to do in the early days of their tenure. A corollary to the short fuse items were the **low-hanging fruit items –** things that could be accomplished quickly that would show some indications of success. (We even occasionally held back on some items to accomplish them after the arrival of the appointee so they could be claimed as *their* successes.) *Fifth*, we always included a section we called **legacy items**. These were things that the appointee could try to accomplish or on which they could make progress "on their watch," and this discussion always included who would be helped or benefited by accomplishing these items. If we could have honest and frank discussions on these areas during our briefing, we felt that we were serving the appointee's interests (and ours as well) and ensure that we would get off to

a good start with the appointee. If the atmosphere of these briefings could bear it, we might look for opportunities to inject some humor in the briefings. This would only be beneficial if a friendly relationship looked possible based on how the briefing was proceeding.

5 Moral courage is necessary when a public servant is asked to do something that violates his/her oath of office (that oath is presented as the opening of Chapter 1 of this book), or witnesses inappropriate behavior by a colleague, supervisor, a senior manager, or a politically-appointed leader of an agency. This is a rare situation for a public servant (fortunately, one that I never had to face in my 40 years of public service).

6 As a senior manager at the U.S. Environmental Protection Agency, I launched a multi-year project to develop more meaningful performance measures for the national compliance and enforcement program. This involved multiple iterations and experiments identifying better performance measures, setting up data flows to support new or refined measures, and seeing how the measures affected operations and outcomes. This effort occurred over four years during my time as the Director of the Office of Compliance.

7 Andrew Zolli and Ann Marie Healy, *Resilience/Why Things Bounce Back* (Simon & Schuster, New York, NY, 2012) pages 6 and 7.

8 For most of my tenure in the Senior Executive Service I held an Adjunct Faculty appointment in the Master's in Public Administration program at George Mason University in Fairfax, Virginia. This allowed me to stay abreast of the current thinking on the academic side of public affairs/administration. And being a practitioner at the same time, I was able to apply many of the ideas of the literature in the projects and programs I managed. I think this gave me a distinct advantage in my public service career.

9 Parker J. Palmer, *On the Brink of Everything, Grace, Gravity, and Growing Old* (Berrett-Koehler, Oakland, CA, 2018), page 45. Parker Palmer is a writer, teacher, activist, and founder of the Center for Courage and Renewal.

10 Coy Barefoot, *Thomas Jefferson on Leadership, Executive Lessons from His Life and Letters*, 2nd Edition (Mariner Publishing, Buena Vista, VA, 2008). Throughout my career, I have collected a series of quotations from various writers and public figures, the equivalent of the "commonplacing" book that Jefferson kept. I was not aware that this habit was one of Jefferson's, but I was aware of the value of compiling memorable quotes which I wanted to remember, and which had an uplifting effect during difficult moments in my career. My version of a commonplacing book appears as Appendix of this book.

11 Palmer, *On the Brink of Everything*, pages 34, 37, 38.

12 During the early years of my career, I benefitted greatly from being mentored by two members of the Senior Executive Service. One, named Kirke Harper, was a strategic thinker always asking whether our mission was being fulfilled, and always on the lookout for better ways to achieve it. Very much an "ideas man" and a visionary, he was a useful presence in the organization, making people consider questions about what the organization was doing and why. He was the first executive I encountered who was truly a "reflective practitioner." My other mentor was Bert Simpson, who was a deadline-oriented project manager, the kind of person who "always made the trains run on time." Not one for considering big existential questions, he was considered a very effective manager. By working with both of these men early in my career, I learned the value of the visionary leader and the on-time manager, and tried to incorporate their strengths into my leadership style, setting aside the weaknesses of their respective styles. My career was given a huge push forward by observing and learning from these two esteemed public servants.

13 During my time in public service, I regularly served as a mentor for many employees, and I developed an interest in coaching public servants. In my last two years of public service, I earned a Leadership Coaching Certificate from Georgetown University and began taking on coaching clients at my agency, the U.S. EPA, and I continue coaching in my retirement, through my LLC, Stahl Strategic.

Bibliography

Barefoot, Coy. *Thomas Jefferson on Leadership, Executive Lessons from His Life and Letters, 2nd Edition.* Buena Vista, VA: Mariner Publishing, 2008.

Healy, Ann Marie and Andrew Zolli. *Resilience: Why Things Bounce Back.* New York, NY, Simon and Schuster, 2012.

Kennedy, Robert F. "Day of Affirmation Address." June 6, 1966. Cape Town, South Africa, MPEG-4, 33:52. www.jfklibrary.org/asset-viewer/day-of-affirmation-address-june-6-1966.

Palmer, Parker J. *On the Brink of Everything: Grace, Gravity, and Growing Old.* Oakland, CA: Berrett-Koehler, 2018.

3

A PHILOSOPHY FOR REFLECTIVE PRACTITIONERS

Creating Public Value and Solving Public Problems

Those who are responsible for doing the business of the public, whether as members or managers of public programs, need a philosophy to help guide their thoughts and actions. They belong to the set of actors who are the practitioners of public service, and a set of abiding beliefs, values, and principles can serve them well as they navigate laws, statutes, policies, and practices through the years of their careers.

The idea of a "reflective practitioner" has been defined in various articles and books in the management literature.[1] A composite of those definitions would include someone who engages in reflective practice i.e., the ability to reflect on one's actions to engage in a process of continuous learning. A reflective practitioner then, is someone who, at regular intervals, looks back at the work they do and the work processes, and considers how they can improve. Put another way, a reflective practitioner is an individual who believes in learning constantly and updating their knowledge by reflecting on activities done by them in the past.

The laws, statutes, and policies that give rise to the formation of public programs were **usually created in response to a problem that needed solving, so the work of the public servant is to help further define that problem and to devise strategies to ameliorate or eliminate the problem**. The public servant gets the opportunity to develop a precise understanding of the public problem and to devise solutions and test their efficacy over time. These problems can present themselves as pervasive, long-term issues, which need multiple legislative attempts to solve all aspects of the problem, or shorter term issues that need a burst of public attention to address the problem.[2]

DOI: 10.4324/9781003266235-4

Creating Public Value

In 1995, Mark H. Moore of the Kennedy School of Government at Harvard University published his seminal book about public management, titled *Creating Public Value, Strategic Management in Government* (Harvard University Press, 1995). His stated purpose was

> to lay out a structure of practical reasoning to guide managers of public enterprises. It presents a general answer to the question of what public managers should think and do to exploit the particular circumstances they find themselves in to create public value.

Further, Moore states that the book offers several different kinds of ideas, such as (1) setting out a *philosophy* of public management which, among other things, defines what constitutes virtue in the execution of their offices; (2) providing *diagnostic frameworks* to guide managers in analyzing the settings in which they operate; and (3) suggesting particular kinds of *interventions* managers can make in their political and organizational settings. Moore says that "… while I address primarily those who hold line management positions in executive branch or independent agencies, I speak as well to the others who define the context for managerial action." Moore offers these eloquent descriptions of the role of public servants …

> **public managers are explorers who, with others, seek to discover, define, and produce public value …** public managers have a bundle of assets entrusted to their stewardship … the task of public managers is to judge in what particular ways assets entrusted can be redeployed to increase value of the enterprises for which they are responsible.[3]

It is the job of managers in the public sector to work conscientiously at the task of defining publicly valuable enterprises as well as producing that value. They must be prepared to adjust and reposition their organizations in their political and task environment, in addition to ensuring their continuity. Managers need an account of the value their organizations produce. Their organizations consume public resources, and they produce real consequences for society – intended or not. Moore says that "if the manager cannot account for the value of these efforts with both a story and demonstrated accomplishments, the legitimacy of their enterprises is undermined and, with that, their capacity to lead."[4]

The Strategic Triangle. Public sector organizations need a strategy if they are to produce value for the public. Moore says that such strategies need to meet three broad tests. First, the strategy must be *substantively valuable*, i.e., that the organization produces things of value to overseers, clients, and beneficiaries at low cost in terms of money and authority. Second, the strategy must be *legitimate and politically sustainable*, i.e., the enterprise must be able to continually attract both authority and money from the political authorizing environment to which it is ultimately accountable. Third, the strategy must be *operationally feasible* in that the authorized, valuable activities can actually be accomplished by the existing organization with help from others who can be induced to contribute to the organization's goal.

If the strategy lacks operational capacity, what happens to the strategy? The goal will be rejected as unfeasible or the political world will find a different vehicle for accomplishing it. If the strategy lacks political support, what happens to the strategy? The goal will be doomed by lack of capital and resources. If the strategy lacks substantive significance, what happens to the strategy? The organization will fail in the long run because it will eventually be viewed as wasteful. If the strategy is substantively valuable but has no political support or administrative feasibility, what happens? The ideas fail and become academic.

These tests are effective because they identify the necessary conditions for production of public value in the public sector. Moore says the triangle ...

- Encourages managers to maintain a sense of purposefulness that allows them to challenge and lead their organization toward the production of greater public value.
- Encourages managers to scan their authorizing environments for potential changes in the collective, political aspirations that guide their operations.
- Allows them to search their substantive task environments for emergent problems to which their own organizations might contribute some part of the solution.
- Encourages managers to review the operations of their own and other organizations in search of new programs or technologies that their organizations could use to improve performance in existing or new missions.
- Focuses managerial attention outward to the value of the organization's production, upward toward the political definition of value, and downward and inward to the organization's current performance.[5]

Thinking strategically in the public sector requires managers to assign equal importance to *substance, politics, and organizational implementation.*

Producing Value. Public managers should seek, find, and exploit opportunities to create public value. Greater public value can be produced by (1) increasing the quantity or quality of public activities per resources expended; (2) reducing the costs (in terms of money and authority) used to achieve current levels of production; (3) making public organizations better able to identify and respond to citizens' aspirations; (4) enhancing the fairness with which public sector organizations operate; and (5) increasing their continuing capacity to respond and innovate.

What Managers Need ... Managers need to exhibit a certain kind of consciousness: they need to be imaginative, purposeful, enterprising, and calculating.

They focus on increasing the value of the organizations they lead to the broader society. In search of value, their minds range freely across the concrete circumstances of today, seeking opportunities for tomorrow.

The job of a public manager is psychologically demanding, then, because public sector executives must strike a complex balance between two commonly opposed psychological orientations. First, they must have strong enough convictions about what is worth doing that they are willing to work hard for them and to stake their reputations on the values that they pursue. Yet their convictions cannot be so strong that they are impervious to doubt and the opportunity of continued learning. Their views, the ones for which they labor so mightily and with which they are closely identified, must be held *contingently*. Second, they must be willing to act with determination and commitment while retaining a willingness and a capacity for thought and reflection.

As Moore states, "Those who would lead public organizations need an appropriate managerial temperament — a cool, inner concentration which combines the psychological strength and energy that come from being committed to a cause coupled with a capacity for diagnosis, reflection, and objectivity." Moore further argues that the required repertoires of public sector managers need to change. The role of public sector managers needs to be elevated from the role of *technicians*, choosing from well-known administrative methods to accomplish purposes defined elsewhere, to the role of *strategists*, scanning their political and tasks environments for opportunities to use their organizations to create public value. It also changes their administrative job from assuring continuity and efficiency in current tasks to one of improvising the transition from current to future performance. Public sector executives serve to position the organization they lead to create public value, not simply to deploy resources to accomplish mandated purposes. Public sector managers must feel authorized to search their environments with purposeful, value-seeking imaginations and then act on any opportunity they see through interactions with their political authorizing environments and innovations within their own organizations. If they succeed in finding and exploiting opportunities to create value, it will be because they earn their success in the tough institutional environments in which they find themselves, not because their world has become less demanding.

How Problems Get on the Public Agenda

In his book, *Agendas, Alternatives, and Public Policies* (Harper Collins College),[6] John W. Kingdon offers a model for understanding how public issues emerge from the interaction of "three streams" to land on the public agenda for action. The three streams — *problems, politics, and policies* — interact to identify and select certain issues for public attention.

Problems gain attention through the following: *indicators* that characterize or quantify changes in conditions; a *focusing event* such as a crisis, or a natural disaster, or an existential concern (e.g., global warming); and *feedback information* that indicates a failure of some type.

Politics can be a source of items for the public agenda, sometimes through: a change in administrations (e.g., at the presidential or gubernatorial level) who puts a different set of priorities on the public agenda; changes in the ideological or partisan distribution of legislative bodies; and interest group campaigns to keep an issue visible and continue pressuring an administration or a legislative body to take action.

Policies are developed and selected through policy *communities* composed of specialists on a given subject matter, and policy *entrepreneurs* who advocate on behalf of a set of ideas. Policy ideas need to meet several criteria to survive to selection: they need to be technically feasible; they need to be acceptable within values held by the community and they need to anticipate the constraints the proposals will face.

When these streams converge, they open a window for a change in the public agenda. Policy advocates act as surfers, who need to be ready to meet the big wave (an event, etc.) that will bring them to shore. Kingdon also uses the analogy of a space expedition, which needs a launch window, a time when planets are in proper alignment, and the opportunity to complete the mission exists. The likelihood of reaching the public agenda is dramatically increased if all three streams – problems, politics, and policies – are joined. Policy entrepreneurs play a central role in "coupling the streams at the window."

The Problem-Solving Framework of Public Management

When public problems are an acknowledged part of the public agenda, they often become the province of government agencies, where problems need to be considered on a more granular, operational level. Malcolm K. Sparrow, Professor of the Practice of Public Management at the Kennedy School of Government at Harvard University, has over the course of his academic career developed and refined the ideas of the problem-solving approach as the framework for government agencies involved in controlling risks. These ideas are captured in several of Sparrow's books, especially *The Character of Harms* (Cambridge University Press, 2008).[7]

Sparrow says the summary phrase he uses for regulatory audiences to label the operational approach he advocates is, "Pick Important Problems, and Fix Them." Sparrow points out that even though the phrase is a simple one, "it turns out that organizing around carefully selected and important pieces of a risk – rather than around traditional programmatic or functional tasks, or around core high-volume operational processes – is extraordinarily difficult for agencies or institutions to do."[8]

The acronym ROPE (recognize, organize, perform, explain) serves as a crude but useful way of diagnosing the progress that risk-control agencies have made in mastering the art of harm reduction. Many organizations engaged in risk control have been organized around *functions*. Lawyers in one branch, investigators in another branch, and so on, each specializing in using particular *tools* and advocating for their use in solving specific problems, each pursuing their own priorities and agendas. Other organizations engaged in risk control have been organized around *processes*. Agencies set up core, high-volume processes to deal with whatever flows in, and it is these processes that can break open the functional silos.

From Sparrow's perspective as a teacher of many regulatory officials over many years, the five most common categories of harms are these:

- Invisible harms: where low rates of reporting or detection make the bulk of the problem invisible;
- Harms involving conscious opponents: where those responsible for control find themselves engaged in a dynamic game played against adaptive opposition, each side seeking to outsmart the other;
- Catastrophic harms: involving calamities of enormous consequence but of very low probability;
- Harms in equilibrium: some systems rest in harmful equilibrium states which require an initial "big shove" sufficient to overcome the gravitational pull of the starting position;
- Performance-enhancing risks: usually involves unlawful behavior under the general heading of unlawful organizational conduct that derives from an organization's performance goals. This often happens when the organization's social context puts greater emphasis on achieving the ends than on restricting the means. This category is frequently driven by a core performance imperative that is unambiguous and has a clear and objective metric.

Sparrow has developed a six-stage problem-solving protocol to guide agencies trying to move toward the problem-solving approach as an operational framework. The protocol has the following elements:

Problem-Solving Protocol

1. **Nominate and Select Potential Problems for Attention**
2. **Define the Problem Precisely**
3. **Determine How to Measure Impact**
4. **Develop Solutions/Interventions**
5. **(a) Implement the Plan**
   (b) Periodic Monitoring/Review/Adjustment
6. **Project Closure, Long-Term Monitoring/Maintenance**

Stage 1, the nomination process, may occur long before the launch of the project, maybe initiated by people who become part of the project team, or may even come from suggestions that are from parties outside the organization. Stage 2, defining the problem, stands as a distinct category in order to emphasize the significant analytical work necessary in developing an accurate problem specification. It recognizes the complexity of the choices involved in setting the scale and picking the right dimensions by which to characterize a harm. Stage 3, in which Sparrow calls for the most critical piece of methodological rigor in the problem-solving process, *obliges a project team to consider relevant metrics carefully, and to do so before they consider or select any intervention plan* (in Stage 4). The order of the protocol, in which developing metrics precedes the development of an intervention strategy, is important to avoid the inevitable temptation to measure the organization of, or compliance with, *the plan* rather than measuring the plan's impact on *the problem*.

By splitting Stage 5 into parts (a) and (b), highlighting the need for periodic review, the protocol makes it clear that picking an action plan is not necessarily a onetime thing. Sometimes the most effective solutions were not the first ones tried. To get to the second or third action plan, an organization has to be able to recognize when a plan is not working and be prepared to abandon it so they can try the next idea. Finally, Stage 6 formally recognizes the need for project closure, even in circumstance in which closing a project usually involves accepting some residual level of harm. Projects might be closed for two general reasons. The project *succeeded*, with the concentration of harm sufficiently mitigated (even if the resulting level is not zero) that this particular concentration no longer represents a special priority. Another reason for closure would be the realization that, for whatever reason(s), there was no real prospect for success, and the problem was *utterly intractable*.

Managing a portfolio of projects is different from managing one project to conclusion, and that portfolio demands a management infrastructure. Sparrow suggests that such an infrastructure include the following components:

- a nominating system to invite and generate nominations;
- a selections system for assessment of nominated issues, and prioritization of issues to proceed;
- assignment of responsibility and allocation of resources;
- project records;
- managerial oversight and periodic review;
- reporting system for channeling account of project-based accomplishments;
- support systems for teams and managers in an oversight capacity;
- a system for learning and to pool knowledge.

Sparrow's ideas and writings provide the blueprint for agencies and programs whose missions involve controlling risks and reducing harms. His contributions enable agencies to become more effective in protecting people from risks and harms of all types. The challenges of implementation are formidable and will demand a long-term effort to transform these agencies to become more effective.

Epilogue

The ideas of Moore, Kingdon, and Sparrow form a coherent philosophy that can be beneficial to public servants, especially to those who ascend to management ranks in their programs and agencies. It will be particularly useful to *reflective practitioners*, those who blend their practical experience with the ability to occasionally pull back and consider larger questions about the mission of their organizations, and their means of achieving it. These are the practitioners who ask questions about: whether their mission is producing public value; are the capabilities present in their agencies to achieve the mission; are their programs focused on addressing the right problems; are the performance measures of the agency or program focused on the right outcomes. These practitioners are able to focus simultaneously on the details of implementing and operating programs while never losing sight of the larger mission with which they are entrusted.[9]

Key Concepts

1. Moore's description of public managers as **"explorers who, with others, seek to discover, define, and produce public value"** is a very useful, if somewhat aspirational definition of the job of public managers. His view that public managers are **"entrusted with a bundle of public assets"** that they can deploy in their search for public value is a handy way to view the task facing any public manager.

2. Moore has also contributed his **strategic triangle**, a device for evaluating whether an organization's strategy for achieving public value meets three tests: is it **substantively valuable**, that is, whether the organization produces things of value at low cost in terms of money or authority; is it **legitimate and politically sustainable**, i.e., is it able to continually attract money and authority from the political authorizing environment to which it is accountable; and, third, is it **operationally feasible**, i.e., the valuable activities can be accomplished by the existing organization. Moore says thinking strategically in the public sector requires managers to assign equal importance to **substance, politics, and organizational implementation**.

3. Kingdon's model explaining how issues get on the public agenda for action involves "three streams," which converge to open a window for change. The three streams – **problems, politics, and policies** – combine to propel an issue onto the public agenda. These issues are aided by *focusing events, policy communities*, and *policy entrepreneurs*, who help push ideas for public attention.

4. Sparrow's problem-solving framework for public management of agencies involved in controlling risks and harms. His summary phrase for this approach

is **"Pick important problems, and fix them."** Sparrow describes common categories of harms, among them: *invisible harms* with low rates of reporting and detection; *harms involving conscious opponents* where there is an adaptive opposition who must be outsmarted; *catastrophic harms* involving calamities of enormous consequence but very low probability.

5. Sparrow offers a six-step problem-solving protocol: (1) **nominate and select problems for attention**; (2) **define the problem precisely**; (3) **determine how to measure impact**; (4) **develop solutions/interventions**; (5) (a) **implement the plan** (b) **periodic monitoring/review/adjustment**; (6) **project closure, long-term monitoring/maintenance**.

6. Sparrow also offers a model for the management infrastructure needed to oversee a portfolio of problems to solve.

Notes

1 One attempt to characterize the reflective practitioner concept can be found in Donald A. Schon, *The Reflective Practitioner: How Professionals Think in Action* (Basic Books, New York, NY, 1983).

2 An example of a long-term, pervasive problem that needed multiple judicial and legislative interventions to address the problem's many aspects is the attempt to promote racial desegregation in American schools. Through several decisions of the Supreme Court and Acts of Congress, attempts were made to address various parts of the problem, including the Civil Rights Act of 1964.

On the other hand, the problem of asbestos in schools was addressed primarily through two Acts of Congress (the Asbestos School Hazard Abatement Act, and the Asbestos Hazard Emergency Response Act.) Passed within two years of each other, the former authorized $50 million in loans and grants to school districts each year for asbestos abatement, and the latter gave EPA regulatory authority to require school inspections and abatement of asbestos. These two statutes working side-by-side for several years seemed to adequately address the problem.

3 Mark H. Moore, *Creating Public Value, Strategic Management in Government* (Harvard University Press, Cambridge, MA, 1995) pages 20, 16, 39. I first became familiar with this book when I replaced my boss as an enrollee at a Harvard University Executive Education seminar at which I heard Mark Moore speak. During my graduate school years and in the first years of my career in the U.S. government, I had become very disillusioned with the public administration literature, which I felt offered little of value to practitioners who were involved in the day-to-day leadership of government programs. But Mark Moore was different, because his ideas were based on his scholarly knowledge, but also on what he had learned from practitioners, whom he seemed to hold in esteem, and his views of their role and the ideas he offered them were very practical, *and so useful*!! Here, finally, was an academician with something valuable to say to practitioners. He was a source of ideas throughout my career, as was his colleague at the Kennedy School, Malcolm Sparrow, who I will cite later in this chapter.

4 Moore, *Creating Public Value*, page 57.

5 Ibid., page 73.

6 John W. Kingdon, *Agendas, Alternatives, and Public Policies* (second edition, Harper Collins College).

7 Malcolm K. Sparrow, Professor in the Practice of Public Management at the Kennedy School of Government at Harvard University (and a colleague of Mark Moore at the Kennedy School) is the leading scholar and proponent of the "problem-solving approach" to public management. Through the course of his many writings in his academic career, including four of his books *Imposing Duties, Government's Changing Approach to Compliance* (Praeger, Westport, CT, 1995), *The Regulatory Craft, Controlling Risks, Solving Problems, and Managing Compliance* (Brookings Institution Press, Washington, DC, 2000), *The Character of Harms, Operational Challenges in Control* (Cambridge University Press, Cambridge, 2008) and *Handcuffed, What Holds Policing Back and the Keys to Reform* (Brookings Institution Press, Washington, DC, 2016). Sparrow has been a leading thinker and advocate for problem-solving as the organizing framework for policing and regulatory agencies interested in doing a more effective job in protecting the public from all manner of risks. A former Detective Chief Inspector in the British Police Service, Sparrow went on to a remarkable academic career at Harvard without losing the soul of a practitioner. All his ideas are of benefit to the practitioners of public service who populate agencies trying to eliminate or control risks. Originally focusing primarily on police agencies, he quickly realized that many agencies of government had responsibilities for controlling risks, they faced a similar set of challenges, and, most importantly, they could all learn from each other through his Executive Programs at Harvard on regulatory and enforcement strategies. I attended his executive programs in January 1973, and September 1977, and I encountered an academician who not only knew exactly the challenges I was facing as a manager in a compliance and enforcement program, but seemed to have great ideas about how to conquer them. Over a period of years, I became friends with Malcolm, followed the evolution of Malcolm's ideas, and worked with him as a contractor to my Office of Compliance at EPA.

8 During my years as the Director of the Office of Compliance for the U.S. Environmental Protection Agency, we used many of the concepts of Sparrow's problem-solving approach to set national enforcement and compliance assurance priorities for the Agency. We began our priority-setting process with a round of nominations from our internal staff: the inspectors who brought their observations from the field about patterns of noncompliance; the enforcement attorneys who developed the cases stemming from the inspections; compliance assistance staff who contributed their knowledge about assistance information that was most in demand; and managers in the enforcement and compliance program who brought a sensitivity to the resource demands for the nominations suggested. We then published a list and a description of each nominated priority in the *Federal Register* and solicited comments from the public. This provided interesting input from parts of the regulated community that were suggested as nominees for priority status, who argued that they did not deserve that designation from EPA, and that other regulated sectors were much more worthy! The comment process also yielded information (e.g., from environmental and labor groups) that helped define the problem more precisely. A set of EPA managers collected and analyzed the information and then proposed a final list of priorities to senior management, which included the Assistant Administrator for Enforcement and Compliance Assurance, and the Agency's Deputy Administrator and Administrator. Once a list was agreed to by the senior managers, it was published in the *Federal Register*, and then internal implementation teams were formed to manage each priority initiative. These teams were responsible for ensuring progress

on solving the environmental problem embedded in the priority, making adjustments in the strategy in response to changing conditions, and devising measures of success to guide the performance of the programs involved. That issue, selecting the performance measures, proved difficult for the implementation teams. Over time, some priorities were adequately addressed and moved off the list, others were continued for multiple years, and others became a precursor for larger Agency initiatives. This process served to: put certain regulated entities on notice that they were going to be an object of attention; help the national enforcement and compliance program gain a sense of momentum against certain environmental problems; and helped provide (in spite of the problems of measurement) an account of performance that was helpful in explaining our accomplishments to overseers.

9 This ability to balance a detailed understanding of the operational side of managing with the larger public purpose of the organization was something I always sought in any person I had a hand in hiring, especially for people seeking positions as a manager. It was the main indicator that I watched for in the development of subordinate managers who worked with me in my career. I viewed people who had this balance as prime candidates for advancement in my, or other, organizations.

Bibliography

Kingdon, John W. *Agendas, Alternatives, and Public Policies, 2nd Edition*. Upper Saddle River, NJ: Pearson Education, 1995.

Moore, Mark H. *Creating Public Value, Strategic Management in Government*. Cambridge, MA: Harvard University Press, 1995.

Schon, Donald A. *The Reflective Practitioner: How Professionals Think in Action*. New York, NY: Basic Books, 1983.

Sparrow, Malcolm K. *Imposing Duties, Government's Changing Approach to Compliance*. Westport, CT: Praeger, 1995.

Sparrow, Malcolm K. *The Regulatory Craft, Controlling Risks, Solving Problems, and Managing Compliance*. Washington, DC: Brookings Institution Press, 2000.

Sparrow, Malcolm K. *The Character of Harms, Operational Challenges in Control*. Cambridge: Cambridge University Press, 2008.

Sparrow, Malcolm K. *Handcuffed: What Holds Policing Back and the Keys to Reform*. Washington, DC: Brookings Institution Press, 2016.

4

IMPLEMENTING PUBLIC POLICY AND USING NETWORKS

Those involved in the actual implementation of public policy can be guided by a set of ideas and principles that can help bring order to the implementation process.[1] The ideas and principles can be used as a stepwise process to guide thoughts and actions that are necessary for implementation of public policy. This stepwise process is depicted in Table 4.1.

Model of the Public Policy Implementation Process

The process begins with: (1) a **public issue** that rises to the public action agenda – these issues can take the form of harms (in Sparrow's parlance), risks or threats, inequities, conflicts, failures, breakdowns, scandals, or inefficiencies. Then there is a period in which various alternatives are considered for[2]: (2) a **public response** which can range from passage of a new law, or a change in current law or policy; the expansion or change in an existing program; a court prescribing a solution through a ruling in response to a case; a call for more study of the issue; a market correction; or a decision to do nothing. Usually, the issue becomes the responsibility of an executive agency, so: (3) a **program plan** is developed involving a suite of activities such as developing a strategic plan, which normally leads to setting goals and objectives, developing and implementing measures of success, requesting and then allocating resources. Next, the: (4) **program implementation** occurs, which might involve any of the following – developing and operating processes, executing specific functions, collecting data, and serving customers. Finally, the: (5) **evaluation and measurement** phase in which data about results and outcomes are analyzed, and program impacts are identified and evaluated.

This process should be thought of as being **cyclical** in nature. In other words, the evaluation and measurement phase of the process can lead to returning

DOI: 10.4324/9781003266235-5

TABLE 4.1 Model of the Public Policy Implementation Process

(1) Public Issue	(2) Public Response	(3) Program Plan
TYPES: Risks, Harms, Inequities, Conflicts, Failures/Breakdowns, Inefficiencies	TYPES: New Law, Change in Law, Expand/Change Existing Program, Court Prescription, More Study, Do Nothing, Market Correction	ACTIVITIES: Develop Strategic Plan, Set Goals and Objectives, Develop Performance Measures, Allocate Resources
ACTORS: Media, Academia, Interest Groups, Legislatures, Executive Branch Agencies	ACTORS: Exec., Legis., Judicial Branches, Interest Groups	ACTORS: Agency Mgmt. and Staff, Contractors, Co-producers

(4) Program Implementation	(5) Evaluation and Measurement
ACTIVITIES: Execute Functions, Operate Processes, Collect Data, Serve Customers	ACTIVITIES: Review Results/Outcomes, Evaluate Impact, Consider Program Modifications
ACTORS: Agency Management and Staff	ACTORS: Agency Management and Staff, Legislatures, Oversight Agencies, Interest Groups

to the public issue phase to consider redefining the problem in light of a new understanding discovered during an evaluation. Or such evaluations can point to needed changes in the public response phase, such as changing the statute, or refining the existing program to take a new aspect of the problem into account, or even launching an effort at more study of an aspect of the problem that has just come to light.

It should also be noted that each phase features a **different set of actors** that are prominent in each phase. During the phase when the *public issue* is being defined, it can be discovered and publicized by: (1) the media; (2) academia (which can contribute studies that shed new light on the issue or key aspects of it); (3) interest groups which can demonstrate how an issue is affecting particular groups or economic sectors; (4) legislators and their staff who are often contacted by affected individuals and interest groups; and (5) executive branch managers who have been working on the issue in its initial iteration and who are discovering new aspects from their day-to-day experience with the issue. There is benefit in these actors continuing to talk to each other throughout the implementation phases, though, regrettably, this often does not happen after the initial push to pass the legislation has concluded.

In the *public response* phase, the principal actors maybe those in the legislative and executive branches, though they may find consultations with interest groups and academic experts to be very beneficial to drawing up the right response. In the *program planning and implementation* phases, the principal actors are the government officials developing the goals and objectives and carrying out the implementation activities. In the *measurement and evaluation* phase, an entirely new set of actors may come into play in the form of inspectors general, agency evaluation teams, and academic evaluators. These groups will most times, but not always, work with the officials who planned and implemented the program to develop recommendations for improvements.

There are numerous observations to be made about this phased implementation model. First, the model may depict events in a more orderly fashion than is the normal reality in the policy-making process. The model does not always march inevitably through the phases in the order depicted. Particularly in the earliest phases, progress may be in fits and starts, moving back and forth between the public issue and the public response phases. Similarly, there may be many instances of back-and-forth between the program plan and the program implementation phases. Second, the public issues that pass through the model's steps are very diverse and include a wide range of public problems, and the types of responses are equally diverse and wide-ranging. Third, the boundaries between the different phases can be very fuzzy, with various events and activities in one phase influencing or contributing to the adjoining phases. Fourth, the roles of the actors in each phase can be shared or fragmented across phases. Lastly, this process is usually known more for its inefficiency than its efficiency. It can be, and usually is, very messy and not straightforward.

Implementation Variables

The academic literature has made contributions to practitioners involved in the implementation of public policy. In their influential book, *Implementation and Public Policy* (University Press of America, Inc., Lanham, Maryland, 1989),[3] Daniel A. Mazmanian and Paul A. Sabatier offer their *framework for implementation analysis* which is provided as a tool for evaluators and academicians to analyze the effects of implementation efforts, but which also, and more importantly, provides a set of variables for the *implementers* of public policy to troubleshoot the potential and actual difficulties in their efforts to implement public policy.

Mazmanian and Sabatier offer a definition for implementation, it is the

> carrying out of a basic policy decision, usually incorporated in a statute but which can take the form of important executive orders or court decisions. Ideally, that decision identifies the problem(s) to be addressed, stipulates the objective(s) to be pursued, and in a variety of ways, "structures" the implementation process.[4]

Implementation analysis identifies crucial variables which affect the achievement of legal objectives throughout the implementation process. The variables can be divided into three broad categories: (1) the tractability of the problem(s) being addressed, (2) the ability of the statute to structure favorably the implementation process, and (3) the net effect of a variety of political variables on the balance of support for statutory objectives. These categories are depicted in Figure 4.1.

In the category of **tractability of the problem**, several variables are at play: the first variable is **technical difficulties**, wherein "the achievement of a program goal is contingent upon a number of technical prerequisites, including an

Tractability of the Problem

- Technical difficulties
- Diversity of target group behavior
- Target group as a percentage of the population
- Extent of behavioral change required

Ability of Statute to Structure Implementation

- Clear and consistent objectives
- Incorporation of adequate causal theory
- Initial allocation of financial resources
- Hierarchical integration within and among implementing institutions
- Decision rules of implementing agencies
- Recruitment of implementing officials
- Formal access by outsiders

Non-statutory Variables Affecting Implementation

- Socioeconomic conditions and technology
- Public support
- Attitudes and resources of constituency groups
- Support from sovereigns
- Commitment and leadership skill of implementing officials

FIGURE 4.1 Variables in the Implementation Process

ability to develop inexpensive performance indicators and an understanding of the principal causal linkages affecting the problem."[5] Another variable in this category is the **diversity of target group behavior**. "The more diverse the behavior being regulated or the service being provided, the more difficult it becomes to frame clear regulations and thus the greater discretion which must be given to field-level implementers."[6] The next variable in this category is **the target group as a percentage of the population**.

> In general the smaller and more definable (i.e., capable of being isolated) the target group whose behavior needs to be changed, the more likely the mobilization of political support in favor of the program and thus the more probable the achievement of statutory objectives.

The final variable in this category is **the extent of behavior change required**. Mazmanian and Sabatier describe this variable as:

> The extent of behavior modification required to achieve statutory object- ives is a function of the (absolute) number of people in the ultimate target group and the amount of change required of them. The basic hypothesis is the greater the amount of behavioral change, the more problematic will be successful implementation.

This framework recognizes that some problems are far more tractable than others. Mazmanian and Sabatier suggest that

> problems are most tractable if: (1) there is a valid theory connecting behavioral change to problem solution, the requisite technology exists, and measurement of change in the seriousness of the problem is inexpensive; (2) there is min- imal variation in the behavior which causes the problem; (3) the target group constitutes an easily identifiable minority of the population within a political jurisdiction; and (4) the amount of behavioral change required is modest.[7]

In the second category of variables, **the ability of the policy decision to structure implementation**, the authors argue that original policymakers (i.e., legislators passing a statute, appellate court decisions, or executive orders) can sub- stantially affect the attainment of legal objectives by utilizing the levers at their disposal to coherently structure the implementation process.[8] The first variable in this category is **precise and clear ranking of legal objectives**, which can serve as an indispensable aid in program evaluation, as unambiguous directives to implementing officials, and as a resource to supporters of those objectives. Another variable in this category is the **validity of the causal theory**. An adequate causal theory requires (1) that the principal causal linkages between governmental and the

attainment of program objectives be understood; and (2) that the officials responsible for implementing the program have jurisdiction over a sufficient number of
critical linkages to actually attain the objectives. The authors point out that "inadequate causal theories lie behind many of the cases of implementation failure."

Another variable in this category is **the initial allocation of resources**.
A threshold level of funding is necessary if there is to be any possibility of achieving
statutory objectives, and the level of funding above this threshold is (up to some
saturation point) proportional to the probability of achieving those objectives.
Hierarchical integration within and among implementing institutions
is another variable in this category of the ability of the policy decision to structure implementation. The difficulty of obtaining coordinated action within any
given agency and among the numerous semiautonomous agencies involved in
most implementation efforts is well-documented in public administration literature. It is best if the authorizing statute focuses on hierarchically integrating the
implementing agencies. That integration is determined by (1) the number of *veto /
clearance points* involved in the attainment of legal objectives; and (2) the extent to
which supporters of those objectives are provided with inducements and sanctions
sufficient to ensure acquiescence among those who have a potential veto.

Among the variables in this category are the **decision rules of implementing
agencies**. The authorizing statue needs to provide clear and consistent objectives,
few veto points, and adequate incentives for compliance, but the statute can further influence the implementation process by stipulating the formal decision rules
of the implementing agencies. **Officials' commitment to statutory objectives** is an important variable in the implementation process. The attainment
of legal objectives which seek to significantly modify target group behavior is
unlikely unless officials in the implementing agencies are strongly committed to
the achievement of those objectives. Any new program requires implementers
who are sufficiently persistent to develop new regulations and standard operating
procedures and to enforce them in the face of resistance from target groups and
from public officials reluctant to make the mandated changes. The final variable in
this category is **formal access by outsiders**. Statutes which permit citizens to
participate as formal intervenors in agency proceedings and as petitioners in judicial review are more likely to have their objectives attained.

In commenting on this set of variables, the authors recognize that statutes and
other policy decisions often do not structure the implementation process very
coherently. This is particularly true at the federal level, where the heterogeneity of
interests effectively represented, the diversity in proscribed activities, the multiple
vetoes and weak party system in Congress, and the constitutional and political
incentives for implementation by state and local agencies make it extremely difficult to develop clear goals, to minimize the number of veto points, and to assign
implementation to sympathetic agencies.

The third category of variables identified by Mazmanian and Sabatier is the
non-statutory variables affecting implementation. Implementation has an

"inherent dynamism" driven by two important processes: (1) the need for any program which seeks to change behavior to receive constant or periodic infusions of political support if it is to overcome the delay involved in seeking cooperation among large numbers of people; and (2) the effect of changes in socioeconomic and technological conditions on the support for those objectives among the general public, interest groups, and sovereigns.

The first of the variables in this category is the **socioeconomic conditions and technology**. Variation in socioeconomic conditions can affect perceptions of the relative importance of the problem addressed by a statute (or other basic policy decision). In the case of policies on environmental or consumer protection or worker safety which are directly tied to technology, changes or the lack of changes in the technological state of the art over time are obviously crucial. The next variable, **public support**, often works in a cyclical fashion in which there is an initial awakening of public concern, followed by a decline in widespread support as people become aware of the costs of "solving" the problem, as other issues crowd it off the political agenda, and, conversely, public support may be temporarily reawakened by dramatic new evidence that the problem persists, e.g., another oil spill or a nuclear power accident. This episodic, or perhaps cyclical, nature of public concern creates difficulties for the successful implementation of any program requiring periodic infusions of support from sovereigns.

Mazmanian and Sabatier offer as the next variable in this category **attitudes and resources of constituency groups**. Changes in the resources and attitudes of constituency groups toward statutory objectives and the policy outputs of implementing institutions play a part in the implementation process. The basic dilemma confronting proponents of any program that seeks to change the behavior of one or more target groups is that public support for the program will almost invariably decline over time. The next variable in this category, **support from sovereigns**, concerns those institutions which control the legal and financial resources of implementing agencies, normally including: the legislatures (especially the relevant policy and fiscal committees); the chief executive; the courts; and in intergovernmental programs, hierarchically superior agencies (though one of the major difficulties in the implementation of intergovernmental programs is that implementing agencies are responsible to different sovereigns). The final variable in this category is the **commitment and leadership skill of implementing officials**, and there are two components to this variable. The first component is the direction and ranking of statutory objectives in officials' priorities. The second component is the officials' skill in realizing those priorities, i.e., their ability to go beyond what could be expected in using available resources.

Six Conditions of Effective Implementation

One of the features of their book on policy implementation which makes it especially useful to practitioners, Mazmanian and Sabatier offer *Six Conditions of*

Effective Implementation.[9] The authors organize the statutory and political variables into conditions so that a statute or policy decision can produce "a substantial departure from the status quo … and achieve its desired goals" if it can be guided by these conditions.

1. The enabling legislation or other legal directive mandates policy objectives which are clear and consistent or at least provides substantive criteria for resolving goal conflicts.
2. The enabling legislation incorporates a sound theory identifying the principal factors and causal linkages affecting policy objectives and gives implementing officials sufficient jurisdiction over target groups and other points of leverage to attain, at least potentially, the desired goals.
3. The enabling legislation structures the implementation process to maximize the probability that implementing officials and target groups will perform as desired. This involves assignment to sympathetic agencies with adequate hierarchical integration, supportive decision rules, sufficient financial resources, and adequate access to supporters.
4. The leaders of the implementing agency possess substantial managerial and political skills and are committed to statutory goals.
5. The program is actively supported by organized constituency groups and by a few key legislators (or a chief executive) throughout the implementation process, with the courts being neutral or supportive.
6. The relative priority of statutory objectives is not undermined over time by the emergence of conflicting public policies or by changes in relevant socio-economic conditions, which weaken the statutes causal theory or political support.

Practitioners can use these conditions to forecast potential trouble in the implementation process. If any of these conditions (especially conditions #1–5) appear to be unmet in the initial phases of implementation, actions will need to be taken early in the process to bolster these conditions. Similarly, condition #6 can provide a warning system to anticipate and explain why a program may be in need of a course correction. In any case, the six conditions can help practitioners be more effective as implementers since they can serve as a diagnostic tool to help steer implementation.

Designing and Managing Networks

The "network model" of governance has emerged as a method for organizing resources of government and partner organizations to address public problems and needs. In their seminal book explaining this phenomenon, Stephen Goldsmith and William D. Eggers, describe the movement toward networks as the "new shape of the public sector" (**Governing By Network**, Brookings Institution Press, Washington,

DC, 2004). Goldsmith and Eggers say that twenty-first century challenges and the means of addressing them are numerous and more complex than ever before. Problems have become both more global and more local as power disperses and boundaries (when they exist at all) become more fluid. One-size-fits-all solutions have given way to customized approaches as the complicated problems of diverse and mobile populations increasingly defy simplistic solutions. The authors suggest that the rise of government by network has been fueled by the confluence of four influential trends that are altering the shape of the public sector worldwide.

1. *Third-Party Government:* for decades the increase in using private firms and nonprofit organizations – as opposed to government employees – to deliver services and achieve policy goals.
2. *Joined-up Government:* the increased tendency for multiple government agencies, sometimes even at multiple levels of government, to join together to provide integrated service.
3. *The Digital Revolution:* the relatively recent technological advances that enable organizations to collaborate in real time with external partners in ways previously not possible.
4. *Consumer Demand:* the increase in citizen demand for more control over their own lives and more choices and varieties in their government services, to match the customized service provision technology has spawned in the private sector.

These factors, particularly the rise of third-party government, are transforming the public sector from a *service provider* to a *service facilitator*. Goldsmith and Eggers say there are six types of networks that should be considered by officials looking to use a networked approach for providing a service or addressing a problem. These types of networks should be considered:

1. Service contract – service agreements with contractors and subcontractors are used to create an array of vertical and horizontal relationships;
2. Supply chain – deliver complex products (e.g., jet fighter) by assigning production tasks to various parties;
3. Ad hoc – usually formed in response to a specific situation (often an emergency);
4. Channel partnership – companies and nonprofits conduct transactions on behalf of government (e.g., buying a fishing license at a sporting goods store);
5. Information dissemination – using partners to spread, distribute, and sometimes integrate information for use by the public;
6. Civic switchboard – government uses its broader perspective to connect diverse organizations to augment each other's capacity to produce a public service or outcome (e.g., forming a network of food pantries to help shelters take care of the homeless).

These network types can be placed on a spectrum according to the degree of government involvement in operating the network. The network which requires the most government involvement is the service contract network (#1 above), followed by the supply chain network (#2). The ad hoc network (#3) and the channel partnership network (#4) are in the middle of the spectrum. The networks with the least government involvement are the information dissemination network (#6) and the civic switchboard network (#5).

To choose the right type of network for the task it can be helpful to answer the following questions: What is our overarching purpose – deliver a service, provide information, build a tangible product? Is the need ongoing or one-time? How much money is available? What is the relative importance of accountability versus flexibility?

To manage the network, there is a need to consider what processes should be integrated and who should do the integrating. Governments who use the networked approach have three choices about how to manage the network: they can be their own integrator and manage the network in-house; they can delegate all the integration tasks to the prime contractor; or they can hire a third party to coordinate the network.

Networks are often necessitated by the nature of the problem to be addressed; the logic is that collaboration is needed to deal with problems that don't fit neatly within the boundaries of a single organization.[10] When the purpose and the task form the organizing principle for the network, there are generally four types of networks that can be considered. First, there is the *service implementation network* that is generally funded to deliver services to clients, and the services are often based on joint production for vulnerable clients such as the elderly, families on welfare, or the mentally ill. The second type of purpose-based network is an *information diffusion network* whose purpose is to share information across governmental boundaries to anticipate and prepare for problems such as earthquakes and hurricanes. The third type of network is a *problem-solving network*, the purpose of which is to solve a proximate problem (i.e., a problem which we know will happen, but we don't know when or where they will happen, such as wildfires). A fourth type of network is the *community capacity-building network*, whose purpose to build social capital in a community so that it is better able to deal with a variety of ongoing and future problems, such as substance abuse among youth.

Effective network management can be facilitated by taking care of certain key tasks.[11] One task is the *management of accountability*, because networks operate without a chain of command, both network managers and managers of organizations in networks must successfully negotiate who is responsible for what and how to respond to free riders who don't contribute their fair share but continually demand more resources. Another task for effective network operation is the *management of legitimacy*, since, unlike a public organization created by law, a network is usually a cooperative venture that must continually negotiate its legitimacy, especially if its boundaries cross the public, private, and nonprofit sectors.

Management of conflict is the third crucial task of network managers. Conflict can develop from differing goals among the organizations in the network, so it is important that network managers provide mechanisms for conflict resolution. There are design choices for networks, and the *management of design* (or governance structure) is an important issue. Early in the evolution of a network if may be appropriate to operate on the basis of consensus. But as a network expands and attains a diversity of members the initial governance structure can fail. Sometimes when a network becomes sufficiently large, it might be a good idea for the network to create a specific organization or committee whose task it is to manage the network. The *management of commitment* in a network where most salaries are paid by individual organizations is a continuing task for managers of networks. Managers must first recognize that all organizations in the network and all individual representatives are not equally committed to the network and its goals. Network-level managers must build and maintain the commitment of all network members, recognizing that not all members will be involved to the same extent.

Epilogue

It is tempting to think that implementing programs is a dying art in government agencies, what with shrinking agency budgets, the lack of congressional and legislative initiatives to address public problems, and the resultant lack of new program enactment in government. But, as more public problems are addressed through network models, there will always be a place inside government for managers who have the skills necessary to implement new programs or bring change and improvements to existing programs.

The talents necessary to design and operate networks to accomplish public goals will be in great demand as networks become the predominant vehicle for achieving common purposes. As public problems become more complex and intertwined, and rarely fit within the boundaries of one organization, collaboration, and network management will increasingly be the essential skills for public managers.

Key Concepts

1. The process model for program implementation has the following phases: public issue; public response; program plan; program implementation; program evaluation and performance measurement.
2. Mazmanian and Sabatier offer three categories of variables to analyze program implementation efforts: tractability of the problem; ability of statue to structure implementation; and non-statutory variables affecting implementation.
3. Mazmanian and Sabatier offer six conditions of effective implementation: (1) enabling legislation provides clear and consistent objectives; (2) enabling

legislation incorporates a sound theory identifying principal factor and causal linkages affecting policy objectives; (3) enabling legislation structures the implementation process so as to maximize the probability that implementing officials and target groups will perform as desired; (4) implementing officials possess substantial skills and are committed to statutory goals; (5) program is actively supported by organized constituency groups; and (6) priority of statutory objectives is not undermined by conflicting public policies.

4. Goldsmith and Eggers identify six different types of operating networks: service contract; supply chain; ad hoc; channel partnership; information dissemination; and civic switchboard. Milward and Provan suggest network types that are based on the task for which they have been formed: service implementation; information diffusion; problem solving; community capacity building.

5. Milward and Provan also suggest network managers need to pay attention to management of certain key tasks: management of accountability; management of legitimacy; management of conflict; management of design; and management of commitment.

Notes

1 Many of the concepts in this chapter were from a course I taught for many years entitled *Program Planning and Implementation* at the School of Public Policy, Government, and International Affairs at George Mason University in Fairfax, Virginia. Serving as a practitioner at the time I was teaching, I made sure this course had a very practical orientation. It was taught to graduate students who were in government service and aspired to be managers in their agencies at the federal, state, and local levels, or in their nongovernmental organizations (NGOs).

2 One of my EPA colleagues used to say of the Inspector General personnel at EPA that their job was "to show up on the field after the battle was over and shoot the wounded." It was a view that I agreed with from my own observations.

3 Daniel A. Mazmanian and Paul A. Sabatier, *Implementation and Public Policy* (University Press of America, Inc., Lanham, MD, 1989). Their model is depicted in Figure 4.1.

4 Mazmanian and Sabatier, *Implementation and Public Policy*, page 20.

5 Ibid., page 22.

6 Ibid., page 23.

7 Ibid., page 24.

8 In implementing the Asbestos School Hazard Abatement Act (ASHAA), which authorized the U.S. Environmental Protection Agency (EPA) to distribute annually $50 million in loans and grants to schools for asbestos abatement projects, the statute structured a process to evaluate schools' applications for funds. It stated that EPA was to examine the degree of asbestos hazard faced by the school and take the financial need of the school district (or Local Education Agencies – LEAs) into account. It did not specify what criteria should be utilized in evaluating degree of hazard and financial need, so our EPA team set about developing a formula to consider these factors. We developed criteria to assess the hazard: the asbestos material had to be friable (breaking apart into fragments that caused particles to be distributed into the ambient air) and type

of asbestos material. For financial need, EPA economists felt that the best measure to assess financial need was the per capita income of the residents of the LEA, which gave a sense of the financial wherewithal of the residents to provide funds to the LEA for the project. This was used to determine how much of the request EPA would fund and the mix of loan vs. grant to be awarded. Finally, the projects were rank-ordered by the exposure hours for that particular space in the school, so that classrooms or gymnasium which were in constant use by many students or school staff throughout the day were ranked higher than other less-used areas.

Combining these criteria produced a way of establishing a list of awardees that was easily understandable, using the transparent criteria that were provided in the LEA application and verified by EPA staff (often through EPA inspections). This method allowed us to target the funds at the projects with the highest impact on the schools and was not challenged successfully in all the years of operating this program.

9 Mazmanian and Sabatier, *Implementation and Public Policy*, page 41.

10 H. Brinton Milward and Keith G. Provan, *A Manager's Guide to Choosing and Using Networks* (IBM Center for the Business of Government, Networks and Partnerships Series, 2006).

11 Ibid., pages 18–24.

Bibliography

Goldsmith, Steven, and William D. Eggers. *Governing by Network*. Washington, DC: Brookings Institute Press, 2004.

Mazmanian, Daniel A., and Paul A. Sabatier. *Implementation and Public Policy*. Lanham, MD: University Press of America, 1989.

Milward, H. Brinton, and Keith G. Provan. *A Manager's Guide to Making and Choosing Networks*. Washington, DC: IBM Center for the Institute of Government, 2006.

5

PERFORMANCE-BASED MANAGEMENT

An Opportunity Squandered

Among the many challenges facing government agencies and programs, one that has persisted for decades in spite of many efforts to address it, is the defining and measurement of performance. Identifying, developing, and using performance indicators for government programs has proven devilishly hard to do, but is necessary to manage programs and to demonstrate the value of government in the face of the anti-government forces lined up in the political environment. Legislation designed to authorize ways to address complex social problems often does not state goals and objectives clearly, does not mandate collection of information that would aid in measuring performance, and does not set timelines for completion of problem-solving initiatives.

What Is Performance-Based Management?

As Joseph Wholey described in his seminal article on this subject,[1] both in government and in the not-for-profit sector "leaders and managers are grappling with closely related problems that include tight restrictions on resources, increased demand for effective services, low levels of public trust, and increasing demand for accountability." One solution that has emerged is *performance-based management*, that is, "the purposeful use of resources and information to achieve and demonstrate measurable progress toward agency and program goals." Wholey further states that the

> key steps in performance-based management are (a) developing a reasonable level of agreement on missions, goals, and strategies for achieving the goals; (b) implementing performance measurement systems of sufficient quality

DOI: 10.4324/9781003266235-6

to document performance and support decision making; and (c) using performance information as a basis for decision making at various organizational levels.

Many countries around the world have mounted efforts to move in the direction of performance-based management.[2] For example, in the United Kingdom a report by Sir William Beveridge back in 1942 led to a fundamental rethinking of services such as public health, education, and housing. Then, when Tony Blair's so-called New Labour Government took office in 1997, performance measurement became a cornerstone of its governing policies. Using public service agreements (PSAs) with outcomes and specific targets for each central government department, Prime Minister Blair personally kept the heat on Cabinet secretaries to review key agency performance targets.

In Canada, after performing audits on a series of well-performing public agencies, in 1996 Canada enacted the Planning, Reporting, and Accountability Structure (PRAS) policy framework, that provided departments and agencies with a basis for planning and management which served as a solid foundation for communicating performance information. The PRAS framework was replaced by the Management, Resources, and Results Structure, a policy under which a government agency's activities are tracked in relation to the overall outcomes which they contribute to. Finally, in April 2005, the Canadian government adopted a Management Accountability Framework that "focuses on management results rather than required capabilities; provides a basis of engagement with departments; and suggests ways for departments both to move forward and to measure progress."

The movement to define and manage outcomes occurred in many countries around the world. In Singapore and Japan, for example, there has been a strong effort to bring a focus on performance management in government. In 2001, France crafted a five-year agenda to shift to a results-oriented form of management that integrated outcome measurement with budgeting.

Legislating Performance-Based Management in the United States

President Bill Clinton signed into law landmark legislation called the **Government Performance and Results Act (GPRA) of 1993**[3] that required federal agencies to develop three key elements of an effective program performance measurement system: (1) *strategic plans* that cover a five-year period with updates every three years, (2) *annual performance plans*, and (3) *annual performance reports*.

In the findings and purposes of the third aspect, Congress states what the Act needed to achieve –

(1) improve the confidence of the American people in the capability of the Federal Government, by systematically holding Federal agencies accountable

for achieving program results; (2) initiate program performance reform with a series of pilot projects in setting program goals, measuring program performance against these goals, and reporting publicly on their progress; (3) improve Federal program effectiveness and public accountability by promoting a new focus on results, service quality, and customer satisfaction; (4) help Federal managers improve service delivery, by providing them with information about program results, and service quality; (5) improve congressional decision making by providing more objective information on achieving statutory objectives, and on the relative effectiveness and efficiency of Federal programs and spending, and (6) improve internal management of the Federal Government.

Over the years since the passage of GPRA, the implementation and use of its requirements to provide and utilize performance information has been a mixed bag. It has not really been the panacea for government reform its sponsors imagined it could be. Many agencies treated it as a gratuitous exercise in paperwork rather than as an effective tool to improve management of federal programs. Congressional appropriators and overseers have not availed themselves of the tools that GPRA has provided. In short, they don't speak the language of outcomes created by GPRA when making budgetary decisions or conducting oversight of programs. If Congress itself would focus on outcomes and makes spending decisions with outcomes in mind, agencies would have more incentive to focus on them.

Defining the Terms of Strategic Planning

As government agencies and programs work to develop strategic plans, there are several steps and components necessary for developing a successful strategy. These steps form an interlocking structure, with each part supporting the others, in essence a scaffolding that provides the planning architecture for the agency or program. First, it is necessary to develop a statement of the program's *mission*, a concise statement of the agency's or program's purpose, usually by answering the following questions: "What are we doing, why, and for whom?" Second, statements of *goals* need to be developed. These are statements of outcomes to be achieved by the agency or program, usually by answering the question "What are the general ends embodied in the mission?" Next, statements of *objectives* are necessary. By answering the question, "What are the expected results?" programs or agencies can establish measurable targets that describe the results a program is expected to achieve in a given time period. Establishing meaningful *indicators* or *measures* is challenging but vital to the successful operation of any program or agency.

Within the category of indicators or measures, there are four types which are considered necessary to manage programs or agencies effectively. *Inputs* are the personnel, funds, or other resources that contribute to an activity. *Outputs* are quantitative or qualitative measures of activities, work products or actions. For example, an output may be defined as the number of enforcement actions taken in a given year. *Intermediate outcomes* are changes in knowledge, behavior, or conditions that result from program activities and are needed to achieve the end outcome – for example, pounds of pollution reduced from enforcement actions. Finally, *end outcomes* are the ultimate results the program is designed to achieve, such as improvements in air or water quality. Table 5.1 defines and describes the types of performance measures, and their advantages and disadvantages.

Purposes Served, Benefits Derived from Measuring Performance

Performance indicators/measures serve many purposes that make public programs and agencies more effective.[4] One of the most basic purposes served by measures is to *control* program operations, ensuring subordinates are focused on the right activities, and enabling managers to increase, decrease, or shift inputs.

Another purpose served by measures is to *motivate* personnel to improve performance by comparing real-time outputs with production targets. A third purpose served by measures is to *promote*, by demonstrating that the agency or program is doing a good job by communicating easily understood aspects of performance about which citizens actually care. A fourth purpose served by measures is to *recognize* worthy accomplishments through significant performance targets that provide a real sense of personal and collective accomplishment. Performance measures can be an aid to *budgeting*, helping to figure out how best to spend public funds, sometimes using efficiency measures (i.e., outcomes or outputs divided by inputs). Importantly, performance measures can also help agencies or programs *learn* what is working or not working, and help discern why or why not, usually through disaggregated data that can reveal deviances from the expected. Another important purpose of performance measures is to *evaluate* how well we are performing by analyzing outcomes, combined with inputs and related factors. The final and arguably most important purpose for performance measures is to *improve*, by raising questions about what we should do differently to improve performance through examining patterns and relationships that link changes in operations to changes in outputs and outcomes.

The benefits of performance measures are: (1) improved control of program operations, (2) improved ability to set goals and develop strategies, (3) improved decision-making for resource allocation, (4) improved ability to identify and correct performance issues, (5) improved ability to motivate employees, and (6) improved ability to communicate with the public. This last benefit, communicating with the public, is very important in ensuring continuing support from constituents, stakeholders, and overseers in the legislative and executive branches.

TABLE 5.1 Categories of Performance Measures

	Output	Intermediate Outcomes	End Outcomes
Definition	Tabulation, recording of activity or effort usually in quantitative terms	Progress toward end outcome, such as change in behavior or other contributing results, expressed in quantitative or qualitative terms	Ultimate result(s) program is designed to achieve
Purpose	Track amount of activity being produced in a specific time period	Track amount/type of results produced by outputs during a specific time period	Track progress toward achieving larger social goal
Example	No. of enforcement actions issued in FY 08	Amount/types of pollution reduced due to completed enforcement actions in FY 08	Amount/types of health benefits achieved due to FY 08 enforcement actions
Accomplishment Statement	"In FY2008, EPA referred 250 cases to DOJ"	"In FY 2008, EPA enforcement actions resulted in 2.3 billion pounds of pollution reduction"	"In FY 2008, EPA enforcement actions reduced health care costs by $3.8 billion, premature deaths from heart/lung disease by 500…"
Advantages	-Relatively easy to collect data to count activities and report to public -Provides a sense of what is produced with available resources	- Provides a sense of how outputs contribute to end outcomes - Direct causal connection between activity and result - Results occur in relatively short time	- Helps make definitive connection between gov't activity and end result - Provides insight about whether goals/mission is being achieved
Disadvantages	No insight about results, consequences that flow from activities	Not as meaningful as end outcomes	End outcomes may not occur for extended period - Technical challenges in measuring complex social conditions - Many forces contribute to end outcome
Notes	Counts activity or behavior of persons *internal* to program or organization		Counts activity or behavior of persons *external* to program or organization (i.e., target population)

Developing Performance Measures

> Not everything that can be measured is important.
> Not everything that is important can be measured.
>
> *Albert Einstein*

The process of developing performance measures can be thought of as a three-stage model. (See this process depicted in Table 5.2.)

The first stage in the model is **Identifying Potential Measures**. The second stage of the model is **Designing Measures**. And finally, the third stage is **Using Measures as a Management** Tool. The best practices should be used in a mostly linear fashion, though the work on some (especially within a given stage) can happen simultaneously.

Stage 1, **identifying potential measures**, involves casting a wide net to determine what is important to measure. The first of the nine best practices in this stage is to *determine the scope* of the measures – is it a national, regional, or local program, and are we measuring a whole program or a specific initiative or approach to a public problem? The second of the best practices is *consulting with stakeholders and staff*. Meetings with these parties can be used to solicit ideas for potential performance measures, ideas for criteria to evaluate potential measures, and ideas for guiding the overall effort to develop and use indicators. This is followed by the

TABLE 5.2 Model for Developing and Using Performance Measures

Stage 1: Identifying Potential Measures	Stage 2: Designing Measures	Stage 3: Using Measures as a Management Tool
Best Practices	Best Practices	Best Practices
• Determine scope • Consult with stakeholders and staff • Apply logic model • Develop guiding principles • Select criteria for evaluating indicators • Develop common definitions for key terms • Inventory existing data sources • Look beyond existing data • Select appropriate combination of indicators	• Use internal teams to determine how to design and test • Conduct pilot projects • Develop in phases • Consult with experts • Monitor design and testing • Create and distribute development plan • Ensure timely and accurate reporting	• Monitor performance with regular reports • Analyze performance of organizational units • Review effectiveness of specific programs • Report to external audiences • Analyze behind the numbers • Assess and adapt indicators

best practice of *establishing definitions for types of measures and applying logic models*. Early in the process of developing measures, it is vital that an agreed-upon set of definitions for terms such as inputs, outputs, and outcomes (both intermediate and end outcomes). Also, in this stage, it is useful to create a "map" of activities and results, using a logic model to identify the full range of results of program activities, with particular attention to intermediate outcomes. This stage is also the time to *inventory existing data sources* to determine whether existing data will support potential measures. Limitations of data sources should not limit consideration of potential measures. The final step in this phase is to *select the appropriate combination of measures for further development*. The criteria for selecting measures to be developed further include: (1) potential measures need to be *relevant* to goals, objectives, and priorities; (2) potential measures need to be *transparent* and promote understanding of the agency or program; (3) potential measures need to be *credible* and based on data that is complete and accurate; (4) potential measures need to be *functional* to encourage constructive behavior; (5) potential measures also need to be *feasible*, i.e., their value to the program outweighs the cost of implementation; and (6) potential measures need to be *comprehensive*, covering important operational aspects.

The second stage, **designing measures**, has seven major practices for getting measures prepared for use in managing programs and agencies. The first of these best practices is to *use internal teams to determine how to design and test measures*. The internal work teams should work to complete the following tasks: (1) define measures in more detail, (2) review relevant data in existing data systems, (3) develop new information collection and reporting processes, and (4) establish schedule for developing and testing measures. The second of the best practices is to *conduct pilot projects*, to try out new or modified measures to see how they contribute to providing an account of performance. Another best practice is to *execute implementation in phases*, for example, by grouping similar measures to be implemented concurrently. A fourth best practice is to *consult experts to resolve technical and methodological issues*, for example, using a statistician to help with any measures that might benefit from sampling. Another best practice is to *monitor closely the design and testing of measures*, perhaps through the use of a management oversight team that examines the benefits and issues associated with the new measures and raises questions at the appropriate times. A fifth best practice is to *create and distribute a development plan* widely inside the whole organization so every member sees the momentum or the impediments to progress. The sixth and final best practice is to *ensure timely and accurate reporting*, by, for example, getting senior managers to promote such reporting in oral and written statements to staff members, and making reporting practices a subject of routine management reviews.[5]

The next stage, **using measures as a management tool**, has six practices for getting measures to aid in the management of agencies and programs. The first of the best practices is to *provide regular reports to monitor performance*, letting staff and managers see the products and benefits of developing measures. Even if the initial reports only provide information on basic outputs of the organization, providing regular reports of things produced by the organization begins to develop a culture of measurement for the organization. Another crucial practice in this phase is to *review performance of organizational units*, such as regional offices that are part of the national program, to get a clear sense of the relative contribution of those units to the program's overall output. Similarly, another is to *review the performance of specific programs*. For example, the air pollution control program of an environmental protection agency can be examined separately from the other program elements. The fourth is to *begin reporting to external audiences*, letting them in early on a new account of agency or program performance, and getting them involved in discussions about what is most valuable for the agency or program to produce and measure. The fifth practice is to *analyze behind the numbers*. This recognizes that measures can only tell that a given output or outcome has increased or decreased, but it cannot tell you <u>why</u> that measure has increased or decreased. Measures, thus, serve as a beacon to draw attention to an area of a program or agency that needs further scrutiny to determine what is actually happening. The sixth and final best practice in the "using measures" phase is to *repeatedly assess and adapt measures*. This practice should occur on a continuous basis, as we learn more from the use of measures and the repeated review of them. We may see things that need to be adjusted or changed in the data collection process or the definition of the measure or we may come to the conclusion that the measure is not valuable enough to afford the cost of collecting data about it.

Having developed and begun using measures, there are several ongoing challenges in the use of measures. For example, the sheer duration of implementation can stretch over multiple years. This provides challenges about the continuity of the effort and to the commitment of senior managers to see it through to its conclusion. Second, the lack of interpretative skill in the corps of managers and staff who will be the custodians of applying the measures, will need to be built up and maintained for a considerable period of time. Third, when the use of measures becomes transparent, they may be subject to misuse or misinterpretation by external audiences. Fourth, there are inherent limitations in the use of measures. For example, as mentioned above, they do not provide an explanation about *why* a measure has increased or decreased, but merely *signal a need for deeper review.*

Obstacles to Performance-Based Management Reforms

When we examine the state of performance measurement in the public sector, we need to understand the factors that have hampered the spread of performance-based management. Four types of obstacles have been present over the years – *institutional, pragmatic, technical, and financial* – and they continue to hamper wider acceptance and applications of performance measurement in the public sector.[6]

Institutional Obstacles. Utilizing performance measures has been unfamiliar to the background and management style of many public sector managers (especially those from non-quantitative disciplines). Many managers are unaccustomed or even unreceptive to using quantitative data as a basis for decision-making. Sometimes managers who have survived previous management fads – e.g., zero-based budgeting, management by objectives – experience "innovation saturation" which leads them to take a cynical view of the latest "management revolution."

Another institutional obstacle to the acceptance and use of performance measurement is a government's degree of openness. If a government is not prepared to work with constituents about questions raised by the performance numbers publicized by a government, that government will choose to avoid the turmoil of opening such a discussion. The "readiness" of a government to use performance measurement depends on a number of factors in an organization, including: the presence of strong political and administrative leadership; an emphasis on making decisions based on facts; trust between management and elected officials; favorable past experiences with innovative budgeting techniques and related productivity/work quality programs; an expectation of organizational stability; and appropriate incentives within government to encourage administrators to move forward with productivity improvement efforts.

Pragmatic Obstacles. The reluctance to apply performance data arises from many reasons. Many officials do not find such data useful or appropriate, or the data do not tell them anything *new* that they can and will use, especially regarding priority issues. Often their experience is that performance information seems to confirm what managers and staff already knew or to provide new information for low priority areas. From the perspective of middle and line management, performance measurement has too often been viewed merely as piles of paperwork to be completed and mounds of information that no one ever looks at. Performance measures have often turned out to be information in search of an application, with substantive uses few and far between.

Thus, the reputation of performance measurement as a distraction of little value is a significant obstacle to its continued use. Performance measurement poorly conducted only contributes to the reluctance of managers to take up measurement initiatives. Conducting these initiatives using the steps outlined above will help ensure success.

Technical Obstacles. Confusion over definitions persists, with terms like "government performance" and "productivity" still casting a fog over initiatives, and operational definitions of types of measures (i.e., outputs, intermediate outcomes, and end outcomes) are still a subject of debate.

A more serious technical obstacle is making performance data available in a timely fashion. For certain programs, there is an inherent lag in getting data about the results of government efforts, such as for research programs, environmental initiatives, employment programs, and many others.

Another technical obstacle to the adoption of performance-based management is the need for multiple measures to understand program performance. This is exacerbated by the many clients, constituencies, and perspectives that need to be considered in assessing government performance. The practical result of having multiple measures for a single program can be information overload that overwhelms potential users with a "rat's nest" of rising and falling trend lines which makes it difficult to synthesize, interpret, and communicate the results and dilutes the importance of individual measures.

In the last analysis, we often have only a vague understanding of why particular results occurred, and what can be done to improve them. Public sector performance measurement is, in effect, like "putting a meter on a black box": we have little knowledge of the mechanism inside and no theory linking inputs, processes, outputs, and outcomes to explain why a particular result occurred or to prescribe what management or organizational adjustments are needed to improve performance.

Financial Obstacles. Measurement of government performance requires the collection and reporting of data at each point along the causal chain – inputs, processes, outputs, and outcomes, as well as external factors. As noted by Wholey and Hatry, "The costs of performance monitoring must always be balanced against the value of performance monitoring in improving government performance and credibility."[7]

Measuring government performance requires resources, including: the staff to collect and analyze data; the systems to ensure the data flows that support each measure; managers who can discern what operational adjustments are suggested by increasing knowledge about the results created, and the reporting mechanisms to involve the public and increase the credibility of the program in the eyes of the public.

Epilogue

When the United States passed the GPRA in 1993, it stood at the brink of what could have been a new age of public management. With the passage of time, it is clear that the Act did not have the impact that was hoped for by its supporters.

The Act was greeted by many agencies as a paperwork requirement, rather than as a tool to improve management and performance. The oversight agencies such as the Office of Management and Budget (OMB) greeted it as just another thing to check in with the agencies about, rather than as an important tool for changing government. Congressional appropriators and overseers did not embrace the Act's requirements as a way to insist on improved performance in the agencies over which they had jurisdiction. Stakeholders and the general public missed an opportunity to familiarize themselves with the services and products of government and to demand better performance from the agencies that provide them.

What could have transpired in the wake of the passage of GPRA was: (1) the development of missions, goals, objectives, and performance measures using a model of public participation that engaged constituencies and the larger public in setting the course for public agencies; (2) the advent of an evaluation ethic among public managers, congressional overseers, and the public that would have motivated continuous improvement in the performance of government programs, and (3) a more enlightened civic discourse about the role of government, how to calibrate its impact, and how to control our investment of resources in government.

This would have taken a conscientious approach to the Act's implementation. But once passed, those responsible for the effort behind the law turned their gaze away, as often happens in the wake of a passage of a law. The effort wanes when the law crosses the finish line and implementation is viewed only as the province of a cadre of bureaucrats in a small number of agencies.

This tendency for supporters to turn their attention elsewhere after the law is passed, is a weakness in our democracy. In the case of the GPRA, the opportunity for important and fundamental reform was squandered.

Key Concepts

1. Performance-based management has been defined as "the purposeful use of resources and information to achieve and demonstrate measurable progress toward agency and program goals." The key steps in performance-based management are as follows: developing a reasonable level of agreement on mission, goals, and strategies for achieving the goals; implementing performance measurement systems of sufficient quality to document performance and support decision-making; using performance information as a basis for decision-making at various organizational levels.

2. Along with various other countries that moved toward performance-based management, the United States passed the GPRA of 1993. GPRA required the development of strategic plans that covered a five-year period, the development of annual performance plans and annual performance reports.

3. Strategic planning requires steps that include defining the mission of a program or agency, developing goal statements to identify outcomes to achieve, identifying objectives to carry out the goals. Performance measures need to be developed such as inputs, outputs, intermediate outcomes, and end outcomes. These steps form an interlocking structure that provides the scaffolding for a planning architecture for the agency or program.

4. The purposes served by measuring performance include: control of program operations; motivation of personnel to improve performance; promote the agency or program by communicating aspects of performance; recognition of worthy accomplishments; budgeting for the best use of public funds; helping agencies learn to what is working or not working; evaluating how well the agency is performing; and, most importantly, to improve by examining patterns and relationships between changes in operations to changes in outputs and outcomes.

5. The benefits of performance measures are the following: improved control of program operations; improved ability to set goals and develop strategies; improved decision-making for resource allocation; improved ability to identify and correct performance issues; improved ability to motivate employees; and, improved ability to communicate with the public.

6. The three-stage model for developing performance measures includes: *identifying potential measures*, including nine best practices; *designing measures*, including seven best practices; and *using measures as a management tool*, including six best practices.

7. There are several obstacles to performance-based management reforms, and they divide into four categories, including *institutional obstacles*, *pragmatic obstacles*, *technical obstacles*, and *financial obstacles*.

8. The United States did not take full advantage of the GPRA and its potential to reform government and make it fully performance-oriented. Failures by implementing agencies, oversight agencies such as the OMB, congressional appropriators and overseers, constituencies and stakeholders, all contributed to minimizing the impact of the GPRA.

Notes

1 Joseph S. Wholey, "Performance-Based Management, Responding to the Challenges," *Public Productivity & Management Review*, Vol. 22, No. 3, March 1999, 288–307.

2 This discussion of international efforts to move to performance-based management is from Martin Cole and Greg Parston, *Unlocking Public Value*, (Josh Wiley & Sons, Inc., Hoboken, NJ, 2006).

3 Report of the Committee on Governmental Affairs, U.S. Senate to accompany S. 20 the *GPRA*, June 16, 1993.

4 This discussion of purposes is from an article by Robert D. Behn, "Why Measure Performance? Different Purposes Require Different Measures," *Public Administration Review*, September/October 2003, Vol. 63, No. 5.

5 The performance-management initiative that I helped direct in the compliance and enforcement program at the U.S. EPA was greatly aided by two of the Assistant Administrators who presided over the program during the years of the initiative. When they began to ask questions in our in-person reviews of regional program office programs about their reporting practices, especially about intermediate outcomes such as pounds of pollution reduced by enforcement actions, staff and managers finally understood the importance of reporting these accomplishments. They instantly began taking the measure seriously and even began targeting their enforcement actions at facilities where they could achieve significant pollution reductions.

6 John M. Greiner, "Positioning Performance Measurement for the Twenty-First Century." In *Organizational Performance and Measurement in the Public Sector: Toward Service, Effort, and Accomplishment Reporting*, edited by Arie Halachmi and Geert Bouckaert, (Quorum Books, Westport, CT, 1996), pages 11–43.

7 Joseph S. Wholey and Harry P Hatry, "The Case for Performance Monitoring," *Public Administration Review*, Vol. 52, No. 6, November/December 1992, 604–610.

Bibliography

Behn, Robert D. "Why Measure Performance? Different Purposes Require Different Measures." *Public Administration Review* 63, no. 5 (2003): 586–606, accessed September 9, 2021, https://academic.udayton.edu/richardghere/IGO%20NGO%20research/Behn_Robert_D.pdf

Cole, Martin, and Greg Parsten. *Unlocking Public Value: A New Model for Achieving High Performance in Public Service Organizations.* Hoboken, NJ: Josh Wiley & Sons, 2006.

Greiner, John M. "Positioning Performance Measurement for the Twenty-First Century." In *Organizational Performance and Measurement in the Public Sector: Toward Service, Effort, and Accomplishment Reporting*, edited by Arie Halachmi and Geert Bouckaert, 11–43. Westport, CT: Quorum Books, 1996.

Wholey, Joseph S., and Harry P. Hatry. "The Case for Performance Monitoring." *Public Administration Review* 52, no. 6 (1992): 602–610.

Wholey, Joseph S. "Performance Based Management: Responding Through the Challenge." *Public Productivity and Management Review* 22, no. 3 (1999): 288–307.

6

GREATEST ACHIEVEMENTS
OF GOVERNMENT

Sitting inside a bureaucracy, as a member of a team or branch, which is part of a division, which is part of an office or program, which is part of an agency, which is part of the executive branch of government, it is often difficult to see a direct line from your contribution to the mission or major accomplishments of the program or agency or to the larger purposes of the work you are doing. One way to gain some perspective to counter the feeling of being "buried in the bureaucracy" is to reflect on some of the greatest achievements of government and the roles someone in the bureaucracy contributed to make that happen.

Identifying the Greatest Achievements

Fortunately, Paul Light's book entitled *Government's Greatest Achievements: From Civil Rights to Homeland Security* has provided a very comprehensive description of the many things that government has accomplished over the 55-year period of 1944–1999. His results were derived from a survey of 450 history and political science professors. The survey focused on the federal government (though many of these accomplishments were dependent on state or local governments). He said that the survey suggests that the federal government not only aimed high but also suggests that it often succeeded in changing the nation and the world. The report suggests that "government deserves more credit than it receives."[1]

The report focuses on what the federal government actually sought to achieve and does not address whether the Congress should have asked government to undertake the endeavors it achieved, nor whether the federal government should have given greater energy to fewer priorities. The report asks, **what did the federal government try to do and what did it achieve?**

DOI: 10.4324/9781003266235-7

Building on previous research by Congressional scholars, 538 major statutes were identified as a base for building a list of greatest endeavors. They were selected on the basis of their significance, visibility, and/or precedent-setting nature. The laws range from the creation of new programs or government agencies to the passage of constitutional amendments and ratification of foreign treaties, and they cover virtually all areas of federal endeavor, from health care to economic deregulation, food and water safety to national defense.

The 538 statutes were sorted into 16 policy areas: agriculture, arts and historic preservation, civil rights, crime, the economy, education, health, housing and urban development, foreign policy and defense, government performance, income security, natural resources and energy, safety, science and technology, trade, and transportation. After sorting into policy areas, the statutes were sorted again based on the problem to be solved. This second sorting produced an initial list of the federal government's 67 major endeavors of the past half century.

That list was further winnowed to the final 50 based on the level of effort involved in each of the endeavors. The 17 endeavors that were not included in the final 50 were not unimportant. They included things such as ending discrimination in the armed services, providing help to the victims of natural or man-made disasters, promoting the arts, reforming the nation's campaign finance system. These endeavors were important, but they earned less attention from the federal government than the 50 endeavors that made the final inventory.

Most of the 50 finalists involve tight collections of laws organized around a consistent strategy for addressing a focused problem (e.g., crime, water quality, or arms control and disarmament). The list of 50 finalists is best viewed as the product of a good-faith effort to identify the problems that the federal government tried hardest to solve over the half century of 1949–1999.

Discussion of the Greatest Achievements of U.S. Government

The scoring and ranking of the achievements were based on the survey of 450 history and political science professors. It should be noted that this survey population has certain biases. The respondents are overwhelmingly white and male, highly educated (most with PhDs), and are not very representative of the population as a whole. They were chosen for their familiarity with public issues and the responses of government. Table 6.1 lists the top 10 highest ranked endeavors of the 50 greatest achievements of government during the 55-year period 1944–1999.

Regarding degree of **importance** of the endeavors, the survey used a point scale ranging from not difficult (1) to very difficult (4).[2] Respondents gave 50 endeavors an average rating of **2.9**. Finally, regarding the **success** of the endeavors, respondents were asked to rate the endeavors on a four-point scale from not successful (1) to very successful (4). Respondents gave 50 endeavors an average rating of **2.5**.

TABLE 6.1 Top 10 Ranked Achievements

The List of the Top 10 Highest-Ranked Greatest Government's Achievements on the List of 50 Greatest Government's Achievements

Rank	Endeavor	Ranking Based on Importance, Difficulty, Success		
1.	Rebuild Europe after world war	2	14	1
2.	Expand the right to vote	1	19	2
3.	Promote equal access to public accommodations	5	12	5
4.	Reduce disease	13	23	11
5.	Reduce workplace discrimination	4	3	20
6.	Ensure safe food and drinking water	8	36	18
7.	Strengthen the nation's highway system	40	49	3
8.	Increase older American's access to health care	12	31	9
9.	Reduce the federal budget deficit	34	7	6
10.	Promote financial security in retirement	18	38	10

Descriptions of the Top 10 Achievements

Though each of the top 10 achievements was significant in its time, some of them seem very distant from today's problems. Sometimes this is due to the problem being fully addressed so that it has faded from view as a concern for the public agenda. For example, the rebuilding of Europe after World War II seems a very distant accomplishment 60 years later. Others on this list, still seem unsolved (e.g., expanding the right to vote) or seem to be resurgent (e.g., reducing disease) with the advent of Covid-19.

Paul says there are three parts to the endeavors that he identifies. First, **every endeavor involves a problem.** Some problems are more difficult to solve, while others are easier. Some problems are more important, while others are judged less significant. Finally, some problems can be solved if the federal government takes the lead, while others are better handled by state and local governments, the non-profit sector, private groups, or individual citizens or families.

Second, **every problem involves a solution.** Some solutions can be found in passage of a law or laws, other solutions can be found in Supreme Court decisions, while others result from presidential orders. An endeavor demands tangible, not symbolic, action. Some problems involve more than one kind of solution.

Third, **every endeavor involves some level of effort.** This can be measured by the number of laws passed, pages of regulations written, the amount of money spent, or the number of employees hired. Great endeavors require more than great intentions: they usually require sustained action over time.

Here are summary descriptions for the top 10 achievements of government from 1949 to 1999.

#1. Rebuilding Europe after World War II. Rebuilding Europe is the oldest and only inactive endeavor on the top 10 list, and it is anchored in the Foreign Assistance Act of 1948 (better known as the Marshall Plan). Launched with the Bretton Woods Agreement of 1945, the nation could declare success for this endeavor by the end of the 1950s.

Nearly 60 years after the United States completed its most significant work in rebuilding Europe, this endeavor resonates as one of the greatest of the federal government's achievements. The roads, railroads, factories, and bridges that had been bombed into rubble had to be rebuilt; the economies that had been devastated by labor shortages needed to be rekindled; and the hunger, homelessness, and unemployment that marked the end of the war had to be addressed to get the war-torn continent healed. (This effort, which became known as the Marshall Plan, is discussed in more detail in Part II of this book in the profile of General George Marshall.)

By helping the economies of Western Europe, this endeavor simultaneously helped alleviate suffering abroad, contain communism, create a vibrant market for American goods, and establish America as the preeminent world power. This endeavor was central to the nation's broader effort to protect free people from terror and oppression. As President Harry S. Truman said in 1947, "The seeds of communism are nurtured by misery and want. They spread and grow in the evil soil of poverty and strife. They reach full growth when the hopes of a people for a better life has died."[3] The Marshall Plan, at its most basic level, was aimed at the restoration of hope.

George Marshall had served as Army Chief of Staff during World War II and had joined the Truman administration as Secretary of State. Marshall had created a Policy Planning Staff at the State Department, and he gave them the charge to design a relief program that would be accepted at home and abroad. Marshall then chose the delivery of a commencement speech at Harvard University to announce the plan. He said of the European Recovery Plan, as it was formally titled, "Our policy is directed not against any country or doctrine but against hunger, poverty, desperation, and chaos."[4] Marshall had seen and been deeply affected by the poverty and despair he witnessed firsthand as he traveled through Europe in March 1947.

The Marshall Plan provided about $12 billion in aid to increase economic production, expand European trade, encourage new economic ties between former enemies, and put an end to the rampant inflation of the time. The program was limited to four years, either succeeding on that timetable or not. The program demanded cooperation from the nations it was designed to help. Nations could only receive funding if they created a new organization to distribute the funding. Twenty-two nations were invited to the first organizational meeting in the summer of 1947, but only 16 showed up, as the Soviets and their communist allies in Europe chose to develop their own relief program.

There was substantial opposition in Congress from Republicans and Democrats who wanted to protect U.S. workers from new competition abroad. Many Americans opposed help to Germany and Italy. But in February 1948, the government of Czechoslovakia fell to the communists, and the opponents softened their opposition.

The Marshall Plan was adopted in the late spring of 1948 and had almost immediate success. Within two years economic production across Europe had risen almost 25 percent over prewar levels, and within four years it was up 200 percent. By 1952 unemployment, homelessness, and inflation were all trending downward.

The Marshall Plan was a stunning foreign policy success, but it was also a great moral victory for America. General Marshall received the Nobel Peace Prize in 1953 for his work restoring Europe.

#2. Expanding the Right to Vote. Ten statutes comprise this broad effort to protect and expand the right to vote. Although the Voting Rights Act of 1965 is the list's flagship, it shares the endeavor with three extensions in 1970, 1975, and 1982, three earlier statutes (the 1957, 1960, and 1964 Civil Rights Act) and two constitutional amendments (the 24th outlawing the poll tax, and the 26th lowering the voting age to 18), making it an endeavor of notable endurance.

In 1870, African-American men finally won the right to vote under the 15th Amendment, a simple one-sentence amendment prohibiting states from denying the right to vote on account of race, color, or previous condition of servitude. But states in the South quickly invented a variety of devices to raise the costs and risks of voting for African-Americans. Some states imposed a poll tax on voters, requiring citizens to vote in a given election, while other states created literacy tests that required citizens to recite the constitution of the state before being allowed to even register to vote. Still other states defined primary elections as private events, thereby evading the 15th Amendment by creating a whites-only system for nominating white candidates who often ran unopposed in the general election.

By 1940 only about 12 percent of African-Americans were registered in the South. African-American registration rates climbed to 40 percent over the next 20 years, due in part to federal pressure on a handful of southern states, and in part to the civil rights movement itself, which urged African-Americans to protest a host of injuries. Voting rates also increased after the passage of the 24th Amendment in 1964, abolishing the poll tax in national elections, though it did not apply to state and local elections, which meant that African-Americans faced serious obstacles converting their right to vote into reality.

Then came Bloody Sunday on March 7, 1965, marking the bloodiest confrontation of the civil rights movement, when 600 protesters led by the Rev. Martin Luther King, Jr. began walking from Selma, Alabama toward Montgomery, Alabama. King had selected Selma as the target for his voting rights campaign. Acting under orders from Governor George Wallace to stop the march, state troopers went into the crowd with tear gas, whips, police dogs, and ropes, clubbing the protestors and eventually driving the marchers back nearly a mile to the spot where the march began. These events were televised, and many Americans saw the brutality as it happened.

President Johnson called Bloody Sunday "an American tragedy" and he convened a special session of Congress on March 15 to demand immediate action on voting rights. In his speech, Johnson reminded Congress that

> it is wrong – deadly wrong – to deny any of your fellow Americans the right to vote in this country. We have already waited a hundred years or more, and the time for waiting is over. Their cause is our cause too, because ... really it is all of us, who must overcome the crippling legacy of bigotry and injustice. And we shall overcome.[5]

Bloody Sunday not only propelled the Voting Rights Act to passage within five months but also made the bill much tougher than it otherwise would have been. The final law included seven separate sections that guarantee voting rights, including giving the federal Department of Justice the authority to dispatch federal examiners to register citizens to vote in seven states. The law began to achieve results almost immediately – within a year adding 124,000 African-Americans to the voting rolls, and by the end of 1966 nearly a million more. Nearly 45 million new voters had registered under the law by 2000.

But the right to vote is perpetually under assault. Voter suppression practices were still in place for the 2020 presidential election, with some states limiting the number of polling places, and engaging in other practices designed to make access more difficult. After the 2020 election, many Republican-controlled state legislatures in the South and elsewhere introduced many voter suppression laws which devised many new provisions for limiting access through new registration requirements, curtailing vote by mail procedures, and limiting the availability of polling places. Ensuring the right to vote remains a work in progress, due to Republican efforts to keep likely Democratic voters from voting.

#3. Promote Equal Access to Public Accommodations. This endeavor involves three statutes, beginning with the Civil Rights Act of 1964, expanding with the Open Housing Act of 1968, and concludes with the Americans with Disabilities Act of 1990. Thus, it shares one of its three statutory foundations with the effort to eliminate workplace discrimination, and expand the right to vote, confirming the enormous impact of the Civil Rights Act as a core statute for the top 10 lists. It is arguably the single-most important statute on the original list of 538.

The campaign to open public accommodations to all Americans involved decades of struggle. The effort was not over when the nation ratified the 13th Amendment abolishing all forms of slavery in the United States. Nor was it over when Congress enacted the Civil Rights Acts of 1866, 1867, 1870, 1871, or 1875 which gave citizens "of every race and color the right to make and enforce contracts, sue and be sued, participate in politics, vote, and be given the full and equal enjoyment of public accommodations such as hotels, transportation, or theaters." Nor was it over when the nation ratified the 14th Amendment in 1868, even though the intent of the amendment is unmistakable: "No state shall make or enforce any law which shall abridge the privileges or immunities of citizens of the United States; nor shall any State deprive any person of life, liberty, or property, without due process of law …."

But various Supreme Court decisions upheld the "Jim Crow" laws that many states had passed to classify and segregate Americans by race. As African-Americans formed new organizations (e.g., the National Association for the Advancement of Colored People (NAACP)) to continue fighting those laws in the courts, they also began demanding change through a social movement around civil disobedience and boycotts. The successful Montgomery, Alabama bus boycott in 1955, in which African-Americans stopped riding city buses after a seamstress named Rosa Parks was arrested for violating the city's Jim Crow law by refusing to move to give up her seat on a city bus to a white citizen. The boycott ended after 381 days when the Supreme Court ruled that bus segregation was unconstitutional, and it gave a young minister named Martin Luther King, Jr. his first national victory as a civil rights leader.

Then *Brown v. Board of Education* gave a major victory to African-Americans, in a case that shows how important the federal judiciary is to many of the federal government's greatest endeavors. Brown actually was a blend of five school desegregation cases (from Delaware, Kansas, South Carolina, and Virginia). As the *Brown* cases swept away hundreds of laws, they provoked intense opposition. Many southern politicians vowed to block schoolhouse doors, and some Southern states encouraged their school districts not to comply with the Supreme Court's order.

The movement to break down the color barrier hit its peak with the 1963 March on Washington, which included a powerful speech from Martin Luther King, Jr. He addressed 250,000 demonstrators at the Lincoln Memorial in one of the most moving speeches in American history. King's speech had a dramatic effect on public opinion but failed to move many in Congress, which easily derailed a new civil rights bill through a Senate filibuster. As the end of 1963 approached, the civil rights movement was stalled. But then came the assassination of President John F. Kennedy. President Lyndon Johnson demanded immediate legislative action on Kennedy's civil rights bill, as a way to honor the fallen president. Johnson rallied public opinion to the effort, finally overcoming a two-and-a-half-month filibuster.

With the opposition exhausted, the Senate finally passed the Civil Rights Act of 1964 in June. Unlike the previous versions of the act, the 1964 act authorized the U.S. Attorney General to withhold funds from any government program that was not desegregated to bring lawsuits in federal courts to force action and gave citizens the right to appeal certain kinds of discrimination.

#4. Reducing Disease. The obligation to protect the nation from foreign and domestic threats involves more than fighting wars and enforcing laws. It also involves protecting Americans from hidden threats such as disease, pollution, and unsafe foods. As science has learned more about preventing disease, the federal government's role has grown, whether through funding for advanced scientific research or programs to make sure all Americans are vaccinated against life-threatening illnesses. The Polio Vaccine Act of 1955, and the Polio Vaccination Act of 1965 are the starting points for the most eclectic group of statutes on the top 10 list. Alongside vaccinations assistance, the effort to reduce disease also includes targeted research on heart disease, cancer (the National Cancer Act of 1971), and stroke, bans on smoking, strengthening the National Institutes of Health (NIH) and lead-based poison prevention. Despite this dispersion, the endeavor reflects a clear commitment to reducing disease, whether through specific interventions or broad research investments. Federal involvement in buying and distributing vaccines has saved countless lives and billions of dollars spent on the costs of treating preventable diseases.

The federal government's reputation in reducing disease may no longer deserve recognition as one of government's greatest achievements as that achievement has taken quite a hit from the Trump Administration's blatant incompetence in handling the Covid-19 pandemic.

The federal role in vaccinating children against life-threatening diseases dates back to the beginning of the vaccination era in the late 1940s and 1950s, when Congress passed a set of acts in 1955 and 1961 to help state governments immunize all children against polio, diphtheria, whooping cough, and tetanus by the age of five. The Polio Vaccine Act was a desperately needed act for a desperate time. Americans were not quite sure how, when, or why the highly contagious poliovirus was transmitted. Some victims were permanently paralyzed, others were condemned to live in an iron lung machine, while others were strapped into leg braces to help them walk.

Although the disease was never as widespread as smallpox, its crippling effects were so terrifying, its victims so young, and its causes so unclear, that its spread created widespread panic. Fear led to quarantines, and quarantines led to greater fear.

The federal government stepped up its involvement in the crisis in 1955 when Jonas Salk finally developed a vaccine against the virus. Now the nation knew how to prevent the disease so the challenge was how to make sure that every child would be protected. Under the 1955 Polio Vaccine Act, Congress provided funding to make sure every child received the vaccine, and it required the Surgeon General to set standards for the testing and distribution of the vaccine to millions of children, without regard to their families' ability to pay.

The federal government continues to promote vaccinations against childhood disease through the National Immunization Program at the Centers for Disease Control (CDC). The CDC was created by Congress in 1946, and though it has been recognized as the world's pre-eminent authority for disease control, it acquired a black eye to its reputation during the Covid-19 debacle of the Trump Administration.[6]

Designed to help states and localities educate parents about the need for vaccinations and monitor the supply of vaccines, the immunization program has been a remarkable success. Since the 1950s when the federal government began distributing vaccines, the incidence of most childhood diseases has fallen by 95 percent or more. The number of polio cases dropped from 15,000 a year in the 1950s to zero today, while German measles has virtually disappeared from the Western Hemisphere.

The program has also produced a huge return on investment. Every dollar spent immunizing children against measles, mumps, and rubella saves $21 in future health costs, while every dollar spent on vaccinations for diphtheria-pertussis-tetanus saves $29.

The CDC does more than operate the national vaccination program. They also conduct in-depth research on some of the nation's most serious health issues, which has contributed to significant reductions in heart disease and significant gains in cancer survival rates. The CDC's disease detectives have been at the forefront of identifying a host of baffling illnesses, including the respiratory illness that came to be identified as Legionnaire's Disease, toxic shock syndrome in 1980, hepatitis C in 1989, and tracking down the causes of food poisoning outbreaks. The CDC also has a role in preparing the nation for a possible biological attack.

The CDC is not the only agency involved in reducing disease. The NIH was started in 1887 when the federal government began to study infectious diseases carried to the United States on passenger and cargo ships. As the number and types of infectious diseases grew, so did the federal government's involvement in health care research. By 2001, the NIH had 27 separate institutes on a 300-acre campus in Bethesda, Maryland. The investment has made a dramatic difference in the quality of life for most Americans. Deaths from heart disease are down by more than a third since the mid-1970s; five-year cancer survival rates are up by 60 percent; schizophrenia and depression are much more treatable. Although there are still significant differences in disease rates between the rich and poor and among African-Americans, Native Americans, and whites, Americans in general are living longer, healthier lives because of the federal effort to reduce disease.

The increase in life span is largely due to a decline in death at early ages. More children are surviving childhood as vaccinations and better nutrition and sanitation now prevent many of the illnesses that killed many in previous generations. Many more of today's middle-aged Americans will live to retirement age as medical research renders once-deadly diseases manageable. And more 65-year-olds will live into their 80s due to improved survival rates for heart attacks and cancer.

#5. Reducing Workplace Discrimination. The effort to prohibit employers from discriminating on the basis of race, color, religion, gender, national origin, age, or disability spanned several decades, and included laws such as the Equal Pay Act of 1963, the Civil Rights Act of 1964, the Age Discrimination Act of 1967, and the Americans with Disabilities Act of 1990. The United States has one of the most diverse workforces in the world. Currently, only 15 percent of new workers are white males, compared to almost 50 percent in the early 1980s.

As employee diversity has grown, so have calls for expanded protections against workplace discrimination. Many of these disputes have been settled in the Supreme Court. Women, older Americans, and the disabled have won a series of victories using the 1964 Civil Rights Act, the 1967 Age Discrimination Act, and the 1990 Americans with Disabilities Act to advance their cause. The endeavor illustrates that laws are not self-implementing, they often must be interpreted and enforced by presidents, federal agencies, or courts.

The women's rights movement, having been frustrated for over a century in their campaign to limit sex discrimination, won a big victory when Congress added the word "sex" to the prohibitions against discrimination on the basis of "race, color, religion, or national origin" in the 1964 Civil Rights Act. Once the bill passed, women had the lever they needed to demand workplace protection. However, they needed help from the Supreme Court to make sure the laws were interpreted and enforced.

A series of cases through the 1980s and 1990s began to expand workplace rights of women. For example, in 1998 *Faragher v. City of Boca Raton*, a 7-2 majority agreed that employers, not just individual employees, are responsible for preventing sexual harassment in the workplace. Even if they do not know that a supervisor is harassing an employee, employers can be held liable for damages.

Those with disabilities also won the full force of the laws protecting them through court cases that dealt with particular forms of discrimination. The effort to reduce workplace discrimination demonstrates the importance of both law and its enforcement in creating government achievements. Much of the progress in expanding voting rights, opening public accommodations, and addressing workplace discrimination have been a combination of legislation and judicial action. Congress can pass all the laws it desires, but it must rely on the federal courts to make those laws work. Similarly, the courts can make all the decisions they wish but they need Congress, the president, and the federal bureaucracy to make those judgments real.

#6. Ensure Safe Food and Drinking Water. There are nine statutes that comprise this long-running bipartisan effort, including the Federal Insecticide, Fungicide, and Rodenticide Act (FIFRA) of 1947 (signed by Democrat Harry S. Truman), Poultry Products Inspection Act of 1957 (signed by Republican Dwight D. Eisenhower), Wholesome Meat and Poultry Acts of 1967 and 1968 (signed by Democrat Lyndon B. Johnson), Federal Environmental Pesticide Control Act (signed by Republican Richard M. Nixon), the Safe Drinking Water Act of 1974 (signed by Republican Gerald R. Ford), and the Food Quality Protection Act of 1996 (signed by Democrat Bill Clinton).

The federal government has been working to protect citizens from tainted food and unsafe drinking water since 1906 when Congress passed the Food and Drug Act and the Federal Meat Inspection Act. The country was stunned by the publication of Upton Sinclair's *The Jungle* (see Part II of this book for a profile of Sinclair) in which the muckraking Sinclair reported about the appalling practices of the meatpacking industry, leading Congress to prohibit interstate commerce in misbranded food and drugs, which in turn gave the federal government authority to demand truth in labeling and inspect food processing plants. Congress then created a new program within the Agriculture Department to inspect all cattle, sheep, pigs, goats, and even horses at the slaughterhouse.

These two laws provided the platform for repeated expansion over a period of years. The Agriculture Department added the poultry industry to its inspection list in the 1920s, and Congress expanded the effort under the 1957 Poultry Products Protection Act. Congress also rewrote the Food and Drug Act in 1938 to give the Food and Drug Administration (FDA) new powers to make sure that food and drugs were not just properly labeled but safe to eat and use, then expanded it again and again over the years to keep pace with scientific breakthroughs and new threats to public safety, including bioterrorism.

Public demand for protection increased in the 1960s in part due to the publication of Rachel Carson's *Silent Spring* (see the profile of Carson in Part II of this book) which heightened public worries about pesticides. The creation of environmental interest groups also heightened awareness. Groups such as Ralph Nader's Public Citizen, the Natural Resources Defense Council, and Greenpeace joined forces with existing organizations like the Sierra Club, and the Wilderness Society. Between 1965 and 2000, Congress passed a long list of laws to protect citizens from environmental harm.

Having a Congress controlled by one party and the presidency controlled by the other party is often characterized as the worst possible circumstances for passing legislation. Certainly "divided government" makes passage of legislation more difficult, but Congress has passed some of the nation's most important legislation during just such periods.

The Safe Drinking Water Act is a good example of bipartisan lawmaking. The first version of the statute was passed by voice vote in 1974 by a Democratic Congress and signed into law by a Republican president; the first set of amendments was passed in 1986 by a Republican Congress and a different Republican president; and a third and final set of amendments in 1996 by a Republican Congress and a Democratic president. The Safe Drinking Water Act has been a success almost entirely because of legislative actions by a divided government.

The Act also established national drinking water standards for any system serving at least 25 people. The Act also gave the Environmental Protection Agency (EPA) the authority to regulate a number of threats to water purity, including bacteria, nitrates, metals, lead, and copper, all of which endanger human health. Congress also transferred responsibility for regulating pesticides from the farmer-friendly

Agriculture Department to the EPA in 1974, giving EPA the power to regulate all threats to water purity.

In future years, merely keeping up with population growth imposes substantial pressure on the federal government's public health agencies. Some Americans still drink from contaminated wells and aquifers, packing plants still have problems with cleanliness and bacteria, and advertisers often overstate the health benefits of various nutritional supplements, vitamins, and even teas.

#7. Strengthen the Nation's Highway Systems. Eight statutes underpin the ongoing federal effort to augment the national highway system, most notably the 1956 Interstate Highway Act. The multi-billion-dollar expansions of highway aid under the 1991 Intermodal Surface Transportation Act (ISTEA) and the 1998 Transportation Equity Act for the Twenty-First Century make this the most recently amended endeavor.

The federal government has long been in the business of roadbuilding, first becoming involved in building roads when the first Continental Congress appointed Benjamin Franklin as the first Postmaster General who was responsible for delivering the mail, which included building the roads. But building the roads was about more than delivering the mail, roads were a way of building the economy by facilitating interstate commerce.

The federal government has now built nearly 43,000 miles as part of the interstate highway system. Although that system represents just one percent of all highways in the country, it carries nearly one quarter of all roadway traffic and more than 60 times as much traffic as all passenger rail services. The interstate system has proven to be much safer than the old two-lane highway system it replaced. The Federal Highway Administration estimates that the system may have saved 200,000 lives since the first mile of pavement was laid in 1957.

The system did not come cheap. Established by Congress under the Interstate Highway Act of 1956, the system has cost roughly $350 billion to build, of which the federal government has contributed 90 percent. It is easy to argue that the benefits of the system far outweigh the costs. Lower accident rates saved billions of dollars in health costs and property costs, while the savings in time and shipping costs and thousands of transportation jobs have helped the economy grow. Reduced accident rates also saved thousands of lives.

Some experts argue that the construction of more highways to combat congestion actually adds to that congestion, pointing out that new roads lead to "induced travel," by people who might otherwise use mass transit (e.g., buses, subways).

The federal government has done much more than to build the interstate highway system, however, as it has invested billions in helping states and localities build roads, bridges, and highways. In doing so, they promoted the time-honored practice of pork-barrel politics. The $217 billion Building Efficient Surface Transportation and Equity Act of 1998 (BESTEA) is the latest in a long list of highway construction bills that provided federal aid back home. The primary sponsor of the bill, 12-term representative "Bud" Shuster (R-Penn) always defended the billions reserved for special projects earmarked by individual members of Congress. Even the Senate, which had long protested the earmarks as wasteful spending, offered a list of 360 projects worth $2.3 billion as the bill was moving to the final passage just before a scheduled recess.

The current efforts of the Biden Administration to enact a massive infrastructure bill to fund repair and replacement of parts of the nation's highway and railway systems show the need for the continuing commitment to invest in infrastructure systems over many years. It remains to be seen whether infrastructure investment will remain a bipartisan initiative or whether it will succumb to partisan bickering that prevents progress across many areas of current public policy.

The success of this endeavor may explain the failure of the federal government's effort to strengthen urban mass transit. By building highways instead of mass transit systems such as subways and light rail, the federal government encouraged Americans to travel to and from work by car, likely stimulating much of the urban sprawl that vexes commuters today, while diluting public support for urban mass transit. Thus, one endeavor's success can sometimes precipitate the failure of another endeavor.

#8. Increase Health Care Access for Older Americans. John F. Kennedy made Medicare for the elderly his top priority in 1961. But the endeavor actually dates back to the late 1940s when Harry S. Truman offered a much more comprehensive national health insurance program. It was Lyndon Johnson, with his mastery of the legislative process, who usually gets the credit for winning passage of the 1965 Medicare Act, which created an entirely new federal health insurance program to provide health care access for older Americans.

From the outset of the debate, the major barrier to action was the 150,000 members of the American Medical Association (AMA) who were adamantly opposed to what they labeled as "socialized medicine," be it for all Americans or just the elderly. The AMA had claimed credit for defeating Truman's proposal in 1950 and keeping health insurance off both party platforms in the 1952 and the 1956 presidential elections.

The tide began to turn in 1956 when labor unions won passage of a new Social Security program covering the totally and permanently disabled. The AMA was increasingly isolated in their opposition as the American Nurses Association and the American Hospital Association endorsed Kennedy's plan in 1961. But in spite of this growing public support, Democrats did not have the votes on the House Ways and Means Committee needed for passage, and Medicare slipped from the legislative agenda.

But the 1964 elections, which brought 65 new Democrats to Congress, changed everything. Emboldened by his landslide reelection, Johnson made Medicare his top priority, and congressional Democrats put the bill at the top of the legislative agenda in both chambers. Knowing that the bill was likely to pass, almost half of the Republicans voted for its passage. Johnson signed the bill at the Truman

Library in Independence, Missouri on July 30, 1965, and Harry and Bess Truman were enrolled as the first two recipients the same day.

The future of the Medicare program is clouded by upcoming financial uncertainties. By 2030 almost a quarter of all Americans will be eligible for Medicare, driving the cost up from an amount equal to 2.6 percent of gross domestic product today to roughly 5.3 percent in 2040 and consuming roughly a third of the entire federal budget. The looming financial crisis has three simple causes. First, the ratio of taxpayers to beneficiaries is about to fall rapidly as the baby boom cohort retires. Second, life expectancy continues to rise, meaning that older Americans will draw benefits longer. So, the good news for the health of older Americans has been bad news for the Medicare budget. Third, medical costs are rising much faster than other costs in the rest of the economy, making Medicare the fastest growing item in the federal budget. This strain will be exacerbated by the recently enacted coverage of prescription drug costs.

#9. Reducing the Federal Budget Deficit. Six statutes are part of the effort to balance the federal budget through caps, cuts, and tax increases, Including the Gramm-Rudman-Hollings Anti-Deficit Act of 1985, and the 1987, 1990, 1993, and 1997 deficit reduction/tax increase packages that contributed to budget surpluses. Launched in the mid-1980s as budget deficits swelled, this is the most recent endeavor on the top 10 list.

In the summer of 1999, the federal government had its first budget surplus in over 20 years. Although Congress and the president had set the process in motion with budget agreements in 1990, 1993, and 1997, the surplus showed up nearly three years ahead of schedule and was much larger than expected. The long economic expansion of the 1990s had done much of the work by increasing employment, and Congress and the president deserved much of the credit for restraining federal spending. Between 1990 and 1998, the discretionary portion of the federal budget actually fell by 11 percent, in inflation-adjusted terms. There were many good breaks that aided the budget outlook. For example, the end of the cold war produced a 26 percent cut in defense spending over the decade, allowing for a highly successful effort to close obsolete military bases.

What actions and forces led to the deficits that needed to be addressed in the 1990s? When President Reagan was elected in 1980, he became an advocate for the theory called supply-side economics, which argued that federal tax cuts would actually reduce inflation while balancing the budget through an infusion of revenues stimulated by economic growth. But these tax cuts (enacted in 1981) did exactly the opposite, because they reduced federal government revenues dramatically. Supply-side economics produced the largest federal deficits in American history.

By 1985, Congress realized it needed a means to restrain federal spending and it enacted the Balanced Budget and Emergency Deficit Control Act, which set annual targets for reducing the budget deficit, and required the president to reduce the federal budget by a uniform percentage if Congress exceeded the annual targets.

This approach worked well until the budget ceilings had to be revised in 1990, just before they would have been exceeded. Facing an $85 billion across-the-board cut, Congress set aside the Gramm-Rudman-Hollings law and entered negotiations with President George H.W. Bush on a package of tax increases and budget caps that yielded progress toward keeping the budget under control. Both parties exhibited the will needed to restrain spending, with the president agreeing to targeted tax cuts and Democrats agreeing to cuts in sacred-cow programs such as Medicare, welfare, and job training. Two additional compromises in 1993 and 1997 produced the first balanced budget in almost 40 years.

Reducing the budget deficit is a never-ending challenge. Social Security benefits owed to the retiring baby boom generation will be an enormous challenge far into the future. Additional spending during the George W. Bush administration (e.g., homeland defense, prescription drug coverage under Medicare), and the Affordable Care Act of the Barack Obama administration continue to present challenges to controlling the budget deficits.

And recently, during the Donald Trump and Joe Biden administrations, billions invested on several economic stimulus packages designed to provide relief to individuals and businesses during the Covid-19 pandemic, which will provide more challenges to the goal of getting and keeping the federal budget deficit under control.

#10. Promote Financial Security in Retirement. This endeavor began with the passage of the landmark 1935 Social Security Act. The program began with barely 200,000 beneficiaries who received the first checks in 1937. The program now provides benefits to 46 million Americans at an annual cost of more than $350 billion. It is financed by a payroll tax on wages, the Federal Insurance Contribution Act (FICA) tax is now collected from 152 million workers, compared to 46 million workers in 1937. Social Security is the federal government's single largest program, and it is the most popular program. (For an account of the development of the Social Security program, see the profile of Francis Perkins in Part II of this book.)

Social Security is both an **insurance** program, in which citizens contribute "premiums" in the form of payroll taxes in return for retirement "annuities" in the form of monthly checks, and a **welfare** program, in which the benefit formula is weighted to give low-income beneficiaries a much higher "rate of return" on their taxes, thereby providing a floor against poverty. Social Security is a classic "pay as you go" system in which today's taxes are mostly spent on today's benefits. Social Security's financing depends almost entirely on having enough workers and employers paying taxes into the program to cover the cost of benefits going out.

As the program gained public support, Congress and the President began expanding available benefits. There have been numerous instances of increasing benefits over the years. Congress established the Supplemental Security Income (SSI) program in 1972 to provide additional cash payments to the elderly, poor, and passed the Employee Retirement Income Security Act two years later to protect private pension plans. Together these programs have increased financial security for older Americans while cutting the poverty rate in this group from 35 percent to just 12 percent between 1970 and 2000. Without Social Security, almost half of Americans over the age of 65 would be living in poverty.

By 1981, the Social Security program was in financial crisis. In response, the Reagan administration proposed a deep cut in Social Security benefits. The proposal was denounced by all, so the Reagan administration hurriedly appointed a National Commission on Social Security, chaired by future Federal Reserve Board chairman Alan Greenspan, to resolve the crisis. Two years later the commission produced a $168 billion package of benefit cuts and tax increases to close the short-term deficit.

The compromise was a product of a brokered agreement between opposing parties. Business groups opposed an acceleration of the 1977 payroll tax increases, the American Association of Retired Persons (AARP) opposed any benefit cuts, and labor unions opposed any increases in the retirement age. These locked-in positions constituted the makings of a compromise, which meant that Congress and the president would have to hurt all sides equally. The White House and commission members created a "gang of nine" to develop a final package on which the White House, the Commission, and then the Congress could agree.

But the future of Social Security is dependent on future rescue efforts which will make the 1983 effort look easy. The situation is guaranteed to worsen in future years due to inevitable changes in the pool of beneficiaries. In 1935, there were 46 taxpayers for every beneficiary; by 2000 there were just three for one and in the 2010s the program spends more in benefits than it collects in taxes; by 2030 there will be only two taxpayers for one beneficiary, and it will exhaust the $2 trillion in savings it has been collecting. And the system will again be in crisis.

Though the sense of future crisis around the program has not grown enough to result in recent legislative action, the future crisis could be averted by raising the retirement age to 70 over the next decade, boosting tax rates by half a percentage point or so, and reducing the annual cost of living adjustment (COLA) by a fraction.

It is very unlikely that the day will come when American citizens will tolerate the collapse of Social Security. There will need to be a rethinking about the way to generate funds to pay the benefits that so many people count on for living their life with some financial security and sense of dignity. Finding a way to have an adequate funding base and reduced pool of beneficiaries will be one of the major challenges for those in government service over the next 30 years.

Lessons of the Great Achievements

A few things stand out from the list of the top 10 achievements. The first observation is that racial and other forms of discrimination are the basis for several of the highest rated endeavors. The presence of expanding the right to vote (#2 on the list), promoting equal access to public accommodations (#3 on the list), and reducing workplace discrimination (#5 on the list), speaks to the pervasiveness and intractability of prejudice (racial, gender, religious) in American life. In addition, reducing disease (#4 on the list) is tinged with racial overtones with African-Americans and Native Americans suffering higher rates of disease than other segments of the population. These discrimination-based problems are by no means solved and will show up in various forms in any future list of government "achievements." Also, the baby boomer generation has, predictability, confronted Americans with the challenges of providing health care to older citizens (#8 on the list) and providing financial security in retirement (#10 on the list).

Paul has not just compiled a list of the achievements; he has also tried to summarize the principal lessons to be learned from the successful efforts of government. In general, "achievement appears to be the product of endurance, consensus, and patience."[7]

Achievement seems to have firm roots in a coherent policy strategy. The government's top 10 achievements center on a mostly unified regulatory or spending strategy that is anchored in a relatively clear description of the problem to be solved and is supported by enough resources, budgetary or administrative, to succeed. Also, the top 10 achievements also involve relatively clear and measurable results. It is easy to tell whether government is actually making progress expanding the right to vote, reducing disease, building roads and bridges, and so forth.

Achievement appears to reside at least partly in the moral rightness of the cause, whether a belief in human equality, a commitment to world peace and democracy, or a commitment to honor promises to previous generations. In many of these achievements, the government acted by taking the moral high ground despite significant resistance.

Achievements reflect government's determination to **intervene where the private and nonprofit sectors simply will not go**. In this era of promises for smaller or more limited government, "it is useful to remember that the federal government seems to do best when it exercises its sovereignty **to take big risks that no other actor could ever imagine taking**."[8]

In looking at the patterns of these endeavors, the first lesson that Paul Light observes is that despite the focus of scholars on breakthrough statutes such as Medicare, **most of government's greatest endeavors involved a large number of statutes passed over a relatively long period of time**. Only 8 of the 50 greatest endeavors involved fewer than three major statutes: the remainder of the 50 great endeavors have approximately nine statutes per endeavor.

Second, it is difficult to give any single president, party, or Congress the primary credit for launching and maintaining more than a handful of the endeavors. Nine of the 50 greatest endeavors can be credited primarily to Democratic presidents, 5 can be credited to Republican presidents. The rest span Democratic and Republican administrations. As a result, even though Democrats controlled

Congress for the vast majority of the past 50 years, only six can be tied to unified party control of government. Almost by definition, **government's greatest endeavors reflect a stunning level of bipartisan commitment**, whether reflected in repeated raises in the minimum wage or the ongoing effort to contain communism. As Paul Light points out, "achievement appears to be the direct product of endurance consensus and patience"[9]

Third, government's greatest endeavors involved **a mix of policy strategies**. Twenty-six of the 50 endeavors focused primarily on *federal spending* as a policy tool, including programs to provide health care to the elderly, increase homeownership, and stabilize agricultural prizes. Another 20 focused on *regulatory strategies*, including programs to improve air and water quality, end workplace discrimination, and make government more transparent to the public. The final four involved a *mix of both spending and regulation*. In addition, only 13 of the 50 involved targeted benefits for a specific group such as the elderly, poor, veterans, or racial minorities. The rest diffused benefits across the nation more generally.

Future Challenges for Government's Attention

As this chapter was being completed, we have passed through the 2020 presidential election, and are in the beginning years of the Biden Administration. The voters have turned out an incumbent president in favor of a former vice president who exhibited throughout his campaign a level of competence, experience, and calm presence that built a bond with a record 80 million voters.

This presidential campaign was not as issue driven as others, but there was still discussion of many important issues by the candidates and others paying attention to the campaign. There is still much of that discussion hanging in the air as this book was being finished. Based on that discussion and some of the demographic and other trends taking shape, we can anticipate some of the looming challenges that government will confront over the next few decades.

Eliminating the Coronavirus and Preventing Future Pandemics. The first order of business for government achievements will be to get the world past the Covid-19 pandemic, and to prevent any future pandemics from wreaking the public health and economic devastation of the Covid-19 pandemic.

It would not be an exaggeration to describe the Trump administration's failure to protect the American people from the Covid-19 virus as one of the greatest failures of government in U.S. history. At this writing, the United States is entering the winter of 2020–2021, and over 700,000 Americans have died at the hands of the pandemic. The failure of the federal government to fully encourage and model even the basic preventive steps that all people can take to prevent the spread of the virus, is surely one of the great failures of the federal government. To not call on the American people to make these sacrifices, and to not summon the American people to be altruistic for the sake of their fellow citizens, is not only irresponsible but insulting to Americans.

Can the Biden Administration summon the altruistic spirit of the American people to do the things they can do to get the virus under control (such as restricting gathering in groups, wearing a mask, practicing social distancing, and frequent handwashing)? Will the Biden Administration put science at the center of their response to the virus, convincing the American people that in this matter and in others (such as climate change) that being guided by science is the right path to choose? Can the Biden Administration manage national supply chains to produce adequate amounts of personal protective equipment to safeguard medical personnel? Will the Biden Administration be able to use the vast resources of the federal government to distribute safe and effective vaccines to the groups in descending order of priority? Finally, can the Biden Administration provide adequate and timely testing for the virus to properly characterize the extent to which people will be experiencing symptoms and need to be isolated?

Progress on Climate Change. This was discussed mostly among the various Democratic campaigns during the 2020 primary elections, since President Trump still considered climate change a "hoax" that did not warrant the development of a plan to address it. Joe Biden made a good-faith effort to bring in many of the more progressive wing of his party to blend their ideas on climate change with his.

President Biden has rejoined the Paris Climate Accord. Administratively, this can be done easily, though our foreign allies and counterparts would be justified in wondering about the seriousness of the American commitment, which may make them less willing to be cooperative with American ideas and proposals going forward.

The Democratic platform and the Biden campaign expressed support for seeking major reductions of greenhouse gasses, though this will likely take considerable restructuring of various industrial and manufacturing practices (such as in the energy sector), to which there will be formidable opposition. It will take many years to reach substantial reductions in emissions of greenhouse gasses.

But setting goals (and making progress toward) these reductions has been made more urgent by the four-year hiatus occasioned by the Trump administration's total lack of activity in this endeavor. Look for the United States to make more progress in addressing climate change, and for entrenched U.S. industries to be dragged kicking and screaming toward that progress.

Can the Biden Administration and their successors convince Americans that the dangers of climate change are already manifesting and therefore need to take measures to combat it? Can the Biden Administration and their successors work with industry groups on the reduction of greenhouse gas emissions from their production processes? Can the Biden Administration summon the American people to follow certain practices (as buyers and consumers of products) to help alleviate climate change?

Resolving Health Care Policy. America has struggled to provide adequate health care to its citizens for several decades. Starting in the administration of

Harry S. Truman, many attempts were made to devise a health care system that would cover the needs of all citizens, especially the elderly. The Medicare Act of 1965 was the landmark legislation that provided health insurance for senior citizens.

But in the 2020 presidential election, there was much discussion about options for better health insurance coverage not just for the elderly, but for everyone. Particularly among the Democratic candidates in their primaries, there was much discussion about approaches for health insurance coverage, ranging from improvements to the Affordable Care Act (i.e., Obamacare), developing a public option for coverage, a Medicare for All approach, and other permutations. For his part, President Trump repeatedly promised development of a "great health care plan" that would lower costs, increase access to great health care, and cover pre-existing conditions. Regrettably, no such plan from the President ever materialized.

In fact, the Affordable Care Act is the only significant health care reform over the past 50 years. It is responsible for providing health care insurance to an additional 23 million people who previously could not afford coverage. If there was an analysis of the greatest achievements of government from 2000 to 2050, the Affordable Care Act and its successor Acts might be the first entry for that list.

Confronting Systemic Racism in Policing Systems. Perhaps the next frontier in confronting America's deep-seated racial prejudice is to address the problem in police departments across the nation. In "Race and Policing: An Agenda for Action," David Bayley, Michael Davis, and Ronald Davis observe that race remains an "American Dilemma," especially for police, and they lay out a very broad agenda:

> American police confront issues of race daily, in almost everything they do. They confront race in the geographic distribution of criminality and the fear of crime as well as in assumptions of what criminals look like. They confront race in the suspicion and hostility of many young African American men they encounter on the street. They confront race in complaints from ethnic communities about being either over- or under-policed. They confront race in charges of racial profiling and unequal justice. And they confront race in decisions about hiring, promoting, and assigning police officers.[10]

In his book *Handcuffed – What Holds Policing Back, and the Keys to Reform*, Harvard University's Malcolm Sparrow asserts that with respect to levels of police violence, other advanced democracies have also had their problems. "But the level of police violence in the United States, and sometimes the nature of it, seem both remarkable and appalling."[11]

It is only relatively recently that statistics have been kept about deaths at the hands of police violence. Police in America are currently shooting people dead at an average rate of three per day, while in the United Kingdom, by contrast, in the five-year period 2010–2014 police killed a total of four people, averaging less than one *per year*.

Is it possible that the police interaction with criminal suspects so frequently involves use of firearms because permissive U.S. gun laws have made guns so pervasive that the criminals the police are apprehending engage them fully equipped with firearms? Could the American phenomenon of having police interactions with suspects, African-Americans or otherwise, result in killings be attributed to a failure of police training – i.e., not teaching how to de-escalate confrontations, so that they inevitably escalate into violent resolutions? Could the police killings be a product of the culture within the police organizations, where they view themselves not as a community resource, but as an occupying army with an "us vs. them" orientation?

Perhaps the problem of police killings could be reduced by a combination of these ideas – more restrictive gun laws, better police training, and cultural changes in police departments.

Key Concepts

1. The selection of the government's greatest achievements was the product of a survey of history and political science professors, who examined the collection of major legislation from 1949 to 1999. This survey group had biases in gender, education, and ethnicity, but also was a group uniquely suited to be informed about the achievements of government over a long period.
2. The list of the greatest achievements has many endeavors designed to address the "American dilemma" of racism, for example, with respect to voting rights, access to public accommodations, and workplace discrimination.
3. The top 10 of the achievements – rebuilding Europe after World War II, expanding the right to vote, promoting equal access to public accommodations, reducing disease, reducing workplace discrimination, ensuring safe food and drinking water, strengthening the nation's highway system, increasing older Americans access to health care, reducing the federal budget, and promoting financial security in retirement – reflect the efforts of many public servants (not only those in government service) who saw problems in need of addressing and put their energy into solving them for the nation.
4. The lessons of the great achievements include: (1) most of government's greatest achievements involved a large number of statutes passed over a relatively long period of time; (2) government's greatest endeavors reflect a stunning level of bipartisan commitment; and (3) government's greatest achievements involved a mix of policy strategies, involving federal spending and regulation.

5. Government will be challenged by many difficult problems in the future including solving the current pandemic, implementing a climate change strategy, resolving health care policy, and addressing racism in policing.

Notes

1 Paul C. Light, *Government's Greatest Achievements of the Past Half Century*, Reform Watch Brief 6/18/01 (Brookings Institution, Washington, DC), page 1.
2 The value of having a deadline or sunset provision in developing and conducting a government program was demonstrated to me in my own career. As one of the managers responsible for distributing $50 million dollars in loans and grants to schools for asbestos abatement under the Asbestos School Hazard Abatement Act (ASHAA) of 1984, the statute imposed a deadline for distribution of the money to the schools of June 6, 1985. In many of the statutes that EPA administered, there were Congressional deadlines for completing statutory provisions, and the EPA had developed a habit of ignoring these deadlines, asserting that implementation takes longer than Congress realizes. In the ASHAA program, we were given a ten-month period from passage to deadline. We decided that we were going to try to complete the first round of fund distribution by the statutory deadline. When it became clear to the rest of EPA that we were on a quest to meet the deadline, other parts of the Agency that were expected to give us help in administering the program (e.g., the grants administration division, the economists in a division of our office) gave our requests higher priority as they did not want to be singled out as the reason we would not meet the deadline. On June 6, 1985, we met our deadline and distributed $50 million dollars to schools around the country.
3 Light, *Government's Greatest Achievements*, page 67.
4 Ibid., page 68.
5 Ibid., page 72. Johnson's speech was so moving that it is said to have moved Martin Luther King, Jr. to tears.
6 The politically appointed leadership installed at the CDC during the Trump Administration, Dr. Irwin Redfield (Director of the CDC) earned a black eye from public health experts for his willingness to water down guidance from the CDC to the states during the pandemic. However, the career public servants at the CDC, particularly Dr. Anthony Fauci, maintained public confidence and escaped unscathed from legitimate criticism, though President Trump seemed to grow increasingly willing to criticize Dr. Fauci as the election campaign neared and Trump began to realize he might lose the election largely due to his mishandling of the virus.
7 Light, *Government's Greatest Achievements*, page 63.
8 Ibid., page 64.
9 Light, Reform Watch Brief page 11.
10 Report quoted in Malcolm K. Sparrow, *Handcuffed, What Holds Policing Back and the Keys to Reform* (Brookings Institution Press, Washington, DC, 2016), page 30.
11 Ibid., page 31.

Bibliography

Bayley, David, Michael Davis, and Ronald Davis. "Race and Policing: An Agenda for Action." Office of Justice Programs, United States Department of Justice. June 2015. www.ojp.gov/ncjrs/virtual-library/abstracts/race-and-policing-agenda-action.

Light, Paul C. *Government's Greatest Achievements: From Civil Rights to Homeland Security.* Washington, DC: Brookings Institution Press, 2002.

Light, Paul C. "Government's Greatest Achievements of the Past Half Century," Reform Watch Brief. Washington, DC: Brookings Institution, November 2000.

Sparrow, Malcolm K. *Handcuffed: What Holds Policing Back and the Keys to Reform.* Washington, DC: Brookings Institution Press, 2016.

7

QUALITIES NEEDED BY FUTURE PUBLIC SERVANTS

> Public managers are explorers who, with the help of others, seek to discover, define and produce public value.... Greater public value can be produced by: 1) increasing the quantity or quality of public activities per resources expended; 2) making public organizations better able to identify and respond to citizens' aspirations; 3) enhancing the fairness with which the public sector organizations operate; 4) increase their continuing capacity to respond and innovate.
>
> *Mark M. Moore, from* Creating Public Value, Strategic Management in Government

When people hear the term "public servant," they think of presidents, governors, legislators, cabinet secretaries, agency directors – the political officials featured on news broadcasts, on political talk shows, and in newspapers and various websites. These officials are an important component of our system of governance, deserving of our scrutiny, praise, or sometimes our disdain. But they are only a small portion of the legion of people responsible for governing the nation.

The nation's career public servants implement the laws, carry out the programs, deliver the services, and manage the resources that keep the nation functioning. Many of them are public managers responsible for directing the programs and organizations of federal, state, and local government. They are selected through merit systems designed to ensure competence and continuity in the operation of government. They often operate in a hostile environment, in which criticism, cynicism, and resistance greet the actions of government.

Public managers also operate in an environment that affords many opportunities to improve the lives of others and contribute to the proper functioning of a democracy. The ability of the nation to address the most pressing and complex

DOI: 10.4324/9781003266235-8

problems largely depends on the effectiveness of public managers. The nation's most daunting challenges – those often beyond the capacity of the market and other institutions – are assigned to government, and the hard work of finding solutions falls uniquely on public managers.

Too many public managers emphasize operating and perfecting processes, procedures, functions, and hierarchical structures. The rules and accountability structures of large organizations impose this orientation on them, but public programs are expected to solve complex public problems. The traditional orientation of public managers does not position them to squarely confront public problems, which appear in myriad forms and do not fit neatly within the authority of one law, jurisdiction, or organization.

A successful public service that helps lead the country by addressing its public problems requires managers and leaders who understand and embrace the new imperatives of public management. These new imperatives mean that public managers need to serve as strategists and entrepreneurs, masters of improvisation, champions of effectiveness, reflective practitioners, and stewards of the public interest.

Strategists and Entrepreneurs

Public managers can no longer succeed if they remain in their traditional roles as technicians and administrators concerned only with controlling and refining organizational functions and processes. They now need to be *strategists and entrepreneurs* who identify emerging needs and demands, frame new opportunities for their programs and organizations, and reposition those programs to respond more effectively.

Public managers operate in an onrushing stream of public problems that emerge in many forms: risks, threats, inequities, conflicts, breakdowns, failures, and inefficiencies, to name a few. These problems compete for a place on the public agenda. Simply put, the formal mandates to which public managers hold title are often inadequate to address these problems, which do not fit neatly into existing laws, programs, and hierarchical organizations.

Effective public managers now need to develop the diagnostic skill and discipline to anticipate and identify problems, analyze them to understand their causes and interrelated parts, characterize their severity and urgency, and triage them to set priorities for action.

Public managers also need the skills and discipline to devise and implement appropriate responses. To do so, they must develop: a set of tools (policies, programs, and capabilities) that can be applied to problems; select the appropriate combinations of these tools to apply to each problem; look beyond their organizational boundaries for partnership opportunities with parties that offer resources, expertise, and authority for solving the problem; exercise both agility and persistence in implementing solutions; and measure the progress made.

Masters of Improvisation

Public managers need a broad perspective not fixed strictly on the status quo. They must be comfortable with constant surprise, able to function amid significant change, and anticipate a wide range of future scenarios.

Public managers often find themselves surrounded by ambiguity – about the problem they are asked to address, the authority they can bring to bear on that problem, resources available over the long-term, challenges they will encounter, and difficulties measuring success. They need to develop an appetite for dealing with ambiguity, turning ambiguity from a liability into an asset. In ambiguity lies opportunity, the chance to fill the gap left by statutory language, better define a public problem, and design tailor-made solutions.

The worsening crisis in public spending (exacerbated by the massive expenditures for coronavirus relief) will be a constraint or barrier to innovation or improvement, but it also provides an incentive or mandate for public managers to be more creative, innovative, and improvisational. Although resources (funds and personnel) are likely to continue their decline, demands for government intervention are likely to continue and expand, and the problems assigned to government may well become more complex and threatening (e.g., climate change).

Public managers need to be masters at developing adaptive business models that allow programs and organizations to adjust to new circumstances and still produce valuable results. They need to adapt to being conveners, leaders, or members of networks and other collaborative structures that combine the resources, expertise, and authority of multiple organizational entities. Such networks offer opportunities for new creative partnerships that can address problems and deliver services more effectively and comprehensively. In doing so, public managers need to be mindful of the tradeoff between the improved capabilities the networks provide and the difficulty of ensuring accountability of the multiple public and private partners in these networks.

Champions of Effectiveness

Public managers need to be relentless advocates for creating and measuring results and outcomes. They need to use performance-based management to ensure that their programs and organizations use resources wisely, produce useful activities and quality services, and achieve outcomes that support the mission or purpose for which they were created.

The principle tool available to public managers who wish to focus on results and outcomes is a set of meaningful performance indicators. A critical skill for effective public managers is a keen ability to identify, design, and use performance indicators or measures. Such indicators need to be: *relevant* (to goals, objectives, and priorities); *transparent* (promoting clarity and understanding); *credible* (based on complete and accurate data); *functional* (encouraging effective and constructive behavior); *feasible* (cost-effective); and *comprehensive* (addressing important operational aspects).

Most programs have some capacity to count or measure activities or *outputs* (such as the number of enforcement actions taken by a regulatory agency). Some programs attempt to measure *ultimate outcomes* (such as an improvement in ambient air quality or industrial workplace safety) though the program may only be one influence on these results. *Intermediate outcomes* – the territory between outputs and ultimate outcomes – hold the greatest promise for achieving performance-based management.

These intermediate outcomes (such as reduction or elimination of noncompliant behavior) have several advantages: (1) they provide a more meaningful account of program performance than outputs, offering a more compelling story about program accomplishments for the public and political overseers; (2) in contrast to ultimate outcomes, they directly relate to outputs; (3) measuring them presents fewer technical challenges than measuring final outcomes; (4) they manifest more quickly than ultimate outcomes; (5) they provide insight for managers and others about whether activities contribute significantly to final outcomes.

Identifying, developing, and using performance indicators is an iterative, incremental exercise: a journey rather than a destination. The benefits for public programs – better control of operations, stronger justification for scarce budget resources, enhanced understanding of patterns and relationships between activities and outcomes, and clearer demonstration of program effectiveness – are well worth the considerable effort.

Reflective Practitioners

Effective public managers continuously examine current practices, reviewing whether procedures and policies still make sense and evaluating the impact of their programs and organizations. They also continuously scan for ideas and approaches, assessing their applicability and potential for improving their effectiveness. They do not allow the press of day-to-day business to hamper their ability to raise issues about current reality or search for new ideas. Moreover, they create a "marketplace of ideas" in their organization and convey constant openness and receptivity to better ways of doing business.

Practitioners should cultivate an active dialogue with academic experts and thought leaders in public management and public policy as sources of fresh thinking. Any gulf between public management practitioners and academicians is unfortunate as they have much to learn from each other, and both would be strengthened by a closer relationship. Practitioners can help improve academicians' relevance, and academicians can help improve practitioners' effectiveness.

Given the magnitude and complexity of the public problems government must address, the public manager's success can no longer be left to ad hoc approaches to learning about supervision, management, and leadership. Instead, public managers need the formal, continuous education other professions – such as doctors and lawyers – use to stay current with developments in their professional field.

Stewards of the Public Interest

The "public interest" is a lofty and vague concept, but individual public servants and managers *can* contribute to the public interest through their day-to-day activities in their particular sphere of public policy and administration. They can objectively view the nature and causes of public problems and the options for addressing and resolving them. They can ensure balance and fairness in decisions affecting competing or conflicting interests. They can open public policy processes for participation in collaborative efforts to make decisions on public issues. They can use public funds and resources prudently and effectively. Finally, they can embody a passionate commitment to the mission of the organization and serve as a model for its members.

Our public discourse is often driven by chronic partisanship and short-term political gain. The tactics of those who practice this type of discourse include fear, distortion, intellectual dishonesty, and a cynical brand of simplification that obscures the complex nature of public problems and solutions. Our political culture often glorifies and celebrates individual freedom without regard for the common good, social equity, and the need for shared sacrifice.

This situation suggests a broader, emerging stewardship role for public servants. In these times, the nation desperately needs citizens who have not lost sight of the public welfare and demand that the public good receives the deference it deserves. Joining these citizens can be public servants who, as they tend to the public good in performing their jobs, provide a balancing force or countervailing influence on the excesses of our public discourse and political culture. They can help form the core of public-spirited citizens who still believe we have obligations to each other, responsibilities to preserve democratic ideals for future generations, and a need to be constructive citizens of the world.

Answering the Call to Public Service

The public sector is usually called on to address the nation's most serious, sweeping, and intricate problems, and career public servants must devise and take practical steps to identify and implement solutions. The conventional wisdom is that government is broken (a view aided by the Trump Administration's failure to deal with the coronavirus), that it is incapable of addressing even simple tasks, and is not up to the challenges of the future. Contrary to that conventional wisdom, government also has an impressive record of achievement (see Chapter 6 for a discussion of these achievements).

There is no shortage of challenges on the horizon that will be assigned to public servants. In the immediate future, getting the nation and the world past the coronavirus pandemic by: using the available tools and resources of the public and private sectors to correctly characterize the problem (through adequate and available testing); distributing appropriate Personal Protective Equipment to front-line health care workers; and developing and distributing safe therapeutics and vaccines. Another mega-issue is the growing income disparity between upper-class and working-class Americans which might be solved by a variety of economic tools that lead to wage increases and tax reductions. Finally, and most challenging of all, consider the magnitude and complexity of solutions needed to reduce and reverse global climate change, including: finding ways to reduce the emissions of greenhouse gases; developing alternative energy from renewable sources; educating people about myriad earth-friendly practices they can use daily to reduce their impact on climate change. And all of these things will need to be done in a way that does not "break the bank" with exploding deficits that will set the nation back for decades.

Key Concepts

1. The new imperatives for public servants mean that they need to serve as strategists and entrepreneurs, masters of improvisation, champions of effectiveness, reflective practitioners, and stewards of the public good.
2. Public managers can no longer succeed if they remain in their traditional roles as technicians and administrators concerned only with controlling and refining organizational functions and processes. They now need to be strategists and entrepreneurs who identify emerging needs and demands, frame new opportunities for their programs and organizations, and reposition those programs to respond effectively.
3. Public managers need a broad perspective not fixed on the status quo. They must be comfortable with change and anticipate a wide range of future scenarios. They need to be comfortable with ambiguity and see it for the opportunity it can be. The declining resources available to government also add great uncertainty and compel public servants to be comfortable with and skillful in using improvisation.
4. Public managers need to be advocates for creating and measuring results and outcomes of government programs. They need to become experts at identifying, developing, and using performance indicators, leading their organizations on a journey to better control of operations, stronger justifications for scarce budget resources, enhanced understanding of patterns and relationships between activities and outcomes, and clearer demonstrations of program effectiveness.
5. Reflective practitioners continuously examine current practices, reviewing whether procedures and policies still make sense, and always evaluating the

impact of their programs and organizations. The need for reflection should lead practitioners to partnerships with public administration academicians to engage in active dialogue about new ideas and approaches.

6. To be a steward of the public interest, public servants need to remain conscientious in carrying out their duties. But they should go beyond that role to join citizens interested in promoting the public good to provide a balancing force or countervailing influence to the excesses of our public discourse and political culture.

7. The challenges of the future will be daunting, from emerging from the coronavirus, to addressing income inequality, to reducing greenhouse gasses and getting climate change under control. These challenges will require public servants of the highest caliber, responsive to the needs and demands of people, skillful at using the considerable capabilities of the government.

Bibliography

Light, Paul C. *Government's Greatest Achievements: From Civil Rights to Homeland Security.* Washington, DC: Brookings Institution Press, 2002.

Moore, Mark H. *Creating Public Value, Strategic Management in Government.* Cambridge, MA: Harvard University Press, 1995.

Sparrow, Malcolm K. *The Regulatory Craft, Controlling Risks, Solving Problems, and Managing Compliance.* Washington, DC: Brookings Institution Press, 2000.

PART II

Examples for Effective Public Service

Profiles of Public Service Heroes

8

ABRAHAM LINCOLN

His "Sacred Effort" to Keep the Union Together

DOI: 10.4324/9781003266235-10

Abraham Lincoln gave his Second Inaugural Address on March 4, 1865. The speech, which was written by him with a few useful suggestions from select Cabinet members, is considered his best speech (among many great speeches he had written over his career); it has become a model of statesmanship; it summoned his countrymen to meet the high aspirations of the founders of the nation. He used only four paragraphs, 703 words, of which 505 would be but one syllable. He conveyed the speech to his audience in his high-pitched and sometimes piercing voice in only 6 minutes, compared to his First Inaugural address which took 35 minutes. Reaction to the Second Inaugural speech at the time was mixed.

After the inaugural festivities had finished for the day, Lincoln held a large reception at the White House to greet well-wishers. When Fredrick Douglass tried to enter the reception, he was restrained by security guards. When he explained that he had been invited by the President, he was held until they were able to ask the President if they should let Douglass proceed to the reception. Once inside the reception he made his way to Lincoln. When Lincoln saw him he immediately went to Douglass and addressed him in a voice loud enough to be heard by many onlookers, "Douglass, I saw you in the crowd today, listening to my inaugural address. There is no man's opinion I value more than yours; what did you think of it?" Douglass replied, "Mr. Lincoln, it was a sacred effort." Douglass later said of the speech, "the address sounded more like a sermon than a state paper."

Setting the Stage: America in March 1865

By February 1865, the Confederacy was beginning to come apart as Lincoln prepared his inaugural speech. General William Tecumseh Sherman had taken Atlanta on September 2, and was making his way out of Savannah with 60,000 troops after taking it on December 21. They slashed through South Carolina, and wreaked havoc in the state that had been the well spring of secession. Lincoln ordered a nighttime illumination in Washington, DC to celebrate victories in Columbia and Charleston, South Carolina, and Wilmington, North Carolina. Crowds celebrated these achievements as the beginning of the war's end.

Around this time, General Ulysses S. Grant was besieging General Robert E. Lee's troops near Petersburg, Virginia, 20 miles south of Richmond, Virginia, the capital of the Confederacy. Though Confederate General Robert E. Lee had shown many times he could elude defeat, it was evident that his badly outnumbered troops could not hold out much longer. In Virginia, General Phil Sheridan had driven General Jubal Early and his troops out of the Shenandoah Valley in mid-October. All signs pointed to a Union victory in Petersburg and in the war overall, and these victories were helping to assure Lincoln's victory in the upcoming election.

Lincoln was indeed victorious over his Democratic opponent, George McClellan, the Union general who Lincoln had removed in 1862, for his bad judgment in whether to engage Confederate armies as the General of the Army of the Potomac. Lincoln had won 55 percent of the popular vote over McClellan, which could legitimately be considered a popular mandate, unlike the 39.8 percent of the popular vote he had received four years earlier. But Lincoln seemed to take little comfort in his military or electoral success, still carrying an apparent sadness on his lanky frame.

There was much apprehension accompanying the hopeful feeling that a victory was imminent. Washington was full of rumors that desperate Confederates, sensing that defeat was upon them, would attempt to abduct or assassinate the President. Secretary of War Edwin M. Stanton took extraordinary precautions. Roads leading into Washington had been heavily guarded and the bridges were being patrolled with "extra vigilance." The 8th Illinois Cavalry was sent out from outside Washington to look for "suspicious characters." Large numbers of Confederate deserters now roamed the capital. Stanton posted sharpshooters on the buildings surrounding the inaugural ceremonies. Plainclothes detectives roved the city keeping track of questionable persons. A "weariness of spirit pervaded the nation."[1]

The scale of the human loss in the Civil War was enormous. It is estimated that approximately 700,000 persons died in the war: 1 out of 11 men of service age was killed between 1861 and 1865. Compared with World War I (117,000 killed), World War II (403,000 killed), the Korean War (54,000 killed), and the Vietnam War (58,000 killed), deaths in the Civil War almost equal the number killed in these subsequent wars. The people of the United States in the early 1860s felt the impact of war down to their small communities.

On March 3, the day before the inauguration, Washington was overcrowded in spite of the inclement weather which had made Washington's roads a sea of mud. Although six decades old, Washington was only an almost-city. Charles Dickens, during his first visit to the United States, in 1842, had called Washington, DC "the City of Magnificent Intentions." He described Washington as "spacious avenues, that begin in nothing, and lead nowhere; streets, miles-long, that only want houses, roads, and inhabitants; public housing that need but a public to be complete."[2]

March 4 dawned with incessant rain. Many visitors avoided the shortage of hotel rooms by showing up on the day of the ceremonies. Fog hung over the city as the crowd began arriving at the east entrance of the Capitol. The inaugural parade took shape and began to move at 11 a.m. from the corner of Pennsylvania Avenue and Tenth Street. The presidential coach moved along the route drawing cheers, though the President had moved to the Capitol earlier that morning to sign bills and meet with lawmakers. Far down the parade line were four companies of black soldiers from the 45th Regiment United States Colored Troops. On this inauguration day for the first time, the new iron dome of the capitol towered above the crowd, finally being completed after approval by the Congress in 1855. Lincoln had insisted that the project proceed to completion, in spite of the difficulties of wartime construction. The statue at the top of the dome, *Armed Liberty* (which held a sword in one hand, symbolizing power, and a wreath of flowers in the other hand), was placed there finally on December 2, 1863.

Inside the Capitol, the ceremonies got underway with a speech by the incoming Vice President, Andrew Johnson, who unfortunately had taken three drinks of bourbon before getting to the podium. He produced a rambling, embarrassing, and cringe-worthy speech that went on much too long. After the speech, as planned, the ceremonies moved outside for the President's address and the taking of the oath of office.

When Lincoln was introduced, the crowd exploded in applause. Though he had been criticized and even mocked during much of his first term, as the war's fortunes began to turn he was gaining in esteem. He moved to a small table that was made from pieces of the dome construction, the only piece of furniture at the inaugural. Lincoln, now 56 years old, looked older than his years. Sitting near Lincoln behind an iron railing was John Wilkes Booth, an actor that Lincoln had seen perform at Ford's Theater the previous November. As he rose to speak, the sun emerged from the clouds and immediately "flooded the spectacle with glory and with light."[3]

Lincoln's Greatest Speech

Lincoln had written his speech well in advance. He was a student of language and rhetoric, and as he grew in his presidency, his texts showed increasing attention to artful detail. He labored over words, writing a few sentences a day and then putting the draft in a drawer and returning to it the next day. He had finished the Second Inaugural speech by around February 26. His speech started with the words, "Fellow Countrymen," a more intimate connection than in most of his speeches, perhaps to suggest that the war had settled the question of whether we were still a nation. Lincoln was going to try in his speech to seek common ground by taking both a religious and prophetic view of the nation's past, present, and more importantly, its future.[4]

The First Paragraph – Setting Expectations

Fellow Countrymen: At this second appearing, to take the oath of the presidential office, there is less occasion for an extended address than there was at the first. Then a statement, somewhat in detail, of a course to be pursued, seemed fitting and proper. Now, at the expiration of four years, during which public declarations have been constantly called forth on every point and phase of the great contest which still absorbs the attention, and engrosses the energies of the nation, little that is new could be presented. The progress of arms, upon which all else chiefly depends, is as well known to the public as to myself; and it is, I trust, reasonably satisfactory and encouraging to all. With high hopes for the future, no prediction in regard to it is ventured.

In the opening paragraph of the speech, Lincoln talks about what his speech is *not* going to discuss – he won't give an extended address, he will not talk about the course to be pursued, and he will not even make a prediction about the war's outcome. Instead, he set about doing two things. He needed to calm down the self-righteous and vengeful impulses of Northerners, and he needed to prepare them for hearing something they did not expect. He seeks to lower their emotions by giving them nothing to cheer at the outset of the speech. It must have raised a question in the minds of the audience: what **is** the President going to say? Questions open minds, and Lincoln's audience needed an open mind to consider the challenge he was going to propose.

Lincoln offered a tone of humility to start his speech. In spite of the stature his six-foot-four-inch height gave him, he wore his sense of loss outwardly, for he had suffered much personal misfortune. His mother had died when he was 9 years old and his older sister and younger brother had died before he was 21. He lost his first sweetheart, Ann Rutledge, when he was 26, a death that prompted thoughts of suicide. He had lost two of his four sons, Edward before age 4 and most recently, Willie, who died of typhoid in 1862, at age 12. His humility was a leadership tool, making him more accessible to people he encountered on train rides, speaking personally to petitioners who came to the White House, and welcoming black leaders, escaped slaves, and abolitionists into the White House. His reluctance to predict a Union victory reflects his humility with respect to steering the course of the war. Showing his humility also subtly conveys to the audience that it is time for them to be humble as well. The personal pronoun "I" appears just once in the opening paragraph.

The Second Paragraph – "And the War Came ..."

> *On the occasion corresponding to this four years ago, all thoughts were anxiously directed to an impending civil war. All dreaded it – all sought to avert it. While the inaugural address was being delivered from this place, devoted altogether to saving the Union without war, insurgent agents were in the city seeking to destroy it without war – seeking to dissole [sic] the Union, and divide effects, by negotiation. Both parties deprecated war; but one of them would make war rather than let the nation survive; and the other would accept war rather than let it perish. And the war came.*

In this paragraph, Lincoln begins the shift in content and tone that would give this speech its distinctive meaning. In a paragraph of five sentences, he employed several rhetorical strategies that are designed to guide and aid the listener. First, he emphasized common actions and emotions, using "all" and "both" to be inclusive of North and South. In sentence one: "All thoughts were anxiously directed to an impending civil war." In sentence two: "All dreaded it – all sought to avoid it." In sentence four: "Both parties deprecated war."

But then Lincoln chose to acknowledge divisions. He talks of the two parties (North and South) and says, "one of them would *make* war rather than let the Union survive, and the other would *accept* war rather than let it perish."

He concludes the paragraph with the words, "And then the war came." The choice of words here is very calculated. Instead of saying "and then we went to war," he speaks of the war as if it arrived inevitably, pushed by larger forces beyond our control, and he speaks of war as having its own agency.

The Third Paragraph

One eighth of the whole population were colored slaves, not distributed generally over the Union, but localized in the southern part of it. These slaves constituted a peculiar and powerful interest. All knew that this interest was, somehow, the cause of war. To strengthen, perpetuate, and extend this interest was the object for which the insurgents would rend the Union, even by war; while the government claimed no right to do more than to restrict the territorial enlargement of it. Neither party expected for the war, the magnitude, or the duration, which it has already attained. Neither anticipated that the cause of the conflict might cease with, or even before, the conflict itself should cease. Each looked for an easier triumph, and a result less fundamental and astounding. Both read the same Bible, and pray to the same God; and each invokes His aid against the other. It may seem strange that any men should dare to ask a just God's assistance in wringing their bread from the sweat of other men's faces; but let us judge not that we be not judged. The prayers of both could not be answered; that of neither has been answered fully. The Almighty has His own purposes. "Woe unto the world because of offences! for it must be that man by whom the offence cometh!" If we shall suppose that American Slavery is one of those offences which, in the province of God, must needs come, but which, having continued through his appointed time, He now wills us to remove, and that He gives to both North and South, this terrible war, as the woe due to those by whom the offence came, shall we discern therein any departure from those divine attributes which the believers in a Living God always ascribe to Him? Fondly do we hope—fervently do we pray—that this mighty scourge of war may speedily pass away. Yet, if God wills that it continue, until all the wealth piled by the bondman's two hundred and fifty years of unrequited toil shall be sunk, and until every drop of blood drawn with the lash, shall be paid by another drawn with the sword, as was said three thousand years ago, so still it must be said "the judgments of the Lord, are true and righteous altogether."

The third paragraph contains about 60 percent of the address, and it tells a story. The tactic of storytelling has been employed by leaders to invite followers to see themselves as part of the story. A story actively engages the listener for a satisfying ending. Lincoln's story is about slavery, "which all knew was somehow the cause of the war." This is a significant turn, a different story line for most of the nation, who thought the cause of the war was to preserve the Union. Lincoln was explaining his new understanding of the meaning of the war. This is one of "the most powerful attempts at presidential leadership in American inaugural history: the war is God's punishment for the institution of slavery."[5]

In his book, *Statesmanship, Character, and Leadership*, Newell suggests that the Second Inaugural can be understood as a series of complex questions Lincoln used to "propel the audience on a learning journey."[6] Starting with: what is fitting and proper to talk about today in the first paragraph; to raising the question of why the war was inevitable in the second paragraph; to asking in the third paragraph how was the slave interest the cause of the war, why has the war lasted so long and when will it end, what is God's righteous judgment, and what are we required to do (which he deals with in the final paragraph), he asks the audience to consider these questions with him as he considers what to do. As he said in his December 1862 State of the Union address:

> *The dogmas of the quiet past, are inadequate to the stormy present ... The occasion is piled high with difficulty and we must rise to the occasion. As our case is new, so must we think anew, and act anew; we must disenthrall ourselves, and then we shall save our country.*

In this address, Lincoln is practicing "meaning making." With the facts of the war not in doubt, but what those facts mean had been widely contested and was still being debated. Leaders gain followers when the meaning they make of the facts is persuasive, enabling followers to see that meaning as part of a broader story in which they have a part. For Lincoln, the meaning of the war had changed from what he suggested in his First Inaugural (preservation of the Union) to the abolition of slavery, which was now center stage. An argument he could not make, politically and perhaps even personally, at the start of the war is now acceptable and perhaps even imperative to saving the Union. He is now ready to turn to his prescription for "saving our country."

The Fourth Paragraph – "... Let Us Strive to Finish the Work We Are in ..."

In his book *Lincoln's Greatest Speech – The Second Inaugural*, Ronald White says the first eight words of the final paragraph proclaim a timeless promise of reconciliation, defining Lincoln's vision for post-Civil War America. White also says that "to appreciate the trajectory of the concluding words of Lincoln's Second Inaugural, we need to hear an unvoiced 'therefore' as the first words of the final paragraph." The unvoiced "therefore" connects paragraphs one through three with the final one. The "therefore" is the tissue between what God has done and what men and women are to do.

> *With malice toward none; with charity for all; with firmness in the right, as God gives us to see the right, let us strive on to finish the work we are in; to bind up the nation's wounds; to care for him who shall have borne the battle, and for his widow, and his orphan—to do all which may achieve and cherish a just, and a lasting peace, among ourselves, and with all nations.*

After four years of war, Lincoln tells the nation (both North and South) that they have a duty to repair the Union and a moral obligation to abolish slavery.[7] Creating the peace is as much their responsibility as it is his. While he remains vague on what the peace will contain, the speech relies heavily on an appeal to core values, particularly: forgiveness, love, caring, and justice. These values serve two goals — to "finish the work we are in" and to "achieve and cherish a just and lasting peace."

Lincoln offers little detail about how to achieve the peace. He chooses to provide his challenge to the nation by offering the values, goals, or purposes, and leave the details to followers. Adding their own details builds commitment and buy-in. He could not possibly have known all the programs and policies that would be needed, and the speech was not the appropriate setting to lay out those details. The flexibility of the speech is one of its strengths, he was inviting both North and South to join in designing the means (i.e., the policies, laws, rules) to achieve the peace.

He summons all citizens to "finish the work we are in" which seems to mean the building of the nation. In his First Inaugural address he refers to his view of the Union, which represented a sentimental attachment to each other and to the idea of a republican government. He says in that First Inaugural address:

Though Passion may have strained it must not break our bonds of affection. The mystic chords of memory, stretching from every battlefield and patriot grave to every living heart and hearthstone all over this broad land, will yet swell the chorus of the Union, when touched, as they surely will be, by the better angels of our nature.

Ronald White says it is a mistake to consider the Second Inaugural speech as an ending, but, rather, it must be considered as a new beginning. Four years earlier the nation had begun "a dark night of the soul." But in the spring of 1865, it was becoming daylight, and Lincoln was the elected leader who would lead the nation into a new era.[8]

Epilogue

Effective leaders challenge followers with goals that are hard to reach.[9] His final paragraph summons citizens to aspire to his driving principle: *victory without malice.* It asks for something seemingly impossible — not just peace, but setting aside all malice and offering charity. It is a message not about the policy prescriptions or legislative measures needed to bring about peace in the nation. Instead, it is a message of hope based on the belief in the forgiving power of human nature, a personal prescription for each individual person, not for broad national policy proposals. Napoleon once said, "A leader is a dealer in hope," Lincoln ended his speech with this challenge, though he knew he was asking much of his "fellow countrymen," and he used his first three paragraphs to prepare them for what he was asking of them. That final paragraph stands as one of the most eloquent and uplifting passages by any political leader in world history, a summoning of a whole nation to reach for the future he knew was possible.

Given that Lincoln was assassinated only six weeks after his Second Inaugural speech, the words he left behind for us in his speech can be viewed as his final guidance for the nation he was leading. He told us to work toward a victory without malice, to preserve and build the Union, and to end the scourge of slavery.[10] He seemed to be pointing the way to a greater tomorrow.

Notes

1 Ronald C. White, Jr., *Lincoln's Greatest Speech, The Second Inaugural* (Simon & Schuster, New York, NY, 2002), page 23.
2 Ibid., page 26.
3 Ibid., page 42.
4 Terry Newell, *Statesmanship, Character, and Leadership in America* (Palgrave, Macmillan, New York, NY, 2012), pages 56–57.
5 Ibid., pages 62–63.
6 Ibid., pages 66–67.
7 White, *Lincoln's Greatest Speech*, page 166.
8 Ibid., page 173.
9 A more recent and well-known challenge issued by a President came in a speech on September 12, 1962 at Rice University by President John F. Kennedy when he said he wanted the United States to land a man on the moon and return him safely to earth in the decade of the 1960s. "We choose to go to the Moon in this decade and do other things not because they are easy, but because they are hard."
10 On June 11, 1963, President John F. Kennedy found it necessary to summon the nation and the Congress to support civil rights legislation, taking to a nationally televised speech to tell the nation,

> We are confronted primarily with a moral issue. It is as old as the scriptures and as clear as the American Constitution. The heart of the question is whether all Americans are to be afforded equal rights and equal opportunities. Whether we are going to treat our fellow Americans as we wish to be treated.

Bibliography

Achorn, Edward. *Every Drop of Blood, the Momentous Second Inauguration of Abraham Lincoln.* New York, NY: Atlantic Monthly Press, 2020.

Goodwin, Doris K. *Team of Rivals, the Political Genius of Abraham Lincoln.* New York, NY: Simon & Schuster, 2005.

Lincoln, dir. by Steven Spielberg. Burbank, Walt Disney Studios Motion Pictures, 2012.

Newell, Terry. *Statesmanship, Character, and Leadership in America.* New York, NY, Palgrave Macmillan, 2012.

Smithsonian Collector's Edition. *Lincoln, America's Greatest President at 200.* Washington, DC: Smithsonian Media, 2009.

White Jr., Ronald C. *Lincoln's Greatest Speech, the Second Inaugural.* New York, NY: Simon & Schuster, 2002.

Widmer, Ted. *Lincoln on the Verge: Thirteen Days to Washington, D.C.* New York, NY: Simon & Schuster, 2020.

9

FREDERICK DOUGLASS

Calling Out the Cruelty and Hypocrisy of Slavery

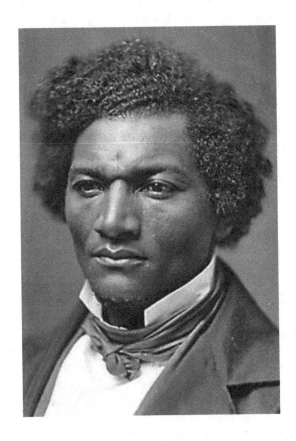

DOI: 10.4324/9781003266235-11

In the early summer of 1852, Frederick Douglass was invited to deliver a Fourth of July address to the Rochester (NY) Ladies' Anti-Slavery Society. The speech was actually delivered on July 5 at Douglass's suggestion, since the date of July 4 had long been sullied in African American communities because it was often the date of slave auctions. For at least three weeks Douglass worked hard on the speech, which was aimed at not just his local audience but beyond the hall to the nation as a whole. He had the speech printed in bulk and sold it in his newspaper as well as out on the lecture circuit at 50 cents per copy.

Douglass's Evolution to Reformer and Statesman

At the time of the speech, Douglass was 34 years old and had established a reputation as a social reformer, abolitionist, orator, and writer. He had escaped slavery on the Eastern Shore of the Chesapeake Bay in Talbot County, Maryland. His mother died when he was 7 years old and he lived with his maternal grandmother who was a slave, and his maternal grandfather who was free. Douglass served as a slave with the Auld family, where he lived in Baltimore. He felt very lucky to live in the city where slaves were almost freemen, compared to slaves on plantations. The Auld family (particularly Sofia, the wife of the master, Hugh Auld) saw to it that he was educated, properly clothed and fed, and slept in a bed with sheets and a blanket. Douglass described Sofia as a kind and tenderhearted woman who treated him "as she supposed one human being ought to treat another." Douglass later worked as a slave for Edward Covey, who whipped Douglass so frequently that his wounds had little time to heal. Now 16 years old, Douglass remembered that the frequent whippings broke his body, mind, and spirit. He eventually fought back against the beatings, and after he won a physical confrontation with Covey, he never tried to beat him again. On September 3, 1838, Douglass (now age 20) successfully escaped by boarding a northbound train. He caught a steam ferry and eventually reached the home of noted abolitionist David Ruggles in New York City. In a letter written to a friend after reaching New York City, he wrote, "I felt as one might feel upon escape from a den of hungry lions. Anguish and grief, like darkness and rain, may be depicted; but gladness and joy, like the rainbow, defy the skill of pen or pencil."

He became a national leader of the abolitionist movement in Massachusetts and New York. He became famous for his oratory and incisive antislavery writings. He was held up as a counterexample to slaveholders' arguments that slaves lacked the intellectual capacity to function as independent American citizens. Douglass wrote three autobiographies which became bestsellers and they were each influential in promoting the cause of abolition. Douglass also actively supported women's suffrage and held several public offices. Douglass believed in dialogue and in making alliances across racial and ideological divides, as well as in the liberal values of the U.S. Constitution. When radical abolitionists (under the slogan, "No Union with Slaveholders") criticized Douglass's willingness to engage in dialogue with slave owners, he replied, "*I would unite with anybody to do right and with nobody to do wrong.*"

Douglass's friends were concerned that his growing notoriety would attract the attention of Hugh Auld, who might try to get his "property" back, so they urged him to tour Ireland, as many former slaves had done. At age 27, he set sail for Ireland on August 16, 1845, and spent two years lecturing in churches and chapels. He drew large crowds of people curious to see this erudite former slave. His supporters in England raised funds to buy his freedom from his American owner, Thomas Auld. They also encouraged him to stay in England but his wife was still in Massachusetts and three million of his brethren in bondage in the United States, he returned to the United States in the spring of 1847.

Upon his return to the United States, and with funds in his pocket from his English supporters, Douglass published his first abolitionist newspaper, the *North Star*, from the basement of a church in Rochester, New York. (The motto of the *North Star* was, "Right is of no Sex – Truth is of no Color – God is the father of us all, and we are all brethren.") In addition to publishing the *North Star* and delivering speeches, he also participated in the Underground Railroad. He and his wife provided resources and lodging in their home to more than 400 slaves. Douglass in 1851 merged the *North Star* with the *Liberty Party Paper* and formed *Frederick Douglass' Paper*, which was published until 1860. Douglass started his last newspaper in 1870, the *New National Era*, which he used to hold the nation to its commitment to equality. In the 1850s, Douglass observed that New York's facilities and instruction for African-American students were vastly inferior to those for whites. He called for court action to open all schools to all children. He said that upgrading the educational system for African-Americans was a more pressing need than political issues such as suffrage. In his later years, Douglass was appointed U.S. Marshall for the District of Columbia. President Harrison appointed Douglass as the U.S. minister resident and consul general to the Republic of Haiti and chargé d'affaires for Santo Domingo in 1889, and in 1891 he was appointed Recorder of Deeds for the District of Columbia

The Fourth of July Speech

In his definitive biography, entitled, *Frederick Douglass, Prophet of freedom*, David W. Blight compares the Fourth of July speech to a symphony in three movements. The first movement sets the audience at ease by honoring the genius of the Founding Fathers, and he placed hope in the youthful nation, which he believed was "still impressible" and open to change, saying there was "consolation in the thought that America is young." Douglass was laying the groundwork of "prophetic irony" for the main argument to come in the second movement. In that movement, as Douglass reminded his largely white audience of their national and personal declension, his theme emerged – the hypocrisy of slavery and racism in a republic. The second movement went on for 14 pages, making his audience squirm as he dragged them through a litany of America's contradictions.

> I am not included within the pale of this glorious anniversary! This fourth of July is *yours,* not *mine.* You may rejoice, I must mourn. ... Above your national tumultuous joy, I hear the mournful wail of millions! whose chains, heavy and grievous yesterday, are today, rendered more intolerable by the jubilee shouts that reach them.

The third movement began calmly with a firm embrace of the antislavery interpretation of the Constitution, calling it a "GLORIOUS LIBERTY DOCUMENT ... full of principles and purposes, entirely hostile to the existence of slavery."[1]

Douglass begins his speech in a positive vein, saying that the fathers of the nation were great statesmen, and that the values expressed in the Declaration of Independence were "saving principles" and the "ringbolt of your nation's destiny," stating, "stand by those principles, be true to them on all occasions, in all places, against all foes, and at whatever cost." He maintained, however, that slaves owed nothing to and had no positive feelings toward the founding of the United States. He faulted America for utter hypocrisy and betrayal of those values in maintaining the institution of slavery.

> What have I, or those I represent, to do with your national independence? Are the great principles of political freedom and of natural justice, embodied in that Declaration of Independence extended to us? **What to the American slave, is your Fourth of July? I answer; a day that reveals to him, more than all other days in the year, the gross injustice and cruelty in which he is the constant victim.**

Douglass also expresses the view that slaves and free Americans are equal in nature. He says that he and other slaves are fighting the same fight regarding the desire to be free that white Americans, the ancestors of the white people he is addressing, fought 70 years earlier. He also says that if residents of America believe that slaves are men, they should be treated as such. True Christians, according to Douglass, should not stand idly by while the rights of others are stripped away.

Douglass, in this instance, is serving the public by identifying and characterizing a problem that he is trying to get on the public agenda for action. This was one of the roles of the abolitionists as the nation moved inevitably toward war: keep the savagery of slavery on the minds of the public, particularly in the North. (Recall the discussion in Chapter 3 about the role of activists in getting attention for an issue and tee it up for some kind of action by legislative or executive branches of government.)

He goes further in this speech to denounce the churches for betraying their own biblical and Christian values. He expresses his outrage at the lack of responsibility and indifference toward slavery that various religious sects have taken across the country. In his view, many churches stand behind slavery and support its continued existence. Douglass, however, argues that religion is the center of the problem, but could be the main solution to it. Douglass is trying to get his audience to realize that they are not living up to their proclaimed beliefs. He points out that they are proud of their country and their religion and how they rejoice in the name of freedom and liberty, and yet they do not offer those things to millions of their country's residents.

Douglass details the hardships past Americans once endured when they were part of the British colonies and validates their feelings of ill treatment. He validates the feelings of injustice the Founders felt and then juxtaposes their experiences with vivid descriptions of the harshness of slavery.

> Attend the auction; see men examined like horses; see the forms of women rudely and brutally exposed to the shocking gaze of American slave-buyers. … Tell me citizens WHERE, under the sun, you can witness a spectacle more fiendish and shocking. Yet this is but a glance at the American slave-trade, as it exists, at this moment.

Douglass criticizes the audience's pride for a nation that claims to value freedom though it is composed of people who continuously commit atrocities against blacks. It is said that America is built on freedom and liberty, but Douglass tells his audience that more than anything, it is built on inconsistencies and hypocrisies that have been overlooked for so long they appear to be truths. Douglass states that true freedom will elude America if black people are still enslaved, but is adamant that the end of slavery is near. Knowledge is becoming more readily available, Douglass says, and soon it will cause the American people to open their eyes to the atrocities being inflicted on their fellow Americans.

Blight says of the speech;

> In both secular and sacred terms, prescient in its vision and powerful in its unforgettable language, Douglass had delivered one of the greatest speeches in American history. He had transcended his audience … into a realm inhabited by great art that would last long after he and this history were gone. He had explained the nation's historical condition and, through the pain of his indictment and the force of his altar call, illuminated a path to a better day. As Douglass lifted his text from the podium and took his seat, nearly six hundred white Northerners stood and roared with a "universal burst of applause."[2]

On February 20, 1895, Frederick Douglass attended a meeting of the National Council of Women in Washington, DC. During that meeting, he was brought to the platform and received a standing ovation. Shortly after he returned home,

Douglass fell to his knees in the front hallway of his home, then laid out fully on the floor. He had suffered a massive heart attack. The man of a million words had gone cold and silent. He was 77.

In his discussion about the aftermath of Douglass's death, Blight says of Douglass, "he is not gone, he is merely dead."[3]

Notes

1 David W. Blight, *Frederick Douglass Prophet of Freedom* (Simon & Shuster, New York, NY, 2018), pages 231–233.
2 Ibid., page 236.
3 Ibid., page 757.

Bibliography

Blight, David W. *Frederick Douglass: Prophet of Freedom*. New York, NY: Simon & Schuster, 2018.

10

IDA B. WELLS

Journalist for Justice

DOI: 10.4324/9781003266235-12

Though Ida B. Wells died on March 25, 1931, the impact of her work in journalism, social service activism, and community organizing continues to be felt in the movement toward racial justice. Her legacy lives on in the specific stories, articles, and reports she wrote during her life. She was awarded a posthumous Pulitzer Prize Special Citation in 2020, the citation reads:

> To Ida B. Wells, for her outstanding and courageous reporting on the horrific and vicious violence against African-Americans during the era of lynching.

The spirit of her writing and activism has inspired the kinds of journalism that challenge authority and help in the organizing that African-Americans still find necessary to do to ensure progress. (Note to Readers: This account of the life of Ida B. Wells describes instances of lynchings and other acts of violence about which she made the world aware through her writings.)

Beginnings in Mississippi and Memphis

Ida Wells was born on July 16, 1862, in Holly Springs, Mississippi. Born to parents who were slaves, her mother was a deeply religious woman whose convictions about the dignity of man were developed under the cruelties of slavery, and her father was a man of independent spirit even in slavery, who sought and attained his full independence in the period after emancipation. As the eldest daughter of a family of eight children, Ida had many responsibilities for raising and caring for the children. Her father was a skilled carpenter and had plenty of work rebuilding homes, industrial plants, and government buildings destroyed during the Civil War. He was also a man of considerable ability and much civic concern and was selected as a member of the first board of trustees of Rust College (originally named Shaw University, founded in 1866). Ida attended Rust all during her childhood (which provided instruction at all levels and grades, including the basic elementary subjects) and she was considered an exceedingly good student.

In 1878, a terrible epidemic of yellow fever struck Holly Springs. Two thousand of the town's population of 3,500 fled, most of whom remained contracted the disease and 304 of them died. Both of Ida's parents and the youngest child, Stanley, ten months of age, died in this epidemic. Two of the other children had died previously. Friends, neighbors, and well-wishers offered to take some of the children. But Ida, at 16, was steadfastly determined to keep the family together. Her father had left some money, and with the help of the Masons, who served as guardians, she cared for all of them.

During this time, Ida studied and passed the teacher's exam, and she was assigned a one-room school in the rural district about six miles from Holly Springs. Her younger brothers were apprenticed to carpenters to learn the trade of their father. In 1882, Ida's aunt, Fannie Butler, who lived in Memphis, Tennessee some 40 miles away, suggested to Ida that she move to Memphis and seek a teaching position there. Ida accepted and first taught in the rural schools of Shelby County while studying for the teacher's examination for the city schools of Memphis.

Ida rode the trains to and from school, and one day while riding back to the school she took a seat in the ladies' coach of the train as usual. When the train started and the conductor came along to collect tickets, he told her that he could not take her ticket there, and told her that she would have to go to the smoker's car. When she proposed to stay put, the conductor tried to drag her out and grabbed hold of her arm, whereupon Ida "fastened my teeth into the back of his hand."[1]

She took the return train back to Memphis and engaged an African-American attorney to file suit against the railroad, but after months of delay she learned that he had been bought off by the railroad. She engaged a white attorney who was a former judge, and the case was finally brought to trial in the circuit court, where she was awarded 500 dollars in damages. The *Memphis Appeal* covered the case with the headline *A Darky Damsel Obtains a Verdict for Damages Against the Chesapeake and Ohio Railroad*.[2] But the railroad appealed the case to the state's supreme court, which reversed the lower courts after Ida refused to negotiate with the railroad on a settlement. She was ordered to pay out $200 in court costs. Having secured her teaching job in Memphis before the railroad case was finally settled, Ida's salary was available to help pay the court costs.

From Teacher, to Journalist, to Newspaper Owner

Much of what Ida knew about life was from reading books, including the Bible and Shakespeare. When she moved to Memphis, the church also became a huge influence. Many of her teachers growing up had been the consecrated men and women from the North who came into the South to teach immediately after the Civil War. During this time, Ida became the editor of the *Evening Star*, a newspaper with a predominantly African-American readership. She was also invited to share some of her writings for the *Living Way*, a paper published by a pastor of one of the leading Baptist churches in the area. In weekly letters to the *Living Way*, she wrote in a plain, common-sense way about the things which concerned African-Americans, keeping her prose simple and straightforward to have maximum impact on her audience.

In 1898, Ida was invited to be a writer on the *Free Speech and Headlight*, a newspaper owned by the pastor of the largest Baptist church in Memphis. She was also invited to become an investor and she bought a one-third interest in the paper. She served as its editor, while the other partners managed the business side of the paper.

When she published an article critical of the condition of the schools set aside for African-American students – criticizing the physical condition of the school buildings and the inferior quality of the teachers assigned to these schools – she stirred controversy. The school board elected not to renew her contract for the following year. Ida felt that she had struck a blow for the students in Memphis through her article, had pointed out an injustice that needed correcting, but lost her job as a result. She now had to make a living from her newspaper work. She took a trip all through the Southern states to increase subscriptions to her paper and was very successful in doing so and setting up a network of correspondents in many of the cities she visited on her trip. One of the paper's co-owners had to withdraw from his involvement in the paper, and Ida bought out his interest.

A Lynching in Memphis, and on to New York City

While Ida was on a trip to Natchez, Mississippi she learned of a terrible atrocity going on in Memphis, Tennessee in her absence. She received word of the lynching of three men – Thomas Moss, Calvin McDowell, and Henry Stewart – who owned and operated a grocery store in a thickly populated Memphis suburb. Ida was a friend of Tommie, who was a letter carrier, married and with one daughter, and a popular figure in town. His partners ran the grocery store while Tommie worked as a postman during the day.

Thomas had established his business in a part of town known as the "the Curve" which put him in competition with a white merchant who had enjoyed the monopoly conditions prior to Tommie's establishment of the People's Grocery Company. The district in which they had both set up their businesses was mostly African-American and many of his customers belonged to Tommie's church or lodge.

One day some white and African-American boys had a fight, which the African-American boys won. But the father of one of the white boys whipped one of the African-American boys and the father and the white grocery store owner swore out a warrant for the arrest of the victors. The owners of the People's Grocery Company had also been drawn into the fight. The resulting case was dismissed with nominal fines, but the vanquished whites let it be known that they were coming on Saturday night to clean out the People's Grocery.

Moss and his partners consulted a lawyer and were told that since they were outside the city limits and beyond police protection, they would be justified in protecting themselves if attacked. But as Moss was preparing to close the store that Saturday night, shots rang out in the back of the store where he had posted guards who had seen several white men stealing through the rear door. Three of these men were wounded, and the Sunday morning papers came out with lurid headlines telling how officers of the law had been wounded in the discharge of their duties, calling People's Grocery Company "a low dive in which drinking and gambling were carried on; a resort of thieves and thugs."[3] That Sunday morning, over a hundred African-American men were dragged from their homes and put in jail by police claiming to be looking for others who were implicated in what the papers labeled a conspiracy. On Sunday and Monday nights, a group of black men guarded the jail to see that nothing happened to the prisoners. On Tuesday, the newspapers announced that the wounded men were recovering and out of danger from their wounds, and so those who had guarded the jail decided the crisis had passed and decided to not guard the jail that night.

But while the prisoners slept, Thomas Moss, Calvin McDowell, and Henry Stewart were taken from their cells, transported a mile north of the city, and horribly shot to death. The papers carried detailed accounts of what had happened, saying that Tom Moss begged for his life for the sake of his wife, his child, and his unborn baby, and that when he was asked if he had anything else to say, told them to "tell my people to go West – there is no justice for them here."[4] Other more lurid details were supplied by the newspapers, which indicated that the one who wrote the news report was either an eyewitness or got the facts from someone who was.

A white mob formed and took possession of the People's Grocery Company. They destroyed what they could not eat or drink, and a few days later the remaining contents were auctioned off. The *Free Speech*, commenting in Ida's absence, said,

> There is only one thing left we can do; save our money and leave a town which will neither protect our lives and property, nor give us a fair trial in the courts, but takes us out and murders us in cold blood when accused by white persons.[5]

Many African-Americans in the Memphis community took the advice of the *Free Speech*, combined with the last words of Thomas Moss before he was shot. Whole church congregations departed, and along with them the profits of many white businesses. The white newspapers in Memphis, who had fanned the flames of prejudice and abetted the lynching, now reported stories of hardship and death among those who had left Memphis and were making their way across difficult terrain, urging those who had not yet left Memphis to stay and remain among friends and the comforts of home.

After visiting Oklahoma where many of her readers had resettled, and taking a trip to Philadelphia for a conference, Ida visited New York City to size it up as a new place to live. Upon her arrival in New York City, she was handed a copy of the *New York Sun* which had a story about a committee of leading citizens in Memphis who had gone to the office of the *Free Speech*, run the business manager out of town, destroyed the type and furnishings of the office, and left a note that anyone trying to publish the paper again would be punished by death. She sent telegrams to her lawyer in Memphis to get more information, and the return telegrams implored her not to return as she would surely be killed.

She was hired by the *New York Age*, where she hoped to continue her fight against lynching and those who practiced it. Her Memphis paper was now destroyed and she had lost every dollar she had invested in the paper. She was given a one-fourth interest in the *New York Age* in return for her subscription lists, and she became a weekly contributor on salary. She spent the early part of her tenure at the *Age* researching many instances of lynchings in the South.

On October 26, 1892, Ida began to publish her research on lynchings in a pamphlet titled *Southern Horrors: Lynch Law in All Its Phases*. She had examined many accounts of lynchings due to the alleged "rape of white women," she concluded that Southerners cried rape as an ostensible reason to hide their real reasons for lynchings: black economic progress, which threatened white southerners with competition, and white ideas of enforcing black second-class status in the society. In many states, whites worked to suppress black progress. Southern states passed laws or new constitutions to disenfranchise most black people and many poor white people through the use of poll taxes, literacy tests, and other devices.

Also during this time, Ida met Frederick Douglass, who complimented her on her writings about lynchings, telling her it was a "revelation" to him. She was very grateful for the chance to meet him and to get to know his wife (who was white). She described how her admiration and love for him deepened and strengthened, describing him as the "biggest and broadest American our country has produced."[6]

On Friday, February 3, 1893, Ida was in Washington, DC at a meeting Frederick Douglass had organized of women in Washington to hear Ida speak about racial injustice. The next morning newspapers told the story that at the time the meeting was going on in Washington, in Paris, Texas one of the most heinous instances of lynching and burnings the country had ever witnessed was underway. The alleged perpetrator was an African-American man who had been accused of ravishing and murdering a five-year-old girl, without a trial and without an opportunity to counter his accusers. School children had been given a holiday to witness the burning alive of the alleged perpetrator, railroads ran special excursions to bring people from the surrounding country to witness the event, and the account included details about how the mob fought over the hot ashes for bones, buttons, and teeth for souvenirs. The man had protested his innocence, and because there was no trial, the truth will never be known about whether he was innocent. But there can be no doubt about the guilt of the mob that murdered and tortured him. Ida felt that this case explained why she must continue advocating for investigations of every lynching to get and publicize the facts, especially in the absence of a trial.

Speaking in Scotland and England, Adopting Chicago as Home

The incident in Paris, Texas became well-known all over the world and caused Ida to be invited to England to spread the truth about the various racial injustices practiced in America and to get support for her demand that those accused of crimes be given a fair trial and punished by law instead of by mob rule. A newspaper from the area of Scotland Ida was visiting described Ida's message in her speeches this way:

The facts that are set forth go to show very clearly that although slavery in the southern states of America is believed to have been abolished when the American war closed, the lot of the coloured people in these parts is little better than when slavery was in full force. These people are uniformly treated as people of an inferior caste, they are subjected to every possible indignity, they are denied all the rights of citizens, and when they give any manner of offence to the white man, they are tried according to the summary methods of Judge Lynch. ... But a case has been made ... that cannot be ignored by those who care for the good name of the United States; and it is no wonder that so much sympathy has gone out to the ladies who have come to tell the people of this country how freedom is mocked in the country that boasts herself the freest in the world.[7]

Ida's lectures and appearances in Scotland and England were drawing very positive reviews and were informing British audiences about the injustices of treatment of African-Americans in post–Civil War America.

When Ida returned to the United States, her first stop was Chicago, where she helped set up a women's organization, with the help of the leading African-American women of the city. The supportive Chicago environment convinced Ida to remain in Chicago, instead of returning to New York City, and she immediately began working on the *Chicago Conservator*, the oldest African-American newspaper in the city, and she worked to further develop the newly established women's club. But Ida was invited to return to England for another speaking tour, and after making all the arrangements, she again sailed for England in February 1894.

Her second time in England was even more successful than her first because a greater number of meetings had been arranged, each with larger audiences than her meetings during her first trip. Her first trip had aroused much interest, and new reports of additional lynchings had raised more concern among English audiences. Starting in Liverpool and Manchester, Ida drew overflow crowds at every appearance. In Manchester, she spoke 12 times in ten days. Also in Manchester, she was given newspaper accounts of two women who had been the victims of lynchings in recent weeks. One of the women was found hanging from a tree in Little Rock, Arkansas with no one who could supply any information for follow-up action. The second woman, in San Antonio, Texas, had been boxed up in a barrel with nails driven through the sides and rolled down a hill until she was dead.

Ida was the guest of many of the most influential clergy in many of the towns in England, all giving her the opportunity to speak of American injustice at their churches or in meetings of various clubs in their areas. Her speeches, along with news reports about specific lynchings, convinced the British people of the truth of American racial injustice. During her six-week stay in London, Ida addressed clubs, drawing room meetings, breakfast and dinner parties, speaking 35 times at various gatherings, and she had more invitations than she could fill from people anxious to know the facts.

Ida found herself wishing that Americans would give her the same opportunity for open discussion on this subject, feeling that it can only be conquered by meeting it fairly. Ida was also accorded much attention by the London Press; she was interviewed by six dailies, six weeklies, and four monthlies who ran lengthy interviews and articles on racial injustice in America. Several cities in the Southern United States began to react to the notoriety Ida was getting in London, running articles and editorials not to deny the lynchings and other injustices happening in their cities, but to attack Ida's character. Ida recognized in her final days in England that the Christian, moral, and social forces of Great Britain had responded to her appeal, and caused the civilized world to acknowledge the evil of lynching. Ida had succeeded in using her travels throughout England to raise awareness of America's racial injustice to audiences who listened to her factual accounts of lynchings and other incidents with alarm, and many formed groups to take various actions in support of the cause. Everywhere she went in England, they showed respect for her intelligence and integrity, were attentive to her needs, and showed her great courtesies at every event. Though they could offer her no salary, they paid all expenses throughout her trip.

Ida Returns to the United States

Upon her return to the United States, Ida began to receive invitations to visit many cities for lectures. After delivering her lectures, she would remain in town to make a personal appeal to the newspapers and speak with ministers of leading congregations. Ida arrived in Chicago around August 7, 1894, where she rested for about a month.

She accepted a speaking engagement in Rochester, New York, where she was a guest of Susan B. Anthony, the well-known suffragist. She had many discussions with Miss Anthony who gave Ida the impression of a woman eager to hear all sides of any question. Ida felt this manner was one of the reasons for her success in the organizations which did so much to give the women of America an equal share in all the privileges of citizenship.

Another benefit of being in Rochester was that it had been the home of Frederick Douglass for many years before and during the Civil War. His body lies buried there, as well his two wives, and the citizens of Rochester erected a monument on one of the public squares of the city to honor his memory. Ida's final time meeting Mr. Douglass was at a joint speaking engagement in Providence, Rhode Island, in November 1894. He died shortly thereafter in February 1895. Ida was in San Francisco at a speaking engagement when he died and the meeting organizers there held a memorial meeting. Ida felt that "in the death of Frederick Douglass we lost the greatest man that the Negro race has ever produced on the American continent."[8]

Other locations were not so hospitable to Ida's anti-lynching agitation. In St. Louis, Missouri, at the close of an otherwise successful meeting at which Ida had spoken, the editor of the *St. Louis Republic* rose to report that he had sent reporters throughout the South to get something to publish against Ida, but regrettably, he was not able to find anything. Ida later learned that many other editors had also spent some time and resources trying to find something to discredit her. She found St. Louis "too strongly southern" to bother doing any of the organizing she did in other cities. She went on to Kansas City, and after a successful speech, she went to a Methodist ministers meeting where she was entangled in a parliamentary quagmire that prevented the meeting from approving a resolution in support of her work. She had a similar experience in San Francisco where a resolution also caused some consternation among Congregationalist ministers.

After conducting greater research, Ida published *The Red Record* in 1895, a 100-page pamphlet with more detail, describing lynching in the United States since the Emancipation Proclamation of 1863, and also covered black people's struggles in the South since the Civil War. *The Red Record* described the alarmingly high rates of lynchings in the United States, which Wells said most Americans outside the South did not realize the increasing rate of violence against black people in the South. Wells noted that since the time of slavery 10,000 Negroes have been killed in cold blood, through lynching without the formality of judicial trial and legal execution. Wells gave 14 pages of statistics related to lynching cases committed from 1892 to 1895 and included pages of graphic accounts detailing specific lynchings. She noted that most of her data was taken from articles written by white correspondents, white press bureaus, and white newspapers. *The Red Record* had far-reaching influence on the debate about lynching.

Ida had been speaking in the United States for a year and was physically and financially depleted, feeling she had done all one person could do to keep the topic of lynching before the public and to stir righteous public sentiment to try to stop it. She returned to Chicago in June 1895 to marry attorney F.L. Barnett and live in the privacy of their own home. After word got out that Ida was about to marry, a protest arose among her African-American colleagues who felt she was abandoning the cause.

But Ida had already decided to continue her work as a journalist. She had already purchased the *Conservator* from its owners, and the Monday morning after her wedding she was at work in the offices of the newspaper. Her activities as the editor, as president of the Ida B. Wells Woman's club, and as a sought-after speaker in white woman's clubs in and around Chicago kept her busy. But on March 25, 1896, she gave birth to Charles, her first son. Ida agreed to make a speaking tour of Illinois with her six-month-old baby, so long as each sponsoring group agreed to provide a nurse for the baby's care at each stop.

When Ida's second son, Herman, was born in 1897, she was thoroughly convinced that the duties of wife and mother were a profession in themselves. She gave up her newspaper, resigned from the presidency of the Ida B. Wells Club after serving in that role for five years. As she left the club, she worked with them to establish a kindergarten in the Negro district at Bethel Church.

Events kept Ida in her public service role, in spite of her attempts to withdraw from public life. In the spring of 1898, a horrible lynching occurred in Anderson, South Carolina; the victim was the postmaster there, and she thought that the federal government would step in and punish the perpetrators of this offense against a federal officer. Citizens of Chicago held a mass meeting in which a resolution of denunciation was passed and a collection was taken up to send Ida to Washington to present the demand that the government should act. Ida was joined by the seven congressmen from the Chicago area in a meeting with President McKinley. The president told his visitors that they had already placed some of the finest of their secret service agents to discover and prosecute the lynchers of the black postman. Ida stayed in Washington for five weeks, talking to key Congressmen about the lynching of the North Carolina postmaster and trying to spark interest in a legislative response to lynching. She returned home to Chicago frustrated by the lack of progress toward any legislative solution.

In response to the murders of more than a dozen people in 1899, Ida wrote *Lynch Law in Georgia*, in which she asserted,

> The real purpose of these savage demonstrations is to teach the Negro that in the south he has no rights that the law will enforce. Samuel Rose (one of the victims) was burned to teach the Negroes that no matter what a white man does to them, they must not resist.[9]

Then in 1900, Ida wrote *Mob Rule in New Orleans* which chronicled widespread mob violence on the Negro community and the horrible demise of Robert Charles, who was murdered in retaliation for defending himself against a police officer.

Also in 1900, the *Chicago Tribune* published a series of articles to argue for the benefits of a separate school system for the races in Chicago. Over a two-week period interviews were printed first with parents of children who had struck in one of the schools in Chicago against having a Negro teacher. Articles were also published containing interviews with superintendents of separate school systems in St. Louis, Baltimore, Washington, DC, and other smaller cities.

It became clear that the *Tribune* was working to abolish the mixed school system of Chicago. Ida considered what action could be taken, telling her husband, "*There must always be a remedy for wrong and injustice if only we know how to find it.*" Ida wrote to the *Tribune* editor pointing out that everybody who had been quoted on the subject of separate schools except those most vitally concerned – the African-Americans. She further asked if he would receive a delegation of colored citizens to hear their views on the subject. Ida did not receive a response to her letter, nor was it published in the "Voices of the People" column of the paper. So she visited the editor in person, uninvited. Their conversation revealed his beliefs that it was not right that ignorant Negroes should have the right to vote and to rule white people even when they were in the majority. The editor further informed Ida that he did not have the time to meet with a delegation, but he would publish as much of her letter as he could find space for, when they got around to it.

After the meeting, Ida, realizing what they were up against, paid a visit to Jane Addams and asked her to reach out to those people of influence who would be willing to take up their cause. She readily agreed to do so and organized a meeting at Hull House the following Sunday evening. The crowd that evening included editors of other daily newspapers, ministers, social service workers, and a member of the Board of Education. Ida spoke to the crowd, outlined the problem with what the *Tribune* was advocating, and described in detail her own meeting with the editor. As a result of the meeting, the group appointed a seven-person committee headed by Jane Addams to speak to the *Tribune* editor. Ida was not a part of the committee, so she was not aware of what the committee did or said, but the series of articles ceased and the effort to separate schoolchildren on the basis of race promptly ended. Ida had found a "wrong and an injustice, had searched for a remedy, and found it."

In the fall, the *New York Age* issued a call to resurrect a national movement started some years before called the Afro-American League. She was urged by citizens of Chicago to attend an organizing meeting in New York. She went to the meeting and stayed as the guest of Susan B. Anthony, and during her stay with Miss Anthony, she mentioned some frustration over the fact that women like Ida, who had a special call for special work, naturally divided their attention when they married and had children. Further, Miss Anthony told Ida that there was "no one in the country better fitted to do the work you had in hand than yourself, but that since you have gotten married agitation seems practically to have ceased."[10] Ida considered this rebuke and thought that the lack of activity was due not to the distraction of motherhood, but the lack of support that, unlike Ms. Anthony, Ida was able to muster. This had discouraged Ida.

During this trip to New York, the Afro-American Council was born and Ida was selected as secretary, launching her again into the public sphere. The Council had called a meeting in Washington in the aftermath of President McKinley's message to Congress in which he had failed to condemn a terrible race riot in Wilmington, North Carolina. The Council passed very strong resolutions condemning the President of the United States for ignoring the riot in his message. In 1899, the first annual meeting of the Afro-American Council was held in Chicago, and the National Association of Colored Women's Clubs was held in Chicago at the same time. During these simultaneous meetings, Jane Addams of Hull House in Chicago invited the leadership of the National Association to have lunch with her. Ida regarded Addams as one of the greatest women in the United States, and though she was not part of the Association at this point she helped organize the meeting with Addams.

Ida could not attend the 1901 meeting of the Afro-American Council in Philadelphia because she was about to have her first daughter, Ida Bell. The National Business League, led by Booker T. Washington, was also in session in

Chicago during this time. In Atlanta during the Business League session, a human being was being burned alive in Alabama, and a delegate to the Business League from Kansas introduced a resolution of condemnation, which was referred to a committee. Mr. Washington, who was the dominant figure of the organization, killed the resolution so that it never received full consideration, arguing that such a resolution could endanger his school (the Tuskegee Institute) if he permitted the resolution to be passed. The organization took no position on the Alabama incident.

In the winter of 1903, Ida was approached by Celia Parker Wooley, a Unitarian woman minister who wanted to establish a center in which white and colored could meet and get to know each other better. She wanted to call it the Frederick Douglass Center and wanted to know Ida's opinion of the idea. Ida indicated that she and her husband would support it most wholeheartedly. Ida pulled together a group of women to raise money for the first payment on a building Ms. Wooley had located. This group of women later became known as the Douglass Women's Club, and Ida agreed to serve as their Vice President, after initially saying that the age of her children prevented her from serving as an officer.

Ida's second daughter Alfreda was born in 1904. Her growing family challenged her to find a balance between her professional life and her burgeoning home life.

In 1906, a riot took place in Atlanta, Georgia in which three innocent African-Americans were lynched by a frenzied mob. J. Max Barber, editor of the *Voice*, a magazine which he had published in Atlanta, was in Chicago as a refugee from the riot and he was invited to address the Douglass Center Women's Club. He reported that a white woman had made a charge of being assaulted by an unknown Negro male. The *Atlanta Journal* had fanned the flames of race prejudice to such heights that not only did the mob lynch three innocent men but also they destroyed much property, and the heads of schools, lawyers, and doctors were humiliated and made to march like criminals up the streets at the command of the mob. Ida felt that the Atlanta riot made clear that the national African-American community had no organization which was really national in character, and which had the financial and numeric strength to do what was necessary to do the work which was needed to make an organized fight against the growing racial injustices.

Establishing the Negro Fellowship League

In 1908, a riot broke out in Springfield, Illinois and continued for three days. Three African-American men were lynched "under the shadow of Abraham Lincoln's tomb" during those three days. None of them had any connection with the original cause of the riot. One of them was an old citizen of Springfield who had been married to a white woman for 20 years and had raised a family by her. When the mob could do nothing else, they went to his home, dragged him out, and hanged him in his own yard. Ida again was frustrated that African-Americans did not have an organization prepared to respond to this and other situations of lynching and racial injustices. At the next session of the Illinois legislature, a law was enacted which provided that any sheriff who permitted a prisoner to be taken from him and lynched should be removed from office.

Ida was teaching a men's Bible study class, and disturbed by the Springfield riot, one day in class she decried the apathy of Negroes in the face of the injustice of the riots. She urged the men in her class to meet outside of the class period to discuss what to do about the situation. This discussion group became the basis for what came to be known as the Negro Fellowship League.

Members of the League were also confronted by another Illinois lynching case, this time in Cairo, Illinois. The body of a white woman had been found in an alley in the residential district and, following the usual custom, the police immediately looked for a Negro. Finding a penniless colored man known as "Frog" James, who was unable to give a good account of himself, so he was locked up in the police station and a crowd began to gather around the station and demanded to see the sheriff. The sheriff, Frank Davis, took the prisoner to the railroad station, got on the train, took the prisoner into the woods, and stayed there overnight. The next morning, the mob had grown very large, and they went up into the country and found the sheriff and his prisoner. They were brought back to town on the train, and when the train came to a standstill, some of the mob put a rope around "Frog's" neck, dragged him from the train to the most prominent corner of the town, the rope was thrown over an electric light arch, and the body hauled up above the heads of the crowd.

Five hundred bullets were fired into the body, some of which cut the rope, and when the body dropped to the ground, the mob seized hold of the rope and dragged the body up the main street of the town. The body was taken to the place where the corpse of the white girl had been found; they cut off his head, stick it on a fence post, built a fire around the body and burned it.

When news of this travesty appeared in the papers, Ida called a meeting of black citizens and a telegram was sent to Illinois Governor Deneen to remind him of his authority to displace the sheriff and to demand that he do so. Newspaper reports indicated that he was hesitant to do this, but he sent a telegram to the sheriff ousting him from his job. As the law provided, the sheriff would have the right to appear before the Governor and show cause why he should be reinstated. The Governor sent a telegram to Ida and her group informing them of the date and time when the sheriff would have his hearing. Ida decided that she would go to the hearing, feeling it was a duty that had to be done, and that no one else in her group was willing to do it.

At the hearing, Ida made a statement based on a brief written by her lawyer-husband. She successfully parried one of the best lawyers in Illinois (who was also a state Senator), making her arguments about the sheriff's negligence in protecting "Frog" James from the mob, and declaring that if Sheriff Davis was reinstated, it would signal all those in Illinois inclined to mob rule to proceed whenever they saw fit. The hearing adjourned, Ida returned to Chicago and awaited the ruling of the Governor. His proclamation was that Frank Davis could not be reinstated because he had not properly protected the prisoner within his keeping and that lynch law would have no place in Illinois. By showing up and choosing to involve herself in the hearing, Ida had turned the hearing into a proceeding which could not ignore the facts and had to consider the views of an aggrieved population.

Ida's main partner in establishing the Negro Fellowship League was Mr. Victor Lawson, owner and publisher of the *Daily News*, who agreed to help establish a place for a reading room and other services and to pay the expenses for a year. On the first day of May 1910, the Negro Fellowship Reading Room and Social Center was opened at 2830 State Street, in the midst of all the temptations of the neighborhood. Very soon after opening the Center, they added a men's lodging house upstairs where men could get a place to stay overnight for 15 or 25 cents. At the end of their first year, they averaged 40 or 50 persons a day who came in to read, play checkers, or hunt for jobs. At the end of the year, they had placed 115 young men in places of employment.

Meanwhile, things were beginning to stir in the effort to form a national group to speak for African-American interests, sometimes in response to significant events like riots or lynchings or more subtle forms of racial injustice. The country at large seemed to be supportive of Booker T. Washington's ideas on industrial education as the focus of education for Negroes. But others agreed with Dr. Du Bois that it was impossible to limit the aspirations and endeavors of an entire race within the confines of the industrial education program. It was decided that a committee of 40 should be appointed to spend a year devising ways and means for the establishment of an organization. Known as the National Negro Committee, their report was to be completed in a year.

At the meeting a year later, the name National Association for the Advancement of Colored People (NAACP) was adopted, and the decision was also made to establish their own publication called *Crisis*. Ida felt that the NAACP did not get off to the kind of prominent and energetic start that she had hoped for, as its first chairman of the executive committee was too centered in New York City.

Ida began to have trouble with continued funding for the Negro Fellowship League, as her original sponsors now needed to end their commitment for funding the operation. Judge Harry Olson, the chief justice of the municipal court, called a committee to consider ways of helping the League to continue its work. Ida moved the headquarters of the League as a cost-cutting step, and Judge Olson recommended Ida for an appointment as an adult probation officer, which would pay her $150 per month. Judge Olson told Ida she could carry on the work of probation officer in conjunction with her work at the League, and she used her salary to supplement the budget of the League.

At the end of the 10 years, she had spent working with the Negro Fellowship League, no one who came in looking for food was not given a card to a restaurant nearby, everyone who came in looking for lodging was accommodated, and nobody who applied for a job was ever turned away.

Ida Organizes the Alpha Suffrage Club

All during her residence in Illinois, Ida had been a member of the Women's Suffrage Association, and in 1914 the Illinois legislature was considering the question of enfranchising the women voters of the state. Ida and some of her suffrage friends organized the Alpha Suffrage Club in January 1913 and turned out many voters in city council elections. The Alpha Club was visited by representatives of the ward organization, who had taken note of the impact of the Club on the vote totals in the ward. The representatives said they now recognized that there was now a demand for a colored candidate and said the organization would itself nominate one at the next vacancy. The Alpha Club was founded as a way to further voting rights for all women, to teach African-American women how to engage in civic matters, and work to elect African-Americans to city offices. They played a significant role in electing the first African-American alderman in Chicago.

At this time, the National American Woman Suffrage Association (NAWSA) was organizing a suffrage parade in Washington, DC, scheduled for the day before President Woodrow Wilson's inauguration. Suffragists from across the country were gathered to demand universal suffrage. Ida went to Washington with a delegation of members from Chicago. On the day of the March, the head of the Illinois delegation told the Chicago delegates that the NAWSA wanted to keep the delegation entirely white, apparently in response to Southern delegates who were concerned that support for suffrage would erode if African-American women were too prominent in the parade. They were asked to march at the end of the parade in a "colored delegation."

Instead of going to the back of the parade, however, Wells waited with spectators as the parade got underway, and stepped into the white Illinois delegation as they passed by. She visibly linked arms with her white colleagues for the rest of the parade route.

Documenting Injustice

Ida continued her civil rights work in 1917 by writing a series of investigative reports for the *Chicago Defender* on *The East St. Louis Massacre: The Greatest Outrage of the Century*, in which she chronicled the horrific violence against an entire African-American community. With the shortage of workers during World War I, the effort to employ recent migrants from the South led to tensions in East St. Louis which caused death and destruction of an entire African-American community. The National Guard was called into the community but did little to protect people or property – thousands were killed and those that survived were displaced and lost all of their property.

Ida went to investigate in the aftermath of the riot and interviewed people firsthand to learn what had happened. She then wrote her *Massacre* pamphlet and met with Illinois governor Frank Lowden to try to ensure accountability for those who had created the situation. Ida's approach to investigative reporting of these incidents was designed to take control of the narrative of the situation, or, at least, to offer an alternative to the narrative developed by law enforcement organizations who were often complicit in exacerbating the riots.

In August 1917, a race riot in Houston, Texas occurred involving black soldiers at Camp Logan. A predominantly black army unit was sent from New Mexico to guard the construction of Camp Logan on the edge of Houston. They were met with hostility from racist white police officers, racist civilians, and the white workers building the camp who hated the presence of the soldiers. Tensions grew between the black soldiers and the police officers.

On August 23, a black soldier witnessed a white police officer attempting to arrest a black woman. When the soldier attempted to defend the woman, he was clubbed and then arrested. A black military police officer went to find the soldier, and he, too, was beaten. Though he fled, he was later detained. Rumors swirled about what had happened, and the town was in a frenzy. The black soldiers heard that a white mob was coming to attack the camp, so they grabbed rifles and headed into downtown Houston. Over the course of a few hours, total chaos erupted as soldiers, police, and local residents became embattled. It resulted in the arrest of 118 enlisted black soldiers, and 63 of them were charged with mutiny. Their trial was a mockery, with due process rights repeatedly ignored, and the soldiers were given no chance to appeal. Thirteen black soldiers were found guilty and sentenced to death, and two weeks later they were hanged. An additional seven were hanged weeks later, seven were acquitted, and the rest were sentenced to various prison terms.

When Ida was rebuffed by Chicago-area pastors in her effort to hold a memorial service for the Houston soldiers, she had 500 buttons made to commemorate the soldiers who were killed in the "legal" lynching. She distributed the buttons, to make sure that the soldiers' deaths did not go unnoticed. Ida was later visited by two Secret Service agents who warned her to stop distributing the buttons. They warned her she could be brought up on treason charges. Ida scoffed at the suggestion that distributing these little buttons was a treasonous act, and told the agents that if they were going to proceed to charge her with treason, they had better be sure of their facts.

In 1919, Ida was invited to attend the Paris Peace Conference, organized by Marcus Garvey's Universal Negro Improvement Association to take stock of the world situation after World War I. Ida was under investigation by the FBI at the time and her passport to the conference was denied. Also in 1919, more than 25 race riots broke out around the country, labeling the year as the "Red Summer." One of the riots that summer was in Elaine, Arkansas.

Her approach to documenting situations of racial injustice was used again when she went to Elaine, Arkansas in 1920 to investigate the deaths of a group of black sharecroppers and the sentencing of 12 to Death Row. Through interviews she conducted, she learned their alleged crime had been an effort to form a labor union and secure better pay for cotton industry workers. Ida's pamphlet *The Arkansas Race Riot* countered the prevailing narrative and told the story of what happened from the black people's point of view, leaving behind a firsthand account of what actually happened.

Final Years

In the 1920s, Ida Wells participated in the struggle for African-American workers' rights, urging black women's organizations to support the Brotherhood of Sleeping Car Porters, as it tried to gain legitimacy. She lost the presidency of the National Association of Colored Women to Mary Bethune. In 1930, she unsuccessfully sought elective office, running as an Independent for a seat in the Illinois Senate against the successful Republican Party candidate.

Ida B. Wells died of kidney failure (uremia) in Chicago on March 25, 1931, at the age of 68.

Epilogue

During her long journey in public service, Ida Wells crossed paths with Frederick Douglass, Susan B. Anthony, Jane Addams, W.E.B. Du Bois, and Booker T. Washington. She was unmatched in adhering to her convictions, undaunted in her courage, fearless in her propensity for action, guided always by facts, and determined to speak out and act against injustice.

She was labeled a "Negro adventuress," a "Negro agitator," a "sensational Negro lecturer on lynching in the South," and she came to be seen as too radical to take a leadership position in the emerging civil rights organizations.

Her greatest contributions to public service were (1) her tenacity in investigating and communicating about racial injustices across the United States in post–Civil War America; (2) her willingness to organize African-American women through civic clubs in their cities; and (3) her years providing social services for African-American men who had migrated from the South to find better lives for themselves and their families.

Notes

1 Ida B. Wells, *Crusade for Justice – The Autobiography of Ida B. Wells* (University of Chicago Press, Chicago, IL, originally published in 1970, updated in 2020), page 17.
2 Ibid., page 18.
3 Ibid., page 44.
4 Ibid., page 45.
5 Ibid., page 46.
6 Ibid., page 72.
7 Ibid., page 80.
8 Ibid., page 195.

9 Michelle Duster, and Hannnah Giorgis, *Ida B. the Queen, The Extraordinary Life and Legacy of Ida B. Wells* (Simon & Schuster, New York, NY, 2021), page 112.

10 Wells, *Crusade for Justice*, page 213.

Bibliography

Duster, Michelle. Giorgis, Hannah, *Ida B. The Queen: The Extraordinary Life and Legacy of Ida B. Wells*. New York, NY: Simon & Schuster, 2021.

Wells, Ida B. *Crusade for Justice: The Autobiography of Ida B. Wells, 2nd Edition*, edited by Alfreda M. Duster. Chicago, IL: University of Chicago Press, 2020.

11

UPTON SINCLAIR

Author, Socialist, and Muckraker

Upton Sinclair was born on September 30, 1878 into relative prosperity in Baltimore, Maryland. Most of his life was spent as a writer, with a distinctive point of view, once describing himself as a socialist propagandist. His ability as a writer led to publication of *The Jungle* in 1906 (at 27 years of age), which detailed

DOI: 10.4324/9781003266235-13

the horrors of the meatpacking industry and the products they produced, and contributed to the passage of the Safe Food and Drug Act to improve practices in that industry. In spite of the success of *The Jungle*, critics dismissed him as a mere muckraker, an investigative reporter bent on stirring up trouble. He would bounce back with a series of popular nonfiction attacks in the 1920s on religion, the press, and modern education (called the Dead Hand series). After age 60, he began a series of 11 novels of historical fiction about the wars of the twentieth century including *The Dragon's Teeth* about the rise of Nazi Germany, for which he won a Pulitzer Prize in 1943. He also tried his hand at running for office on the Socialist Party ticket, losing in 1920 for the U.S. House, losing again for the U.S. Senate in 1922, and then for Governor in 1926 and 1930. He then ran as a Democrat for Governor of California earning 879,000 votes. He was unsuccessful in all these attempts.

During the early years of his life, Upton Sinclair knew Mark Twain, Jack London, and Theodore Roosevelt. In his middle years, he formed a political alliance with Franklin Delano Roosevelt and built admiring friendships with Albert Einstein, Charlie Chaplin, Thomas Mann, and George Bernard Shaw. And as an old man, he was corresponding with Carl Jung and Albert Camus. In 1967, President Lyndon Johnson honored him at a White House ceremony. He was a straitlaced puritan about sex (which was a troublesome issue in his first marriage, which ended when his wife ran off with his best friend), he despised alcohol (mostly due to his mother's puritanical streak, and because as he grew up he saw alcohol's bad effects on his father), he was not a good father (though his second wife saw to it that he was estranged from his only child). His insistence that he knew best what was right for everyone else fed extreme views of him from both admirers and detractors. Many felt that he was self-righteous and petulant.

His typical plot in his many books sent a naïve seeker in search of truth, and he especially loved Don Quixote whose wanderings prompted Sinclair to ask the question that guided him throughout his life: 'What shall be the relation of the idealist, the dreamer of good and beautiful things, to the world of ugliness and greed in which he finds himself?'[1]

Early Years as a Writer

In the fall of 1893, at only 15 years old, Upton Sinclair became one of the youngest freshmen at the City College of New York. In addition to his studies, and some freelance writing, Upton found the time to study the violin with a former classmate as his tutor and picked up an even greater passion for the newly fashionable game of tennis. (He would win a half-dozen amateur tournaments over the next 50 years.) With money he earned from his freelance writing, and after graduating from City College with little regard for his grades, he began graduate studies at Columbia University in September 1897 to prepare for a career as a lawyer. But he quickly changed his plan when he discovered that he could add and drop classes almost at random, with no additional cost, so he sampled 40 classes over two years, attending most just long enough to get the reading list and assess the professors' attitudes and presentation methods. As he grew older and more certain of his intellectual gifts, he came to see himself as blessed with superior skills, capable of doing almost anything he tried.

By 19 he was a self-supporting writer of published novels, mostly juvenile entertainments. He was commissioned to write a continuing saga about life at the U.S. Military Academy at West Point, just a half a day's ferry ride up the Hudson River. He would spend several days wandering around the academy, soaking up the atmosphere, and talking to cadets about details of their lives there. After a few days, his research turned into a 30,000 word novel, authored by "Frederick Garrison, USA." He subsequently did an additional series from the Naval Academy in Annapolis, under the pen-name "Ensign Clarke Fitch, USN."

In 1900, at 22 years of age, Upton made a conscious decision to become a literary artist of the first rank. He had undeniable gifts, his powers of observation, understanding, and memory were extraordinary, and he awed everyone he knew with his capacity for the hard work that writing entails. He developed a burning sense of mission, of being specially selected to do great things. He knew that he was destined to be a pure artist and would give up writing for money and devote himself wholeheartedly to a career as a serious novelist.

In April 1900, Upton moved into a log cabin at Lake Massawippi near the border between Quebec and Vermont to write *Springtime and Harvest* about a woman in a quandary about her choice of a husband, which suffered from his lack of experience with his subject. But publishers showed little interest because of its cluttered plot, unconvincing characters, and its stilted language.

Also during this time at Lake Massawippi, he carried out a summer romance with Meta Fuller, a woman he had known through family connections. They married on October 17, 1900. Unwilling to give up on his novel, Upton borrows money from an uncle, prints a thousand copies of his book, and sends them to friends and potential reviewers at newspapers and magazines. A brief burst of publicity results. A ray of hope appears when *Springtime* is published under a different title, though only about 2,000 copies were sold. But this is enough to rekindle Upton's hopes for a writing career. Meta announces she is pregnant, unwelcome news to both Upton (because he views Meta and his family as a distraction from his writing) and Meta (who wants more of Upton's attention and wants a more secure financial footing before beginning to raise a family).

In June 1901, he and Meta travel to camp for the summer in the Thousand Islands at the mouth of the St. Lawrence River, and he begins work on his second novel *Prince Hagen*, which he regards as his first work of social criticism. Meta enjoyed the summer idyll less than Upton did, because she was saddled with cooking, cleaning, and morning sickness.

In correspondence from this time, Upton explained that his whole purpose in life was to work, but not for money.

> I want to give every second of my time and of my thought, every ounce of my energy to the worship of my God and to the uttering of the unspeakable message that I know he has given me. I have no other joy or care in the world but this.[2]

Meta gave birth to a baby boy they named David on December 1, 1901, after 14 hours of painful labor. He did not object much when Meta's father and mother took Meta and David home with them soon after David's birth, telling Upton not to come see them until he had a job.

After a meeting with prominent socialists, Upton begins to form a coherent philosophy based on socialism. In his third novel, *The Captain of Industry*, he develops a properly vicious capitalist villain. But the novel reads like a revenge fantasy, a "melodrama gone haywire," and it was as much a failure as *Springtime and Harvest*. It would not be seen by readers until after publication of *The Jungle*. But Upton moved on to his next project, a tribute to America in the form of a Civil War trilogy, which he saw as his attempt to write a work worthy of comparison to the greatest of all epics, Homer's *Iliad*.

Upton, Meta, and David moved to a farm near Princeton, New Jersey in May 1903, and he turned the page to a life in which his formal education and his difficult beginnings as a novelist were behind him. His early novels had been failures because his true gifts were as a teacher and a preacher but his stories lacked both practical lessons and moral coherence. In Princeton, he would find his lasting subject — *the conflict between idealism and materialism in America* — the wellspring of his belief in socialism. He was basing his Civil War epic on his research skills with the set of personal narratives on hand in the Princeton Library. He took time off only to assist a team of carpenters build a small cabin, his family's first real home, built in large part to help brighten Meta's mood. When they settled in, David's health immediately improved and Meta finally had time to begin the reading program that Upton had designed for her, with wide readings in philosophy, economics, political science, and books by feminist authors.

The first book of the Civil War trilogy, *Manassas*, was nearing completion in February 1904. His theme was the *triumph of idealism over the threat of destruction from immoral forces, chiefly those related to slavery*. His confidence in the quality of the novel was offset by the long, painful, and inexorable deterioration of his marriage. He surmised that his wife had more of a need to give and receive love, whereas he was dedicated to the stern call of duty. He thought it was foolish to strive to be happy, but to be *useful* was what one should strive for in life. The highest use was to live the "heroic life," striving against great difficulties for "the good of all." He felt that the work he was now doing as a writer was of this nature. Meta's depression had deepened and she tried to mount the courage to commit suicide.

In early May, Sinclair received an offer to publish *Manassas* in August of the following year. He was working with the same publisher who had steered *The Call of the Wild* through publication, and there was a sense that Upton had finally arrived as a serious author. But in spite of some strong reviews, *Manassas* was not the masterpiece that Upton had hoped for, selling less than 2,000 copies in 1904.

Becoming a Muckraker

Born in 1878, Sinclair was the youngest and the last of the muckrakers. Ida Tarbell, who had denounced John D. Rockefeller in her 1904 book, *The History of the Standard Oil Company* was born in 1857. Charles Edward Russell, whose series of articles on the meatpacking industry in *McClure's* magazine became *The Greatest Trust in the World*, was 18 years older than Sinclair. Arthur Brisbane, the Hearst editor who sometimes campaigned for reform and later became Sinclair's friend, was 14 years older. Ray Stannard Baker was born in 1870 and his groundbreaking study of race, *Following the Color Line*, did not appear until after *The Jungle* in 1908. David Graham Phillips, who wrote about malfeasance in Washington in *Treason of the Senate* in 1905, was 11 years older. The dean of the muckrakers was Lincoln Steffens, who influenced Sinclair and whose friendship he cherished. Born in 1860, his greatest work, *The Shame of the Cities*, was published in March 1904 as Sinclair was finishing *Manassas*. *Shame of the Cities* started as a collection of articles on municipal corruption in Pittsburgh, Chicago, and other cities that had appeared in McClure. Sinclair wrote a long letter to Steffens about *Shame* to say that he was thrilled by what he had written, though he regretted that Steffens failed to advocate socialism as the cure for the corruption he had so vividly described.

Sinclair began to tire of the idea of the Civil War trilogy, though he was struck by the parallels between "chattel slavery" of blacks before the Civil War and the "wage slavery" of the workers in the early 1900s. He was approached to write a series of articles about wage slavery, and he asked for a stake of $500, enough to live on for a year. Sinclair also approached his previous publisher about turning the articles into a book. He described his goal for the book: he "intended to set forth the breaking of human hearts by a system which exploits the labor of men and women for profits."[3] His clear intention was to write something popular. His publisher agreed to advance $500 against the royalties on the promised novel. He now had $1000 in the bank, two publishers in his pocket, so he left his wife and child behind and set out for Chicago, where he would see for himself what life was like for the wage slaves in the slaughterhouses.

In Chicago, Sinclair showed up at the Transit House, a huge rambling hotel near the Union Stockyards that was always jammed with cowboys, ranchers, and cattle dealers. Upon his arrival, he exclaimed, "Hello! I'm Upton Sinclair! And I've come to write *The Uncle Tom's Cabin* of the Labor Movement!" The comparison was apt, since his subject was to be the working conditions that he thought approximated slavery. His argument would be that the capitalist system behind such conditions should give way to socialism. He had virtually no interest in persuading readers that their meat was rotten except as a means of dramatizing the sad conditions of the workers who prepared it for them.

The challenge faced by the meatpacking industry was to turn living creatures into products. The work involved was unpleasant at best and dangerous for workers – it entailed not only the risks of injury, but also infection and disease at every turn both for the workers and the meat they turned out. In addition to these hazards were others imposed by innovations in modern science and technology. Chemical preservatives inhibited the process of decay in fresh meat, but raised questions about meats "embalmed" with formaldehyde, as detailed in a series of articles in the Hearst newspapers. Such preservatives were blamed for killing more American soldiers in Cuba than had died fighting the Spaniards. On the scientific front, Dr. Harvey Wiley, the chief of the Bureau of Chemistry in the U.S. Department of Agriculture and his "poison squad" looked into adulterated foodstuffs, including meat. When Theodore Roosevelt became president, the "Rough Rider" hated the packers for poisoning his troops in Cuba, and he vowed to target them among the great "trusts" that he wanted to take legal action against.

Though the Hearst stories had brought attention to the practices of the meatpackers, Sinclair believed that only a novel equivalent to *Uncle Tom's Cabin* would move readers on the emotional level needed for action. Only through fiction could writers concerned about social problems and ideas hope to reach the widest audience. Sinclair agreed with Frank Norris (the author of the novel *The Pit*, about the Chicago commodities market) that a novel could be as effective as a sermon in changing people's attitudes, and he agreed with Shelley's claim that writers and poets should lead the way to social change as the **"legislators of mankind."**

Sinclair was aided by many who wanted to share their experiences in the plants. Sinclair stayed at the University of Chicago Settlement House, run by Mary McDowell, known as "the Angel of the Stockyards" for her sympathetic devotion to the workers in the stockyards. Her expertise and access to influential friends were helpful to Sinclair. He was able to interview plant foremen and laborers, priests and bartenders, policemen, politicians, and undertakers. He wandered unimpeded through the vast Armour facilities, memorizing details of what he saw and then returning to his room to write everything down. Gifted with an ability to absorb sights and sounds and information, driven by a messianic sense of purpose, he had nearly enough within a few short weeks to write the novel. But he was worried that he had no story, he needed characters, he needed a plot, and he needed a new style that he could adapt to his unique situation.

But wandering aimlessly through the "back of the yards" on a Sunday afternoon, Sinclair found a Lithuanian wedding party in a saloon, who generously invites him to join them. There, he was inspired to find his characters, watched them for the entire afternoon and into the night, and fitted them into his story. He wrote it all down later, turning paragraphs into pages exactly as he had memorized them.

This opening chapter of *The Jungle* has been hailed as one of his best and one of the best in American literature: "one of the most poignant sketches in American literature of a common experience of immigration: the loss of a culture in all its complexities, and the acquisition of poorly understood fragment of a new one."[4] He had devised a narrative that combined documentary realism with the traditional novelistic elements of character and plot. He could now attack "wage slavery" through the eyes of its victims, interpreting what they saw in his own words that he hoped would move his middle-class readers to sympathy and to action.

After seven weeks of gathering harrowing information about life in the stockyards, Sinclair was certain that he had in his hands the greatest story of his life. He returned to Meta and David a few days before Christmas. On his return, he had to attend to the purchase of a house, as Meta had informed him that she did not intend to spend another winter in their dilapidated home on the marsh. With his new novel on the way, they should be able to afford to borrow the money necessary to buy what Meta wanted: a nice country house. Their current landlord owned a small farm a half mile away. After touring the farm house, which was a short distance from their own house, Meta suggested that they seek a loan from the clergyman that had married them. The clergyman at first refused to help, but Sinclair told him of his concern for his wife's health, explaining that she had already attempted suicide and he was concerned for her mental health if she spent another winter in their current home. This convinced the clergyman to help, and Meta was thrilled at their good fortune.

On Christmas morning 1904, Upton Sinclair sat down in his tiny study and began to write *The Jungle*. But when he began to turn out the drafts for publication as a series of articles, interest among his publisher and his readers began to wane, and his book publisher's interest began to dissipate as well. He had met with both to work out the revisions they wanted made, but struggled to resolve the problems they had noted. Sinclair did concede that he had written a book that lagged in its later sections as he tried to pack everything into the book that he knew about the Socialist movement. He later pruned some of the excesses and circulated the book among other publishers. While waiting for several publishers to decide about *The Jungle*, he resolved to publish and promote the book himself. He was aided in this attempt by a rousing plug by Jack London that proclaimed that all good socialists should be heartened by *The Jungle*, which did for the "wage slaves of today" what *Uncle Tom's Cabin* had done for black slaves.

But on December 16, he received an excellent offer from a reputable New York publisher to publish *The Jungle*. The publisher was Doubleday, Page: a former reporter named Isaac Marcosson, who had written favorable reviews of some of Sinclair's earlier works, was now at Doubleday. He had taken the manuscript home, read it in one evening, and described himself as "spellbound" by its power and originality. Hours later, he burst into his boss's office and declared that if it were properly merchandised it was destined to become a huge success. He was convinced that *The Jungle* had real news value and could be a real moneymaker for the company. The manuscript was sent to the *Chicago Tribune* for a factual review of its contents by a reporter, who produced a damning report about its accuracy.

But the *Tribune* was published by Robert McCormick, who despised outsiders who presumed to criticize local industry, and Sinclair suspected that the report was an effort to silence him. The publisher sent Marcosson and the company's attorney, Thomas McKee, to Chicago immediately. McKee later learned from a publicity agent for the meatpacking industry that they had prepared the report for the *Tribune*, making Sinclair's charge that the report was a fraud obviously correct. When McKee returned from Chicago, Sinclair agreed to sit with him to take out anything in *The Jungle* that seemed libelous or likely to offend readers needlessly. Doubleday wanted to market a book that exposed the meatpacking industry and by so doing prompted reform: Sinclair had hoped to arouse enough outrage about wage slavery to provoke a socialist revolution. Encouraged by Sinclair's pliability, along with the boxes of documentation that support his remaining assertions, Marcosson and McKee persuaded Doubleday that they were ready for any backlash that might come from the industry in reaction to publication.

Sinclair signed his contract with Doubleday on January 8, 1906: six weeks later the first printing of 20,000 copies was nearing completion. When review copies became available, Marcosson sent copies to the Associated Press and United Press for distribution to their newspapers. He also sent a copy to President Roosevelt, and when Sinclair sent one to Roosevelt they began a lively and prolonged correspondence.

In a meeting with Sinclair, Roosevelt praised the book for pointing out problems that needed to be investigated. Roosevelt had decided to send a small team of investigators to Chicago, including his commissioner of labor, Charles P. Neill, and a younger man, James R. Reynolds, who was known to Sinclair from his previous settlement work in New York. Sinclair met with the men immediately but did not accompany them to Chicago as Roosevelt had requested, instead returning to Princeton. Sinclair was met there the very next morning by a businessman who offered him a large quantity of shares in a new "independent packing company," in return for which Sinclair would let his name and reputation be used to promote the company. The businessman came back several times after Sinclair's initial refusal of his offer, eventually raising the offer to $300,000 worth of stock, an amount equivalent to $6 million today.

Failing in their attempt to buy him off, Sinclair's opponents then set about on a line of attack using articles under Ogden Armour's name in the *Saturday Evening Post*, which attacked Sinclair's book and burnished the image of the meatpackers. Sinclair countered by setting up a small publicity office in New York, which he used to give interviews and issue statements to the press.

The report from Neill and Reynolds had more than confirmed Sinclair's charges in *The Jungle*: they told him that they thought he had actually understated the disgusting conditions they had witnessed. Their report was not yet in writing, so could not yet be made public. On May 22, a bill by Senator Albert Beverage was passed in three days due, in part, to the spotlight focused on members by *The Treason of the Senate*, without the Neill and Reynolds report having to be made public at all.

Industry supporters in the House were attempting to bury the Beveridge bill. But then Sinclair became the first in a long line of activists throughout American history who make their case by leaking documents to the *New York Times*. By publishing the report as it had been conveyed to him orally, he hoped to force Roosevelt to release the entire report in writing. During his presentation to the *Times*, ten stenographers took down his story in shifts over three hours, and by 1:00 a.m., it was ready to go to press. It appeared on the front pages on Monday, May 28, without his byline, it was ostensibly written by a *Times* reporter in Washington. Personalizing the dispute, he published a blistering letter to the *Times*, daring Armour to sue him. He summarized in the latter the charges he had gathered from a variety of sources in Chicago:

> the selling for human food of the carcasses of cattle and swine which had been condemned for tuberculosis, actinomycosis, and gangrene; the converting of such carcasses into sausage and lard; the preserving of spoiled hams with boric and salicylic acid; the coloring of canned and potted meats with saline dyes; the embalming and adulterating of sausages – all of these things mean the dealing out to hundreds and thousands of men, women, and children of a sudden, horrible, and agonizing death.

Roosevelt then ordered Neill and Reynolds to have their report on his desk within 48 hours. The report was released to the public on June 4th, and it was a disappointment to Sinclair as it was only eight pages long and contained only those things that Neill and Reynolds had seen with their own eyes and guided tours through packing plants. Even so, the plants revealed an indifference to sanitation and a sense of "universal uncleanliness." It was obvious that meat products coming out of such conditions were a menace to the health of their consumers. Though dry and factual in its presentation, the report managed to catch the public's attention.

The release of the report foiled the packer's scheme of delaying the vote on the Beveridge bill until after the summer. A compromise food and drug bill was passed on June 23rd and was signed by Roosevelt on June 30, 1906. Roosevelt did not acknowledge Sinclair's work during the bill signing, instead limiting his praise to Senator Beveridge. Roosevelt later wrote that he had come to see Sinclair as "hysterical, unbalanced, and untruthful," later calling him a "crackpot."

Sinclair's biographers have concluded that the contribution of *The Jungle* had been to set forth issues and fears of long standing; it did not set in motion the drive to pass the Pure Food and Drug Act but helped push it across the finish line, persuading many of the need for the legislation. Sinclair was bitterly disappointed with the outcome of the battle. Hoping to rouse sympathy for the workers, he said, he had "aimed at the public's heart and by accident I hit it in the stomach." The wage slaves he had sought to save were left alone and helpless in their cells. His conviction that the system was fixed against the possibility of reform was confirmed. His entry onto the great stage of national affairs had only convinced him of the impossibility of real change within the existing system.

Critics have noted Sinclair's strengths in *The Jungle*. They lauded his powerfully descriptive prose, a sense of truthful authority, and an inspiring moral fervor. The book made Sinclair a considerable sum of money, though that was not important to Sinclair. By midyear he had realized more than $30,000 from sales of the book. He was also famous, which he wanted to be. By the end of 1906, there were 100,000 copies in print, and untold millions of Americans soon knew his name. He was now a man of influence, able to count on drawing supporters to his various crusades.

His Later Years in California

Sinclair and his second wife, Mary Craig Kimbrough, a woman from an elite Greenwood, Mississippi family, who he met when she attended one of his lectures, were married in 1913 and lived near Los Angeles in the 1920s. Sinclair wanted to get involved in politics, and after founding the state chapter of the American Civil Liberties Union, he began seeking elective office. He twice ran on the Socialist Party ticket for the U.S. House of Representatives and then ran for the U.S. Senate for the Socialist Party in 1922. He was also the Socialist Party candidate for governor of California in 1926 and in 1930. He was unsuccessful each time.

He then ran for governor as a Democrat in 1934. He ran on a platform known as the End Poverty in California (EPIC) movement, gained much support in the Democratic Party, and secured its nomination. He earned 879,000 votes in that election, making it his most successful effort, but not enough to defeat incumbent Governor Frank Merriam, who earned 1,138,000 votes, defeating Sinclair by a sizable margin.

Sinclair's plan to end poverty was a controversial issue, with conservatives considering his proposal an attempted communist takeover of the state. They used propaganda to portray Sinclair as a staunch communist. At the same time, American and Soviet communists disavowed his candidacy, considering him a capitalist.

After his loss to Merriam, Sinclair abandoned politics and EPIC and returned to writing. In a 1935 book explaining his defeat in the governor's race, Sinclair's most well-known line from that book has become well known and used by various political figures: "It is difficult to get a man to understand something, when his salary depends upon his not understanding it." He also said of his gubernatorial bid that the American People will take Socialism, but they won't take the label, pointing out that he got 879,000 votes running as a Democrat on the slogan to "End Poverty in California."

In 1961, Sinclair's second wife, Mary Craig Kimbrough died. Later that same year, Sinclair married his third wife Mary Elizabeth Willis, they moved to Arizona before returning east to Bound Brook, New Jersey, where Sinclair died in a nursing home on November 25, 1968, a year after his wife. They are both buried in Rock Creek Cemetery in Washington, DC.

Notes

1 Anthony Arthur, *Radical Innocent, Upton Sinclair* (Random House Publishing Group, New York, NY, 2006), page xiv.
2 Ibid., page 18.
3 Ibid., page 42.
4 Sinclair quote summarizing findings from book, contained in his letter to Armour (page 11).

Bibliography

Arthur, Anthony. *Radical Innocent: Upton Sinclair.* New York, NY: Random House, 2006.
Sinclair, Upton. *Dragon's Teeth.* Safety Harbor, FL: Simon Publications, 2001.
Sinclair, Upton. *The Jungle.* Mineola, NY: Dover Thrift Publishing, 2001.

12

ALICE PAUL

Tireless Champion of Women's Rights

DOI: 10.4324/9781003266235-14

When Alice Stokes Paul was born in Mount Laurel, New Jersey on January 11, 1885, her parents could not have foreseen that they were bringing into the world one of the most influential advocates for women's rights in the history of the United States and the world. She spent 50 years as the leader of the National Women's Party (NWP) working on the passage of the 19th amendment to secure women's right to vote, the Equal Rights Amendment, and provisions of the Civil Rights Act of 1964 protecting women against discrimination.

This profile focuses on Paul's contributions to the suffrage fight, where she became one of the most creative and energetic advocates pushing the passage of the 19th amendment.

Early Years – Education, England, and Discovering the Suffragist Movement

Alice was the oldest of four children, she was a descendant of William Penn (the founder of Pennsylvania), she was raised in a Quaker household, with an emphasis on public service. Her mother was a member of the National American Woman Suffrage Association (NAWSA) and Alice would sometimes join her at suffragist meetings.

Alice attended Moorestown Friends School, went on to Swarthmore College (an institution cofounded by her grandfather) where she earned a bachelor's degree in biology in 1905. She had helped form a labor union while she earned another degree, this one at the New York School of Philanthropy. She then completed a fellowship at the College Settlement House in New York City's lower east side. This experience taught her about the need to right injustice, but it also helped her decide that social work was not going to be her path to achieving that goal. She wanted to attend Princeton for further study, but they did not accept women or black men. It would be the first of many times in her life that Woodrow Wilson, then in his role as Princeton's President, stood in the way of her aspirations. Instead, she earned a master of arts degree from the University of Pennsylvania in 1907, taking courses in political science, sociology, and economics.

Having earned three degrees in three years – 1905, 1906, and 1907 – her thirst for learning led her to continue her studies at Woodbrooke Quaker Study Center in Birmingham, England, while taking economics classes at the University of Birmingham. She supported herself by doing social work. During her time at Woodbrooke, she attended a lecture by Christobel Pankhurst that would change her life. Christobel and her mother Emmeline were active in the suffrage movement in England and had a growing reputation as militants. The lecture was disrupted by angry men shouting at the speakers, but Alice was riveted by the composure of Christobel and her description of the suffrage struggle in England, which had been going on for decades. When the lecture was over, Alice "could feel the electricity in her body ... unlike anything she had ever felt before."[1] Alice later moved to London to study sociology and economics at the London School of Economics, where she joined a militant suffrage group, the Woman's Social and Political Union (WSPU) led by Christobel and Emmeline Pankhurst. Alice was repeatedly arrested during suffrage demonstrations and served three terms in jail while working with the Pankhursts.

At the first of two suffrage rallies Paul attended in England, she met women from the American suffrage movement, including Dr. Anna Howard Shaw, NAWSA. She marched in the procession with the Americans and attended the indoor rally to hear the various speakers.

The next event Paul attended was "Suffrage Sunday" organized by the WSPU. The march terminated in Hyde Park where 20 platforms had been set up to accommodate the many passionate suffragist speakers. When she began attending classes in the fall at the London School of Economics, among the few women at the School, Paul met Rachel Barret, a WSPU organizer, who invited her to pass out suffrage literature on street corners. Tolerating verbal abuse through it all, Paul earned a reputation for her perseverance, and was then asked to do public speaking on street corners, at train stations, and inside trains.

After spending two years in England, Paul was ready to return home, and she had received a letter from her mother imploring her to do so. But she had also received a letter asking her to accompany Mrs. Pankhurst in a delegation to see the Prime Minister, a confrontation that might put her in danger of being arrested and imprisoned. After some deliberation, Paul responded in her own letter by committing to spend the summer working for the WSPU. Her first assignment was a march with Emmeline Pankhurst to the House of Commons, where they were promptly arrested. In the police station, Paul introduced herself to a redhead wearing an American flag lapel pin. Her name was Lucy Burns, a Catholic from Brooklyn. She had come to Europe to study for two years at the University of Berlin, after Vassar and Yale, before signing up with the suffragists in England. The two talked for hours, forming a lasting bond. When they were released by the police, the two women were exhausted but emboldened. Their next assignment was to confront a rising politician named Winston Churchill at an event he was attending, who did not believe that women should have the right to vote.

Also during this time, Paul and Burns participated in various actions that got them arrested and imprisoned. In an act of protest, Paul refused all food, taking only water. She also refused the prison clothes she was offered deciding instead to remain naked. Sometimes these self-deprivation tactics led to her early release from jail, but they took a toll on Paul. At one point, Paul had been arrested six times in the previous six months and gone on two hunger strikes. She was becoming both a celebrity and an oddity, an American woman sacrificing so much of her time and health to fight alongside British women for their voting rights.

In prison, Paul would lay shivering in her bed weak from refusing food for several days and cold from refusing the prison clothes. But then the guards wrapped her in blankets, took her to another cell, and the largest female guard sat across Paul's knees and pinned her shoulders to the cot, while two other guards sat on either side of her and held her arms. They wrapped a towel around her throat as a doctor came up from behind and forced her head back while shoving a tube (up to six-feet long and thick as a finger) up her nostril. They would pump a mixture of eggs and milk down her throat. Each time the ordeal ended, she trembled, cried, bled from her nose, and lay drenched in sweat. She endured this twice a day for nearly three weeks, causing physical damage that would plague her for the rest of her life.

On January 6, 1910, she boarded a ship back to America, to return to her family which greeted her at the dock as reporters descended on her to ask her questions about the cause for which she had sacrificed so much. It was not long before she craved another challenge, and that following September she entered the Doctoral program at the University of Pennsylvania, where she was a star who drew admirers to her. One of them was a graduate assistant named William Parker from upstate New York, who wrote to her after he left the university and told her, among other things, "if you only don't break yourself to pieces, you will conquer the world."[2] Though she would not let herself be distracted by a relationship during her time in school, their paths would cross again in Washington, DC.

The Suffrage Procession in Washington, DC

When Woodrow Wilson was traveling by train to Washington, DC for his inauguration as President, the U.S. Capitol was also preparing for another event: a massive suffrage procession timed to coincide with Wilson's arrival at 3:45 p.m. The platform and public areas were crowded with those arriving on "Suffragette Specials" from many cities near and far; thousands of women were expected to participate in the protest.

The plans that Alice Paul and Lucy Burns had started three months earlier were starting to materialize. They had joined the NAWSA, the organization that had been headed by Susan B. Anthony until she died in 1906, and it was now led by Anna Howard Shaw. NAWSA's strategy was to change the laws at the state level rather than the federal level because it assumed a federal amendment could not be achieved.

Paul and Burns asked Shaw if they could try a more aggressive strategy for a federal amendment by forming a committee dedicated to this cause within the NAWSA. Burns was especially convincing, and she was developing a reputation as a sophisticated public speaker after attending upper-crust schools such as Vassar, Yale, Oxford, studying abroad at the University of Berlin, and traveling with the Pankhursts throughout England and Scotland. In January 1913, Paul and Burns established the Congressional Committee headquartered in Washington, DC, as a part of the NAWSA.

Throughout the planning for the procession, Paul had stressed that the event needed to exude dignity and poise to counteract the cultural assumption that it was unladylike for women to be out walking on their own. She wanted the procession to show strength and intelligence, to remind the audience how hard women work in all fields. Paul wanted to include black women and invited them to participate. But some in her organization expressed concern and wanted to avoid a "race war." Paul considered this issue and decided that black women would be scattered among the northern and Quaker groups in the parade. She wanted to win voting rights so that *all* women would benefit.

The procession was headed by Inez Milholland, a beautiful 27-year-old woman who was a suffragist and the daughter of a wealthy inventor. She had a law degree and a practice in New York City devoted to women and striking laborers. Paul put her at the head of the parade with a starred crown, riding a white horse. The procession of 8,000 women began to march with signs reading *we demand an amendment to the United States Constitution enfranchising women of this country*. Two police cars carved a clear path ahead of the front of the line. The officers of the NAWSA walked behind Milholland, and the crowd, bustling with agitated men, closed in behind her. After moving with reasonable ease for six blocks, it became difficult for the women to make progress walking on the street.

The procession continued to force its way forward. In the middle of the procession was the Illinois delegation which included Ida B. Wells, a prominent African-American journalist who, among other things, had helped found the National Association for the Advancement of Colored People in 1909. The march itself was a radical act and racially integrating the procession was even more so. When Ida Wells lined up with the Illinois delegation to begin the parade, some in the delegation saw Wells and questioned whether she should be there. Black women marched with the Delaware, New York, West Virginia, and Michigan delegations. When word spread that Mary Church Terrell, a prominent African-American would lead a group from the National Association of Colored Women, southerners threatened a boycott, so the men's section offered to march between these black and white groups.

Procession participants were fighting their way to make progress through a mass of onlookers that had clustered at the Treasury Department. Alice Paul became concerned about the chaos. She, Lucy Burns, and others jumped into cars to more easily monitor the mayhem, moving slowly up to the front. All around them men cursed, shoved, and jeered at the marchers while the police did little to intervene, with the police chief waiting at Union Station for Woodrow Wilson to arrive. The marchers did not lash out, but some began to quit when the mob turned vicious, dragging women out of the procession. Over the course of six hours, 100 people were injured. The police made no arrests.

The procession, designed to be a dignified and educational call for women's voting rights, had devolved into an unmanageable, frightening, frustrating, and violent event. About 2,000 of the 8,000 suffragists completed the procession, and they made their way to a pre-planned rally at the multilevel auditorium that served as the headquarters of the Daughters of the American Revolution. The gathering was supposed to be a celebration of the day and its participants meant to acknowledge and inspire. But speakers focused on the police's failure to maintain order, stoking the outrage to generate more sympathy for their cause. Anna Howard Shaw issued a statement to the press charging not only the police but the "whole official government" in Washington with making a determined effort to interfere with the success of the parade because they were annoyed that it interfered with Wilson's inaugural. Press accounts largely credited the suffragists with behaving well and took the police and other authorities to task for their handling of the event.

The procession had pleased Shaw because it successfully drove more women to the cause. But Shaw wasn't entirely content because she felt threatened by the young activist Paul and her influence within the suffrage movement and in the public domain. Paul was becoming a powerful force.

Woodrow Wilson's Recalcitrance, Women's Organizations Sort Themselves, and the Launch of *The Suffragist*

Two weeks after the suffrage procession, Alice Paul decided she needed to capitalize on the momentum created by the procession. She scheduled a face-to-face meeting with President Woodrow Wilson, and she carefully curated a group of women from the NAWSA to attend the meeting, choosing each suffragist for her political muscle.

The meeting with the women began with Paul urging Wilson to raise in his initial speech to Congress the need for an amendment to the Constitution giving women equal suffrage with men throughout the United States. Others in the group of women chimed in with various reasons and arguments in support of the amendment. Wilson sat stiffly as others in the group read his own words back to him from his speeches. Others in the group urged him to do better than his two Republican predecessors did on women's right to vote.

Wilson *refused their request* to include a mention of women's suffrage in his address to Congress, claiming the public agenda was getting crowded and there were items he considered higher priority, such as currency and tariff reform. He also mentioned that as a southerner who believed in state's rights, he felt that states should decide about suffrage on their own by referendum. Paul realized that their ten-minute discussion hadn't changed his opinion and that the only way she could force him or Congress to act on a federal amendment was by converting public opinion.

A week later, still having heard no final decision from Wilson about the content of his upcoming speech, she decided to visit Wilson again. With a different set of women, they again made the case to Wilson about the importance of the amendment and the need to include it in his address to Congress. For the *president asserted that the House and Senate would be occupied with tariff and currency reform*, and he would, therefore not ask them to consider the suffrage question.

Time was running out before the President's scheduled address to Congress on April 8. Paul waited only three days before requesting a third meeting with Wilson, this time with her largest delegation yet. One aspect of their message to Wilson was that at some point voting women could turn against the party that was impeding women's progress. In spite of their pleas, Wilson *held to his view that he only wanted to call attention to currency and tariff reform* to focus the efforts of Congress. He *refused them a third time*, and Paul was certain it would take more than a few meetings with Wilson to change his mind.

The day before Wilson's speech, Paul had organized a rally and procession to the U.S. Capitol Building. Beginning at the Columbia Theater on F Street, where speeches by noted suffragists had been scheduled, followed by a procession of 531 women – two from every state and one from each congressional district – each carrying small envelopes with a copy of a petition for her representative in Congress.

Wilson's address indeed did not include anything about suffrage, and Paul was now convinced that Wilson had no intentions of taking up suffrage. She believed that NAWSA needed a large, well-funded entity solely focused on pushing legislation on Capitol Hill. NAWSA still favored a state-by-state strategy. After studying NAWSA's bylaws, Paul devised a proposal for a new entity called the Congressional Union (CU), and their focus would be pushing for a constitutional amendment on Capitol Hill. When Paul and Burns met with Shaw about their proposal, she approved their idea but told them they would have to cover all of their own expenses. They set an intention to secure a hearing before the Senate Woman Suffrage Committee and began organizing suffrage demonstrations nationwide throughout the summer.

By mid-summer of 1913, an "auto brigade" campaign devised by Alice Paul was traveling throughout the country gathering signatures on petitions that would be driven to Washington. The stunt generated so much publicity that the CU headquarters was flooded with mail and it awakened opposition groups who became more active. CU members delivered the signed petitions to the Senators, and for the first time in 26 years, the chamber struck up a floor debate on suffrage. Over two hours, 22 senators spoke in favor of the amendment and three spoke against it. One senator suggested that suffrage be set aside in order to leave time for the tariff debate. With that, the activism that led to what the press called the "siege of the Senate" ended without a vote on the amendment itself.

Paul launched another project that summer, a weekly newspaper called *The Suffragist*. Sometimes producing more than 20 pages of copy, containing news updates, editorials, profiles of activists, photographs, and pointed cartoons on the cover, Paul saw the newspaper as an important tool, one that could educate and inspire and also fund the movement through subscriptions. The paper debuted on November 15.

Two days after the launch of *The Suffragist*, Paul learned that a delegation of 73 women from Wilson's home state of New Jersey was still awaiting a reply from the White House about a request for a meeting. The women were now in Washington waiting for their reply. Paul called the White House to get a meeting scheduled and told them that as it seems impossible to find out what hour the President can meet with the group, they will come to the White House and wait there until he is ready to receive them or would definitely refuse to meet with them. The women began their seven-minute walk to the White House, and when they arrived, two guards met them at the gate and allowed them to pass toward the executive office unchallenged. An attendant asked that two of the women be selected to go into the Oval Office to meet the President. Wilson greeted them warmly and told them that he had been talking just yesterday to members of Congress regarding the Suffrage Committee in the House. He assured them "the subject is one in which I am deeply interested, and you may rest assured that I will give it my earnest attention." The women left the meeting feeling they had won a small victory. Wilson had shifted from "suffrage is not on my agenda," to a place where it could be. Such was the glacial pace of progress in convincing Woodrow Wilson to support suffrage.

But all was not harmonious in the ranks of the suffrage movement. Lucy Burns, in particular, drew the ire of Anna Howard Shaw about some of her tactics which Shaw considered rash, risky, and a threat to the long-term success of the movement. Paul and Burns helped organize and lead the fifth annual convention of the NAWSA. They both had gained notoriety for their recent work in the CU, and they spoke in the early stages of the convention. While Paul was pale, thin, and businesslike, Burns was ruddy, solid, and belligerent, her fiery mane an expression of the burning passion at her core, while Paul's language was direct and as unadorned as the inside of a Quaker meeting house. Burns was more engaging, and spoke in a way that was almost musical, her cadence reflective of her broad life experience. But these complimentary differences in personality and approach were the recipe for the pair's unique balance.[3]

The next day, Wilson delivered his first annual address to Congress, and the suffragettes were hopeful that he would mention their cause, but he only vaguely acknowledged the need for a more equal democracy in America, not mentioning the need for action to assure women's right to vote. That evening the NAWSA delegates talked about Wilson's latest snub. Even Shaw was outspoken about her anger toward the President's position on suffrage.

After the convention concluded, there was a meeting scheduled with President Wilson, this was the fifth visit and it was the largest delegation to visit Wilson. He immediately began to explain why he could not promote suffrage in the House and Senate. "I am merely the spokesman of my party. I am not at liberty to urge upon Congress policies which have not had the organic consideration of those for whom I am the spokesman." Shaw immediately rejected Wilson's argument and asked him to send a message to the House and Senate encouraging them to enfranchise women, and urged him to create a suffrage committee in the White House. Shaw further pressed Wilson by asking who would speak for them if not the President or his party. Wilson replied with a broad smile that they seemed more than able to speak for themselves. The suffragists ended the meeting and left the White House.

After the new year, there were discussions between the NAWSA leadership and the CU about the future direction of the movement and about its leadership. Paul approached these meetings with hope that the relationship between the two groups could be repaired. However, Paul realized in the meeting that the disagreement between the groups about the federal amendment versus the state-by-state approach would not be reconciled. She quit the NAWSA.

Paul, now 29 years old, was emotionally and physically depleted. Gaunt and worn out, Paul realized that she needed to follow the advice of many of her friends and admit herself to a hospital to recover. She checked into Woman's Hospital of Philadelphia, a Quaker facility that was founded by a female doctor, and served as a rare training ground for women in medicine. She got the treatment and rest she needed, but, while in the hospital, she did not disengage from the movement and the newly independent organization she created – the Congressional Union for Woman Suffrage (CUWS) – so she began dictating letters to raise funds. She remained in the hospital for three weeks, then stayed with a friend for an additional week. When she returned to her offices in Washington, she needed to find a replacement for the editor of *The Suffragist*. She appointed Lucy Burns as editor, and the two of them launched a wildly successful campaign to boost subscriptions. In the meantime, Paul also began organizing demonstrations across the country, scheduled for May 2.

As America moved into the summer, the president was growing concerned about foreign affairs. But he was also distracted by his wife's health, which was rapidly deteriorating, though Dr. Grayson, the White House doctor, had been downplaying the seriousness of her illness so as not to upset the president. But now that she had become bedridden, other doctors were called into her diagnose her condition. They concluded she had Bright's disease; her kidneys were failing, and she would not recover. Wilson was informed, and he climbed the stairs to Ellen's second floor room and sat vigil by her bed, where he worked at her bedside over several days. Then, one of the doctors advised Wilson to call in the family because the end was near. Wilson openly wept.

Ellen held on for two more days. Moments before she died she drew Dr. Grayson near and asked them to "take good care of Woodrow, doctor." He promised he would. At 5 p.m., in the presence of her family, Wilson folded her hands across her chest, walked to a window and sobbed.

Meanwhile, Paul had organized a meeting of suffragists to be held at the opulent home of a wealthy suffragist in Newport, Rhode Island. Paul and Lucy Burns wanted to have a discussion with these women about some of their ideas for advancing the cause. Burns began with a discussion of the political situation. The Democratic Party was in full control of the legislative and executive branches of the federal government, President Wilson had now been asked seven times to support the suffrage movement, *and seven times he refused*. Democratic leaders in the Senate had blocked the amendment by bringing the amendment to a vote when they knew it would be defeated. The House Rules Committee had consistently blocked the measure because, according to the Democratic Chairman, it was in keeping with the policy of the Democrats. For these reasons, Burns said that the upcoming midterm elections would be essential to the suffragist cause. (This was also true because this was the first election since the newly ratified 17th Amendment, which held that voters – not the legislators from their home states – would directly elect senators for the first time.) Suffragists might be able to tip the balance in the midterms to elect more Republicans to Congress. "It is up to all of us … to guide voters toward the GOP," Burns said. The election was only a couple of months away and the CU should try to defeat the Democrats. Paul then turned to a discussion of their strategy for defeating Democrats at the polls.

> We are determined to get the amendment through the next Congress, or to make it very clear who had kept it from going through … The point is first, who is our enemy, and then how shall that enemy be attacked?[4]

Paul had an ambitious and expensive plan to defeat a blacklist of 18 key Democrats who were not moving suffrage forward and could be voted out by women casting ballots in their home states, sending a strong message to the national party that the movement was advancing beyond talk to direct mobilization with national political implications. She wanted to send two suffragists to each of the western states where women could vote, one would speak at rallies in the largest cities, and the other one would organize the distribution of literature to every household.

This would be the first venture into a national election for the suffragists, a shocking concept that betrayed nearly seven decades of America's polite suffrage legacy. But Paul and her allies were ready for something new that used the advantages they had gained in recent years. In mid-September, the western campaigners left from Washington's Union Station. When the election ended, the CUWS took credit for defeating three candidates and for influencing the results in three other races. This was a small number but all that could be expected from an eight-week sprint using inexperienced staff spread thinly across half the country. Nationwide, the Democrats picked up four Senate seats, but in the House they lost 60 votes, leaving them with only a 34 vote majority, a shrinking margin that distressed Wilson greatly. Publicity around the midterm efforts gave Paul more credibility. As her national stature grew, Wilson was confined to the White House collapsing emotionally, over the loss of his wife three months earlier and the results of the mid-term election. He also did not know what to do about the continuing disintegration of Europe, a distressing emergency. Among its impacts on the United States was slowing exports that dragged down the fragile economy.

On May 7, 1915, Wilson was just finishing lunch when he received the first bulletin about the sinking of the *Lusitania*. Instead of going to his scheduled round of golf, he went for a reflective drive. He was trying to stay out of the war, but the torpedoing of innocent Americans turned many neutral or noninterventionist Americans into hawks. Two days later, Wilson, speaking at a naturalization ceremony in Philadelphia, justified the reasons for maintaining neutrality as a nation, but also impressed upon Americans that they should be prepared to fight.

After their western campaign, Paul's CUWS had been organizing every state at a grassroots level, culminating in a local convention to formulate a plan of attack for Congress. At the same time, Paul had developed a plan to drive a petition with women's signatures across the country. Two Swedish women, taken with the cause of suffrage, volunteered to drive their new car (dubbed the "Suffrage Flier") across the country with a suffragist speaker selected by Paul (Sara Bard Field of Oregon) accompanying them. They left from San Francisco with a crowd of 10,000 people gathered to see them off. As they progressed, Field would call Lucy Burns who shaped her reports into articles for *The Suffragist*, creating a serial adventure.

When Field arrived in Washington on December 6, she ascended the Capitol stairs, trailing the four-mile-long petition on spools behind her, no elected official would meet with her. Rebuffed, the suffragists walked down Pennsylvania Avenue to the White House. Wilson agreed to receive a few of the suffragists in his office, and Field encouraged him to embrace the amendment, both personally and for the upcoming congressional election. She had held up the scrolls and asked him to look at the signatures. He unfurled a section, smiled, and told his visitors

> I hope it is true that I am not a man set stiffly beyond the possibility of learning. I hope that I shall continue to be a learner as long as I live. I can only say to you this afternoon that nothing could be more impressive than the presentation of such a request in such numbers … Unhappily it is too late to for me to consider what is going into my message, because that went out to the newspapers about a week ago.

Plus, he noted his message to Congress was focused on preparing for war.

Around this same time, Anna Howard Shaw, for a variety of reasons, acknowledged that people were losing faith in her leadership, so she announced she would cede control of the two million-member NAWSA to Carrie Chapman Catt. For Wilson during this time, the White House announced on October 6, his engagement to Edith Bolling Galt, a 43-year-old widow who had been married to a man who owned one of the premier jewelry stores in Washington, which she continued to operate successfully after his death. The engagement was announced with an accompanying statement that Wilson intended to vote for women's suffrage in the next month in New Jersey, which might have been an effort to quell criticism that Wilson was remarrying less than a year after the death of his wife.[5]

As the nation focused its attention increasingly on the war in Europe, Paul was developing strategies to keep suffrage at the forefront of the nation's consciousness during the election year of 1916. She wanted to coalesce all of the women voters in America into a force for change. She created the National Woman's Party as an alternative to the Democratic and Republican parties, and it stood for one issue: passage of the woman's suffrage amendment.

During the campaign of 1916, Paul organized one last campaign out West, a dash through dozens of cities in suffrage states in a short span of 38 days. A set of women thrust themselves into the campaign, working hours that were so long many of them became sick. Among them were Inez Milholland, her sister Vida, and Lucy Burns, who is 37 years old and having devoted her entire youth to suffrage, now confessed to Paul that she wanted to return home to Brooklyn. Milholland, speaking to a large audience in Los Angeles, responded to the President's directive to women to be patient, "How long must women wait for liberty?" whereupon she collapsed on the floor and was carried off the stage as her colleagues tried to revive her.

By the end of Election Day, November 7, 1916, Wilson believed he had been beaten by his Republican opponent Charles Evans Hughes, a supporter of women's suffrage. But on November 10, Wilson learned that he had won California by 3,806 votes, becoming the first Democrat elected to a second consecutive term since Andrew Jackson in 1832. Two weeks later, Inez Milholland succumbed to what had been diagnosed as "pernicious anemia," and was dead at 30 years of age. Members of the CUWS were devastated, vigorously angry, and wanted to channel their grief into action.

With Paul as their leader, the women had: marched four years ago in the largest and most outrageous protest procession; assembled an 80-car brigade to deliver signatures from all over the nation; testified, editorialized, and reorganized; formed their own political party; held May Day parades in every state in the union; raised funds and actively worked to defeat Democrats; staffed a booth at a global exposition, collected a miles-long scroll of signatures and drove it cross-country from San Francisco; dropped leaflets from the sky, and a banner from the House chamber's balcony; and they had sacrificed one of their own. None of these actions had accomplished the objective of getting the amendment near passage. Some new approach was necessary to galvanize support, mobilize action, and move the Congress to approve the amendment.

The Silent Sentinels

Alice Paul had a new idea: a silent vigil in front of the White House until Wilson's inauguration in March, standing beside the gateway where he must pass in and out so that their constant presence would pressure him and make him realize the tremendous earnestness and insistence behind the suffrage amendment. Paul instructed those who would stand at the White House gate: don't be provoked into a physical or verbal confrontation; don't make eye contact with angry bystanders; stay quiet, and keep your backs to the gate for safety, and make sure the public can read the signs.

The first group arrived outside the White House and took their positions on either side of the east and west iron gates. They were positioned geographically, with women from the West (who could vote) on one side and women from the East (who could not vote) on the other. They stood silently, and held their signs, which asked questions –

Mr. President, What Will You Do For Woman Suffrage?

How Long Must Women Wait For Liberty?

The women had been in position for only 40 minutes when Woodrow Wilson appeared, returning from a golf outing. The group did not notice Wilson and he passed without incident. The public response to the sentinels was more apparent – government clerks, tourists, diplomats, and various pedestrians were stunned to discover the protestors. Some of them mocked the protestors, others shouted encouragement. The news of the ongoing protest drew overwhelmingly negative response, including from other suffragists. Even close allies were upset by the brazenness of the protest, now viewed as socially inappropriate.

The Silent Sentinels persevered, relying on clothing drives led from their nearby headquarters, as well as wheelbarrows full of warm bricks for them to stand on. They had banners using words from Wilson's book *The New Freedom*:

"Liberty is a fundamental demand of the human spirit." Wilson refused to be held hostage by the sentinels. He resumed his walks, and when he strolled through the gates and passed the women, he would tip his hat in a sarcastic manner.

In June of 1917, the Russians sent a delegation to Washington to discuss war strategy with their allies, and the United States was proud to show off its own government's stability and congratulate the guests on revolting against a monarchy to establish liberty and democracy. But Russia's revolution has produced one outcome that the United States had not: after some demonstrations by women, they were granted suffrage.

On the day the Russians were to visit the White House, a car dropped off Lucy Burns and others in front of the White House about an hour before the Russians were expected. The women unfurled a ten-foot sign, which read:

To the Russian Envoys

President Wilson ... is deceiving Russia when [he] says "we are a democracy, help us with the world war so that democracy may survive." We, the women of America, tell you that America is not a democracy. Twenty million American women are denied the right to vote. President Wilson is the chief opponent of their national enfranchisement. Help us make this nation really free. Tell our government it must liberate its people before it can claim free Russia as an ally.

As passersby stopped to read and comprehend the sign, they were outraged about the attack on the President so directly in front of diplomatic guests. The Russians, arriving by motorcade, passed quickly through the gate but took enough time to read the sign. Several bystanders took the initiative to tear down the sign. There were no arrests that day, either of the suffragists or the attacking bystanders. DC police met with the White House staff and promised to arrest the suffragists if this was attempted again. Wilson, in a letter to his daughter Jessie, wrote of the fracas, "They certainly seem bent upon making their cause as obnoxious as possible."[6]

Twenty-four hours later, a new batch of silent sentinels was back at their posts, carrying signs that read:

We demand democracy and self-government in our own land. And Mr. President, what will you do for woman's suffrage?

The suffragists were arrested and appeared in court on charges of obstructing the sidewalk in front of the White House. They were offered one of two punishments – they could pay a $25 fine or serve three days in jail. They all chose the jail time, knowing this would garner more attention for their cause. They were released without incident after three days.

Paul, at work on her next idea, a Bastille Day protest, collapsed and was hospitalized. She was initially diagnosed with Bright's disease, a kidney affliction, and doctors warned that she might not live two weeks. She was taken to Johns Hopkins Hospital for a second opinion, where she was told she needed only to take two months to rest. She immediately received a letter from William Parker her sometimes-suitor from her graduate school days, who expressed concern for her health and also congratulated her on her work on the suffrage amendment.

The participants in the Bastille Day protest appeared in court after their arrest and were given the choice to pay a small fine or serve two months – almost their entire summer – in the Occoquan Work house, DC's most secure facility about one hour from the city. All elected to serve the jail time. But after they had served just three days, President Wilson decided to issue pardons to all of them. Alice Paul, still resting in the hospital, was contacted by a reporter for her reaction. She thanked the President for pardoning the suffragists but promised that they would be picketing again next Monday.

On August 15, the pickets returned to their posts, with Paul among them. Police were nowhere to be found, and soldiers began assaulting the women. Paul was knocked down three times, a sailor brutally dragged her 30 feet along the White House sidewalk tearing her suffrage sash, and gashing her neck. The protesters kept up the pressure, and by the end of September, two dozen suffragists were confined at the Occoquan Workhouse. But donations and new members continued to pour into the NWP.

On October 20, Paul was at the White House gates, picketing with three colleagues. Her banner displayed the President's own words: *The time has come to conquer or submit. For us, there can be but one choice. We have made it.* Another protester had a sign which read: *Resistance to tyranny is obedience to God.* Police arrested the picketers and instructed them to come back for trial in a few days.

Anticipating that she would receive a sentence for lengthy jail time, Paul prepared others to take on her various responsibilities. The judge sentenced her to spend seven months in jail, the largest sentence ever given to a suffragist. In response to a reporter's question, Paul declared, "I am being imprisoned not because I obstructed traffic, but because I pointed out to President Wilson the fact that he was obstructing the cause of democracy and justice at home, while Americans fight for it abroad." Ten days into her stay, some of which she had spent in solitary confinement, the conditions and food were making Paul very weak. The jail's staff, worried about Paul's condition, summoned her own doctor who was shocked by her frail condition. She could not convince her to stop her hunger strike and she told the press that the protest would continue.

During this time, New York made history, becoming the first eastern state to pass a woman's suffrage referendum. The National Women's Suffrage Association had been urging the President for weeks to meet face-to-face. He finally met with them on November 9, and he was urged for the first time to support the federal amendment. **He refused.**

The jail staff, who had convinced themselves that Paul would break her hunger strike when she became truly hungry, were now becoming concerned about her health. They called in the jail doctor who told Paul that she would be forcibly fed if she did not end her hunger strike. A psychiatrist was called to consult on Paul's case, an attempt to find reasons to label her as insane. He invited her to talk about suffrage. Paul later said she delivered one of the best speeches of her life in response to the psychiatrist. After her speech, the doctors consulted and agreed that Paul should be fed by force.

Paul, just as she had been in England, was strapped down, a tube was stuck up her nose, and milk and eggs were funneled down her throat. This was done three times that first day and force-feedings continued for the next two weeks. News reports from the jail said that Paul was taking the treatments without protest. But on November 10, 41 women protested outside the White House about Paul's treatment. Thirty-one of the women were arrested, including Lucy Burns, and she was sentenced to the largest penalty: six months at Occoquan Workhouse. The women were subjected to treatment that was so harsh an attorney took their case and presented it to a judge as cruel and unusual punishment. He ordered that the women should be transferred from Occoquan to the city jail. And by November 28, Paul, Burns, and 20 other suffragists were ordered released.

At noon on January 8, 1918, Woodrow Wilson stood at the podium in the chamber of the House of Representatives prepared to deliver a foreign policy speech. Now known in American history as the Fourteen Points for peace, a roadmap to end the war. He had given the Congress only 30 minutes' notice that he would address them, but a team of 150 social and political scientists had been gathering information and produced 2,000 reports and documents to help analyze the economic, social, and political facts that could arise during peace talks. Calling for freedom on the seas and open trade; a reduction in armaments; the enemy evacuations of Russia, Belgium, and France; the redrawing of Italy's borders; the sovereignty of Turkey; and an independent Poland. His boldest suggestion was the creation of a general association of nations that would guarantee fairness throughout the world.

Congress Approves the Suffrage Amendment

As Wilson enjoyed the accolades the next day for his visionary speech, the House was about to vote on woman suffrage, and 11 Congressmen descended upon his office to discuss the matter, and learn where the President actually stood on the question of the constitutional amendment. Wilson declared that his personal position had not changed – leaving the states to decide was the appropriate course. But he also said that America and the world had changed, there was growing public sentiment in favor of votes for women. The Congressmen, astonished by his answer, asked if he would write it down so they could share it accurately with the press. Wilson provided this summary: "... he very frankly and earnestly advised us (the Congressmen) to vote for the amendment as an act of right and justice to the women of the country and the world." After the roll call, there were 274 yeas to 136 nays, exactly the two-thirds margin needed.

Wilson earned some credit for the outcome, as he worked behind the scenes on the phone, in letters, and in telegrams, and had swung six votes toward suffrage. (Republicans favored the amendment four to one, Democrats were divided, with those from the South generally against it.) It is not clear why Wilson had his change of heart, whether he was tired of being the object of suffragist scorn, recognized the inevitability of passage of the amendment, or felt more compelled to support the expansion of voting rights in the days after he espoused democratic ideals in his Fourteen Points speech.

The reaction to the victory among the suffragists was both joyful and reflective. The date of passage was the one-year anniversary of the start of their White House protests. For Paul, it was the eve of her 32nd birthday, and she pointed out that they still needed eleven votes before the Senate would approve the amendment.

After the victory in the House, Paul turned to the battle in the Senate. Lucy Burns, determined to reclaim a normal life, had been offered a teaching position at a Brooklyn high school. As she was home considering the offer, Paul begged her to return. Burns agreed to help but asked to remain in the Northeast to campaign in places where senators were against the amendment. Paul also dispatched others to contentious states.

Paul's NWP knew who their Senate opponents would be and how they might be convinced to change their minds. Since Wilson now appeared to be supporting suffrage, they sought a meeting with him to discuss their mutual goal of forcing a vote in the Senate. But one of Wilson's aides convinced him that the NWP was "militant," so **Wilson declined the meeting.** And the President stayed on the sidelines as the women prepared to approach the Senate, which had decided to put the vote off until the fall.

Paul planned the date of their next protest to commemorate the birthday of the late Inez Milholland on August 6. One hundred suffragists marched from NWP headquarters in a single file line to the statue of Marquis de Lafayette in the park across from the White House. There they hoisted banners high enough to be seen in the White House. With Wilson doing nothing to push a vote or promote passage in the Senate they displayed a sign designed to embarrass Wilson:

> We protest against the continued disenfranchisement of American women, for which the President of the United States is responsible. We condemn the President and his party for allowing the obstruction of suffrage in the Senate. We deplore the weakness of President Wilson in permitting the Senate to line itself with the Prussian Reichstag by denying democracy to the people. We demand that the President and his party secure the Passage of the suffrage amendment through the Senate. In the present session.

Before the first speaker could begin, the police swooped in and began arresting the suffragists. The police took four dozen women, including Lucy Burns, to jail. When an officer spotted Paul who had been organizing reinforcements from some distance, they took her to jail too. Once in jail, two dozen of the women began hunger strikes. A steady stream of elected officials came to see the women and report to the public on their conditions. Outrage sped up the prisoners' release and they walked out in five days, without completing their sentences.

After a speech from Wilson encouraging the Senate to pass the amendment, a vote was taken: 34 nays to 62 yeas, two votes shy of the necessary two-thirds majority. For the remainder of October and into November, the NWP moved its protest location from the White House to the U.S. Capitol and the Senate Office Building, where they focused on lobbying southern senators, while maintaining a picket line in the face of civilian harassment. There was a series of bookings and releases. But the suffragists would not surrender.

Wilson was preparing to go to France to negotiate a plan for a lasting peace, with the armistice agreement in hand. This was Wilson's chance to implement the principles of peace outlined in his Fourteen Points plan. Before setting out for

Paris he used his annual address to Congress to urge the House and Senate to pass the suffrage amendment:

> And what shall we say to the women — of their instant intelligence, quickening every task they touched; their capacity for organization and cooperation, which gave their action discipline and enhanced the effectiveness of everything they attempted ... the least tribute we can pay them is to make them equals of men in political rights as they have proved themselves their equals in every field of practical work they have entered ... We shall need their moral sense to preserve what is right and fine and worthy in our system of life as well as to discover just what it is that ought to be purified and reformed. Without their counseling we shall be only half wise.[7]

Wilson planned to stay in Europe only three weeks, hoping to return to the United States well before the Congressional session ended in ten weeks. But the peace talks were slow to develop and dignitaries from all over Europe wanted Wilson to visit their country. While Wilson was in Europe giving speeches, the NWP was monitoring his every word. They started a new form of protest, creating a "watch fire" outside the White House gates, into which they would throw the most recent quotes from Wilson's European speeches. As the speech excerpts were tossed in the fire, two suffragists held a wide banner that read:

> President Wilson is deceiving the world when he appears as the prophet of democracy. President Wilson has opposed those who demand democracy for this country. He is responsible for the disenfranchisement of millions of Americans. We in America know this. The world will find him out.
>
> Although the President had publicly stated he supported suffrage, the NWP was skeptical about what Wilson was actually doing to help it pass. The "watch fires" protests drew heavy negative reaction at the gates of the White House, with some of the suffragists being attacked by onlookers. Paul's idea for these protest was to keep an "eternal flame" burning, periodically throwing Wilson's speech excerpts as quickly as he uttered them. As this protest went into a second straight week, hostility against the women intensified. A group of men attacked the NWP headquarters, and they were not arrested, though the suffragists, including Lucy Burns, were. Three dozen women were sent to prison and went on hunger strikes.

Another Senate vote on suffrage was scheduled, with the composition of the chamber little changed. This time, the suffrage amendment failed by one vote, 63 years and 33 days. The NWP analyzed the votes and determined that they might be able to flip one of two senators, Frederick Hale, a Republican from

Maine, and Democrat Edward James Gay of Louisiana. NWP decided to focus on
these states and any other states where suffrage seemed close to passage. They also
greeted Wilson on his return to the United States from Europe with signs asking,
Mr. President, How Long Must We Wait for Liberty?

Paul ultimately decided to focus the NWP's efforts on Senator William J. Harris,
a Democrat from Georgia, as the senator that could be flipped. She learned that
Harris was in Italy and arranged through intermediaries a meeting between him
and the President in Paris. Wilson convinced him to support suffrage and then
called for Congress to meet in Special Session on May 19 to take up the suffrage
vote. He then sent a persuasive cable

> It seems to me that every consideration of justice and of public advantage
> calls for the immediate adoption of the Amendment and its submission
> forthwith to the legislatures of the several States. Throughout all the world
> this long delayed extension of the Suffrage is looked for: longer, I believe,
> than anywhere else, the necessity for it, and the immense advantages of it
> to the national life, has been urged and delayed by women and men who
> saw for it and urged the policy of it when it required steadfast courage to
> be so much beforehand with the common conviction; and I, for one, covet
> for our country the distinction of being among the first to act in a great
> reform.

The day after Wilson sent his message, the House again passed the amendment
by an even bigger margin than their previous vote, this time with 304 yeas and
89 nays. The Senate scheduled a vote for June 4. The outcome was so certain
(56 yeas to 25 nays) that Paul did not even bother attending, instead of working
on the next steps in the process – getting approval of the amendment in 36 states.

The States Ratify

On June 10, Wisconsin, Michigan, and Illinois approved and a second burst of
ratifications happened on June 16, with New York, Ohio, and Kansas approving.
Pennsylvania followed on June 24 but not without a significant effort by the
NWP. Massachusetts followed. Then on June 28, Texas ratified the amendment.

After signing the Treaty of Versailles ending the war, Wilson returned home to
face the task of getting the Senate to ratify the treaty, which included provisions
for establishing the League of Nations. The Senate, and much of the general
public, was skeptical of the League of Nations, wanting nothing more to do with
entanglements with other nations which might involve the United States in other
wars. Wilson, in ill health, due to a small stroke he had suffered in Paris, felt he
needed to rally the country to support the treaty and the League of Nations. He
decided on a campaign-style whistle stop tour to promote the League of Nations,
in spite of his ill health. Wilson was now 62 years old, giving as many as five

speeches a day, and as the tour went on, it was becoming apparent to the press that he was in terrible condition.

As the train made its way back toward Washington, Wilson made a stop in Pueblo, Colorado. He stumbled through his speech and brought the audience to tears with an emotional address in which he told his audience of visiting a cemetery in France filled with soldiers from the recently-concluded war and saying that he wished those opposing the League of Nations "could feel the moral obligation that rests upon us not to go back on those boys, but see this thing through."[8]

When he returned to the train that evening, he summoned Edith to his cabin, complained of his health, and asked her to call Dr. Grayson. "From that hour," Edith wrote later, "I would have to wear a mask – not only to the public, but to the one I loved best in the world; for he must never know how ill he was, and I must carry on."[9] After he returned to the White House, Wilson was stricken again. He reported no feeling in his hands, and when Edith helped him to the bathroom and called Dr. Grayson she heard a noise and discovered Wilson slumped on the floor unconscious. Dr. Grayson recognized immediately that Wilson had suffered a massive stroke, paralyzing the left side of his body.

A second doctor (Francis X. Dercum of Philadelphia) was brought in and confirmed the diagnosis of Dr. Grayson. In a conversation with Dr. Dercum about caring for her husband, he advised Edith that he must be removed from every problem that could bring about anxiety because his nerves were crying out for rest. But he advised that if he were to resign, he would be removing his main incentive for recovery. He suggested that she take on the task of managing the matters that came to him as part of his presidential responsibilities. She could read the materials he needed to read, consult with Cabinet secretaries as needed, discuss some pending matters with him, and keep his administration afloat. Wilson's aides told the press that he was suffering from nervous exhaustion and needed some rest. Edith Wilson thus became the de facto first female president of the United States. No one was allowed to see Wilson, and no one outside the inner circle knew how truly incapacitated he had become.

Meanwhile, over the course of the summer, Alice Paul was managing the ratification campaign, and the South remained her biggest concern. At the end of July, the NWP was pushing hard for a ratification victory in Georgia, but the state rejected the amendment. But there were other victories that month in Arkansas, Montana, Iowa, and Missouri. In August, Nebraska ratified, followed by Minnesota, New Hampshire, and Utah in September, bringing the total to 17 states in the yes column.

In November, California ratified, followed by Maine, North Dakota, and Colorado to round out the states approving in 1919. In the first month of 1920, five states approved the amendment: Rhode Island, Kentucky, Oregon, Indiana, and Wyoming. Then Nevada passed it in February. The ratification process in New Jersey was difficult, with Paul swooping in to activate everyone she could find – they ratified on February 10. In March, Idaho, Arizona, New Mexico, Oklahoma,

West Virginia, and Washington ratified, but four states defeated the amendment – Mississippi, South Carolina, Virginia (for the second time), and Maryland. Needing just one more state to win, suffragists turned their attention to Delaware, but the state rejected the amendment, in spite of the efforts of Paul and nine colleagues who actively campaigned there.

Suddenly, with nowhere else to turn, Tennessee was suddenly in play, though no one thought they would vote on the amendment. Paul went to Nashville to join the fight. They arranged for influential Democrats from all over the country to contact Tennessee governor Albert Roberts to urge his legislature to take up suffrage. Wilson, in a telegram likely written by the first lady, pointed out that the future viability of all Democrats was at stake. "It would be a real service to the Party and the Nation if it is possible for you to ... consider the Suffrage Amendment. Allow me to urge this very earnestly." Nashville began to swell with the most strident believers for and against the suffragist amendment. The Hotel Hermitage, near the capital, was ground zero, where special interests plied targets with bourbon, cut backroom deals, and set Machiavellian maneuvers into play.

On August 10, the resolution was introduced in both the House and Senate, with the Senate voting first, on the next day. The vote in the Senate was 25 yeas and 4 nays, a strong margin which was not lost on the House members. There were two representatives whose vote no one was sure of: Banks Turner and Harry Burn. Burn first told the suffragists that he could be counted on to vote their way, but then a few days before the vote he told them, "I cannot pledge myself, but I will do nothing to hurt you."

On the day of the vote, however, Burn received a letter from his mother. In her letter, she told her son that she missed him, he should write more often, and said, "Hurrah and vote for suffrage and don't keep them in doubt. I've been waiting to see how you stood, but have not seen anything yet." Burn was called on to vote, took a deep breath, and said, "Aye."

Paul was at NWP headquarters in Washington and when she received word of Tennessee's approval. She walked out on the balcony, looked across Lafayette Park toward the White House, and unfurled a long suffrage flag, with a star hand-sewn on for each state's ratification, now totaling 36. She hung the flag triumphantly over the rail, and looked on the sidewalk where she saw the women who had sacrificed so much. But not everyone she had hoped would be there for this momentous occasion was there. Lucy Burns, the last suffragist to be arrested in America, who had spent more time than any other NWP protester in jail, was in Brooklyn to begin her time raising her niece after her sister had died in childbirth.

Epilogue

Woodrow Wilson was physically depleted and politically battered at home when he left office. In 1920, he was awarded the Nobel Peace Prize for drafting the League of Nations covenant. The award was the capstone of his career. He and

Edith had moved to a house near the White House, where he spent three quiet years before he died in February 1924. Edith was by his side when he died.

Alice Paul earned a law degree in 1922 from American University, as well as a master's and doctorate in law within that same decade. She spent many years working to pass the Equal Rights Amendment. She lived for many years in a new headquarters of the NWP, which went on to draft 600 pieces of legislation to improve the rights of women, half of those bills became law. Paul also played a significant role in adding protections for women into the Civil Rights Act of 1964.

When Paul moved from Washington to a tiny cottage in Ridgefield, Connecticut in 1972, she lived alone, though not too far from her admirer William Parker. Neither of them ever married. As her health began to fail, a nephew moved her into a nursing home about a mile from her family farm in New Jersey. Having spent most of her life relying on the generosity of donors, she was now almost penniless.

In 1977, at 92 years of age, Alice Paul died.

Notes

1 Tina Cassidy, *Mr. President, How Long Must We Wait?: Alice Paul, Woodrow Wilson and the Fight for the Right to Vote* (Simon & Schuster, New York, NY, 2019), page 6.
2 Ibid., page 22.
3 Ibid., page 85.
4 Ibid., page 103.
5 Ibid., page 117.
6 A. Scott Berg, *Wilson* (The Berkley Publishing Group, New York, NY, 2013), page 489.
7 Ibid., page 494.
8 Cassidy, *Mr. President, How Long Must We Wait?*, page 233.
9 Cassidy, *Mr. President, How Long Must We Wait?*, page 233.

Bibliography

Berg, A. Scott. *Wilson*. New York, NY: Berkeley Publishing Group, 2013.
Cassidy, Tina. *Mr. President, How Long Must We Wait?: Alice Paul, Woodrow Wilson, and the Fight for The Right To Vote*. New York, NY: Simon & Schuster, 2019.
"The Vote," directed by Michelle Ferrari. *PBS American Experience Series*, 42nd Parallel Films Production, 2020.
Von Garnier, Katja, dir. *Iron Jawed Angels*. New York, NY: Home Box Office Films, 2004, DVD.

13

PLAIN-SPOKEN PRESIDENT

Harry S. Truman, *"Tireless, Fearless, and Decisive"*

DOI: 10.4324/9781003266235-15

Early Years and Formative Experiences

Harry S. Truman was born on May 8, 1884 in Lamar, Missouri, not far from Independence, Missouri, just ten miles from Kansas City, Missouri. Truman once described Independence as "a place where right is right and wrong is wrong, and you did not have to talk about it." Harry wore thick-lensed glasses, spent much of his youth by himself reading books and playing the piano, dreaming of being a concert pianist, though he had more perseverance that talent.

His father was a not-so-successful farmer, and when Harry graduated from high school in 1901, his father did not have the funds to send him to college. Harry worked through a series of jobs, on a railroad and as a clerk at Kansas City banks. At his father's request, Harry returned to the family farm in Grandview, Missouri, where he toiled in obscurity from 1906 through 1917. His father's get-rich-quick schemes, including investments in oil wells and mining operations, all ended in failure.

On April 13, 1918, Harry Truman began the formative experience of his life, when he landed in France as a 33-year-old captain in the U.S. Army during World War I. He took command of an artillery battery, grew into his command, and by war's end, was a respected and well-liked officer.

Harry returned to America in June 1919 and resolved a life-long quest by marrying his childhood sweetheart Elizabeth "Bess" Wallace. He had been in love with Bess since meeting her in Sunday school as a boy and made many proposals of marriage to her over many years. Harry's life-long love for Bess stands as a great love story, and it is the centerpiece of his life, even when Bess repeatedly preferred staying home in Independence during Harry's years living in Washington, DC as a senator and as President.

Returning from the war, Harry opened a haberdashery in Kansas City, but it failed in 1922, leaving Harry financially devastated. In 1922, Truman won election for a judgeship in rural Jackson County, with virtually no qualifications, but with the support of Tom Pendergast, the corrupt "boss" of the corrupt Kansas City Democratic machine. In 1934, Truman is elected U.S. Senator under dubious circumstances, again largely due to the corrupt Kansas City machine. Critics labeled him the "Senator from Pendergast." Against all odds, due to the stain of the Pendergast support, Truman wins a second term in the U.S. Senate in 1940.

In 1941, Truman begins his work as Chairman of the Senate Select Committee to Investigate the National Defense Program, which becomes known as the "Truman Committee." The committee was investigating corrupt practices among defense contractors and suppliers. Truman gained his first national recognition for the operation of the committee between 1941 and 1944.

Becoming Vice President

At the 1944 Democratic National Convention, Truman becomes the compromise candidate for Vice President, personally selected by Franklin Roosevelt, though Truman had rarely interacted with the President. They are elected on November 7 for FDR's fourth term as President.

After almost no opportunity to work with the President or to receive any briefings about pending international matters, Truman is summoned to the White House after 82 days as Vice President. He is told by the first lady that the President has died. After taking the oath of office, Secretary of War Henry Stimson pulls Truman aside to tell him that there is a project underway to develop a new explosive of almost unbelievable destructive power.

The night he learned of Roosevelt's death, Truman wrote in his diary, "I was very much shocked … I knew the President had a great many meetings with Churchill and Stalin, I was not familiar with any of these things and it was really something to think about." Also on that night, Truman called his 92-year-old mother to tell her what had happened and that he might not be able to call her as frequently. His mother tells him, *"Be good, Harry. But be game, too."* [1]

The next day, April 13, his first as President, was the 27th anniversary of the day he landed in France as a First Lieutenant in the American Expeditionary Force. On that day, Truman arranges lunch at the Capitol with 17 senators and representatives. When he leaves the lunch, he stops to talk to the press and tells them, "when they told me yesterday what had happened, I felt like the moon, the stars, and all the planets had fallen on me." [2]

Serving as President

Hitting the Ground Running. The first four months of Truman's presidency were filled with momentous events that were thrust upon him. These months saw the collapse of Nazi Germany, the founding of the United Nations, firebombing of Japanese cities that killed many thousands of civilians, the liberation of Nazi death camps, the suicide of Adolph Hitler, the execution of Benito Mussolini, the capture of war criminals including Hitler's deputies. Also occurring in these months were the fall of Berlin, the victory at Okinawa, the Potsdam Conference, during which the new President sat at the negotiating table with Winston Churchill and Joseph Stalin in Soviet-occupied Germany in an attempt to map out a new world. Humanity saw the first atomic explosion, the nuclear destruction of Hiroshima and Nagasaki, the dawn of the Cold War, and the beginning of the nuclear arms race.

Truman settled into his role as President by seeing himself as the chief decision-maker. He said,

> It is my duty as President to make the decisions because I can't pass the buck to anybody, and if I get all the facts, I have found that the decisions I make as a result of all the facts are satisfactory to everybody.

He also said of his decision-making, "Once I made the decision, I did not worry over it. If I made a wrong decision, I just made another one to correct it." Truman's sense of duty reflected his Midwestern pragmatism. "There are probably hundreds of people better qualified than I am to be President, but they weren't elected."[3]

The Truman Doctrine. The behavior of the Soviet Union during the immediate postwar period of negotiating settlements of borders and other matters, lead the U.S. State Department to push for a strategy of containment of Russia. Truman looked for a way to describe an American foreign policy that intended to contain Russian aggression.

On March 12, 1947, Truman appeared before a joint session of Congress to explain his policy. In an 18-minute speech, Truman said,

> I believe it should be the policy of the United States to support free peoples who are resisting attempted subjugation by armed minorities or outside pressures ... I believe we must assist free peoples to work out their own destinies in their own way ... I believe our help should be primarily through economic or financial aid which is essential to economic stability and orderly political processes.

This policy became known as the Truman Doctrine, and the speech is considered by many historians to be the start of the Cold War.

The Marshall Plan. Senior Truman Administration officials who had been on the ground in Europe in the weeks following the end of the war were reporting that much of Europe was in ruins, and in dire need of economic assistance to begin recovering. Truman sent Dean Acheson to fill in for him on a foreign policy speech, and the speech was to be the alarm bell that Truman wanted to sound about the need for economic aid for Europe. Acheson said Europe needed everything and could afford nothing, stressing the objective was the revival of industry, agriculture, and trade, and he said that massive funding was necessary if Europe was to be saved.

Secretary of State George Marshall received a report about helping Europe from his own staff at the end of May. Truman would always insist on giving Marshall full credit for the plan, insisting that the plan be named for Marshall to help ensure its passage by Congress. The Truman Administration set out to convince Americans and the Congress; the appeal would be to American altruism and American self-interest, i.e., lifting up our stricken neighbors by providing them American goods and services. The Europeans immediately organized a conference of nations to define and prioritize needs.

Officially known as the "European Recovery Program," the plan totaled a whopping $17 billion. State Department staff were assigned to sell the plan to Congress while specific plans were being developed in consultation with the Europeans.

Creating the North Atlantic Treaty Organization (NATO). After Truman's triumph in the 1948 election, the United States, Canada, and ten Western European countries joined in a defense pact whereby an attack on any one would be taken as an attack on all. It was the first peacetime military alliance since the signing of the Constitution. Truman was convinced that had such an agreement been in place in 1914, the world would have been spared two terrible wars.

The Truman Doctrine of containment of Russia, providing aid through the Marshall Plan, and the creation of NATO in his second term in 1949 were three initiatives that shaped foreign policy of the United States for decades.

The Berlin Airlift. On June 24, 1948, the Russians set a blockade on all rail, highways, and water traffic in and out of Berlin. Stalin was attempting to force the Western Allies to withdraw from the city. Except by air, the allied sectors were entirely cut off. Two and a half million people faced starvation, since stocks of food would only last a month, and coal supplies would only last six weeks. Truman's immediate response: "We stay in Berlin." On Monday, June 28, after considering several approaches on how to respond, Truman ordered a full-scale airlift, ordering two squadrons of B-29's to Germany. Truman later increased the airlift, and another airfield was built, largely by Berliners.

On May 12, 1949, the Russians ended the blockade. The airlift was over after a year and two months – after 277,804 flights delivered 2,325,809 tons of food and supplies.

The Struggle for Civil Rights. In his 1948 State of the Union address, Truman announced he would be sending a first-ever message on civil rights, saying, "Our first goal is to secure fully the essential rights of our citizens." His own Civil Rights Commission proposed the strongest civil rights program ever proposed by a President. Truman asked for a law against the crime of lynching, effective statutory provisions to protect the right to vote, a law against the poll taxes that existed in seven Southern states, the establishment of a Fair Employment Practices Commission with authority to stop employment discrimination by employers and unions alike, and an end to discrimination in interstate travel by rail, bus, and airplane. He also announced that he had directed the Secretary of Defense to review discrimination in the military and to stop it as soon as possible.

Truman was deeply moved by anecdotal information about Negro soldiers just back from overseas being dumped out of Army trucks in Mississippi, or the murder of four blacks by mob gunfire in Georgia. Truman felt that as President he could no longer do nothing in the face of glaring injustice.

Truman delivered a speech to 10,000 people on the steps of the Lincoln Memorial, as part of the Convention of the National Association for the Advancement of Colored People (NAACP). He pledged that "Full civil rights and freedom must be obtained and guaranteed for all Americans."

At the Democratic Convention in July, on the day Truman's nomination and acceptance speech were scheduled, Minneapolis Mayor Hubert Humphrey, an emerging leader of the liberal wing of the party, pushed for a more definitive platform plank on civil rights to replace the more moderate plank currently in the platform. Humphrey's more expansive plank carried the day, ensuring the support of African-Americans in the general election.

By the end of his time in office, Truman achieved less than he had wanted to on civil rights. He had created the Commission on Civil Rights, which has set forth an ambitious road map of reforms for the nation and pushed his party forward on civil rights. He had ordered desegregation of the armed forces and the federal Civil Service and done more than any other President since Lincoln to awaken the American conscience to the issue of civil rights.

Winning His Own Term: Give 'Em Hell Harry

As he approached the beginning of 1948, Harry Truman had developed a taste for the Presidency, and he decided he wanted to be remembered as more than Franklin Roosevelt's replacement. He wanted to carve his own legacy by serving another term.

The prevailing wisdom was that Truman had little chance of being reelected in his own right. The Republicans were expected to nominate New York Governor Thomas Dewey (described by actress Ethel Barrymore as the "bridegroom on the wedding cake"), who was widely expected to trounce Truman, should he choose to run. But Truman had fought uphill battles in his previous elections and found a way to win.

Truman's campaign strategy was to go directly to the people, make the case in sharply partisan terms, hammering home a message that the Democratic Party was better for the farmer, the union member, and for the whole middle class. His idea was to take a train across the country reaching many small towns and cities, talking in plain terms to people who he thought were being harmed by the Republican Party. As the train prepared to leave Union Station in Washington, DC, on September 17, 1948, Truman's Vice President Alben Barkley posed for photos on the rear platform of the train, Barkley exclaimed, "Mow 'em down, Harry!" Truman replied, "I'm going to give 'em hell!" foreshadowing the trip's theme.

With that, the Whistlestop Campaign got underway. It would travel 21,928 miles, first cross-country to California for 15 days, then a 6-day tour of the Middle West, followed by a final 10 days in the big population centers of the Northeast and a return trip home to Missouri.

As Truman explained in many locations on the tour, the difference between Republicans and Democrats was a difference in attitude. The typical Truman stump speech on the tour included this assessment by Truman,

> the basic issue of this campaign is as simple as can be: the special interests against the people. I'm here on a serious mission, and because it is so serious, I propose to speak to you as plainly as I can ... Now use your judgment.

Keep the people in control of the government. I not only want you to vote for me but I want you to vote for yourselves. And if you vote for yourselves, you'll vote for the Democratic ticket.

At each stop, Truman would introduce Bess ("Mizz Truman") and would also introduce his daughter ("Miss Margaret").

David McCullough, the author of the definitive Truman biography, wrote of the effect of these visits on their audiences:

> It could be said that they had seen and heard for themselves a President who was friendly and undisguised, loyal to his party, fond of his family, a man who cared about the country and about them, who believed the business of government was their business, and who did not whine when he was in trouble, but kept bravely, doggedly plugging away, doing his best, his duty as he saw it, and who was glad to be among them. His beliefs were there beliefs, his way of talking was their way of talking. He was on their side. He was one of them.[4]

Dewey was a sharp contrast to Truman. Dewey had been running for President for years, telling friends "it is written in the stars." To reporters who covered him, he seemed aloof and haughty, and they joked that he was the only man who could strut sitting down. The strategy of his campaign was to say as little as possible about pressing issues to avoid controversy. With two weeks to go in the campaign, a Gallup poll showed Dewey's lead cut to six points. At no point in the entire campaign, through the grueling and endless train travel, did any of his staff, the press, or his family ever see Truman show a sign of failing stamina, of failing confidence.

The final rally of his campaign, and the last platform appearance Harry Truman would make as a candidate for public office, was at Kiel Auditorium in St. Louis, in his home state of Missouri. He went on the attack one last time at the Republican Congress, the Republican press, the Republican "old-dealers," and Thomas Dewey himself. The cheering crowd urged him on. He then returned home to Independence, the campaign finally at its end. At 6 a.m. on the day after the election, Harry Truman was driven to the Muelbach Hotel in Kansas City, the site of his victory party. He called Bess and Margaret, who burst into tears at the sound of his voice. By 8:30 a.m., Ohio went for Truman, putting him over the top with 270 electoral votes. At 9:30 a.m., Truman was declared the winner in Illinois and California, and it was clear by this time that the Democrats had won control over both houses of Congress. By 10:14 a.m., Dewey conceded the election.

At the end of the day, Truman returned home to Independence to find a huge crowd gathered in the town square. Truman got behind the small podium, visibly touched by the largest gathering in the history of the town, with the courthouse where he started his career behind him, and called his victory a celebration not for him, but for the country.

The country was flabbergasted by Truman's victory, publications calling it "a startling victory," "astonishing," and "a major miracle." He carried 28 states with a total of 303 electoral votes and defeated Dewey by more than 2.1 million votes. Democrats won 54 Senate seats, and in the U.S. House Democrats soundly beat the Republicans 263 seats to 171. To the Truman loyalists and White House staff who had campaigned with him, it was clear why he had won. "He had done it by being himself, never forgetting who he was, and by going to the people in his own fashion."[5]

Truman headed back to the White House in the early morning of Thursday, November 4, boarding his train for the journey. He made a brief stop in St. Louis, when someone handed him a copy of his least favorite newspaper, the *Chicago Tribune*. Spread across the top of the front page was the soon-to-be famous headline DEWEY DEFEATS TRUMAN. Holding the paper up over his head with both hands, grinning from ear to ear, the victorious President seemed to be saying in America it is the people who decide. The photo conveyed the spirit and the moment perfectly.

Big Challenges: The Korean Conflict and the Insubordination of Douglas MacArthur

During a quick trip back to Missouri in late June, Truman received a call from Dean Acheson, who reported that North Korea had invaded South Korea. Acheson had already notified the Secretary General of the United Nations to call a meeting of the U.N. Security Council. Truman later received word that it appeared that the attack constituted the beginning of an all-out offensive against the Republic of Korea. After a second update from Acheson the next day, Truman flew back to Washington.

According to a report the next day from General Douglas MacArthur, who was on the ground in Korea, it appeared that the South Koreans were incapable of stopping the North Korean advance: "Our estimate is that a complete collapse is imminent." Truman began to take steps to prepare the military for intervention in Korea, but not authorizing any action above the 38th parallel. At a meeting at the White House on Tuesday, June 27, Truman received undivided support from Cabinet officials and Congressional representatives alike for military intervention in Korea. He was advised to proceed on the basis of Presidential authority and not bother to call on Congress for a declaration of war resolution.

After several days of reports that North Korean troops were overwhelming South Korean troops, cities, and remaining U.S. troops, Truman authorized actions to expand all military services and seek huge increases in military spending to send more men, equipment, and supplies to Korea, signaling that from this point on he was committed to the Korean conflict. Notably, he never used the word "war" to describe the action that was to be taken in Korea.

During this time, Truman was becoming more dissatisfied with Douglas MacArthur. His dissatisfaction with MacArthur originated in 1945 at the peak of MacArthur's popularity when Truman described him in his journal as "Mr. Prima Donna, Brass Hat." Even John Foster Dulles, the most prominent Republican spokesman on foreign policy, after returning from a series of meetings with MacArthur in Tokyo, advised Truman to retire him before he caused trouble, feeling that he was well past his prime and a growing liability. Truman did not want to stir controversy by relieving MacArthur while America contemplated options for progress in Korea.

Meanwhile, MacArthur had come up with a daring new plan. He proposed to make a surprise amphibious landing on the western shore of Korea at the port of Inchon. The drawback for this plan was the formidable conditions at Inchon – tides of 30 feet or more, no beaches on which to land, and sea walls which further complicated landings. Truman was advised of the difficulties of the plan, and General Omar Bradley, the fellow Missourian whom Truman had grown to like and trust, felt the plan was the riskiest military plan he had ever heard.

After a series of intense White House meetings, the strategy was approved in principle, though General Bradley reported "the gravest misgivings." Around this time, MacArthur gave a speech to the Veterans of Foreign Wars, to speak out about U.S. policy in continental Asia. Truman was livid at MacArthur for his blatant overstepping of authority, and Bradley called it "the height of arrogance" on MacArthur's part. In spite of MacArthur's insubordination, Truman decided to approve MacArthur's plan for the invasion at Inchon, authorizing the Joint Chiefs to notify MacArthur to do the invasion by September 15.

The invasion force included 70,000 men, and Inchon fell in one day, Seoul was retaken in 11 days, and part of the U.S. forces broke out and proceeded north. The invasion has been a success, a dramatic turn in fortune. By September 27, about half of the North Korean Army had been trapped in a huge pincer movement, and by October 1, U.N. forces were at the 38th parallel and South Korea was in U.N. control. Back in Washington, the invasion was viewed as a great success, the nation exultant, calling it a "military miracle." A jubilant Truman cabled MacArthur: "I salute you all, and say to all of you from all of us at home, 'Well and nobly done.'"

The United Nations quickly urged that all appropriate steps to be taken to ensure conditions of stability. But just days later, MacArthur sent the Eighth Army over the 38th parallel. Truman immediately announced that he will meet with MacArthur in the Pacific to confer with MacArthur on the "final phase" in Korea. They met at Wake Island, Truman arriving at 6:30 a.m. on October 15. Truman and MacArthur greeted each other cordially. When they stepped into the car to take them to their meeting, Truman immediately began to express his concern over Chinese intervention in Korea. MacArthur assured him that victory was won in Korea, and that the Chinese would not attack. Their 30-minute private conversation seemed to reassure each about the other.

During the larger discussion with all of the staff present, MacArthur was asked about the likelihood of intervention by the Chinese or the Russians in Korea. He explained that Chinese intervention was very unlikely, but the Russians might be called on by the Chinese to provide airpower support. MacArthur committed to being able to release a division to return to duty to Europe. Truman wrapped up the session quickly and suggested everyone have lunch, but MacArthur demurred saying he needed to return to Tokyo.

On the way home, Truman stopped in San Francisco to deliver a speech, in which he explained that it was fortunate for the world that General MacArthur, the exact right man for the job was available to do it, and to make clear there was "complete unity in the aims and conduct of our foreign policy."

But then, on Tuesday, November 28, General Bradley contacted Truman to say he had "a terrible message" from MacArthur. The Chinese had launched a furious counterattack with a force of 260,000. The Chinese had come in with both feet. MacArthur declared that we are "facing an entirely new war" and called for reinforcements of the "greatest magnitude." He wanted a naval blockade of China, called for bombing the Chinese mainland, and asked for authority to broaden the conflict. At a National Security Council meeting that same day, the decision was made not to let the crisis in Korea, however horrible, flare into a world war. This *decision stands as one of the triumphs of the Truman Administration*. General Bradley and General Marshall both advised that the war should be limited and the United States should not fall into a trap, they and others felt it was imperative to find a line that could be held, and to hold it.

Inside the Administration, there was growing concern about MacArthur's actions and performance. MacArthur sent a series of increasingly desperate reports to Truman in which he urged rash actions (including dropping 30–50 atomic bombs on cities in China). Truman still refused to reprimand MacArthur, treating him with infinite patience. But many of those around Truman had concluded that the general was "incredibly recalcitrant" and fundamentally disloyal.

Then came a series of promising reports about and from General Matthew Ridgway regarding his progress in restoring the Eighth Army, which he had taken command of after its previous commander was killed in an accident. Suddenly, Ridgway had emerged as an alternative to MacArthur, particularly among the people advising Truman. With a force of 365,000 men, Ridgway faced an enemy force of 480,000 and by the end of March, he was at the 38th parallel having inflicted immense casualties on the Chinese. Ridgway's progress seemed only to distress MacArthur, and he took several actions to upstage Ridgway.

Truman ordered preparation of a cease-fire proposal, which was submitted to the seventeen U.N. nations that were fighting alongside U.S. forces in Korea. The Joint Chiefs sent MacArthur portions of the proposed agreement to review, and this made him realize that there was not going to be an all-out war with Red China as he had been urging. Years later, Bradley would speculate that MacArthur's realization that his war on China was not going to happen "snapped his brilliant but brittle mind." And on Saturday, March 24, MacArthur tried to seize the initiative by issuing his own proclamation to the Chinese, which in effect was an ultimatum. MacArthur concluded by saying he "personally stood ready at any time" to meet with the Chinese commander to reach a settlement.

Senior advisers around Truman viewed MacArthur's action as a major act of sabotage and called it insubordination of the grossest sort. Bradley termed it an "unforgivable and irretrievable act." In his memoirs, Truman said this was the point at which he felt he could no longer tolerate his insubordination. Truman responded to this latest affront from MacArthur by sending a restrained reprimand that reminded him about his recent order forbidding public statements that had not been cleared by Washington. Then, the House Minority Leader took the floor to read a letter he had received from MacArthur in which he was again arguing for a full-scale effort against the Chinese.

Truman remained calm, talking with advisors over a period of oddly quiet days. Truman convened his advisors – Acheson, Marshall, Bradley, and Harriman – to discuss what to do. Earlier the Joint Chiefs had met and concluded that from the military point of view, MacArthur should be relieved. In his meeting, each of his aides urged Truman to relieve MacArthur. Truman revealed, for the first time, that he had reached the same conclusion. Papers were delivered to MacArthur while at lunch in Tokyo with his wife. (The papers had been delivered by the Army Secretary who was already in Korea. Truman said, "He's not going to be allowed to quit on me. He's going to be fired.")

When the story broke across the front pages of American newspapers, the reaction was more than even Truman and his aides had anticipated. Republican outrage in Congress reached a fever pitch. Though there was considerable editorial opinion on Truman's side from many major metropolitan newspapers, who spoke up for the principle of civilian control of the military and who cited Truman's strength of character.

Upon his return to the United States after a 14-year absence due to military duty, MacArthur was given a hero's welcome. He was invited to speak to a joint session of Congress, which had a television audience of 30 million, and his performance was masterful. He was provocative and defiant and resounding cheers and applause interrupted him 30 times in 34 minutes. MacArthur held them spellbound, his voice dropping as he began the stirring, sentimental, and ambiguous peroration that the speech would be remembered for:

> The hopes and dreams have long since vanished. But I still remember the refrain of one of the most popular barracks ballads of that day which proclaimed most proudly that, "Old soldiers never die. They just fade away." And like the old soldier of the ballad, I close my military career and just fade

away – an old soldier who tried to do his duty as God gave him the right to see that duty … Goodbye.

Truman had not listened to MacArthur's speech, or watched on television. He had spent the time at his desk in the Oval Office, having his usual round of Thursday meetings, after which he went to the residence for lunch and a nap.

In the late spring of 1951, the Senate Foreign Relations and Armed Services committees held joint hearings to investigate MacArthur's dismissal. MacArthur was the first witness, testifying for three days, and becoming increasingly self-absorbed and seemingly disinterested in global issues. He would admit to no mistakes, no errors of judgment. The turning point in the hearings was the testimony of Marshall, Bradley, and the Joint Chiefs, who refuted absolutely MacArthur's claim that they agreed with his strategy. Truman had known from the start he needed full support of his military advisors before making his decision. Through 19 days of testimony, he had gotten their full support. They not only gave weight and validity to his decision but also discredited MacArthur in a way nothing else could have. The fidelity of the military high command to the principle of civilian control of the military was total and unequivocal.

Finishing His Term and Returning to Independence

On January 5, 1952, Winston Churchill paid a visit to Truman, who viewed Churchill as the greatest public figure of the age. They dined on the presidential yacht, the *Williamsburg*, and after the table was cleared, Churchill turned to Truman, and said slowly, "The last time you and I sat across a conference table was at Potsdam, Mr. President." Truman nodded and Churchill went on, "I must confess, sir, I held you in very low regard then. I loathed you taking the place of Franklin Roosevelt. I misjudged you badly. Since that time, *you more than any other man, have saved Western civilization.*"

Also in early 1952, Truman felt the need to find his successor, since he had decided some months previously that he was not going to run for reelection. He first approached Supreme Court Chief Justice Fred Vinson, who Truman called the "most logical and qualified." Vinson declined – he was in declining health and would die two years later at age 61. He then approached the nation's number-one hero, General Eisenhower, now serving as the head of NATO. But at a lunch in the first week in November, Eisenhower explained that he and his family were lifelong Republicans, and on January 7, he announced that he was ready to accept the Republican nomination.

Truman then turned to Illinois Governor Adlai Stevenson, who Truman saw as able, progressive, the governor of a major industrial state, a champion of honest government, and a relatively new face. He was very different from Truman, a graduate of Princeton, well-born, a prosperous lawyer, eloquent, witty, urbane – and divorced. At a meeting between the two on January 22, 1952, he asked Stevenson to run for the Presidency. But Stevenson refused and was flabbergasted at the offer. Truman refused to give up, and on March 4, they met again at Stevenson's request. But Stevenson again refused when Truman again offered, having announced that he would run for reelection in Illinois.

Truman considered running again. Then, at the Jefferson-Jackson Day Dinner in Washington, DC, after a fiery, lively speech in which he attacked the Republicans and touted his own record, he revealed,

> I shall not be a candidate for reelection. I have served my country long, and I think very efficiently and honestly. I shall not accept a re-nomination. I do not feel it is my duty to spend another four years in the White House.

As the Democratic Convention opened in Chicago, Senator Estes Kefauver (who Truman referred to derisively as "Cowfever") was in the lead for delegates, against a field of Sen. Richard Russell, Averill Harriman, and Stevenson (with a mere 41 delegates). But Stevenson skillfully rallied his forces and rallied to win the nomination. During the campaign, Stevenson kept Truman at arms-length (perhaps because Truman's approval ratings hovered in the low 30s), and Truman felt he was being treated as a liability and limited his participation. Eisenhower's victory was overwhelming.

As Truman was winding up his time in office, a clearer picture of his accomplishments in keeping the economy vibrant began to emerge. New census reports confirmed gains in income, standards of living, education, and housing since Truman took office were unparalleled in American history. In his final State of the Union message to Congress on January 7, 1953, 62 million Americans had jobs, a gain of 11 million jobs in seven years. Farm income, corporate income, and dividends were at an all-time high. There had not been a failure of an insured bank in nine years. He could rightly point with pride to the fact that the postwar economic collapse that was expected had not materialized. Through government support (i.e., the GI Bill), eight million veterans had been to college, Social Security benefits had been doubled, and the minimum wage increased. Millions of homes had been built through government financing. Prices were higher, but incomes had risen even more. Real living standards were considerably higher than seven years earlier.

Truman held his last press conference (his 324th!!) and was applauded vigorously by the 300 reporters in attendance. His friend Winston Churchill arrived for a farewell visit and a dinner for "Harry" at the British Embassy. Truman hugely enjoyed seeing him again.

Truman delivered his farewell address from the Oval Office on radio and television on the night of January 15, 1953. David McCullough described the speech:

> It was a speech without rhetorical flourishes or memorable epigrams and it was superb, Truman at his best … He was clear, simple, often personal, but

conveying overall a profound sense of the momentous history of the times, the panoramic changes reshaping the world, and the part that he inevitably had to play since that desolate day he was summoned to the White House and told of Roosevelt's death. It was not a nostalgic farewell ... To millions who listened ... it seemed a striking expression of the best instincts of America.

Truman ended his farewell speech with these words:

When Franklin Roosevelt died, I felt there must be a million men better qualified than I to take up the Presidential task. **But the work was mine to do, and I had to do it. And I have tried to give it everything that was in me.**
Good night and God bless you all.

As the Trumans prepared to leave Washington by taking the train to Independence, Dean Acheson provided a farewell lunch for them, a chance to say goodbye to their closest colleagues and staff. Thousands were at the train station to see them off. Talking to a reporter as the Trumans boarded the train, Acheson said, "*There's the best friend in the world. There's nothing like that man.*"

Harry Truman had been on a long road from Independence to the White House, and now he was headed home.

Back in Independence. Now back home as a private citizen, Truman received offers of jobs paying $100,000 for a small commitment of time. He turned them all down, saying his name was not for sale. He missed the pace of the Presidency, life felt strange without the constant pressures. He missed the people most of all. When he wrote to thank Dean Acheson for the farewell party, he said, "I hope we never lose contact."

He began to put his time into writing his memoirs, for which he had received an advance and a deadline for producing a draft. He also spent much of his time on the planning and development of his Presidential library, including examining the architectural design and the content and themes of the exhibits. The town had donated a town park as the site for the library. Truman threw himself into the task of raising money for the library, attending dinners, and giving speeches around the country. In a year and a half, he raised more than a million dollars.

After turning 70, Truman was rushed to the hospital for an emergency operation to have his gall bladder and appendix removed. After the surgery, an infection set in, but fortunately the crisis passed. Truman continued writing his memoirs, and on his 71st birthday, he turned the first spade of earth at a groundbreaking ceremony for his library.

On the morning of his 72nd birthday, Harry and Bess left Independence bound for England to accept an honorary degree from Oxford. He and Bess had long dreamed of a chance to travel abroad, they considered it the trip of their lifetime.

They first went to Paris, and when Harry was spotted in sidewalk cafes, he was greeted with cheers and applause. When he and Bess went to Rome, he received a tumultuous welcome when they arrived at the train station. He and Bess had a rare Sunday audience with Pope Pius XII. At Naples, crowds had tossed flowers in his path.

Arriving at Oxford to receive an honorary degree as a Doctor of Civil Law, the Chancellor described him as, "Truest of allies, direct in speech and in your writings, *and ever a pattern of simple courage* ..." The applause lasted for a full three minutes. Truman was moved to tears, and he smiled broadly when he recovered. He was also celebrated at two white-tie dinners, and at one, he gave a speech in which he offered some advice from his fellow Missourian, Mark Twain, "*Always do right. It will please some people and astonish the rest.*"

Finally, before returning to America, they went to Chartwell, the Churchill family estate south of London. Truman greeted Churchill warmly, they walked in the garden together, and after lunch they said goodbye not knowing if they would see each other again, and they did not. The London newspapers did not wait to praise Truman's visit. *The Daily Telegram* described him as "the living and kicking symbol of everything that everyone likes best about the United States."

Returning to America, on June 7, 1957, Margaret presented Harry and Bess with a new grandson. On July 6, The Truman Library was dedicated before a crowd of five thousand, including many of his colleagues from the Truman Administration. The main speaker was the Chief Justice of the Supreme Court Earl Warren, who described Truman as a man of action, "tireless, fearless, and decisive."

Now the two things he had said he wanted most after leaving the White House – to become a grandfather and to see his library established – had both happened within days of each other. It was often said that the most interesting thing on display at the Truman library was Truman himself.[6] In total, he was there six and one-half days per week for nine years. The crowning touch for the library was a mural at the inside entryway painted by Missouri native Thomas Hart Benton. At first the two men did not like each other, but as they discovered a mutual liking for bourbon, they enjoyed each other's company.

When George Marshall died in October 1959, it was a heavy personal blow for Truman in a succession of deaths of members of his former official family. He called Marshall's wife and attended his funeral in North Carolina. Later he told Acheson in a letter, "*Do you suppose any President of the United States ever had two such men as you and the General?*"

In May 1960, Margaret had a second grandchild. To mark his 75th birthday in May, the Democratic National Committee staged a nationwide celebration, a star spangled television celebration with many stars of the arts and other celebrities.

On Tuesday, October 12 at his farm in Sandy Spring, Maryland, Dean Acheson was found slumped over his desk in his study, dead of a heart attack at age 78. On the afternoon of Tuesday, December 5, Truman was taken to the hospital leaving his house on North Delaware for the last time. He was suffering from lung congestion and the hospital rated his condition on admission as "fair." Margaret immediately flew back to Independence.

By Christmas Eve he had grown progressively weaker and was in a deep coma and near death on Christmas morning. Truman died in Kansas City's Research and Medical Center on Tuesday, December 26, 1972, at 7:50 a.m. An elaborate funeral plan had been developed years earlier, but it was scaled back to be more what Bess wanted. The body was taken to lie in state in the lobby of the Truman Library, the streets were lined with soldiers, and an Honor Guard was posted at the Library steps. Over almost two days, an estimated 75,000 people passed by the closed casket in the lobby of the Truman Library, in front of the Benton mural. "This whole town was a friend of Harry's" one man told a reporter. On Thursday, December 28, as he wished, he was buried in the courtyard of the Library.

He was remembered in print and over the air waves, in the halls of Congress and in large parts of the world as a figure of courage and principle. As David McCullough has written:

> He had held to old guidelines: work hard, do your best, speak the truth, assume no airs, trust in God, have no fear. Yet he was not and had never been a simple, ordinary man … He was the kind of president the founding fathers had in mind.

Bess Truman lived on North Delaware Street for another ten years. She died there on October 18, 1982, and was buried beside Harry in the courtyard of the Truman Library.

Epilogue

Harry Truman may well have been summing up his own career when he said, "do your duty and history will do you justice," and, "do your best and history will do the rest." Truman left nothing of his immense store of energy unused for his service to the country. And perhaps his attitude about serving the public was best captured when he said, *"I would much rather be an honorable public servant and known as such that to be the richest man in the world."*[7]

Notes

1 Albert Baime, *The Accidental President* (Houghton Mifflin Harcourt Publishing Company, New York, NY, 2017), page 37.
2 David McCullough, *Truman* (Simon & Schuster, New York, NY, 1992), pages 352, 353.
3 Baime, *The Accidental President*, page 36.
4 McCullough, *Truman*, page 353.
5 McCullough, *Truman*, page 717.

6 I once had the pleasure of talking to Harry Truman at his library in Independence, Mo. On many of the days he was present at the library he would send the docents out to tell visitors that the President was going to hold a "press conference" in the auditorium, we would be able to ask him questions. I was there with my family, we went to the auditorium, I huddled with my older brother to devise a question to ask him. On the stage was a piano, and an elderly man emerged from behind the curtain, and after playing the Missouri Waltz on the piano, Harry Truman began to speak. His voice was not filled with the certitude of his earlier years, but he began to take questions from the audience. I raised my hand, and he called on me!! I asked him who he thought was the greatest president and why? He thought for a brief moment and then explained that his choice was George Washington, because, he said he was operating without any precedents, he literally had to decide many things that had never been done before, and his good judgement about not acting like a king set up the presidency as an office with much power, but still with separation of powers among the three branches.

I have thought about this answer in light of Truman's experience in taking over the Presidency after Roosevelt's death, when he received none of the preparatory briefings and spent almost no time with Roosevelt about his plans and about the state of world affairs. He may have felt a kinship with Washington over the feeling of "flying blindly" into the Presidency.

7 Ralph Keyes, *The Wit and Wisdom of Harry Truman* (Gramercy Books, New York, NY) page 52.

Bibliography

Baime, Albert J. *The Accidental President: Harry S. Truman and the Four Months That Changed the World*. Buena Vista, VA: Mariner Books, 2017.

Keyes, Ralph. *The Wit and Wisdom of Harry Truman*. Bexley, OH: Gramercy Books, 1999.

McCullough, David. *Truman*. New York, NY: Simon & Schuster, 1993.

Scarborough, Joe. *Truman, The Cold War, and the Fight for Western Civilization*. New York, NY: HarperCollins, 2020.

Steinberg, Arthur. *The Man from Missouri: The Life and Times of Harry S. Truman*. New York, NY: Putnam Publishing, 1962.

"The Presidents: Truman," dir. by David Grubin. *PBS American Experience Series*, David Grubin Films, 1997.

14

FRANCES PERKINS

The Driving Force of the New Deal

DOI: 10.4324/9781003266235-16

Early Years: "Be Ye Steadfast"

Fannie Coralie Perkins was born on April 10, 1880, in Boston, but the place she considered home was where she spent her childhood summers, with her beloved grandmother at a homestead built by her great-great grandfather near New Castle, Maine, near a bend in the Damariscotta River.

She grew up as a middle class shopkeeper's daughter in Worcester. Her family was faithful (Congregationalists) church-goers, and her family had strains of brilliance, traces of manic depression, and a propensity for acts of public altruism. Fannie was an exceptional child, unusually verbal and articulate, and she discovered she had more in common with her father than with her mother and sister, with whom Fannie's affection was dutiful rather than heartfelt. Her father grasped what a remarkable child he had in Fannie, while her mother did not. He taught her to read Greek when she was only eight and began to prepare her for college. She attended Worcester Classical High School, where she learned the traditional curriculum, including Latin and Greek.

New ideas about giving women a broader social role were becoming more prominent, and Fannie's father, while on a business trip, attended an evening lecture on women's suffrage by Anna Howard Shaw, the militant physician and orator. He was very impressed by the address and returned home a convert to the idea that women should have the right to vote.

In her earliest years, Fannie had developed an ability to feel other people's pain and lamented their suffering. Her mother frequently tended to the needs of poor neighbors and encouraged her daughter to befriend them as well. She was also affected by tales brought back by foreign missionaries, their descriptions of the plight of hungry children touched Fannie.

After high school, Fannie enrolled in Mount Holyoke, the women's college near her Worcester home. It was a school that sought to prepare girls for lives of high purpose as missionaries and teachers. The school's founder had a motto: "Go forward, attempt great things, accomplish great things." Perkins majored in chemistry and physics but was most interested in her American economic history course for which she visited factories and other workplaces to interview workers. It gave Fannie her first look at modern industrial life, and it was not pleasant.

An important development during her college years was the arrival of Mary E. Woolley as Mount Holyoke's new president, who wanted to make the college into a top-flight institution. She was not married, and she sought friendship from female friends. Woolley's life presented to the students the novel idea that marriage was a possibility for the future, but not a requirement for a satisfying life. During these years, she also met Florence Kelley, executive director of the National Consumers League, who came to the college on a national speaking tour to talk about the organization she was building to abolish child labor and eliminate tenement work and sweatshops. Kelley was fiery, energetic, infused with idealism, but also pragmatic. She was also one of the most politically radical people whom Fannie had ever met. Kelley also brought new social science methods to her work, some of the same techniques Fannie had learned in her economic history class. Kelley's motto at the Consumer's League was "investigate, record, agitate." In Kelley, Fannie had found the perfect mentor, friend, and guide.[1] Fannie had grown more strong-willed, and more imbued with a sense of mission. When Fannie spoke as class president at the last prayer meeting before graduation, she chose as the text St. Paul's message to the early Christians: "Therefore my beloved brethren, be ye steadfast, unmovable, always abounding in the work of the Lord." The class chose as its motto "Be Ye Steadfast."

After leaving college, she took several teaching jobs, and then she heard about an opportunity to teach science at a women's college in Chicago. She left her family behind and went on to spend her future in a lifetime pattern of moving simultaneously in two worlds – mixing with the elite while advocating reforms to benefit the poor.

Inventing "Frances" Perkins

After arriving at Ferry Hall, a woman's college for affluent young ladies, she changed her name to Frances (perhaps to be taken more seriously), left her family's Congregationalist Church for the Episcopalian faith (which placed her in the most upscale milieu in her town of Lake Forest).

Though Frances was expected to reside at one of the student dormitories at Ferry Hall, she began to spend time at the Hull House in Chicago, a settlement house where she did work in service to the poor. Hull House served as a model for other settlement houses around the country, and its director Jane Addams had achieved some notoriety for her groundbreaking work to develop settlement houses. In addition to meeting important contacts that she would benefit from for the rest of her life (e.g., Upton Sinclair, author of *The Jungle*, the muckraking novel about the meatpacking industry released in 1906), she developed a life-long suspicion of reporters who wrote about Hull House as a nest of political radicals. Her Hull House experience also clarified for Frances that social work was her calling, and she began looking for positions doing social work.

In 1907, Frances pursued a job in Philadelphia that entailed investigating immigrant women pushed into sexual slavery by bogus employment agencies that would lure them into boarding houses that turned out to be bordellos. Frances was to find ways to put pimps and drug dealers out of business – to detect, confront, and bring it to law enforcement's attention. This was considered daunting work even for experienced social workers. She did not hesitate to accept the job when offered and became the general secretary of the Philadelphia Research and Protective Association. She found widespread evidence that European immigrants and young black women from the rural south were being transported to the city for prostitution. She and her associates built a list of reputable boardinghouses to steer young women away from the worst places. She discovered widespread overcrowding and poor sanitation and went on to help shut down four houses by testifying before city public safety officials about what she had seen at these houses.

She realized during this time that she needed to continue her education in order to be more effective in working on economic and labor issues of the time. The Wharton School of Finance and Commerce of the University of Pennsylvania was her obvious choice, as Penn had recently begun accepting women. She had her first serious romance at Penn, where she found Joseph E. Cohen, an intelligent official from the typographical workers union. He was a radical socialist, and she became a committed socialist during this period. The romance did not bloom toward marriage, so she decided to move on. A professor at Penn, impressed by Frances's aptitude, helped her arrange a fellowship at Columbia University. So she returned to New York to make the city her home. She continued to correspond with Cohen; she concealed her Socialist Party membership, insisting she had been apolitical until she joined the Democrats several years later.

Making a Career in New York City

Frances moved into a settlement house affiliated with the Hull House, entered a program to earn a master's degree in Political Science at Columbia University, earning her degree in June 1910. She cultivated valuable connections and benefactors among the Astors and the Vanderbilts. She moved to Greenwich Village, a center of intellectual ferment, living among radicals and writers, painters, suffragists, and ideologues.

Frances developed a talent for gaining the confidence of others and then serving as a sounding board for their dreams and aspirations. She had an uncanny ability to spot people of unusual promise before they were widely recognized by others.[2] One person she singled out as especially interesting was Robert Moses, then a young investigator at the Bureau of Municipal Research who traveled in the same government reform circles as many of her social worker friends. He was arrogant and abrasive and few people took the time to listen to him, but Frances did. She also continued a relationship with the writer Sinclair Lewis, whose career as a newspaperman was floundering, but whose books were gaining attention and put him on the path toward Nobel and Pulitzer prizes. Lewis at one point told several friends that he was in love with Frances and even proposed to her. But Lewis often behaved wildly due to his drinking. Frances also noted the presence of Paul Caldwell Wilson, a young government reformer. Lewis pressed Frances and tried to appeal to her. Frances became active in the woman's suffrage movement, around which she built her closest female friendships. She developed a knack for turning foes into friends through gentle humor.

As her graduate studies neared an end, she was approached by the National Consumers League to head up their office in New York City, a job that offered the opportunity to work on many of the social issues that she was convinced were the cause of many of the nation's problems. The job would also allow her to work closely with Florence Kelly, who had inspired her during a speech at Mount Holyoke and who had been an early resident at Hull House. Kelly's reputation had grown in the intervening years, mostly through research she had conducted into housing, schools, courts, and workplace standards.

On March 25, 1911, Frances attended an afternoon tea near Washington Square. As the tea was beginning, the guests were startled by a disturbance in the street, which turned out to be a fire raging at the Triangle Shirtwaist manufacturing company, a building that was a known firetrap. Employees were jumping from the windows of the building, pushed to the windows by the fire in the center of the building on the top three floors. Many of the employees were hitting the sidewalk below, a horrifying scene. Frances witnessed much of the fire and was stunned by the devastating loss of life. The Triangle fire was a turning point, reorienting Frances's life. The journalist Will Irvin, a close friend, stated, "What Frances Perkins saw that day started her on her career."[3]

In his book, *The Road to Character*, David Brooks describes the course of Frances's life, saying that most people plan their future by looking inside themselves, following their passion, asking what do I want from life? Brooks says,

> Frances Perkins found her purpose in life using a different method ... In this method ... you ask a different set of questions: what does life want from me? What are my circumstances calling me to do? In this scheme of things, we don't create our lives; we are summoned by life. The important answers are not found inside, they are outside.

Brooks further states, people who have not just a career but a calling have a

> certain rapt expression, a hungry desire to perform ... to utmost perfection. They feel the joy of having their values in deep harmony with their behavior. They experience a wonderful certainty of action that banishes weariness from even the harshest days.[4]

For her work at the National Consumers League, Frances lobbied the state legislature for worker safety legislation, where she left behind the prejudices of her upscale New York social set and the gentility of progressive politics, in order to compromise ruthlessly if it meant making progress. Frances had to work with many Tammany Hall politicians who were regarded with horror in the polite circles in which she had previously traveled. After one exchange with a Tammany Hall legislator, Frances wrote in a journal that

> the way men take women in political life is to associate them with motherhood ... I said to myself "the way to get things done [is to] behave, dress, and so comport yourself that you remind them subconsciously of their mothers."[5]

She wore plain black dresses with white bow ties at the neck, pearls, a black tricorn hat, and a matronly demeanor.

Around this time, Paul Wilson, who Frances had met previously, became a close aide to New York's reformist mayor, John Purroy Mitchel. He fell in love with Frances and slowly won her over. They were married on September 26, 1913, in a very quiet wedding in which they did not invite their friends and told their families too late for them to attend. They lived in a gracious townhouse on Washington Square. She continued with her social work, Wilson served in the mayor's office, and their first years were relatively happy. Things deteriorated rather rapidly as Mayor Mitchel was voted out of office, and Wilson had an open affair with a society lady. Frances began to feel stifled in the marriage and asked for a separation. Then she got pregnant, but the boy died shortly after birth. She then had a daughter, Susanna, and wanted to have another child, but by 1918, Wilson was showing signs of mental illness, perhaps manic depression. He made bad investments, spent parts of the next decades in asylums and institutional care, and required a full-time attendant. She worked for most of her life to conceal her private life from public view.

During the time that Al Smith served as Governor of New York, he appointed Frances to the Industrial Commission that regulated workplace conditions across the state and put her in the middle of significant strikes and industrial disputes. During the 1910s and 1920s in Albany, Perkins had opportunities to work with then-state senator Franklin Delano Roosevelt, and she found him shallow and a bit arrogant. Roosevelt disappeared from Perkins's life when he suffered his polio attack, but when he returned, she felt he had changed, purged of the arrogant attitude he had displayed.

When Roosevelt succeeded Smith as Governor of New York after Smith's unsuccessful run for president, he offered Frances the job of Industrial Commissioner to manage the agency she had been part of in Smith's administration. She initially resisted the idea, but she had a growing reputation for a judicial temperament and a strong sense in all situations of what was fair, always open to new ideas, and yet the moral purpose of the law and the welfare of mankind was never overlooked. She took the job and spent the years in Albany with the Roosevelt, getting to know them, staying with them on weekends, and joining their social circle. Frances learned how to work with Franklin, but also how to manage Eleanor, who struggled with feelings of inadequacy (due in part, no doubt, to FDR's continuing affairs with his former and current secretaries).

Whereas Al Smith had been easy for Frances to understand, Roosevelt was extremely complicated. Frances spoke to him every ten days, and she learned the trick of repeating things three times to get something fixed in his memory. She also realized that he wanted to hear a particular point and the story that went with it, and those stories often were used as the most effective kind of political communication.

Perkins eventually excelled at reading Franklin Roosevelt. After he died, she wrote a biography, *The Roosevelt I Knew*, a very astute character sketch. About his decision-making style, she wrote that he had the "feeling that nothing in human judgement is final. One may courageously take the step that seems right today because it can be modified tomorrow if it does not work well." She knew he was an improviser rather than a planner: he took a step and adjusted, a step and adjusted. Gradually a big change would emerge. She saw him as a man who viewed himself as more an instrument than an engineer.[6]

During her time working for Governor Roosevelt, Frances helped him cast himself as a national leader focused on economic issues. The economy was sinking under President Herbert Hoover, and Roosevelt was a proponent of significant government interventions to energize the economy, including "unemployment insurance," and an old-age pension plan. Frances also contributed to Roosevelt's growing national stature by forcefully disputing many of the unemployment statistics that the Hoover Administration was using to falsely claim that the country was not sinking into economic depression.

Becoming U.S. Secretary of Labor

On November 4, 1932, after a long and arduous campaign, Roosevelt was elected President, ultimately capturing 57 percent of the vote. Immediately after the election, Frances's name began to be raised in speculation about Roosevelt's Cabinet choices. Frances publicly denied any ambitions for the job of Secretary of Labor, but she campaigned quietly for the job. Endorsement letters flooded Roosevelt's office, and in January 1933, Justice Brandeis met with Roosevelt and urged him to appoint Frances. For her part, Frances was horrified at the thought of living in Washington, since she needed to supervise Paul's care, knew that the job would be all-consuming, and would open her life to increased public scrutiny.

On February 23, 1933, a week before the inauguration, Frances was summoned to an appointment with Roosevelt. When Roosevelt finally offered her the job, she proceeded to lay out a dramatic plan of action.[7] First, she suggested that the Department needed a significant overhaul, to realign organizational units (including the Bureau of Labor Statistics that had developed the bogus data that Hoover had used to argue that there was not an ongoing depression) and shift resources to the appropriate places. Second, the biggest policy issue was unemployment, and she suggested that some programs of relief should be developed, and a public works program should be implemented in various parts of the country. Third, she also suggested a prohibition against child labor, a reduction of working hours to an eight-hour day, and establishment of a minimum wage. Fourth, in the area of worker health, she recommended worker's compensation be imposed across the country, and she would try to convince states to implement programs to improve working conditions. Finally, she suggested an old-age pension to provide a minimum allotment to the elderly, so they would not burden their families.

Roosevelt reacted negatively to the old-age pension idea, primarily because there was no provision for funding. He agreed to let Frances continue to study the idea, not killing it outright. Frances concluded the conversation by telling Roosevelt that if he did not want these things done, she was not the right person to serve as Secretary of Labor.

FDR told her he would back her ideas; he had promised the American people in his campaign that he would improve their lives, and he intended to do so. She told him that she wanted to talk to her husband before agreeing to the job. Roosevelt told her he wanted her answer by the next evening. Frances knew this would be the hardest job she would ever take on, and she hated the idea of leaving her friends and her surroundings in New York City. She was comforted by the advice her grandmother had given long ago: "If someone opens a door for you, my dear, walk right in and do the best you can. Do the best you can, for it means that it's the Lord's will for you."[8] At 52 years of age, she agreed to become the Secretary of Labor during an economic depression, the first woman to serve in the Cabinet.

The reaction to the appointment was not universally positive. William Green, president of the American Federation of Labor, issued a statement that union officers were "keenly disappointed" over the president's choice, further stating that the Secretary of Labor should be representative of labor, one who understands labor and its problems, and that the new secretary did not meet these qualifications. The *Baltimore Sun* editorial page said, "A woman smarter that a man is something to get on guard about. But a woman smarter than a man and also not afraid of a man, well, good night." At her first press conference, Frances grew testy when reporter's questions probed about Paul or Susanna, now 16 years old, as she had no intention of discussing either. She developed a reputation among reporters as "schoolmarmish" and stuffy.

At Roosevelt's inauguration, Frances listened carefully to his speech, which she described as "a revival of faith." He called for courage and optimism in the face of despair:

> This is preeminently the time to speak the truth, the whole truth, frankly and boldly. Nor need we shrink from honestly facing conditions in our country today. This great nation will endure as it has endured, will revive and prosper. So, first of all, let me assert my firm belief that the only thing we have to fear is fear itself – nameless, unreasoning, unjustified terror with that which paralyzes needed efforts to convert retreat into advance. In every dark hour of our national life, a leadership of frankness and vigor has met with that understanding and support of the people themselves which is essential to victory. I am convinced that you will give that support to leadership in these critical days.[9]

Frances set about tackling the corruption and ineffectiveness she found in abundance at the Labor Department. Frances's enthusiasm for change was part of a feverish spirit that permeated the federal bureaucracy as the Roosevelt Administration began its tenure, with an estimated 13–18 million Americans out of work. She strategized that in the first few weeks of the new administration, there would need to be a pure relief program at the same time when they were developing a public works program. The administration improvised, choosing prominent projects from among the thousands of ideas coming in from around the nation.

Within days of the inauguration, the administration launched the Civilian Conservation Corps (CCC), acting on an idea that Roosevelt suggested about sending the unemployed into rural areas to do forestry work. (This was in keeping with an idea he had supported for many years about forming a universal youth service.) By August 1933, the program included almost 300,000 men. By April 1936, there were 2,158 Civilian Conservation Camps, each with about 160 enrollees. The program was one of the most popular of the New Deal, repeatedly reauthorized and only ceased operation at the beginning of World War II, having enrolled 3.5 million Americans during its nine years of existence. The program's biggest problem was race relations. In the South, local political leaders objected to African-American enrollment in the program and resisted integrating blacks and whites in camps. Some communities objected to having black CCC enrollees located within their boundaries.

A second major relief program was launched simultaneously with the creation of the CCC. On March 21, Roosevelt asked Congress to create a relief program with a budget of $500 million to dispense as state grants. By April, the proposal was approved by a large margin, and the creation of the Federal Emergency Relief Administration commenced. In filling the jobs of the state administrators of the program, some in Congress thought these jobs should go only to Democrats. In Missouri, a middle-aged Democrat named Harry S. Truman was recommended for the job. Truman got the job and this allowed him to build loyalty among hungry job seekers and gave him his first important national contacts and his first official business in Washington. Frances saw Truman as an "unemployed businessman who was just down on his luck."

The Federal Emergency Relief Administration established drought-relief programs, teachers were dispatched to reopen schoolhouses in bankrupt school districts, and jobs and housing programs sprang up for unemployed transients. Across the country, workers earned money for their efforts, working on projects that improved the lives of their fellow citizens.

By July 1933, the U.S. Employment Service had expanded to 192 offices in 120 cities and 23 states, and the National Reemployment Service served many other cities. By June 1934, the U.S. Employment Service had registered 12.3 million people, and by the time the United States entered World War II, it had placed almost 26 million people in jobs.

On the matter of home ownership, the Roosevelt Administration created the Federal Home Owners Loan Corporation in 1933 to help middle-class home owners refinance their homes with government backing, allowing them to pay off their homes at five percent interest over 15 years. The government helped more than one million people between 1933 and 1936. Also, Frances was involved in passage of the National Housing Act, passed in 1934, which utilized Frances' favorite public policy tool: insurance. Through this Act, the Federal Housing Administration (FHA) was created, which allowed private lenders to once again loan money for home purchase with confidence that they would be repaid. This program introduced practices that would revolutionize home purchases for years to come: a 20 percent down payment, mortgages with fixed rates, and payments over a 20-year period.

In spite of her accomplishments, she still managed to avoid press scrutiny. She sometimes actively eluded stories about the Roosevelt "brain trust" of aides and Cabinet Secretaries who were providing the energy behind the plethora of programs that the administration was implementing. She rightly surmised that the term "brain trust" would become an object of scorn.

Frances's preference to house her husband and daughter in New York City caused some financial strain, and she struggled to find suitable living arrangement for herself in Washington. She solved her problem by moving into a Georgetown house with her New York friend, the widow Mary Harriman Rumsey. In addition to having a place to stay, and a friend for company, it also gave Frances a place to entertain at the inevitable Washington parties she was expected to host. Mary was an invaluable ally for Frances, a newcomer to the city trying to build a social network. With Mary's support, Frances functioned more efficiently and with fewer distractions, and Mary was able to draw more top names to her table because of the lure of a presidential Cabinet member living there. Frances and Mary got along well, sharing a pragmatic approach to life. Mary was intelligent and idealistic and had enormous personal energy. It is probably impossible to know whether their relationship was romantic or sexual. They kept their relationship looking like a roommate arrangement, with records of sharing expenses (though much more of the burdens of paying for the house expenses was covered by Mary). Little in the way of personal letters between the two women has come to light, and those that have been discovered have been mostly pleasant business letters. Many of Frances's friends thought that Frances had to live by her wits when it came to finances, needing to cover expenses for Paul's care, wanting to set up a good life for Susanna, and living in a kind of dependent state with women with whom she became close friends.[10]

Developing the Social Security Program

The problem of the indigent elderly had been brought into stark relief with the onset of the great depression. Few of the nation's 6.5 million citizens who were 65 and older had made provisions for their retirement years. Only about 300,000 had public pensions, through the states or federal retirement systems. Another 150,000 received pensions from their private employers or unions. Everyone else was on their own. About 30–50 percent of the elderly sought support from friends or relatives, and adult children found this burden unendurable.

Frances began to look to Europe for models of old-age pensions, which were very common in Europe. She began to focus on ensuring that people could contribute substantially to their own accounts. She looked to the insurance model, in which people pay in when they are employed, so they can get money when they are not.

During Roosevelt's first year in office, officials had been too busy to launch either unemployment or old-age insurance programs. But now Frances was convinced that the time was right, and she told Roosevelt that they should get started on it since this is the only chance in 25 years to get something like this approved by Congress.

Roosevelt gave her the nod, and with joblessness running rampant, Frances decided to try for unemployment insurance first. But unemployment insurance seemed radical to many Americans, with few employers supporting the idea. In March 1934, the House Ways and Means Committee held hearings about the proposed program, with Frances testifying in support. Then Roosevelt wavered as he considered presenting more moderate programs in several areas simultaneously, thinking that more might be accomplished in total. Roosevelt considered the idea of assembling a package of programs under the label of "economic security." He decided to put the unemployment insurance bill on hold to take the time to develop the larger package.

Frances immediately registered her objections to this approach. She got Roosevelt back on track and they began developing more sweeping options, which would create a cradle-to-grave economic security package. The idea was to offer unemployment insurance, old-age pensions, health insurance, and financial assistance for the handicapped and for widowed women with children. Roosevelt set up a Cabinet-level committee to do the groundwork. Roosevelt named Frances the chair and it gave her the opportunity to use all the techniques she had learned over a lifetime about bringing a group to consensus about a difficult policy issue.

On June 8, 1934, Roosevelt formally unveiled the plan. He said he intended to create a program that would provide "security against the hazards and vicissitudes of life." His plan would include state and federal components, with funds raised by individual payroll contributions rather than taxes. In late June, Roosevelt created the Committee on Economic Security, and began to fill the committee with experts who were allied with the thinking of Frances and Roosevelt. She appointed Edwin Witte, chairman of the University of Wisconsin Economics Department, for the job of executive director to oversee daily operations. She found Roosevelt's support remained equivocal. But in spite of these and other challenges, a core of specialists began functioning in concert on the program.

During the deliberations of the Committee, Supreme Court Justice Louis Brandeis, though he could not promote specific legislation, offered some advice about how an unemployment insurance program could pass constitutional muster. He suggested a plan in which contributions to state unemployment reserves could be offset against federal payroll taxes, thus avoiding any problematic direct taxes for this purpose. Brandeis was active in shaping the legislation, believing he could improve the chances of passing the scrutiny of his conservative colleagues on the Court. Meanwhile, Justice Harlan F. Stone, at an afternoon tea party at his home, had a conversation with Frances, who mentioned that she was struggling with the economic security program. Stone leaned in toward Frances and said, "The taxing power, my dear, the taxing power." With two justices suggesting similar ways around the constitutional difficulties, Frances believed that the legal problems could be solved if she did as they directed.

Roosevelt made things more difficult when, during a speech, he publicly took a more cautious stance, saying that he supported unemployment insurance but was uncertain whether this was the time for federal legislation on old-age security. Newspaper reports described this as the "kiss of death." Other accounts portrayed the president as callously abandoning the effort to develop an economic security package. Frances immediately called a press conference to say that the president had been misinterpreted and that FDR actually supported the full range of the programs under consideration.

The proposal finally was forwarded to the Cabinet Committee. Roosevelt had set an arbitrary Christmas deadline for completion of the work, and on December 24, the committee presented their recommendations to Roosevelt, who accepted them and said he would promptly send a message to Congress. On January 17, 1935, about ten months after the process began, Roosevelt presented the economic security legislation and urged Congress to pass it. After an initial period of supportive action in Congress, negative press reports began to take their toll, and Congress began to react with hostility to some parts of the proposed legislation. While the old-age pension system appeared likely to pass, other parts of the program were not faring so well. Hearings were scheduled and brought out both supporters and opponents.

The National Association of Manufacturers strongly attacked the bill, branding it socialistic control of life and industry. The Chamber of Commerce suggested some amendments but generally supported the bill. Many businessmen wrote to Congress to say they supported the concept but opposed the proposed taxes. National health insurance was dropped from the bill, a major disappointment to Frances, largely due to the mobilization of intense opposition of the American Medical Association. But the core of the legislation survived, and on August 14, 1935, FDR signed the measure into law saying it had been constructed in a way that no future politician would be able to tinker with it because it would be funded by workers' own contributions.

After the passage of the Act, many people credited Frances for the economic security program, and for keeping Roosevelt interested and visibly supportive. On the day the bill was signed, Frances issued a statement calling the bill, "one of the most forward-looking pieces of legislation in the interest of wage earners in history."

But on the day when she had achieved a life dream, as she prepared for the bill-signing ceremony, she had learned that her husband Paul had escaped his nurse's care and was roaming alone in New York City. She left Washington immediately after the ceremony, went to New York City, and found Paul later that night.

Frances also suffered the loss of her friend and housemate Mary Rumsey, leaving her to look for another place to live. Frances' remarkable survivor instinct kicked in and she approached Caroline Love O'Day, recently elected congresswoman at large from New York, whose husband was a key associate of John D. Rockefeller. The two women had known each other for more than a decade, and they formed a compatible match.

Her daughter Susanna, now a sophomore at Bryn Mawr, suffered what her friends considered a nervous breakdown. Susanna, hospitalized in Philadelphia, withdrew from her classes, and Frances arranged the best psychiatric care for her. She began to see Susanna frequently, driving from Washington to Philadelphia and back overnight. Frances and Susanna clashed frequently, making her recovery more difficult, but Susanna finally returned to Bryn Mawr to complete her sophomore year.

Frances Faces Impeachment

Frances ran into some trouble with her administration of immigration laws (then the province of the Labor Department), and some in Congress chose to begin impeachment proceedings against her. Charges against Frances stemmed from the successful waterfront strike in San Francisco in 1934. Harry Bridges, an Australian longshoreman, had led the city's workers to an unprecedented general strike, bringing workers together across traditional lines of particular industries. Mass worker actions, the dream of unionists, became a reality, and labor conditions improved across the board. However, businessmen, seeing their worst fears realized, immediately called for Bridges' deportation as a dangerous Communist. Foreigners who had pledged to work for the overthrow of the capitalist system were subject to deportation.

Bridges denied being a Communist, but his connections to Communists were investigated by the Department's immigration officials. The investigation was inconclusive. Frances attempted to ensure that Bridges got a fair hearing and refused to be stampeded into deporting a successful labor organizer on specious charges. As allegations intensified against Bridges, Frances was conducting a private inquiry among her contacts in San Francisco and learned that Bridges was a devoted Catholic, casting doubt on his alleged Communist leanings. Frances even had a talk with Bridges while in San Francisco.

She consulted with Roosevelt, who told her to carry out the law, but not too aggressively. A few months later, Frances set deportation hearings for Bridges. Courts began to rule against Communist-linked immigration cases, throwing such cases in question. The lawyers in the Labor Department favored a strategy of getting a case before the Supreme Court to decide the matter. Frances put her case against Bridges on hold, and the delay drove her critics crazy. In early 1938, the House of Representatives created a Special Committee to investigate Un-American Activities led by Texas Democrat Martin Dies. It generated publicity by arguing that Communism was a greater threat to the nation than Nazism, and accusing various federal employees of being Communists. Soon the Committee put Frances in its sights, and conservative newspapers fanned the flames by accusing her of protecting Communists. Dies specifically attacked Frances for refusing to deport Bridges.

Frances herself became the subject of investigations, and many wild rumors began to circulate, including reports that Frances' niece or her daughter were married to Bridges, or that Frances herself was his secret bride. Finally, in January 1939, Congressman J. Parnell Thomas, a New Jersey Republican introduced an impeachment charge against Frances and several top Labor Department officials. It alleged that they

> had failed, neglected, and refused to enforce the immigration laws of the United States; and have conspired together to violate the immigration laws of the Unites States; and have defrauded the United States by coddling and protecting from deportation certain aliens.

Even in a Congress dominated by Democrats, few rose to her defense.

Roosevelt never mentioned the impeachment events to her, nor did he take action to publicly support her. He did make light of the impeachment attempt in press conferences. In response to a question about the impeachment process, he pretended he had not heard, then said it was not yet time to discuss the matter.

Shaken by the events of this period, she again turned to the advice of her grandmother. Take the high ground. Avoid doing things that will make you appear silly or cheap. She remembered this advice, drew from her New England background, comported herself politely and courteously, hiding the rage she felt underneath. She went to church every morning and sought the support of a higher power.

Her impeachment hearing was held behind closed doors, though she had requested an open hearing. She laid out the facts of the Bridges case, then turned to a critique of the existing immigration laws. When she took questions, she realized that those who were "shaking in their wrath" were those who were angry at "undesirable aliens" who were contaminating the American way of life. She turned to the congressmen who asked her the most outrageous questions and mildly asked them to repeat themselves, knowing that nobody repeats a scurrilous thing a second time.

She left the hearing feeling that she had done the right thing, thinking she would not be impeached. But the hearing had exposed a disturbing split in the Democratic Party. Some members were becoming more conservative and reactionary than their Republican counterparts. Their loyalty to the President was rendered uncertain and undependable. On March 24, 1939, the House Committee unanimously ruled that there were not sufficient facts to support an impeachment charge, bringing the matter to an official close.

As Roosevelt approached his final Inauguration Day, Frances pressed him again to accept her resignation. He beseeched her not to go through with it yet. As Frances later wrote in her own book, FDR then said

> the beautiful words which I shall always think of as our parting; he said them in a voice filled with exhaustion, and I knew it was an effort to speak and that he was saying something that he felt. "Frances, you have done awfully well. I know what you have been through. I know what you have accomplished. Thank you." He put his hand over mine and gripped it. There were tears in our eyes. It was all the reward I could ever have asked – to know that he recognized the storms and trials I have faced in developing our program, to know that he appreciated the program and thought well of it, and that he was grateful.[11]

The two long-time colleagues took the opportunity to express what they had meant to each other through all their efforts to serve the public. Note that what Frances seemed to value most highly was Roosevelt's regard for "our program" they had built together. An article in the August 1944 edition of *Colliers* was titled "The Woman Nobody Knows," squarely identified the New Deal as the creation of Frances Perkins.[12]

The Death of Franklin Delano Roosevelt

Frances learned of Roosevelt's death at Warm Springs, Georgia, in a specially called Cabinet meeting, headed by the new president Harry S. Truman to share the news of the President's death. She went from there to a special church service at St. James Church across from the White House. After leaving the church, she went across the street to the White House gates to join a group of people huddled there. Frances stood next to a soldier, who spoke to her without looking at her. "I felt I knew him." Frances replied "Yes," and the young man paused. "I felt as if he knew me, and I felt as if he liked me," he said.[13]

Roosevelt's body arrived in Washington for a service in the White House, as directed by Eleanor. Frances felt that his popularity and impact demanded that he be given a service at the National Cathedral. Eleanor's composure, dignity, and grace during the service earned Frances's admiration. The mourners boarded a train to Hyde Park, where the president was to be laid to rest.

Frances received many letters of condolence from friends in the wake of FDR's death. She shared one of these with Eleanor, as they sat in the White House on the day Eleanor moved out. Frances's friend Charles Culp Burlingham's letter spoke to FDR's optimism in overcoming obstacles. To Frances, it was the defining characteristic of FDR. Burlingham wrote, "FDR was never disappointed, if things went wrong he took another tack."[14]

Final Years

With FDR's death, she was finally released from her Cabinet duties, as President Truman reluctantly accepted her resignation. Then-President Truman asked her to serve on the Civil Service Commission. Finishing her service in Washington in 1957, a young labor economist asked her to teach a course at Cornell. The job only paid about $10,000 a year, but she needed the money for her daughter's mental health care. She began her time at Cornell living in residential hotels, but then she was invited to live at Telluride House, a kind of fraternity house for some of Cornell's most gifted students. She was delighted by the invitation. While there, she drank bourbon with the boys and tolerated their music at all hours. She attended Monday house meetings, though rarely spoke. She gave them copies of Baltasar Gracian's *The Art of Worldly Wisdom*, a seventeenth-century guidebook by a Spanish Jesuit priest on how to retain one's integrity in the halls of power. Some of the boys had trouble understanding how this small, charming, and unassuming old lady could have played such an important historical role.[15]

She died alone, in a hospital, on May 14, 1965, at age 85. Some of the Telluride boys served as pallbearers. The minister read the "be ye steadfast" passage from I Corinthians as Perkins herself had done upon her graduation at the Mount Holyoke College more than six decades earlier.

Frances Perkins led a summoned life, a life in service to a calling. As David Brooks put it in his book *The Road to Character:*

> Perkins did not so much choose her life. She responded to the call of a felt necessity. A person who embraces a calling doesn't take a direct route to self-fulfillment. She is willing to surrender the things that are most dear, and by seeking to forget herself and submerge herself she finds a purpose that defines and fulfills herself. Such vocations almost always involve tasks that transcend a lifetime. They almost always involve throwing yourself into a historical process. They involve compensating for the brevity of life by finding membership in a historic commitment.[16]

Epilogue

The life of Frances Perkins stands as a testament to what a single person can contribute to their times. She was able to overcome being the solitary woman in a hyper-masculine world, the mental illness of her husband and daughter, decades of political battles and negative press, and the constant crush of obligations, commitments, and new ideas that she had to manage. She was an expert at building and managing "networks" before working with them was even recognized as a necessary skill.

She built Roosevelt's reputation as a man who could use the instruments of government to solve enormous social problems, whose effects were felt at the individual level. An examination of how the New Deal was developed and implemented reveals Frances Perkins standing at the center of it all, working her way through a list of policy proposals and never stopping until the general welfare was secured. It is accurate to say that she made a lifetime study of her principal boss, Franklin Roosevelt, to understand how to work with him and to be the most effective public servant she could be in his administration. She helped him define his agenda, develop specific policies, work for their passage in Congress, and work to implement them in the executive agencies. She was a complete public servant in the fullest sense – developing big ideas, turning them into legislative language, lobbying for their passage in Congress, implementing them in the appropriate agencies. Her career was a showcase of her skills in policy-making, consultation with affected parties, and mapping and carrying out implementation efforts.

Notes

1 Downey, Kirstin. *The Woman Behind the New Deal: The Life and Legacy of Frances Perkins – Social Security, Unemployment Insurance. and the Minimum Wage* (Anchor Books, a Division of Random House, Inc., New York, NY, 2010), page 13.
2 Ibid., page 26.
3 Ibid., page 36.
4 David Brooks, *The Road to Character* (Random House, New York, NY, 2015), pages 23 and 25.
5 Ibid., page 34.
6 Ibid., page 41.
7 During my time managing programs and organizations at the U.S. Environmental Protection Agency, transitions to a new administration, or the arrival of a new politically appointed assistant secretary required briefings of new leaders by those of us in the career staff, to familiarize them with the programs for which they were now responsible. These "transition briefings" that I would conduct always had three components: first, we would explain how the programs operated, including who were the customers and stakeholders, and the base of resources to conduct the program; second, we alerted the incoming appointee about "short-fuse" items, where there was an imminent decision to be made, which needed to be handled carefully so as not to "blow up in the face" of the new boss; third, we offered up some ideas for specific, longer term "legacy" actions that could be taken to build a record of accomplishment during their tenure in the job. By organizing transition briefings in this way, we felt we prepared the new political appointee with the information necessary to both make progress and avoid pitfalls.
8 Kirstin Downey, *The Woman Behind the New Deal, the Life and Legacy of Frances Perkins – Social Security, Unemployment Insurance, and the Minimum Wage*, 2010. page 123.

9 Ibid., page 131. Contrast Roosevelt's summoning of the American people to face the challenge of economic hard times with President Donald Trump's handling of the onset of the Covid-19 virus in 2020. Roosevelt trusts that the American people can handle the news and says, "In every dark hour of our national life, a leadership of frankness and vigor has met with that understanding and support of the people themselves which is essential to victory." Trump's approach to communicating about the virus, as told to Bob Woodward in his book *Rage* (Simon & Schuster, New York, NY, 2020) was to "downplay" the virus because he did not want to "panic" the American people. He told them that the virus would be short-lived, it would dissipate with the warmer weather, the meager number of early cases was under control and was not the harbinger of the inevitable public health emergency that followed, and that his own experts were predicting. Trump seemed to fear that he would be made to own the virus and the sacrifices necessary to suppress it. He showed no signs of trusting the American people to accept the warning, do what was necessary to suppress the virus, and be patient with the economic consequences. He also failed to model the behavior that he should have been urging everyone to follow.

10 Downey, *The Woman Behind the New Deal*, page 166.

11 Frances Perkins, *The Roosevelt I Knew* (Penguin Group, New York, NY, 1946), page 377.

12 Downey, *The Woman Behind the New Deal*, page 312.

13 Downey, ibid., page 344.

14 Downey, ibid., page 346.

15 Brooks, *The Road to Character*, page 45.

16 Brooks, ibid., page 46.

Bibliography

Brooks, David. *The Road to Character*. New York, NY: Random House, 2010.

Downey, Kirstin. *The Woman Behind the New Deal: The Life and Legacy of Frances Perkins, Social Security, Unemployment Insurance*. New York, NY: Anchor Books, 2010.

Perkins, Frances. *The Roosevelt I Knew*. New York, NY: Penguin Classics, 2011.

"Summoned: Frances Perkins and the General Welfare," dir. by Mick Caouette and Joe Paolo. PBS American Experience Series, South Hill Films, 2020.

15

GEORGE C. MARSHALL

From Soldier to Statesman – *Implementing the Plan to Save Europe*

George Catlett Marshall was born on December 31, 1880. Though he was born in Uniontown, Pennsylvania, his family's history and tradition were rooted in Virginia. His ancestors included Thomas Marshall, who fought alongside George Washington in the French and Indian War. He was also a collateral descendent

DOI: 10.4324/9781003266235-17

of John Marshall, the former secretary of state and Supreme Court Chief Justice. But George's father was a failed businessman who favored George's older brother. Periodic illnesses and a slow start to his education were features of a difficult boyhood.

By the time George Marshall began his enrollment at the Virginia Military Institute (VMI) in Lexington, Virginia, he had a mind of logical rigor and precision, which fit well in VMI's culture of discipline and austerity. Marshall had an unusual capacity for these traits. The VMI environment prized the Virginia code of chivalry, promoting a sense of service, gentlemanly conduct, and a dignified bearing. These elements combined in Marshall to give him "extraordinary self-command, the hallmark trait that would come to define his unusual brand of charisma."[1]

In 1914, Marshall was stationed in the Philippines as a 34-year-old captain, when he caught the eye of his commanding officer who told the other officers of his high expectations of Marshall. He was promoted to colonel during World War I and was responsible for planning some of the largest and most successful operations of the war. Based on Marshall's successes, General John J. "Black Jack" Pershing, chief of the American Expeditionary force, scooped up Marshall as his aide. Pershing became a father figure to Marshall, protecting, mentoring, and championing his military career.

At the end of World War I, Pershing recommended Marshall for promotion to brigadier general. But with the return of peacetime, promotions to these positions were frozen, halting Marshall's ascent and consigning him to a series of disappointing positions for the next 20 years. During this time, Marshall lost his first wife Lilly, to whom he was devoted. He also married his second wife, a former actress named Katherine Topper. It appeared for a time that Marshall, now age 59 and only a one-star general, would never get his chance to ascend to higher ranks. But then something unprecedented happened. On Pershing's recommendation, President Franklin Roosevelt reached past 20 major generals and 14 senior brigadier generals to choose Brigadier General George Marshall as Chief of Staff of the U.S. Army.

Eight hours before he was to be sworn in as Chief of Staff, he received word at 3 a.m. that the Germans had invaded Poland. Marshall had inherited the reins of an army of fewer than 200,000 men, ranked 19th in the world, behind Portugal and Bulgaria. His army was ill-equipped and poorly trained.

When Roosevelt offered the Chief of Staff position to Marshall, he warned Roosevelt that he would speak his mind and he wanted to have the right to say what he thought at all times. He insisted that the President not call him George, but General Marshall. He never visited Hyde Park, Roosevelt's estate in New York. He did not laugh at Roosevelt's jokes. He felt it was essential to maintain full independence. Marshall made it clear that he would not be susceptible to Roosevelt's famed charm and powers of manipulation.

After December 7, 1941, Marshall worked seven days a week, seated at his desk by 7:30 a.m., and worked with a ruthless efficiency that terrified his subordinates. During the darkest days of the war in 1942, he seemed to become calmer, recalling that when he worked for Pershing, it was damaging to morale when his staff perceived Pershing as tired or forlorn, so he would not allow himself to lose his temper or show signs of frustration. "I cannot afford the luxury of sentiment, mine must be a cold logic." His wife later wrote that during those years, "it was as though he lived outside of himself and George Marshall was someone he was constantly appraising, advising and training to meet a situation."[2] Marshall also had an even and gracious manner, an ever-present sense of justice, and an evident humanity. He wrote thousands of letters to grieving widows and families of fallen soldiers.

In 1943, as the war began to turn in the right direction for the Allies, their representatives met in Tehran around Thanksgiving Day and agreed on opening a long-anticipated second front with an invasion of Nazi-occupied France. They would have to decide on a general to lead the invasion, and Roosevelt initially wanted Marshall for the assignment. Speaking to Eisenhower in a military plane over Tunisia, Roosevelt said,

> I hate to think that fifty years from now practically nobody will know who George Marshall was. That is why I want George to have the big command. He is entitled to have his place in history as a great general.

Eisenhower did not disagree. Marshall had a commanding vision of each theater of war. He was masterful with Congress and had more experience than Eisenhower. But the notion of Eisenhower serving as Chief of Staff and commanding Marshall was, to say the least, awkward. Roosevelt met with Marshall to try to get him to state a preference, but Marshall refused, saying he would serve in whatever position the President asked. Roosevelt, upon further reflection, decided to give the command to Eisenhower. Roosevelt told Marshall. "I feel I could not sleep at night with you out of the country." Marshall never complained or expressed regret to anyone about Roosevelt's decision to select Eisenhower.

On V-E Day, the day that Hitler's forces surrendered, Secretary of War Henry Stimson called a dozen generals and assorted officers into his office. After they had gathered, Stimson began to speak directly to Marshall:

> I have never seen a task of such magnitude performed by man. It is rare in life to make new friends; at my age it is a slow process but there is no one whom I have such deep respect and I think greater affection. I have seen many great soldiers in my lifetime and you, sir, are the finest soldier I have ever known.

Four months later, after the surrender of Japan, Stimson wrote a letter to President Truman to sum up Marshall's contribution:

> His mind has guided the grand strategy of our campaigns ... It was his mind and character that carried through the trans-Channel campaign against Germany ... Similarly, his views have controlled the Pacific campaign although he has been most modest and careful in recognizing the role of the Navy. His views guided Mr. Roosevelt throughout. The construction of the American Army has been entirely the fruit of his initiative and supervision. Likewise its training ... With this Army we have won a most difficult dual war with practically no serious setbacks and astonishingly "according to plan" ... Show me any war in history which has produced a general with such a surprisingly perfect record as his in this greatest and most difficult of all wars in history.[3]

After the war, Marshall wanted only to return to his estate in Leesburg, Virginia, which he and his wife had dreamed of returning to for many years. He wanted to return home to enjoy his days as a private citizen. But the day after he returned to his estate, he received a call from President Truman, asking him to mediate the civil war in China, an almost impossible mission. Marshall agreed to the mission and hoped he could return expeditiously to Leesburg. But Secretary of State Byrnes tendered his resignation in April 1946 and Marshall again agreed to serve, this time as Secretary of State. Truman remarked on the occasion, "The more I see and talk to him, the more certain I am he's the great one of the age." When he agreed to serve as Secretary of State, speculation began to swirl immediately that he was going to be a candidate for President. Marshall quelled these rumors quickly with a statement, which said, "I will never become involved in political matters, and therefore, I cannot be considered a candidate for any political office." He was taken at his word, and his nomination breezed through the Senate Foreign Relations Committee without a hearing or opposition and was approved unanimously by the full Senate.

Rescuing Europe

Conference of Foreign Ministers

On March 9, 1947, George Marshall and his American delegation arrived in Moscow for a conference with Foreign Ministers of the Allies about the governance of Europe, including which of the Allies would control which of the European countries now attempting to recover from the war. In his large delegation was John Foster Dulles, considered at the time the senior diplomat in the Republican Party, whom Marshall had invited at the request of Republican Senator Arthur Vandenberg. The agenda for the conference included a peace treaty for Austria, border issues in Eastern Europe, claims for war reparations, and the number one issue would be the control of Germany, which many at the conference considered to be the biggest obstacle for lasting European peace. Shortly after the Allies defeated Germany, they had assumed four-part control, with the United States, the Soviet Union, Great Britain, and France all responsible for administration in their sphere, and the powers collectively responsible for administering joint national policy in the Allied Control Council (ACC). Even before the conference, there had been repeated disagreements regarding reparations, Germany's level of production, and other policy matters. The eastern zone, administered by the Soviet Union, was agriculturally oriented, rich in foodstuffs, but poor in industry. The western zone was administered by Great Britain and was the industrial heartland, rich in coal resources, and the core of Germany's war-making capacity. France insisted that Germany's industrial production remain low to prevent it from re-emerging as a security threat. In the meantime, the Soviets were consolidating their economic and political ties in the eastern zone.

As Europe's economic fortunes continued to plummet in the spring of 1947, a new view was beginning to take hold among the American officials involved in the negotiations. They were coming to believe that Germany's rehabilitation was the key to Europe's economic troubles. This view held that the whole economy of Europe was interlinked with the German economy – i.e., keeping Germany in chains, meant keeping Europe in rags. There was, however, much sympathy for the French position of wariness toward the Germans (having been at war with the Germans three times in the last three generations), and Marshall considered the future of France crucial and was aware of the fragility of her internal politics. The Americans saw the oncoming Soviet threat as overshadowing the German one. By January 1947, the scenario most dreaded was Soviet control of Germany and its industrial capacity. Over the course of 1947, America's and Great Britain's interests concerning Germany had converged and concerns about Soviet intentions brought them together.

The conference in Moscow opened on March 10, and by the fifth day, Marshall and the Soviet Union's long-time Foreign Minister Vyacheslav Molotov began to clash over Germany, with the Soviets showing little interest in finding solutions. On March 17, one week into the conference, Molotov brought up the subject of war reparations he felt the Soviet Union had been promised at earlier wartime conferences, arguing that the substantial sacrifices made by the Soviet Union entitled it to the funds. But as Marshall and Great Britain's Foreign Secretary Ernest Bevin saw it, Europe and Germany's economic difficulties were the paramount problem and had placed the reparations questions in a new light. Molotov would not agree to anything until the reparations demand had been met, so it became the ostensible sticking point for the next several weeks. On March 24, Bevin went to the Kremlin to speak with Soviet Premier Joseph Stalin, who was conciliatory and reassuring, though noncommittal. Bevin left the Stalin meeting with more confidence in the prospects of the conference. On April 2, the conference had achieved no meaningful agreement on economic matters, so it moved on to a discussion of the political organization of Germany. The Soviets were alone in urging a strong central government for Germany, interpreted by the American and Great Britain representatives as a preference that would allow them to steer Germany toward their political sphere. This discussion went on for a week, and Marshall moved the conference to the next question. The atmosphere had become strained, with Molotov greeting almost every proposal with counterproposals, amendments, and delays.

Convinced that they would have to act alone, Marshall and Bevin began having daily lunches together, mapping out a strategy for Germany. They decided to try once more to get Molotov to agree to their proposal for demilitarizing Germany. But Molotov responded by offering crippling amendments, and Bevin, now very frustrated at the lack of progress over five weeks of the conference, said, "If we cannot agree to the basic first step of keeping Germany disarmed and unable to wage war, we have indicated to the world a complete lack of unity of purpose in our approach to the German settlement."[4]

Both Bevin and French Foreign Minister Bidault had already had their separate meetings with Stalin, but Marshall had preferred to wait until the negotiations were farther along and most cards were on the table before meeting with Stalin. After 30 fruitless meetings at the Conference, on April 15, Marshall set up his meeting with Stalin. Marshall and Stalin had found ways of cooperating on military matters during the war, and Marshall knew Stalin as a man of his word. He told Stalin he was trained as a soldier and not a diplomat, so he would speak as a soldier, directly and without double meaning. He revealed that he was disappointed at the depth of misunderstanding and differences that were evident at the conference. He explained the U.S. position on Germany, reparations, and the demilitarization proposal and said that it was the U.S. hope that they could do what they could to restore those countries that had suffered economic deterioration and prevent their economic collapse. Stalin reassured him that cooperation would be possible, asserting the economic unity was possible, but would be meaningless without political unity. He desired a strong central government for Germany, so it could not be divided. Stalin and Marshall took turns rehashing their own interpretations of issues discussed at the conference. Stalin's parting words indicated that he did not share Marshall's grave concern about the conference, and he claimed to be more optimistic that agreement on all the main issues was possible.

After his meeting with Stalin, Marshall realized that there was little prospect of any meaningful agreement at the conference. April 24 was the last session of the conference. Marshall and Bevin met and agreed to increase the level of production in their respective zones of Germany, hoping to drive recovery in the rest of the region. On the flight home, as he was reflecting on the discussions at the conference, Marshall became resolved to address Europe's problems with a bold stroke. On Monday April 28, Marshall addressed the nation on a radio broadcast to report on the Foreign Minister's conference. He said prospects for cooperation with the Soviet Union were not good, confirmed that conditions in Western Europe were dire, and that Europe's recovery was essential to U.S. interests. "Disintegrating forces are becoming evident." To stress the urgency of the moment, Marshall put it in plain terms: "the patient is dying while the doctors deliberate."

In mid-March, President Truman addressed a joint session of Congress about aiding Greece and Turkey in their resistance to Soviet aggression. Truman said the United States should take up the responsibility history had placed on its shoulders. It should provide military and financial aid to Greece and Turkey, assuming the role in the Mediterranean that Britain had vacated. Truman spoke in strong and sweeping rhetoric, seemingly committing the United States to support any government anywhere in the world that would stand against "Communist subversion." It was labeled the Truman Doctrine. Marshall found the idea initially irresponsible (especially its sweeping language), but agreed that the United States had a greater role to play in the postwar world, and agreed with the need for strategic provision of aid.

Developing the Plan

After delivering his radio address upon his return from the Moscow conference, Marshall summoned George Kennan, his director of the newly formed Policy Planning Staff, at the State Department to make an assignment to the policy staff.[5] Marshall had decided to move on a plan to aid Europe. Furthermore, if he did not move quickly, Congress would begin to propose ideas, and Marshall felt very strongly that the State Department should lead the enterprise and frame the terms of the debate. Marshall told Kennan that he wanted a report with recommendations on his desk in two weeks. His primary instruction to Kennan was to "Avoid trivia."

Reeling from Marshall's request, Kennan began to look for the sharpest minds in the State Department (on economic, military, and strategic matters) for his workgroup. He found several economists, all working for Will Clayton, Undersecretary of State for Economic Affairs.[6] While Kennan began work with his group on the plan Marshall had requested, President Truman was scheduled to give a speech at Baylor University on U.S. foreign economic leadership in early March 1947, which was to be drafted by Clayton and Dean Acheson, Assistant Secretary of State. During the drafting of the Baylor address, Clayton reached the conclusion that the time for vague warnings had passed. In an internal memo, Clayton called for a concerted U.S. program for European recovery, with an appropriation of $5 billion in the first year to be followed by comparable amounts for several years. He felt that Europe needed more than dollars, but also structural economic reform. In early April, Clayton went to Europe, ostensibly to participate in tariff negotiations but also to see for himself what the situation was on the ground in Europe. He solicited views from old business contacts, selected diplomats, economists, leading industrialists, and he took long walks to talk to shopkeepers. Europe was in far worse shape than he had anticipated.

In the working sessions of Kennan's group, two important ideas were identified. First, the group was convinced that German recovery was essential for Europe's recovery. Second, they also believed that to achieve economic self-sustainability, Europe would have to integrate its disparate national economies. During early May, Truman had to bow out of a speech he was scheduled to give at Delta State Teachers College in Cleveland, Mississippi, so Acheson was asked to substitute for Truman. In his speech, Acheson laid out the problem facing the United States resulting from European economic difficulties. He described Europe as on "the borderline of starvation" and plagued by economic and commercial dislocation. Acheson deeply believed that it was now America's turn to accept the mantle of world leadership, saying it was "our duty and our privilege as human beings" to do so. The speech got little attention in the United States, but before leaving Washington, Acheson had met with three of his British media contacts to give them some advance warning about the speech. It received greater coverage in Europe, with the *Times* of London printing the entire text. When Acheson returned to Washington, *New York Times* reporter James Reston discussed the implications of the speech with Acheson and asked Truman at a press conference if the Acheson speech represented administration policy. Truman answered "Yes" it did. By the middle of May 1947, the State Department was fully mobilized behind the formulation of a policy on European recovery, and the U.S. media began to notice.

In an April 5 column in the *Washington Post*, columnist Walter Lippmann told his readers that Europe was threatened with nothing less than collapse, reporting what he said responsible people were saying, though not publically as yet. He said that political and economic measures of a scale, which no one dared to suggest, would be needed in the next year or so. In a follow-up column on the subject on May 1, Lippmann began to discuss the features and objectives of a recovery plan. Based on the outcome of the Moscow Conference, Lippmann asserted that Russian cooperation was not possible, and the United States would need to support Western Europe alone, if necessary. He further urged that Europe's countries meet to formulate a common plan for their economies. Lippmann's columns planted seeds among his wide readership. In the State Department, the reaction to Lipmann's columns stimulated more strategic thinking and greater speed and furnished junior colleagues with a means to advocate with senior officials. One columnist asserted that State Department strategists had come around to the view that "one way of combatting Communism is to give Europe a full dinner pail."

This speculation about a recovery plan unnerved Marshall and turned up the heat on Kennan. On May 23, Kennan submitted a 13-page memorandum to Dean Acheson with recommendations for a plan to promote European recovery. The fundamental objective of the plan was to provide Europe a self-sustained economic recovery. In addition, Kennan believed that the psychological effect of the plan was an essential part of its impact. The United States needed to provide hope and confidence. Kennan said "… much of the value of the European recovery program will lie not so much in its direct economic effects, which are difficult to calculate with any degree of accuracy, as in its psychological and political by-products." Kennan's memo further stated that "the initiative be taken in Europe and that the main burden be borne by the governments of that area." Kennan had done a brilliant job of combining all the disparate viewpoints discussed in the department and elsewhere in the government.

On his return from Europe, Will Clayton had written a four-page memorandum. His time in Europe had convinced him of the necessity of immediate and bold action. At his request, a meeting was set up with Marshall. The Clayton memo had jolted both Acheson and Marshall. It was now clear that policymakers had underestimated the war's toll on the European economy. The physical destruction of property was obvious to see, but the effects of economic dislocation on production were harder to detect and analyze. Clayton believed that Europe was steadily deteriorating and its political condition was also faltering. Clayton believed there was a real threat to the economy of the United States if Europe collapsed. He had also framed the broad features of a plan, saying it would require $6 or $7 billion of U.S. aid per year for three years. He said the "three-year grant would be based on a European plan which the principal European nations should work out," putting Clayton in agreement with others about one of the principal components of the plan.

The Harvard Commencement Speech

Five months into his tenure as Secretary of State, Marshall was asked to speak at Harvard University's 286th commencement, the first "normal" graduation ceremony since the United States had entered World War II five years earlier. Upon accepting his degree, Harvard President James Conant read the citation, which said that Marshall was "an American to whom Freedom owes an enduring debt of gratitude … a soldier and statesman whose ability and character brook only one comparison in the history of the nation." The comparison was to George Washington.[7]

But Marshall's primary mission that day was not to receive an award and bask in the adulation. No one in attendance knew it, but he was there to give an address that would transform Europe, reconfigure the international order, and launch America forward as a modern superpower with global responsibilities. Marshall spoke in a low and monotonal voice and read speeches in an uninteresting way, never looking up from his text. But Marshal began to lay out Europe's dire economic condition, its dysfunctionality, and its vulnerability. Marshall called for this period of drift to come to an end, stating that the time for action had arrived. He then spelled out in a few simple paragraphs the elements and the contours of the

Plan that would soon come to bear his name. People who heard the speech failed to pick up on its significance, American broadcast media networks did not cover it, and American newspapers were dismissive, most only giving it a few lines.

Marshall had deliberately downplayed the speech, doing little to attract attention to what he was proposing. The British journalists who had lunched with Acheson before his speech in Mississippi did not initially recognize the Harvard speech as the one delivering the plan about which Acheson had told them. But on the other side of the Atlantic, British Foreign Secretary Ernest Bevin did not miss the significance of the speech when he heard it on the BBC: "It was like a lifeline to sinking men. It seemed to bring hope where there was none. The generosity of it was beyond my belief." In spite of Marshall's lackluster delivery, Bevin felt it was "one of the greatest speeches made in world history." In later years, Senator Arthur Vandenberg talked of the "electric effect of a few sentences in quiet sequence."[8]

Marshall stated the objective of the plan was the "revival of a working economy in the world so as to permit the reemergence of political and social conditions in which free institutions can exist." The United States would provide essential aid for three or four years – on a specific time line – to bridge Europe to self-sustainability. The consequences to the United States were apparent – there could be no political stability and no assured peace as long as Europe's economy was stuck in desperation and dysfunction. The plan was rooted in U.S. security and economic interests. Marshall said the "U.S. policy is directed not against any country or doctrine, but in opposition to hunger, poverty, desperation, and chaos." Further, Marshall said that the United States did not wish to dictate terms to participating countries. Instead, the United States wished to empower and embolden Europe to assume control of its own destiny, with the United States serving as a constructive partner. The program "should be a joint one, agreed to by a number, if not all European nations."[9]

Thus, with a few brief paragraphs, Marshall had introduced his plan and delivered his invitation to European nations. Finishing his prepared remarks, Marshall looked out over the scene and offered his impromptu final lines:

> We are remote from the scene of these troubles. It is virtually impossible at this distance merely by reading or even seeing photographs and motion pictures to grasp at all the real significance of the situation. Yet the whole world's future hangs on a proper judgment of just what can best be done, what must be done.

The response to Marshall's proposal in the Harvard speech was very positive. It was an offer to gain resources for European recovery, with the countries being invited to steer the resources in the right direction. Bevin immediately recognized the urgent need for the European countries to get organized to respond to Marshall's offer. The Communist parties of many European countries waited for

Moscow's response. The Soviet ambassador to the United States cabled Moscow with an analysis of the Marshall speech, asserting that the plan was an attempt to stave off collapse in America and Western Europe, and to create an anti-Soviet bloc in the West.

At the White House, presidential aide Clark Clifford suggested to Truman that the emerging plan be called the Truman Plan. Truman wanted to call it the Marshall Plan, to honor Marshall who had taken the lead on European recovery since the Moscow Conference. Naming it the Marshall Plan was also a shrewd political calculation by Truman, since there was an election coming, the Republicans held an overwhelming majority in Congress, and any plan sent to them with Truman's name on it would die a quick death in Congress.

Truman, Marshall, and the others hoping to get approval from Congress knew they would need strong bipartisan support. To achieve that support, they began to look to Arthur Hendrick Vandenberg,[10] the veteran senator from Michigan and a former newspaper editor, who was serving as the Chairman of the Senate Foreign Relations Committee. During his Senate career, he had evolved from Wilsonian internationalist to isolationist. But on January 10, 1945, Vandenberg rose in the Senate to deliver a speech which he had rewritten a dozen times. Vandenberg said that the Atlantic and Pacific were no longer impassable moats; America would have to engage with the rest of the world, broadening the nation's range of commitments. The speech marked a complete break with the foreign policy outlook that he had not only espoused but also had come to embody. It was, therefore, a philosophical about-face, and a courageous political act. Its bipartisan nature was stunning, the kind of act that would not be possible today, given America's current sharp partisan divide.

Reaction was significant: the *Cleveland Plain Dealer* called it "a shot heard round the world," Walter Lippmann and James Reston lauded Vandenberg, and Dean Acheson, using his talent for condescension, called the speech the capstone in Vandenberg's "long day's journey into our times." Vandenberg's reversal seemed to welcome others who had shared his ongoing conversion from internationalism to isolationism and back to internationalism. In late May 1947, when James Reston wrote a detailed account of the Plan being formulated in the State Department, Vandenberg was irate about being kept "out of the loop" about the plan. Marshall went immediately to Vandenberg to offer his case for aid and to hear the senator's views. Vandenberg left the meeting supportive of Marshall's efforts.

In a White House meeting on June 22, which included Truman, Marshall, Acheson, and other key advisors, Vandenberg suggested creating several committees for the governance of the Plan. The most important of the committees would be to assess the Plan's feasibility given American economic needs, offering recommendations for carrying out the Plan. The committee would be composed of leading national figures from business, academia, and public life. Truman, who had worked with Vandenberg in the Senate and had a good relationship with him, liked his ideas for the committee. Secretary of Commerce Averell Harriman was selected to chair the committee, which would have 16 members and would be known as the Harriman Committee. Arthur Vandenberg was making possible a bipartisan spirit for the committee. And as the Committee began, two questions loomed over the fledging Marshall Plan: would the Europeans be able to come together? And what would the Russians do?

Bevin Organizes Europe

Britain's Foreign Secretary Ernest Bevin immediately set out for Paris to have two days of discussions with Georges Bidault. They agreed to form steering committees for reconstruction in key areas such as coal, food, steel, and transport. They also agreed that the Soviets should be invited to participate, but they were not going to permit any delay. Indeed, Bevin and Bidault publicly invited Russia to join in discussions about organizing for the Marshall Plan. The Soviet press expressed the official skepticism of the government, describing the Marshall Plan by saying its purpose was "quick formation of a notorious western bloc under unconditional and absolute leadership of American imperialism."[11] The Soviets agreed to participate in discussions but whether they would work cooperatively or try to block progress remained to be seen.

When the conference opened, Molotov was unusually agreeable in tone and temperament, and he began with a series of questions about what information France and Britain had received from the United States about the details of the Harvard speech, and whether France and Britain had reached any agreements in their earlier conversations about Marshall's ideas. Molotov then proposed that the parties ask the Americans for the exact sum that they were prepared to advance for European recovery. Bevin objected, explaining the American decision about aid would require Congressional action, that Marshall was unable in his speech to offer a specific amount, and that he had merely invited the Europeans to develop a proposal. Further, Bevin stated, it is not the place of debtors to set our conditions to their potential creditors. The parties ended their discussion amicably after four hours, and Bevin and Bidault wondered if the Soviets would continue to participate.

They did not have to wait long for an answer. On the evening of July 1, Molotov sent a cable to Stalin expressing his conclusion that there was no possibility of agreement with Bevin and Bidault. Molotov had asked for time to consider the most recent French proposal, and he owed an answer to the conference about the Soviet view. Stalin's vital need was to maintain control over his eastern sphere, since those states held resources vital to the Soviet Union to fuel their economy. The United States had hoped to lure the Eastern European countries with the promise of aid and economic integration with the West. Stalin could not permit Soviet participation in the Marshall Plan. On July 2, on the fifth and final meeting of the conference, the Soviets showed their hand. After a series of false accusations leveled by Molotov, it became clear that he was ushering the Soviet Union out of participating in the Marshall Plan. Bevin told Molotov that he and Bidault were going to work with those states that wanted to participate in the restoration of war-torn Europe. Bevin told an aide during the meeting that they were witnessing "the birth of the Western bloc."[12]

Bevin and Bidault had performed brilliantly and had now formed a firm axis. The Soviet attitude was now apparent and their obstruction from within would no longer be a delay to recovery. Stalin had instructed Molotov to walk out of the conference because he could not risk Eastern European participation and the loosening of his grip on the region. Stalin had now brought the United States and other capitalist nations together in a grand enterprise to save capitalism and liberal democracy and to prevent European domination by a single totalitarian power. He drove the United States to Europe's aid and he drove the United States into what was becoming a new economic and political bloc and put the United States into a position of being the pre-eminent world power.

Before leaving the conference in Paris, Bevin and Bidault compiled a list of European nations to be invited to a follow-up conference to devise and present a collective request for U.S. aid. The conference was to be held in Paris and would be called the Conference of European Nations. It called for a steering committee to oversee six specialized subcommittees that would each tackle a dimension of Europe's economy. Moscow cabled its ambassadors in Eastern Europe to explain that the Soviet Union had pulled out of the Marshall Plan, but it did not want its Eastern European satellites to do so, instructing them to accept their invitations to the conference. Once there, their objective was to sabotage the plan and not to allow the unanimous adoption of the plan. The satellites were to withdraw from the meeting, taking with them as many delegates from other countries as possible.

Not long after this cable, the Soviets sent a second cable rescinding the first and instructing their satellites not to attend, so all of their satellites withdrew from the conference, except for Czechoslovakia. President Woodrow Wilson created the state after World War I and ensured that it was grounded in democratic traditions. But after having created Czechoslovakia, the West in 1938 had surrendered it to Hitler and the Nazis. Thereafter, a tacit agreement was in place that the Czechs would support the Soviet Union in foreign affairs in return for its independence in domestic matters. Czechoslovakia was currently in need of agricultural goods and financial assistance and they viewed the Marshall Plan as potentially a huge help to their economy. Stalin called the Czech officials who were planning to participate in the conference to Moscow, where he made clear that they were not to participate in deliberations about the Marshall Plan.

The Paris Conference

On Saturday, July 12, the Paris Conference was called to order. The conference agreed to set up a steering committee and a series of technical committees to study Europe's needs and potential for inter-European cooperation. A working committee was appointed to produce a report on the rules and organization for the conference. To get organized, each country attending the conference had to complete a questionnaire describing its resources and its economic state of affairs. Some countries were uneasy about revealing details about their own economies to international scrutiny, in the process showing their weaknesses and vulnerabilities. Britain, for example, was reluctant to expose too much information about its faltering economy.

During the summer of 1947, Will Clayton held a series of low-profile meetings with leading officials and heads of state in Europe. In spite of his efforts to maintain a low profile, the *New York Times* was calling him the U.S. "ambassador to Europe." He had long-standing relationships in Europe, and the stature at the State Department to engage in matters with a degree of latitude. He met with the Executive Committee and stressed the need to produce a report that would help passage through Congress. The report should define a path for getting Europe back on its feet in four years. He tracked the progress at the Conference to make sure that the initiative could be handled by the Europeans.

In early July, Dean Acheson decided to leave the State Department. His position as Undersecretary of State was filled by Robert Lovett, who had served as the deputy secretary of the War Department during World War II. He had Acheson's sharp intellect, but unlike Acheson, he had an easy and genial manner that would make him valuable in dealing with members of Congress. Meanwhile, George Kennan was becoming increasingly alarmed about economic deterioration in Europe. He noted, however, that the Marshall Plan was making it clear that the Communist parties in Europe were trying to slow or block recovery. Also in July, an article appeared in *Foreign Affairs* titled "The Sources of Soviet Conduct," its author listed only as "X." It offered an explanation for Soviet behavior and offered a prescription for meeting the Soviet threat, summoning the United States to begin "a policy of firm containment, designed to confront the Russians with counterforce every time they show signs of encroaching on the interests of a peaceful and stable world."[13] It soon became clear that the author of the article was George Kennan, and his prescription became the organizing concept of the U.S. strategy for the next 40 years: the "containment" of the Soviet Union.

The Conference began to bog down as the attendees began to lose their comity and began to advocate for their national interests. Cooperation began to be replaced by arguing. One impasse involved Great Britain. While the French and the Americans favored maximum European integration, Churchill was calling for a "United States of Europe," and the Labour Party was concerned about integration interfering with British national policy, specifically, the lowering of protective barriers that would subject its labor force and its industry to competition from lower cost producers. A second impasse involved France, the main preoccupation of which was Germany. The French Communists were propagandizing that the Marshall Plan would build Germany up, and they stoked political tensions in France. The conference bogged down over this issue for a period of weeks as economic conditions continued to get worse. American ambassadors began to report that the countries in which they were working were within weeks of economic collapse. That summer John Foster Dulles was sent as an emissary for the Truman Administration on a secret mission to assess the probability of a civil war in France. He reported back that the situation was desperate and the United States needed to do something to bolster the current French government.

Extending past its September 1 deadline, the conference looked like it was failing at its task of developing a plan to apply U.S. funds to the recovery of Europe. American support for a European solution was waning as it appeared that the Europeans were incapable of developing a plan that could pass muster in the U.S. Congress. Feeling that the United States had made a good faith effort to empower Europe to develop a proposal, George Kennan offered two key prescriptions to ensure that the Europeans could remain viable to receive aid. First, he suggested that the European's report from the conference be proffered as a preliminary report to be used only as the basis for continuing discussions. This would give the Plan's supporters greater latitude in upcoming discussions with legislators. Second, Kennan argued that the United States would not be able to formulate a long-term Plan while Europe was mired in desperation. Interim aid was necessary to support Europe, and after Europe was relieved, the United States could then assume the needed long-term perspective.[14] This was a classic "moving the goal posts" strategy. Others in Washington began to pick up the torch for the idea of interim aid. Lovett began to add to the explanation about interim aid, pointing out that the interim aid would give Congress the time it needed to consider all the implications of approving the larger aid package that was to become the Marshall Plan.

In spite of the report's shortcomings, it was still an important achievement. The participating countries had overcome significant doubts, and at least partially subsumed self-interests. They had bet on the United States as an honest broker and showed a level of trust in each other, and as they said in their introduction, the report marks the advent of a new state of European economic cooperation. The Paris Conference and the report it produced took the first steps toward European unification and were the harbinger of the European Union that would follow decades later.

Life magazine called it perhaps "the most important decision of the 20th Century." If it worked, "the Marshall Plan will have proved to be the D-Day of the peace." So Marshall, who was passed over by Roosevelt for the command of the D-Day invasion, and was chosen by Truman to lead the development of the plan that Truman insisted bear Marshall's name, was able to make his own contribution to restoring Europe, containing the Communist threat, and establishing the United States as the world's greatest power.

Generating Support from the American Public and the U.S. Congress

On August 28, 18 members of the U.S. House of Representatives boarded the *Queen Mary*. Assembled by Representative Christian Herter, a Republican from

Boston with a reputation as a scholarly and earnest internationalist, the group was on a mission to see for themselves what was happening in Europe and assess the merits and needs of aiding Europe. The group became known as the "Herter Committee" and included House Foreign Affairs Committee Chairman Charles Eaton and Richard Nixon among its members. Herter was convinced that Europe needed aid and the United States should provide it. He was aware of many of the concerns about the Marshall Plan: (1) the aid would not be effective, (2) it would place a heavy strain on the U.S. economy, and (3) it would bloat the federal budget. Herter hoped that after the mission, returning representatives would come to share his views. The committee was divided into five separate subcommittees, spent 45 days in Europe, and visited every country in Europe except Russia, Yugoslavia, and Albania. Eaton said that the future economic hopes of Europe depended on the committee's findings. One member of the committee reported on his return to the United States on October 10, "We tried to look at Europe in about the way a banker would look at a bankrupt corporation trying to get a loan."[15]

The trip was a win for the Marshall Plan and its prospects. One of the more skeptical members of Herter's Committee, on his return to the United States, expressed a more open mind asking, "What would it cost us not to aid Europe?" But supporters were realistic about the uphill battle they faced in Congress, where some members felt that European aid should be tied to tax relief for U.S. citizens. Meanwhile, the Communists were busy destabilizing France and Italy, in hopes of making implementation of the Marshall Plan more difficult. In Italy, the Communists created many strikes that led to violence with many injured and killed and put the country on the brink of a Communist revolution. In France, the violence associated with the Communist disruptions emptied the streets of Paris. As the agitation and violence continued to rise, Marshall, Molotov, Bevin, and Bidault gathered in London for the fifth Conference of Foreign Ministers. Behind the scenes of the Conference, Bevin met with Marshall to emphasize the need for interim aid for France and expressed concerns over the deliberations of the Congress. Bevin had another suggestion for Marshall. He was concerned over the fear spreading through Western Europe about vulnerability to Russian influences, and he feared it would interfere with the prospects of European recovery. In a meeting with Marshall, Bevin proposed a transatlantic security association to complement the burgeoning economic association taking shape through the Marshall Plan. Marshall liked the idea but felt they would need to discuss it further, given the deliberations in Congress over the Marshall Plan. This was the seed for an extraordinary transatlantic alliance that was later to blossom into the North Atlantic Treaty Organization (NATO).

The effort to get the Marshall Plan approved faced formidable obstacles and would require a well-organized effort to promote its passage – a "Marshall Plan to sell the Marshall Plan," as one Dutch diplomat put it.[16] The American sponsors feared that the United States would retrench into isolationism as it had after World War I. As a response, former Secretary of War Henry Stimson wrote an article in the October 1947 edition of *Foreign Affairs*, urging the United States to assume global responsibility and to support European recovery:

> The reconstruction of Western Europe is a task from which Americans can decide to stand apart only if they wish to desert every principle which they claim [dear to] life … We must take part in this work; we must do our full part, we must be sure that we do enough.[17]

Stimson then agreed to serve as the head of the Committee for the Marshall Plan. Its membership was a collection of bipartisan elite, 300 luminaries from business, religion, academia, agriculture, labor, and other areas of American life, including two newly private citizens: Dean Acheson and Will Clayton. The committee's mission was to educate and inform the American public about the Marshall Plan. They published many pamphlets to increase understanding of the Plan, and they raised funds to employ full-time staff.

Dean Acheson's efforts took him from on-air radio debates to coast-to-coast speeches and even teaming up with Minneapolis Mayor Hubert Humphrey in reception halls that were crowded with people excited to hear from Acheson and Humphrey, who would stand up on a chair and speak about the Marshall Plan for half an hour, then do it over again until they had accommodated all who wanted to hear them.

Endorsements came in from many influencers, including Dwight Eisenhower and presidential hopeful Thomas Dewey, the Republican Governor of New York. Dewey offered an important caveat: the errors of past American aid efforts must be avoided by business-like administration of aid plans, and he offered his own six-point plan to ensure effective administration of any aid offered.

Marshall made it a point to bring Arthur Vandenberg in on the details of the State Department's plans. The two men met secretly each week at Blair House (across from the White House) to discuss what would work best in securing Congressional support. When a reporter questioned Marshall about why he was not making an effort to get Republican support, Marshall knew that his meetings with Vandenberg were still a secret. Marshall later remarked that during that period he and Vandenberg "couldn't have gotten much closer together unless I sat in Van's lap or he sat in mine."[18]

A European delegation arrived in Washington to ensure that the European voice was heard as the State Department reviewed the Paris Conference report. They were able to witness firsthand the political difficulties involved in getting the Plan through Congress. They gained a heightened sense of appreciation for the sacrifice the Americans were making in their support of the Plan. That appreciation gave Lovett added leverage to push the Europeans further into integration, as he pointed out that Americans were taking a calculated risk, and it would be useful for Congress and the American people to see Europe assume a similarly daring risk.

State Department staff were creating "Brown Books" for each recipient country, which laid out each country's financial situation, its needs, and the type of aid the United States would offer. Meanwhile, President Truman called a special session of Congress for November 17 to press for interim aid for Europe. Around this time, Truman held a press conference where he was asked what the United States "would get" for aiding Europe. Truman told the reporters, "We are not doing this for credit. We are doing this because it is right and it's necessary." Truman said in that most plain-spoken way that would be the hallmark of his communication style throughout his presidency. A grueling week of work by State Department staff near the end of November produced a draft of the legislation that was taking shape and nearing completion. That same week, a report was distributed regarding the feasibility of funding the Marshall Plan. The report was something that Vandenberg had counseled Truman to commission. The committee that produced the report was headed by Edwin Nourse of the Council of Economic Advisors and Secretary of the Interior Julius Krug who were directed to look at the capacity of the U.S. economy to take on the kind of commitment required by the Marshall Plan. The report found that a large-scale foreign aid program could lead to acute domestic shortages in certain commodities as well as depletion of natural resources. Even so, the report said the U.S. economy had the capacity to support a large-scale foreign aid program and still preserve national security and standards of living. The report went on to say that the aid program could spur long-term economic growth by strengthening Europe's ability to import U.S. goods. So the potential economic benefit of importing U.S. goods began to gain prominence as a reason to support the Marshall Plan, along with rebuilding war-torn allied countries, keeping Russian influence in Western Europe at bay, and establishing the United States as the pre-eminent world power.

The President's Committee on Foreign Aid was headed by Secretary of Commerce W. Averill Harriman, and Vandenberg also added General Electric Chairman Owen Young and Robert La Follette Jr., former Wisconsin senator, to add bona fides for the skeptical Republicans. The committee had a robust mission: to analyze the principles and policies that should guide the recovery program, to assess the capacity of the U.S. economy to support the recovery, to estimate the volume and nature of the assistance required, and to consider matters of financing and administration.

Harriman also needed someone to spearhead the work of the committee – a kind of executive director – to make sure the committee made progress while Harriman traveled in Europe. Harriman reached out to Richard Bissell, an economist he respected from previous experience working with him, to fill this role for the committee.[19] Arriving in Washington that September, Bissell brought together some trusted colleagues from previous jobs. The most contentious point in the discussions of the Committee was whether the U.S. economy had the capacity to handle the demands of the aid program. The various business, labor, and political luminaries on the Committee sorted themselves into groups, with the most supportive being Robert La Follette, former Republican senator and Vandenberg's pick, and Paul Hoffman, president of the Studebaker Corporation and a Republican. Hoffman believed strongly in the need for large-scale foreign aid, delivering an extemporaneous speech that so moved the committee members that they all rose to their feet in applause.[20] Bissell was so moved by Hoffman's speech that he insisted that Hoffman put his words on paper, and Bissell included them almost verbatim, as the opening remarks in the committee's report. Bissell began to prepare the report, beginning with Hoffman's line that echoed Marshall's Harvard speech, "Only the Europeans can save Europe," and the report went on to deal with all of the key aspects under consideration.

The report pointed out that the United States had three vital interests in European recovery: humanitarian, economic, and political, with the third overshadowing the others because, as the report made clear, the Marshall Plan was fundamentally "an investment in the continued survival of a world economically stabilized and peacefully conducted."[21] The report recommended a new, independent agency to administer the Marshall Plan. It estimated the cost of the Plan at between $12 billion and $17 billion for the entire program. The report contained lucid recommendations and was three inches thick with a vast array of analysis. Upon its release, the *New York Times* called it "exhaustive and eloquent," with similar praise flowing in from the majority of the press. The European reaction was similar, with the *Times* of London saying it was now clear that the Marshall Plan would require real sacrifice from the American people. The report was a public relations home run, and it had great traction with moderate Republicans and the public throughout the subsequent Congressional hearings. By that winter, the various efforts to examine and publicize the Marshall Plan by the Hertzer Committee, the Harriman Committee, and the Committee for the Marshall Plan had managed to create greater public awareness and support for the Plan.

On November 17, President Truman addressed the first special session of Congress convened since Roosevelt had summoned Congress in 1939 when war began in Europe. Several minutes into his speech Truman exclaimed that the United States had achieved great power, and now it must assume great responsibility. The chamber applauded. "The future of the free nations in Europe hangs in the balance," and Truman urged support for both interim aid and the longer term aid called for in the report. To deal with concerns about inflation and price increases, he urged consumer rationing and specific wage and price controls.

A week before hearings began on the interim aid. Senator Robert Taft, Republican from Ohio, a Republican leader and presidential candidate, began to level a series of attacks on the Truman foreign aid program. Taft declared that the Marshall Plan would be inflationary, would mean higher prices, and a large tax burden. He also took aim at previous foreign aid programs run by the Truman

Administration. "The Administration can't get away from the New Deal principle that Government spending is a good thing in itself." He alleged that a carefully planned propaganda campaign for the Marshall Plan, emanating from the State Department, had been launched. Taft was putting forward useful questions for the debate:

> How far shall we make a present to other peoples of the fruits of our labors? Do the advantages to be gained in foreign policy outweigh the disadvantages at home? Let us have all the facts and debate them fully.[22]

Other critics had a bleak view of the prospects for European recovery or even its survival and seemed willing to cede the region to Soviet control. The *New York Times* reported, "Why, it is being asked, if Europe is in danger of being overrun by Communist Russia should this country attempt to rebuild Western European industry when the effort would be to Russia's benefit?" Wisconsin Republican Senator Alexander Wiley wanted the United States to stop being "Uncle Sap" when it came to our generosity on foreign affairs.[23]

Despite the partisan attacks, Vandenberg was able to steer the interim aid package through the Senate with 83 votes for and only 6 against, a near-miraculous achievement. The highly contentious debate in the House opened on December 3, but the Senate vote sent a strong signal to France and Italy that near-term relief was on the way and that longer term aid was increasingly likely. But France and Italy were facing Communist subversion bordering on insurrection, and strikes had reduced coal production significantly in France. After violent clashes that killed innocent civilians, the Communists were overplaying their hand and beginning to lose support. The Italian Communists had also pushed too hard in their pursuit of economic disruption. The availability of interim aid (which became a reality on December 15 when Congress approved $522 million in interim aid for France, Italy, and Austria) from the Americans offered a tangible alternative for economic improvement and made the Communist alternative feel too disruptive.

On December 19, President Truman submitted to Congress "A Program for the United States Support for European Recovery," officially titled the European Recovery Plan, but known as the Marshall Plan. Truman requested $6.8 billion for the 15 months from the end of the interim aid to June 1949, then $10.2 billion from July 1949 to June 1952, totaling $17 billion for a period of four years and three months. The Plan would also create an agency to administer the program. The Plan was received on Capitol Hill primarily as a measure to prevent Communist, and thereby Soviet, expansion in Western Europe.

On Christmas Eve, President Truman presided over the 25th anniversary of the White House tree lighting. The President spoke of the desperation in Europe: "At this point in the world's history, the words of St. Paul have greater significance than ever before. 'And now abideth faith, hope, charity, these three, but the greatest of these is charity.'" He said the "great heart of the American people" would rise to meet the challenge.

During the Christmas recess, with most of his colleagues back home enjoying the holidays with their families, Vandenberg holed up in his Washington apartment making lists of questions and objections likely to be raised in the upcoming debate. Determined to be prepared for the fight, he readied arguments and facts to parry the points that were sure to be raised by his Republican colleagues in opposition to the Marshall Plan. On New Year's Day, he called the Republican governor of his home state to declare definitively that he did not want to be the Republican candidate for president. He was marshaling as much political currency for the contest to approve the Marshall Plan, putting aside his presidential ambitions. Vandenberg was also reading his Republican colleagues to understand and respond to their concerns: many did not want to be bound to an extended commitment; others objected to one Congress binding the hands of the next Congress; others wanted only annual commitments, so they could reduce commitments in future years. Vandenberg's reading was that a four-year commitment was possible, with commitment and appropriations approved annually. He continued to make public statements of support for the Plan, saying that it was indispensable to "intelligent American self-interest." He wanted to set up a great "representative national debate."

On January 8, 1948, George Marshall was to be the first witness at Vandenberg's Senate Foreign Relations Committee hearings. As the hearings opened James Reston wrote that Marshall looked "relaxed and self-possessed" and evinced his "quality of moral grandeur." The members zeroed in on their two most pressing concern: the amount of aid requested and the establishment and operation of the administering agency. Marshall, true to his usual public speaking delivery, was consciously lackluster but his message was forceful. On the amount of aid he said, "An inadequate program would involve a wastage of our resources with an ineffective result. Either undertake to meet the requirements of the problem or don't undertake it at all." Marshall pointed out that the proposed sum was not "an asking figure" in a negotiation, but it was a "realistic appraisal." On the matter of the administering agency, Marshall firmly asserted that the new agency should be folded under the State Department. Finishing his text, Marshall concluded his remarks by saying, "There is no doubt in my mind that if we decide to do this thing we can do it successfully."

During questioning, some of the senators indicated that they did not appreciate Marshall's "all or nothing" approach, pointing out that the Constitution endowed Congress with oversight of government expenditures, and they would not be instructed on that function. Others weighed in on their concerns that the administering agency be independent of the State Department. Vandenberg himself felt that the agency should be run by people with business experience as a results-oriented and pragmatic business enterprise, and that it would need autonomy to function that way. Vandenberg was concerned that the agency would fail unless it was animated by "a new element of business responsibility." A few days later, Marshall testified before the House Foreign Affairs Committee, and he did not change his proposal in any way. He predicted that if the program was not fully funded, it would mean

> economic distress so intense, social discontent so violent, political confusion so widespread, and hope of the future so shattered, that the vacuum which the war created in Western Europe will be filled by the forces of which wars are made.

Moreover, he said that if the United States "did not fill the breach, the regions' political leadership would be dictated by the Soviet Union." Marshall also warned that the United States would be imperiled and would be compelled to push for a comparable or even greater increase in military spending.

Most of his testimony now complete, Marshall spent the next several months traveling the country, targeting pockets of resistance, and taking the fight to the public. As the sitting Commerce Secretary Averill Harriman, emerging as one of the leading champions of the Plan, also testified to its objectives, which he summarized with the phrase "building a stable peace," and further described the Plan as "noble in concept but based on considerations of our own self-interest, and our own self-preservation." Harriman touted the Plan and said its major aim was the promotion of American economic interests and stability.

Stalin did not disappoint the Plan's advocates who were counting on Soviet truculence to boost support for the Plan. A Soviet document obtained by the British Foreign Office in late January summoned German workers and Communist sympathizers to engage in the same acts of sabotage and violence that had raged in France and Italy the previous autumn. Supporters of the Marshall Plan used the Soviet threat to their advantage, asserting that the Plan was the best means of countering the threat. The supporters also argued that the Plan was necessary for another purpose: Europe needed to emerge from the old atomized European economy into a coordinated, efficient, self-sustaining production and trading economy – in short, the Congress wanted to see Europe's economies integrate.

Vandenberg took the unusual step of declaring his office open to any member who had reservations about the Plan. By doing so, he was able to eliminate support for an initiative to create a "Republican Marshall Plan" and he also quashed a potential move by Republicans to lower the figure of the requested aid. Further, to get control of the discussion about finding a satisfactory administrative formula for the administering agency, Vandenberg took the initiative to commission a report from the nonpartisan Brookings Institution. After releasing the report to the public, Vandenberg convinced Marshall and Lovett to cede State Department control of the agency – instead it would be autonomous, an independent agency that could attract a world-class administrator and operate free of the White House or the State Department. When Marshall agreed to this, Vandenberg was able to deliver a critical concession to his Republican colleagues and helped get more support for the Plan.

The only member of Congress with a comparable degree of prestige to Vandenberg, Republican Senator Robert Alphonso Taft, was born into a family of privilege and high expectations in Cincinnati, Ohio. His grandfather was secretary of war and attorney general, and his father, William Howard Taft, was the only man to serve as both Chief Justice of the U.S. Supreme Court and U.S. President. Senator Taft finished first in his class at both Yale and Harvard Law School and was known for wielding a formidable and logical intellect in the cause of conservative ideas.[24] Taft, deeply conservative and a skeptic about the value of government spending of any sort, made clear that he would support aid that was surgically applied to halt the spread of Communism, but he wanted to cut the aid significantly and limit America's commitment to one year. Taft was a brilliant and incisive critic, and his reputation inside the State Department was summarized by the observation, "he has the best mind in Washington until he makes it up." Similarly, Will Clayton said of him "Taft always got the details, but he usually missed the big picture of what we were trying to accomplish."

Opponents also weighed in with other concerns. Former President Herbert Hoover recommended that the $17 billion Plan be reduced to a $4 billion, 15-month commitment. Republican senators called the Plan "state socialism," and "outright communism." Businessmen came forward to criticize the Plan, saying it would lead to severe shortages in essential goods and equipment, driving up inflation. Some predicted depression "more serious than we have ever experienced." Other businessman and some members of Congress were concerned that the United States was building up Europe only to have it compete with America.

After finishing his own testimony in Congress, Marshall went to Pittsburgh to speak to the local chamber of commerce for what was the start of his own campaign of speaking engagements around the country to rally support for the Plan. He did not enjoy stumping or being in front of large crowds, but he traveled thousands of miles per week, going into hostile territory and taking plenty of heat from skeptics. He later reflected on that time, saying he worked "as hard as though I was running for the Senate or the presidency." In front of business-oriented audiences, he framed his argument in business terms: "would we make a capital investment that was within our means to bring long-term gains, or would we spend abundantly for immediate wants in the hope that the day of reckoning could be postponed?"[25] He spoke to the National Cotton Council in Atlanta to address their concerns about being deprived of supplies and equipment, telling them what they stood to gain from European prosperity and trade. The Marshall Plan would finance expenditures for clothing for workers in Europe.

He also traveled to New York and Philadelphia and then took the campaign to the Midwest, where opposition was the strongest. Marshall spoke to women's groups as he believed they would mobilize more quickly than men would. His tone became more urgent, his rhetoric more heated, and his message more anti-Soviet. He was succeeding in quelling dissent and stirring enthusiasm for the Plan. Members of the Committee for the Marshall Plan had also been out promoting the Plan. Dean Acheson promoted the Plan as "the frontline of American security." Will Clayton gave six speeches in one week, moving from St. Louis to New York, to Washington. Behind the scenes, the committee kept a list entitled "Special Cultivation," regarding critical members of Congress. They kept track of their progress in convincing key members. The Committee hired six field staff to go to districts represented by key swing votes to drum up local support. They began publishing weekly fact sheets that went out to members of Congress and leaders across America. They gathered endorsements from 52 prominent national organizations. Marshall came back to Washington periodically, including meeting with Ohio farmers who had just met with Taft. Marshall reported to colleagues that by the time the meeting was over, they now supported the Plan. The combined efforts of Marshall and the Committee for the Marshall Plan were building support from many sectors of American life. Members of Congress were taking note of the increase in support.

International events then intervened. Czechoslovakia was slipping into Communist control, and the Soviets also made threatening overtures to Finland, Norway, and Austria. British Foreign Secretary Ernest Bevin agreed with Churchill that Europe was entering a treacherous period of six to eight weeks. If during that time, the Marshall Plan passed, if Europe proved able to withstand further Communist takeovers, and if the Communists were defeated in upcoming elections in Italy, Europe would have turned a corner. In mid-March, Charles de Gaulle emerged in France, announcing that he would be proud to accept help from the United States. The coup in Czechoslovakia, the Communists' failed policy of sabotage, and the likely passage of the Marshall Plan were all beginning to move public opinion in France. Despite continuing concerns about Germany, it was becoming clear to France that the greater threat to France was from the Soviets, and France began to reconcile itself with the prospect of a rehabilitated Germany as part of postwar Europe.

The Czech coup had far-reaching effects on U.S. foreign policy. First, it motivated the United States to heed Bevin's earlier call for a Western defense association. European leaders quietly met with U.S. defense, military, and diplomatic officials at the Pentagon, under Marshall's orders, to explore a framework for a new association for mutual defense. Second, passage of the Marshall Plan became even more urgent. The Plan's supporters now had a powerful argument to dissolve obstacles to the Plan's passage, and they did not hesitate to use it to promote their cause.

On March 1, 1948, Arthur Vandenberg moved to the lectern in the Senate to make his final speech before a vote in the Senate. His committee's hearings amounted to 1,466 pages, and the hearings in the House totaled 2,269 pages.

Vandenberg's committee had heard from 100 witnesses and received statements from many more. He opened his statement by evoking the ongoing crisis in Czechoslovakia and the one that seemed to be emerging in Finland. He said, "the exposed frontiers of hazard move almost hourly to the west." He acknowledged the concerns of those in opposition, but said, "The greatest nation on earth either justifies or surrenders its leadership. We must choose. There are no blueprints to guarantee results…" He described the Plan as "… the product of eight months of more intensive study by more devoted minds than I have ever known to concentrate upon any objective in all my twenty years in Congress." After 80 minutes, his longest speech of his Congressional career, Vandenberg concluded to thunderous applause, handshakes, and backslapping from members of his committee. Marshall later called the speech "a masterpiece."

In the ensuing weeks, there were more statements from opponents who were concerned that the Plan would offer support to Europe's socialist governments, and that such support would help them on their path to Communism. On the eve of the Senate vote, Taft again spoke out against the Plan, saying if he voted for the Plan, it was with the understanding that it was for a one-year commitment. At five minutes past midnight on March 14, the Senate voted of 69–17 to authorize $5.3 billion for the first year of the four-year program for European recovery. Among those voting aye were Senator Joseph McCarthy and, the most vocal critic, Senator Robert Taft.

The bill moved to the House for deliberation, Marshall set out on the road to generate more support. The Czech crisis was still in progress and the Italian election was on the horizon when he spoke at the University of California at Berkeley and at the University of California at Los Angeles. He was speaking with even more urgency, calling the Marshall Plan a key in the worldwide struggle between freedom and tyranny. The bill quickly moved through the House Foreign Affairs Committee by a vote of 11–8 and moved to the House floor. The bill met a flurry of proposed amendments and objections from Republican leaders. Many of these were to protect special interests in their state or district, but Marshall had done a good job fending off most of the more egregious amendments. During the floor debate, Ohio representative John Vorys read a letter from Herbert Hoover, who had done an about-face and now endorsed the Marshall Plan, calling it "a major dam against Russian aggression." The House passed the bill by a vote of 329 in favor and only 74 against.

President Truman signed the bill into law on April 3, while Marshall was at a conference in South America. Marshall cabled his thoughts from Bogota, calling the legislation "an historic step in the foreign policy of this country." Paul Hofmann called it "probably as well-conceived a piece of legislation as was ever put on the books in the U.S." Leaders in Western Europe were overjoyed when the legislation was signed. British Prime Minister Clement Atlee wrote to Truman to express "our deep gratification at this act of unparalleled generosity and statesmanship."

The decision as to who would administer the European Recovery Program came down to two familiar names. Will Clayton was the first choice of Truman and Marshall, but Vandenberg felt that he would not get much support among Republican senators because he was too tied to the State Department. Vandenberg made clear that his choice was Paul Hoffman and he began sounding out his Senate colleagues about Hoffman. Truman called Acheson to discuss the selection, and Acheson thought highly of Hoffman and told Truman that Hoffman brought a distinct advantage over Clayton. Picking Vandenberg's candidate would keep him supportive of the program, so that when the fight over future funding came up next year, Vandenberg would push for greater rather reduced amounts of funding.

Paul Hoffman was sworn in on April 9, 1948, to lead the European Recovery Program. Vandenberg pushed Hoffman's nomination through his committee in less than an hour. Hoffman commented on his appointment by saying, "It seems that I was the least obnoxious of the Republicans." His Economic Cooperation Administration (ECA) had no offices, 10,000 job applications waiting to be reviewed, and hundreds of requests to get time on Hoffman's calendar. To get some immediate help, he called a local Studebaker dealer for a secretary and a half dozen other employees. Hoffman called Richard Bissell, then a professor at the Massachusetts Institute of Technology, with whom Hoffman had worked on the Harriman Committee. Hoffman convinced Bissell to begin immediately, so he packed for a five-day stay in Washington, and he never returned to live in Cambridge. Bissell emerged as the main architect of the design for how Marshall's aid would be spent. Bissell put Hoffman's vision into practice; the ECA would act as a kind of investment banker for guiding Europe to recovery. But Europe would own its own recovery. Hoffman would say, "The essence of genuine leadership is to share power with people rather than display power over people."

Aid Begins to Flow to Europe

On April 14, 11 days after President Truman signed the Foreign Assistance Act of 1948 into law, the ship *John H Quick* settled under the enormous grain elevators in Galveston, Texas, to take on 900 long tons of grain. Along with five other ships also loaded with grain, fuel, various foodstuffs, feed, chemicals, fertilizers, raw materials, vehicles, and equipment, they all headed out into the Atlantic as the first fleet to bring European Recovery Program (ERP) aid to Europe. Many ships followed the *John H. Quick* in the subsequent days and months, loaded in ports from Texas to New York, bringing all manner of aid to France, the Netherlands, Italy, Austria, Greece, Great Britain, and the rest of the 16 nations in the Marshall Plan.

Hoffman and Tex Moore, who had served as Studebaker's legal counsel, put together a hiring process to draft the best people they could find, choosing mostly businessmen with practical experience in leading others in demanding and competitive enterprises. They wanted their personnel choices to reflect America — including government, business, labor, agriculture, and education. The ECA was to have an office in Europe, the Office of the Special Representative (OSR). Hoffman chose Averill Harriman for the post.

In about 90 days, Hoffman and Moore had hired 400 people and convinced them to come to Washington or move to Europe. British diplomat Sir Anthony Clarke commented on the personnel selected to work on the Marshall Plan, "The quality of personnel provided by the U.S. for this program ... and their enthusiasm – was a most elevating spectacle."[26] Hoffman attributed the quality of the personnel to Marshall's Harvard University speech, which established the Marshall Plan as a noble idea, i.e., the people in the organization wanted to work to contribute to keeping the world free. "The magic was in the Marshall Plan itself," Hoffman said.

By June 30, the ECA had approved grants for goods and services valued at $738 million. While the aid had a substantial near-term material impact, the greater and perhaps more important impact was psychological. The Plan, and the anticipation of what was to come, stirred hope and revived Western Europe's sense of possibility.

In seeking its first round of appropriations, the ECA ran into a buzz saw in the form of House Appropriations Committee Chairman John Taber. He was a small-town lawyer from upstate New York, a fabled curmudgeon, and a fiscal conservative who had isolationist leanings and was skeptical of foreign aid. Taber cut the appropriation by one-quarter and got approval for the cut from his committee. But Vandenberg requested an appearance in front of the Senate Appropriations Committee, in which he said that the cut that the House had proposed would turn the program from one designed for European recovery, to one that could only provide temporary relief to Europeans. Vandenberg's intervention was crucial, and the Senate restored the original appropriated amount. Taber fought for his reduced amount in the conference committee but Vandenberg managed to pressure Taber to support the original amount of the proposal. Vandenberg had rescued the European Recovery Program.

With the appropriation in hand, with 620 employees on board, ECA authorized $750 million in aid. Three quarters went to the United Kingdom, France, and Italy. The categories of aid broke down into 33 percent for food, feed, and fertilizer; 20 percent for fuel; 22 percent for raw and semifinished products; 7 percent for machinery and equipment; 3 percent for other products; and 15 percent for ocean freight.

Seeing the progress of the Marshall Plan, the Soviets and European Communists called the Marshall Plan "an instrument of preparation for war." With European opinion turning against the Soviets, Stalin was witnessing his design for European influence recede. In an attempt to regain momentum in Western Europe, he set his sights on a new target: Berlin.

At a late spring conference in London, Britain, the United States, France, and other countries agreed to several provisions that would enhance Germany's recovery. They raised the ceiling on German steel production, agreed on currency reform in the western zones, allowed western zones "those responsibilities which are compatible with the minimum requirements of occupation," agreed to fuse their zones and create a German Constitutional Assembly, and essentially agreed to create a West German state. This was alarming for Stalin, who did not want to see a revived Germany allied with a western capitalist bloc. A prosperous West German state might attract Germans from the Soviet bloc in the East, who might eventually seek to throw out the Soviets and ally with the West.

Berlin lay 120 miles inside the eastern, Soviet-occupied zone, and the city was split into four zones occupied by the four main powers (the United States, Britain, France, and the Soviet Union). There were 4.2 million Berliners in the Western zones, and they had about a month's worth of food and coal. Without supplies from the outside, they would starve and their industry would shut down. The Allies had 6,500 troops in Berlin, while the soviets had 18,000 and an additional 300,000 in the eastern zones in Germany. It was British General Brian Robertson who suggested supplying western zones through a massive airlift. Given the Soviet advantage in ground troops, Marshall supported the plan, and Truman did not want another war happening as the United States approached the presidential election in 1948. The orders were given to begin airlifts over 120 miles of Soviet-occupied land, to drop 225 tons of food, coal, and other vital materials to the western zones of Berlin. The Soviets made clear that their blockade of Berlin would stay in place until the Allies stopped their plan to create a West German government. By early July, American and British aircraft averaged three flights per day and landed every four minutes. Over time, the number of landings and the amount of tonnage of supplies increased. In late July, Marshall shared his analysis of the Soviets with the Cabinet saying, "The present tension in Berlin is brought about by loss of face of Russia in Italy, France, Finland ... It is caused by Russian desperation in the face of the success of the ERP."

The ERP's mission chief in France was David Bruce, who had worked for Averill Harriman at Brown Brothers Harriman on Wall Street. Bruce had a reputation for being unflappable, and his composure made him a leader that people naturally followed.[27] After the war, he had agreed to join Harriman at the Commerce Department since he knew that Harriman would likely be involved in European reconstruction and he wanted to be part of it. When Bruce arrived in Paris in late June, he expected his tenure to be short, since the looming presidential election looked sure to be a loss for Truman and Dewey would undoubtedly appoint his own loyalist to Bruce's position. Bruce quickly found that his short-term objective should be to do what he could to bolster France's political and economic condition, and his longer term objective should be for French stability, self-sustainability, and prosperity. Bruce found the key to his longer term objective through a partnership with Jean Monnet, who had already devised and set in motion a long-term plan for France's economic growth and industrial modernization and now needed the funds to implement it. Monnet had been a member of the National

Liberation Committee, the government-in-exile of Charles de Gaulle who liked Monnet's ideas about France facing a choice between "modernization or decadence," greatness or obsolescence. With de Gaulle's support, Monnet began to devise a plan that set production targets for key industries such as steel, coal, and transportation. Instead of focusing on the near-term consumer needs, Monnet argued that France needed to harness its limited resources on modernization of basic industries, and he got government ministries and governing coalitions to agree with his approach. In 1946, he served as head of the General Planning Commission and implemented the Modernization and Re-Equipment Plan to spark economic recovery. Monnet was pragmatic, interested in action and results, and Bruce bought into Monnet's vision. An extraordinary collaboration took shape, as the two met several times a week, daily at times. Bruce developed great respect for Monnet, and Monnet respected Bruce as well, finding him the quintessential "civilized man," deliberative, thoughtful, humble, and with a bias for action. The Marshall Plan became the principal funding mechanism for what was commonly known as the Monnet Plan.[28]

As the first term of the Truman Administration drew to a close near the end of 1948, the Marshall Plan had helped Europe make significant progress. About $2 billion of cargo had been delivered, with billions more still on the way from the first year's appropriations. Around $1.4 billion of aid was food, feed, and fertilizer, more than $1 billion worth of raw materials and semifinished products was shipped, and half a billion dollars in machinery and vehicles as well fuel were all sent.

George Marshall Tries (Unsuccessfully) to Step Away

George Marshall had been feeling poorly for some time, and he had postponed surgery to have his kidney removed, but he finally agreed to schedule the surgery after Thanksgiving. Marshall would have served as Secretary of State for two years in January. But with Truman's electoral victory in hand, with the Marshall Plan implementation running at full speed, and with Europe making good progress in its recovery, Marshall felt his duty fulfilled. He told Truman he would like to resign, which was announced in early January to take effect on Inauguration Day.

After leaving the State Department, Marshall served for almost a full year as the head of the Red Cross. But on a vacation with his wife in Michigan, he was summoned to the phone at a country store to take a call from the White House. Marshall had spent months recuperating from surgery and resting at his Leesburg home. But Harry Truman needed him to return to Washington to serve as Secretary of Defense. It was a tough time for Truman. He needed Marshall to manage the war in Korea, and to elevate the stature of the administration with Congress, the press, and the American public. Marshall was confirmed by the Senate by a vote of 57–11.

In December 1950, British Prime Minister Clement Atlee returned from a meeting in Washington with Harry Truman. Atlee announced on his return that

Great Britain needed no more Marshall aid. Ernest Bevin, who had responded to Marshall's Harvard speech by calling European nations together to formulate a plan for Marshall aid requests, wrote the new Defense Secretary: "I sat in the House of Commons yesterday and heard the chancellor announce the suspension of Marshall aid, and had you been there I should have wanted to go and say to you with a full heart 'thank you.'"

With Marshall at the center of so many major events in the previous 20 years, it was probably inevitable that Republican Senator Joe McCarthy's reckless and deceitful campaign to identify and root out Communists in the U.S. government would eventually set its sights on George Marshall. In a Senate speech in June 1951, he accused General Marshall of being at the epicenter of "a Communist conspiracy so immense and an infamy so black as to dwarf any previous such venture in the history of man." McCarthy's assault was 60,000 words long, and McCarthy had been warned by friends not to take on Marshall, who many viewed as one of the true American heroes of World War II and beyond. But McCarthy insisted on attempting to stain Marshall's reputation:

> We have declined so precipitously in relation to the Soviet Union in the last six years. How much swifter may be our fall into disaster with Marshall at the helm? Where will all this stop? This is not a rhetorical question: Ours is not a rhetorical danger. Where will Marshall carry us?

The speech stretched on for three hours and, losing his audience, he inserted the remainder of the speech into the *Congressional Record*. He later published an expanded version of the speech in a thin book, under his own byline (though the speech had allegedly been written by conservative journalist Forrest Davis) and titled it *America's Retreat from Victory: The Story of George Catlett Marshall*. He was so convinced it would sell that he ordered printing of 25,000 copies. Marshall acted unfazed by being accused of treason, saying that if he responded, "I would acknowledge something that isn't true, that McCarthy's accusations are worthy of defense. There is no necessity for me to prove my loyalty to the United States. I have lived that loyalty every day of my life."[29]

During the 1952 campaign, Republican presidential candidate Dwight Eisenhower agreed to appear at a McCarthy campaign event in Wisconsin, putting it off until October 3, since Eisenhower had always been wary of McCarthy. The Eisenhower campaign distributed to the press his intended remarks for the event, which contained a mild repudiation of McCarthy's attack on George Marshall, whom Eisenhower had considered a mentor since their days serving together in World War II. Eisenhower's speech said:

> Charges of disloyalty have in the past been leveled against General George C. Marshall. I am not now discussing any errors in judgment he may have made in capacities other than military. But I was privileged throughout the

years of World War II to know George Marshall personally, as Chief of Staff of the Army. I know him, as a man and a soldier, to be dedicated with singular selflessness and the professional patriotism to the service of America.

But Eisenhower did not read the words, apparently because campaign manager Sherman Adams and others argued to delete this passage. The press immediately took note of Eisenhower's omission, and it tarnished Eisenhower's image as a man of courage.[30]

By 1953, George Marshall had again fallen ill. But in December 1953, he left his sickbed in Leesburg, Virginia, to travel across the Atlantic Ocean one more time. In Oslo, Norway, on December 10, Marshall donned white tie and tails and arrived at a resplendent hall to receive the Nobel Peace Prize. He was the first and only professional soldier to receive it. He was not receiving the award for his role in war, but for his work in the cause of peace. Marshall addressed the international audience, including reflections on a unique life in service and leadership.

It was Marshall who conferred with Stalin at the Moscow Conference in March and April 1947 and became resolved to bolster Western Europe against the internal and external Communist threat. He personally recruited Acheson and Kennan and trusted Clayton, deputized them, and pushed the State Department to work toward a plan for European recovery. Heeding Clayton's call in late May, Marshall determined the time had come for action. Marshall selected the time and place for his announcement address and presented it as an invitation to Europe. In the next month, Marshall lent the full force of his energy and prestige to ensure its passage through Congress. He labored adroitly to construct one of the most extraordinary collaborations in American history. He testified often and effectively, and with the Plan's passage still in the balance, Marshall toured the country, trumpeting the strategic, economic, and humanitarian need for the Plan. It would not have been possible without his vision, his will, his tactical dexterity, his collaboration with Vandenberg, his efforts with the Congress and the American people, and his prestige. By the time it ended in 1951, the Marshall Plan and NATO had decisively secured Western Europe in the U.S. orbit. Soviet domination of Eurasia was thwarted. The objective for which the war had been fought was achieved and the Marshall Plan helped to realize it. Senator Henry Cabot Lodge said, "These achievements in war and peace justify the statement that General George Marshall stands out as the greatest American of the 20th century."

When George Marshall died in October 1959, Harry Truman called Marshall's wife and attended his funeral in North Carolina. In a letter that he sent later to Dean Acheson, he asked "Do you suppose any President of the United States ever had two such men as you and the General?" Truman clearly understood his good fortune in having both Marshall and Acheson working for him, and contributing to his ultimate success.

The success of the Marshall Plan belongs as much to Europe as it does to the United States, since it was designed not as a unilateral exercise or as an initiative imposed upon one side by the other. It is best viewed as a partnership in which Europe and the United States played co-leads. From June 1947 to its termination near the end of 1951, the Marshall Plan provided approximately $13 billion to finance the recovery and rehabilitation of war-torn Western Europe ($100 billion in today's dollars, and as a comparable share of U.S. Gross National Product, it would be in excess of $500 billion). The Plan became the cornerstone of American foreign policy for much of the important postwar years. It employed U.S. capital and a free-market ideology to prop up even socialist regimes, so as to save them from Communist influence. Proposed as an alternative program to save the world from "hunger, poverty, and chaos," it helped trigger the Cold War. Dean Acheson described the Marshall Plan as "one of the greatest and most honorable adventures in history."

The Marshall Plan benefited from relationships formed and maintained by a web of public servants who felt the need to work together and found a way to do it. Truman was able to lead and oversee the work of many talented individuals. His ability to pull together George Marshall, Dean Acheson, Averill Harriman, Paul Hoffman, Will Clayton, and Arthur Vandenberg was important to the success of the plan. Marshall's ability to recruit and work with Acheson, George Kennan, Hoffman, Vandenberg, and Will Clayton was vital to the formation and implementation of the Plan. Vandenberg's willingness to sponsor the Plan in Congress, his ability to persuade his colleagues, and his influence over the Plan's appropriations allowed the Plan to get off to a good start and prove it could be effective. David Bruce's ability to collaborate with Jean Monnet helped save France by paving the way for Monnet's plan to help modernize their economy. Even Senator Taft contributed by constructively opposing the Plan, allowing its sponsors to identify and adjust to possible weaknesses in its administration.

Perhaps one of the best summations of the contributions of George Catlett Marshall was by Winston Churchill, in a July 1958 letter to Colonel John C. Hagan:

> In war he was as wise and understanding in counsel as he was resolute in action. In peace he was the architect who planned the restoration of the battered European economy ... he always fought victoriously against defeatism, discouragement, and disillusion. Succeeding generations must not be allowed to forget his achievements and example.

Notes

1 Greg Behrman, *The Most Noble Adventure, the Marshall Plan and the Time When America Helped Save Europe* (Free Press, A Division of Simon & Schuster, New York, NY, 2007), page 10.
2 Ibid., page 12.
3 Ibid., pages 13, 14.

4 Ibid., page 38.

5 Ibid., page 55. George Kennan was an experienced hand at all things Russian. He was the man who had written and sent the famous "Long Telegram" from his post at the embassy in Russia. Kennan dictated an eight-thousand-word exposition sent to the State Department in five parts, describing the nature of the Soviet threat. He said that the actual mainspring of Soviet intransigence was a deeply rooted national insecurity, the Soviets would respond only to the logic of force, and expressions of goodwill and cooperative efforts would be futile. The United States would have to stand up to the Soviets. The telegram was well received by policymakers hungry for an explanation and a guide for moving forward, the Long Telegram provided both.

6 Ibid., pages 46, 47. Will Clayton assumed his post of Undersecretary of State for Economic Affairs in December 1944, having been recruited personally by Roosevelt, after having risen up by his bootstraps to found an international cotton brokerage firm that made him a multimillionaire and got him on the cover of *Time* magazine, which dubbed him "King Cotton." He had a reputation for unlimited powers of concentration and boundless energy. He would tell his wife "You've got to live the thing you are working on." But he was an astute observer of the larger context of the world around him. During World War II, he had been brought into the government to run the procurement operation for the materials and resources that the Allies needed and did not want the Axis powers to obtain. He accepted no salary for his service. Clayton was an ardent follower of Cordell Hull, who had served as Secretary of State for 12 years, the longest tenure in that position in U.S. history. Hull's vision had become Clayton's, and Clayton was convinced that it was crucial to build an open and prosperous international economic and financial order: he felt it was the key to prosperity, security, peace, and the key to overcoming the mistakes of the past. Some historians believe that Truman offered the position of Secretary of State to Clayton before offering it to Marshall. Truman liked Clayton immensely, and he joined Truman's inner circle of advisors. But Clayton definitively turned down Truman's offer. Marshall was also asked around this time, and it is not clear who was asked first. Truman may not have wanted to ask Marshall because of his impending retirement. Nonetheless, though Clayton's refusal narrowed Truman's options, Truman was fortunate that there was still an excellent man available in Marshall.

7 Ibid., page 2.

8 Ibid., page 3.

9 Ibid., page 69.

10 Ibid., pages 76–80. Arthur Vandenberg was born on March 22, 1884, in Grand Rapids, Michigan, to a family of means whose family's fortune was reduced in the panic of 1893. He was unable to complete his full-time studies at the University of Michigan, so he left after his first year to become a cub reporter at the *Grand Rapids Herald*. When the newspaper's ownership changed, the 22-year-old Arthur Vandenberg was named its editor. Vandenberg thrived in this role, was a consistent supporter of Republican candidates, and when a Republican senator died in 1926 with an unexpired term, the governor appointed Vandenberg. He gained a reputation for his "purple prose" and his booming oratorical style. He wore glasses and a bow tie and carefully arranged a few strands of hair over his bald head. He was considered hearty, vibrant, and affable. He had literary aspirations, publishing three books, including one about Alexander Hamilton, and wrote 100 unpublished short stories, and two published songs. Vandenberg's willingness to change his philosophy toward internationalism and his skill in steering the Marshall Plan through Congress were critical to its enactment.

11 Ibid., page 80.

12 Ibid., page 88.

13 Ibid., page 102.

14 Ibid., page 110.

15 Ibid., page 116.

16 Ibid., page 122.

17 Ibid., page 122.

18 Ibid., page 125.

19 Ibid., pages 130–131. Richard Bissell came from a family that arrived from England in Windsor, Connecticut, in 1636. His ancestor, Sergeant Daniel Bissell, was a spy for George Washington. Bissell was born in the Mark Twain House in Hartford a few years before the start of World War I. His father was president of Hartford Insurance and a prominent Connecticut Republican. He was sent to Groton and Yale University and matured in a culture that valued athletic vigor and achievement. He developed a reputation as a brilliant young thinker. The depression had a profound effect on him as he felt the United States was on the brink of collapse. When he saw Roosevelt step up to meet these challenges, Russell questioned his Republican background and came to believe strongly in the ability of an activist good government to achieve positive ends. He chose economics as his postgraduate degree, taught a course on Keynesian economics, becoming one of Yale's most popular teachers. In the spring of 1941, he left Yale for what he thought would be a temporary period to serve as an economist at the Commerce Department. When Pearl Harbor occurred, he was recruited to join the Combined Shipping Adjustment Board, where his job was to allocate ships and vessels in the United States to various civilian and military programs, becoming the merchant shipping planner for the United States. He won Harriman's respect as "one of the most outstanding economists I've ever known" during Harriman's time overseeing the Lend-Lease program.

20 Ibid., pages 131–132. Paul Hoffman was born in Chicago, Illinois, in 1891 into a prosperous family. As a young boy, he became fascinated with cars, learning all the intricacies of fine cars his father owned. Though a good student, he was mostly uninterested in his courses at the University of Chicago, so he discontinued his studies after his first year. He took his first job as a car salesman at a Studebaker dealership in Chicago, where he discovered he had a talent for sales. Hoffman ventured into rural areas and found untapped markets by taking local bank presidents to lunch in the finest car in his showroom, learning about potential clients in the community. At age 21, he was awarded the company prize for selling the most Studebakers in the country. He moved to Los Angeles in search of larger commissions. He served in World War I, and when he returned home, he bought his own Studebaker dealership. In 1922, the Los Angeles mayor appointed Hoffman chairman of a traffic commission, where he devised a highway plan for the entire city. His work also introduced the first pedestrian crossing lights in America. And he also contributed to efforts to reduce traffic deaths by 30 percent. Hoffman found that the safer the roads, the more people wanted to buy cars, and he learned a larger lesson: intelligent reforms could benefit everyone, including an industry that could flourish with the reforms. He then moved to South Bend, Indiana, to take a senior executive position at Studebaker. Hoffman had a winning manner, and he was earnest, kind, and authoritative in conversation. He was an excellent listener, with expressive eyes and almost always wearing a genuine smile that put people at ease. During the Depression, he was appointed the first president

of the Automobile Safety Foundation and dubbed an "apostle of safety." He was named president of Studebaker and led the company out of receivership and back to profitability. He ensured that labor received good wages and working conditions, and there was never a strike by workers under his leadership of the company. His work at Studebaker during the Depression informed his larger ideology: he would tell fellow businessmen that pursuit of exorbitant profits was actually sabotaging the free enterprise system. Instead, he advocated for tempering self-interest to ensure that others were provided for and enfranchised, pointing out that it was not only humanitarian; when workers were provided for and included, it would always be to the benefit of both the workers and the owners of the company and make the economic system work for everyone. In short, it was enlightened self-interest. In 1942, Hoffman started the Committee for Economic Development, bringing in hundreds of economists and business leaders who produced a series of studies and reports, which reached business and labor leaders around the country, and serving as the engine for the best thinking on America's path forward in the postwar period. Hoffman's testimony on the Marshall Plan before Congress was well received. He was a supporter of the Plan, and a key participant on the Harriman Committee. Vandenberg told Truman that Hoffman was his choice and that of every businessman that he had canvassed on the matter of who should lead the ECA. Marshall also approved the choice and Acheson, in his call with Truman about whether he should select Hoffman, pointed out that choosing Hoffman would irrevocably commit Vandenberg to support the Plan and ensure it was adequately funded. But when Truman offered the job to Hoffman, he was reticent because he did not want to leave Studebaker. He agreed to talk it over with his wife and business colleagues. Vandenberg told Hoffman he had to take the job, and Truman announced his appointment without even hearing back from Hoffman. After going through a pro forma committee hearing and vote in Vandenberg's committee, Hoffman was sworn in as ECA Director, less than a week after the ERP was signed into law.

21 Ibid., page 132.
22 Ibid., page 135.
23 Ibid., page 136.
24 Ibid., pages 148–149. Senator Robert Taft of Ohio was a highly respected member of the Senate. Taft had none of the social attributes of a candidate for high office. He was described as brusque, occasionally tart, aloof to the point of coldness. He wore his trademark rimless spectacles, kept his hat at dead center. Taft was more comfortable on the Senate floor, drafting legislation or formulating political strategy than in a social setting. His wife, Martha, described him by saying "Bob is not austere, he's just compartmentalized." Martha was also a popular Washington personality who was warm, engaging, and humorous and is credited with coining the phrase "to err is Truman." Politically, Taft was a fiscal conservative to the core, wanted to do away with the massive expenditures that were part of Roosevelt's New Deal, and he wanted to tighten the budget, reduce taxes, and limit foreign commitments. America's growing alarm with climbing prices and inflation were giving Taft ammunition in opposing the Marshall Plan. He was running for President and was using his leadership to stop the Plan as an example of what he could accomplish for the nation. He believed that America was best served fortifying its own economic position. He saw the Marshall Plan as a giant European TVA-like effort, a vast "giveaway program."
25 Ibid., page 153.

26 The ability of a mission statement to galvanize an organization, attract and retain highly qualified individuals, and contribute to a daily esprit de corps should not be underestimated. The nobility and magnanimity of the Marshall Plan's mission to secure the economic future of war-torn Western Europe was a contributing factor in carrying out the Plan effectively. My own experience working for 30+ years at the U.S. Environmental Protection Agency (EPA) (many of which I hired people to carry out a wide variety of programs) convinced me of the value of a meaningful mission statement. The short version of the EPA's mission "to protect human health and the environment" was a short-hand way of explaining what a prospective employee would be doing during their time at the Agency. Programs that I managed were easily and succinctly tied to that overall mission of protecting human health and the environment: reducing/eliminating asbestos exposure among school children and employees, increasing compliance with environmental laws, and increasing capacity of other countries to solve environmental problems. The mission of the U.S. EPA kept me engaged and enthused for over 30 years.

27 Ibid., pages 190–192. William Averill Harriman was born on November 15, 1891, the oldest son of E.H. Harriman the railroad tycoon and one of the richest men in America. He grew up on a lavish estate, traveling the world, and attending the finest schools. Harriman's hard-driving father instilled in his son an insatiable work ethic and sense of service and told his son that great wealth is an obligation and a responsibility, and that money must work for the country. In the 1920s, Averill was one of the founders of Brown Brothers Harriman, one of the most prosperous financial houses on Wall Street. Harriman was tall, lean, with slicked-back and jet-black hair, and dark eyes and attracted many female admirers. He was extremely accomplished in athletics, saying "I like recreation that calls for just as much energy as work calls for."

Harriman turned his attention to government through his desire to operate on the world's highest stage. Though born into a Republican family, Harriman grew disenchanted with Republican isolationism and Herbert Hoover's economic stewardship during the stock market crash of 1929. He became an active Democrat, and when fellow-patrician Franklin Roosevelt recruited him to help lead the National Recovery Administration, one of FDR's most important New Deal programs, he thrust himself into the assignment. When war broke out in Europe and FDR decided to send aid to England, he directed Harriman to run the Lend-Lease program, which he ran for the first half of the war. Roosevelt knew U.S.-Soviet relations would be important in the final stage of the war and in the negotiations to follow, so he appointed Harriman U.S. Ambassador to the Soviet Union in late 1943. In early 1946, Harriman left his Moscow post to become U.S. Ambassador to the United Kingdom. When Harry Truman called Harriman back to Washington to become Secretary of Commerce, he had already been a strong champion for European recovery.

Harriman was not a brilliant man; he was a poor speaker, awkward with the press and much more comfortable at the diplomatic conference table or in business meeting than in social settings. He had a rigorous mind with sharp instincts and a businessman's sense of pragmatism. He was known for his proven ability to achieve an objective through his fierce drive and powers of concentration. Among embassy staff with whom he had worked, he offered no human warmth, and they considered him gruff and harsh. He was always loyal to those who were devoted to him; he drove himself hardest of all; he listened and considered subordinates' views carefully and advocated for the embassy's position forcefully and effectively.

It was well know that Harriman had hoped to be the administrator of the Marshall Plan, and his glittering resume as a businessman and a diplomat made him a natural choice. When Hoffman was picked for the position, and he, in turn, offered Harriman the position as Special Representative in Europe, it turned out to be a very effective use of personnel by the Truman Administration.

28 Ibid., pages 217–219, David Bruce had been born into a prominent Virginia family and then married the legendary industrialist Andrew Mellon's daughter. He acquired the tastes and sensibilities of Southern aristocracy. He became a wine connoisseur, gourmand, and an art lover. He spoke fluent French and served in Paris during World War II with the Office of Special Services (OSS) – the elite intelligence unit that included people like Ernest Hemmingway, David Rockefeller, and Arthur Schlesinger – and his affection for French culture and society grew. Bruce saw the ECA mission posting in Paris as a chance to help rebuild the nation that "has for so long nurtured the best hopes and aspirations of Western culture."

29 This discussion of the Joe McCarthy attack on George Marshall is from: Tye. Larry, *Demagogue. The Life and Long Shadow of Senator Joe McCarthy.* Houghton Mifflin Harcourt, Boston, New York, 2020, pages 169–171.

30 Ibid., page 229.

Bibliography

Behrman, Greg. *The Most Noble Adventure: The Marshall Plan and the Time When America Helped Save Europe.* New York, NY: Simon & Schuster, 2007.

Tye, Larry. *Demagogue, the Life and Long Shadow of Senator Joe McCarthy.* Boston, MA: Houghton Mifflin Harcourt, 2020.

Uldrich, Jack. *Soldier, Statesman, Peacemaker – Leadership Lessons from George C. Marshall.* New York, NY: American Management Association, 2005.

16

MARTIN LUTHER KING, JR.

Letter from the Birmingham Jail

DOI: 10.4324/9781003266235-18

King's Early Years – Preparing for the Pulpit

Born on January 15, 1929, in Atlanta, Georgia as **Michael** Luther King, Jr., King grew up in the world of the black elite. His friends called him Mike, and by the time he was five years old, his father, also named Michael, changed both of their names after a trip to the Baptist World Alliance in Berlin. King Sr., the highest paid black minister in Atlanta, went from Berlin to tour Europe and the Middle East and returned to Georgia to a welcome on the front page of the *Atlanta Daily World*. Daddy King, as he was known to friends and family, was born in Stockbridge, Georgia and came from humble sharecroppers. He reinvented himself as a preacher, married Alberta Williams, the daughter of A.D. Williams, one of Atlanta's most successful black pastors. After William's death, King Sr. presided over his congregation at Ebenezer Baptist Church.

King Sr. refused to ride on Atlanta's segregated buses, refused to answer to the term "boy" that white men used to denigrate adult black men, and he would tell black parishioners to embrace political self-determination, saying to a crowd of 1,000 people at a 1939 rally at Ebenezer, "I am going to move forward toward freedom, and I am hoping everybody here today joins me." Young Martin idolized Daddy King as a man of integrity, deeply committed to moral and ethical principles, and it shaped his professional and intellectual aspirations. Martin Jr. both admired and feared his father, who disciplined him using whippings until he was 15.

Martin enrolled at the most prestigious four-year men's school in the nation, historically black Morehouse College, at the time matching a precocious intellect with a growing sense of himself as a potential agent of social change. He found an important mentor and role model in Dr. Benjamin Mays, Morehouse's distinguished president, a friend of Daddy King's, an intellectual who believed in social justice, and who inspired an ethic of leadership and service. Religious classes with Dr. George Kelsey offered a scholarly entrée into the study of Christianity, which King longed for as an antidote to emotional antics of the black Baptist Church (a tradition that Daddy King exemplified).

Around Morehouse, Martin was well-known in his freshman year. His love of fine clothes and his manner of dress earned him the nickname Tweedy. He pursued romantic relationships with the daughters of Atlanta's black elite. Despite his average height, he presented as a good catch, and his baritone voice made him stand out as mature beyond his years. Martin's reputation as a ladies' man made him well-known among the male students at Morehouse. King's plans to study medicine and law were put on the back burner by his growing interest in the intersection of race, religion, and justice. In August 1946, King wrote a letter that was published in the *Atlanta Constitution*. The letter, titled "Kick Up Dust," was in response to the murders of two black couples and one black man by whites in Georgia. In his last year in college, he wrote an essay in the Morehouse newspaper chiding his classmates for aspiring to be middle-class elites who used their education for frivolous or destructive ends. During that last year at Morehouse, he also published a campus newspaper article titled "The Purpose of Education," which criticized former Georgia governor Eugene Talmadge for his segregationist views. He had spent the first three years at Morehouse resisting Daddy King's pleas to join him in the ministry. But in 1947, he finally relented, and at 18 King passed his trial sermon at Ebenezer Baptist Church. In his final year in college, he served as Daddy King's assistant pastor, which immensely pleased Daddy King. Morehouse president Benjamin Mays chose King as a class speaker for the senior sermon, where he dazzled his classmates during the mandatory chapel service.[1]

After his graduation from Morehouse, King spent three years at Crozer Theological Seminary in Chester, Pennsylvania. The school's location near Philadelphia removed him from the domineering Daddy King and enabled him to develop a personal religious philosophy that connected with his interest in social justice. He was one of the 9 black students in a class of 32, a surprising diversity for a prestigious, typically white school. King spent a considerable amount of time in a student hangout – a poolroom beneath the seminary chapel.

During his studies at Crozer, King discovered and embraced the Social Gospel through reading the work of theologian and author Walter Rauschenbusch's *Christianity and the Social Crisis*. The Social Gospel interpreted Christ's teachings as a vehicle for social justice on earth, examining Christianity through the lens of social ethics, and arguing that social justice on earth reflected the greatest manifestation of God's love and King quickly gravitated toward this perspective. Crozer's eclectic faculty of religious scholars, intellectuals, and free thinkers challenged and fascinated King.[2] He studied the writings of Mahatma Gandhi and Karl Marx, and though he was intrigued by Marx he would come to be personally associated with Gandhi. When King read Gandhi, the philosophical concept of satyagraha (rough translation: "truth force" or "love force") held particular appeal for him. King considered Gandhi's nonviolent movement against British colonialism in India as the "collective application of Jesus's love," capable of inspiring "a powerful and effective social force on a large scale." As he studied these ideas from various thinkers, King was seeking a religious and political philosophy that deplored poverty while recognizing love, democracy, and justice as sacred principles. In his first term at Crozer, he wrote a paper outlining the obligation he felt to personally address the forces of economic insecurity. He wrote that preachers "should possess profundity of conviction." He viewed the role of preaching ministry as a "dual process" in which he labored to inspire his flock to transform society "so that the individual soul will have a change."[3]

King was more serious about his academic studies at seminary than he was at Morehouse, but he found time to cultivate a new community of friends, colleagues, and mentors that extended from Chester to Philadelphia to New York. He attended regular dinners at the home of pastor J. Pious Barbour, a King family friend and Crozer's first black graduate. Reverend Barbour became a confidant about romantic entanglements, a debating partner on racial justice issues, and a mentor whose family became a second home for King during his time at Crozer.

He would also take long walks in the afternoon, taking advantage of the scenic beauty surrounding the campus. His communing with nature reflected a deeply meditative side of his personality. He socialized with white students and fell in love with Betty Moitz, the white daughter of Crozer's dietician. He dated Betty while seeing other women in Chester, Philadelphia, and New York, continuing a pattern that began at Morehouse and would continue throughout his life. He considered marrying Betty but decided not to do so, feeling that the relationship would be a burden to his ambitions.

During his final year at Crozer, he discovered Reinhold Niebuhr's 1932 classic *Moral Man and Immoral Society*. It offered him a blueprint for his transition from a preacher with intellectual ambitions to a faith leader and public intellectual who believed that "justice is love's message for the collective mind." King was coming into his own at Crozer as a budding scholar, impactful speaker, and student leader of weekly devotionals. He was elected student body president during his second year, the first black person to win that honor. He grew more intellectually ambitious and politically confident during his time at Crozer, delivering dozens of lectures in churches in Chester and Philadelphia, and he audited a seminar on Ethics and Philosophy of History at the University of Pennsylvania. Gandhi's importance was reinforced after listening to a speech by Howard University president Mordecai Johnson in Philadelphia in 1950. He had returned from a trip to India the previous year, and Johnson railed against Christianity's complicity with Jim Crow and compared the British treatment of Indians to the way America treated colored citizens in Alabama and Mississippi.

King used his years at Crozer to find his own political, theological, and personal voice. In sermons at Ebenezer during the summers, King tested out political themes he had encountered at Crozer. His deep baritone, crisp diction, and southern drawl allowed him to find a rhetorical middle ground between the fire-and-brimstone Baptist preachers, like his father, and the white ministers whose academic preaching style left him cold. He graduated from Crozer on May 15, 1953. He received a $1,200 fellowship to pursue graduate studies. He left Crozer with a deeper sense of his intellectual identity and a clearer sense of the kind of preacher he wanted to be. He had studied a wide range of thinkers and befriended white students and professors. He left Chester with plans to move north because he had secured a scholarship to Boston University to pursue a doctorate of philosophy in religion.

In Boston, the final piece of his eclectic intellectual puzzle was provided by King's doctoral work. He took ten courses from Edgar Brightman, the chief proponent of the school of theology called personalism. King's conclusion that "religion must nurture the individual personality, and his awareness that loss of dignity and self-respect was the insidious result of racism, would underlie the Movement's emotional force and tactical approach."[4]

Also while in Boston, he met and fell in love with Coretta Scott, a classically trained singer, two years older, who was on scholarship at Boston's New England

Conservatory of Music. King told Coretta that he was looking for a wife who possessed "character, intelligence, personality, and beauty" and "you have them all." They married in her native Alabama, just outside of Selma, less than 18 months after their first date.

> It was a complicated relationship, but their early romance eventually flowered into a marriage that became an intellectual and political partnership through which they shared a whirlwind of experiences, public and private, that drew them closer with each passing year.[4]

King's Journey as a Civil Rights Leader Begins

King's coursework was completed in January 1954, and he received an invitation to preach at Dexter Avenue Baptist Church in Montgomery, Alabama. Only two months later, the church offered him the position of pastor with a salary of over $4,000, making him the highest paid minister in the city. Not long after he arrived in Montgomery, King was offered the presidency of the local NAACP, but he turned that down to focus on his church and his new daughter Yolanda (nicknamed Yoki).

Then on Thursday, December 1, 1955, Rosa Parks boarded the bus in downtown Montgomery on her way home from work, and she refused to give up her seat to a white passenger. She was arrested for violating the city's segregation ordinance. A group of black leaders in town met and began to organize a boycott of the buses to begin the following Monday morning. This group became the Montgomery Improvement Association (MIA) and King was selected as the compromise candidate to be president. Twenty minutes after his selection the group was holding its first mass meeting. As part of his remarks, King said, "if we are wrong, justice is a lie." The boycott was effective in reducing ridership on the busses, but the victory was a long time coming for the black people in Montgomery. The city did not back down, but the Supreme Court upheld a district court decision that the city's bus segregation law was unconstitutional. During the yearlong wait, King was arrested and his house was bombed. He got much national recognition, and 10,000 people attended his first New York fundraiser.

However, over the next seven years the movement began to drift. After successes in Montgomery and with the favorable court decision in *Brown v. Board of Education*, the movement drifted for several years. During this period, the Court issued *Brown II*, which called for school desegregation with "all deliberate speed," which had the effect of slowing down the compliance required in the original *Brown* decision. According to King, by 1963 only nine percent of Negro students were attending integrated schools. Segregation laws kept blacks separate in almost all public places in the South – lunch counters, fitting rooms, rail and bus stations, parks, restrooms, even libraries. Five of seven men arrested for Montgomery bombings signed confessions, were indicted, and were acquitted anyway. New city ordinances prevented Negroes and whites from even playing checkers together. King and many of his supporters formed the Southern Christian Leadership Conference (SCLC) in 1957 with King as president, and its focus (at least initially) was to be Negro registration and voting. But it was sometimes late to respond, especially to students who bristled at the more cautious King. Student lunch counter sit-ins in Greensboro, North Carolina began without his involvement. He played catch up again when the Freedom Rides began in May 1961 to integrate interstate transportation facilities. The Freedom Riders were attacked and their bus burned, but the student riders were not joined by King until they arrived in Montgomery.

King had been thrust into a leadership position for which he was not prepared. He had to learn to be not just a minister, but a civil rights leader, politician, strategist, organizer, fundraiser, office and staff manager, and national and international spokesman. Since their victory in Montgomery, he had championed Christian love and nonviolence and that characterized their protests. But the emphasis on Christian love and nonviolence was a philosophy not a plan.[5]

In Albany, Georgia, King was involved in an unsuccessful campaign to test the Interstate Commerce Commission's ruling that interstate transportation facilities were to be integrated. Five black members of the Albany Movement attempted to eat in the bus station dining room on November 22, 1961, and they were promptly arrested. On December 10, a group of Freedom Riders arriving from Atlanta were jailed for trying to integrate the railroad station. On December 16, in town for less than a day, King and Ralph Abernathy led a protest march of 265 people, all of whom were jailed. King had planned to show up only to offer advice, but once there he felt compelled to march. The protest collapsed quickly when a tentative settlement was announced – an unwritten agreement that the city would soon ignore. King was released on bond, he left town dogged by press accounts that credited Albany police chief Laurie Pritchett with peacefully settling the unrest. Convicted for the protest in February 1962, King was sentenced on July 10, he accepted jail rather than pay the fine, but the Albany mayor arranged to have the fine paid to avoid King becoming a martyr. When he announced he would stay in Albany until their grievances were addressed he was confronted by a court injunction against further marches. He decided to honor the injunction, which stopped the Albany effort cold. When lawyers got the injunction lifted, King marched again, was arrested again, and then freed with a suspended sentence. Concluding his presence was doing little good he returned to Atlanta saying his departure would make negotiations easier. The press described the Albany effort as a "devastating loss of face" and "one of the most stunning defeats" of his leadership. Chief Pritchett piled on, boasting that integration had been set back "at least ten years" by King's failure.[6]

On to Birmingham ...

King believed that Birmingham was the most segregated city in America. Only 19 percent of the black population had been allowed to register to vote, it had been the site of more than 50 unsolved bombings over 20 years, it was the only one of 82 southern cities that had no blacks on its police force, its local courts had separate Bibles for blacks and whites taking the oath, and when the city was ordered to integrate its recreational facilities, it chose to close them down instead. One newspaper reporter wrote that "some Negroes have nicknamed Birmingham the 'Johannesburg of America,' and others called it 'Bombingham.'"[7] While progress in Birmingham would be difficult, the level of racism there would magnify anything King could accomplish.

The Birmingham campaign began on April 3, 1962, when the SCLC and the Alabama Christian Movement for Human Rights (ACMHR) coordinated marches and sit-ins against racism and racial segregation in the city. That day the SCLC and the ACMHR delivered copies of the "Birmingham Manifesto" to reporters. The Manifesto demanded (1) immediate desegregation of store facilities, (2) fair hiring practices, (3) dismissal of charges against previous non-violent ACMHR protesters, (4) a merit system to open city jobs to Negroes, (5) reopening of parks and pools on an integrated basis, (6) a biracial committee to focus on other areas.[8] On April 10, a circuit judge issued a blanket injunction against parading, demonstrating, boycotting, trespassing, and picketing. Leaders of the campaign announced, after some deliberation, they would disobey the order. Civil rights leader Andrew Young later recalled, "That, I think, was the beginning of his true leadership."[9] On April 12, (Good Friday), King, Abernathy, and others were arrested and jailed. King was in solitary confinement, interrupted only by a call from his wife that had been arranged by President Kennedy who had called the Birmingham Jail to suggest that they allow a call from Coretta to her husband. Martin was heartened by the President's effort, and took it as a sign of support, and made sure that the President's gesture became well-publicized among the black community. An ally smuggled in a newspaper from April 12, which contained "A Call for Unity," a statement from eight white clergymen against King and his methods. The clergymen agreed that social injustices existed but urged that the battle against racial segregation should be fought solely in the courts, not the streets. The letter provoked a pointed and thoughtful response from King.

His letter, dated April 16, 1963, responded to several criticisms made by the clergymen, who agreed that social injustices existed but argued that the battle against racial injustice was a matter for the courts, not the streets. He first responded to the criticism that he and his fellow activists were "outsiders." As the leader of the SCLC, he was invited to this city by the Birmingham affiliate of SCLC "because injustice is here," in what is probably the most racially divided city in the country, with its brutal police, unjust courts, and many "unsolved bombings of

Negro homes and churches." He asserted "injustice anywhere is a threat to justice everywhere." He also warned that if white people successfully rejected his non-violent activists as rabble-rousing outside agitators, that could encourage millions of African Americans to "seek solace and security in black nationalist ideologies, a development that will lead inevitably to a frightening racial nightmare."

He then addressed the clergymen's disapproval of public actions such as sit-ins and marches. King said that he and his fellow demonstrators were indeed using nonviolent direct action to create "constructive" tension, with the goal of compelling meaningful negotiations with the white power structure without which true civil rights could never be achieved. He said the black community had no alternative but to force negotiations, "We know through painful experience that freedom is never voluntarily given by the oppressor, it must be demanded by the oppressed."

The clergymen also disapproved of the timing of public actions. King replied that recent decisions by the SCLC to delay its efforts for tactical reasons showed that it was behaving responsibly. He also referred to the broader scope of history, saying "wait" has almost always meant "never."[10] African Americans had waited for God-given and constitutional rights long enough, King said "justice too long delayed is justice denied."

Next, King addressed the clergymen's assertion that demonstrations could be illegal. He argued that civil disobedience was not only justified in the face of unjust laws, but also necessary and even patriotic. He said "one has not only a legal but a moral responsibility to obey just laws. Conversely, one has a moral responsibility to disobey unjust laws." He also addressed the accusation that the Civil Rights Movement was "extreme" by first disputing that label and then accepting it. Compared to other movements at the time, King found himself to be a moderate. However, in his devotion to his cause, King referred to himself as an extremist. Jesus and other great reformers were extremists: "So the question is not whether we will be extremists, but what kind of extremists we will be. Will we be extremists for hate or for love?"

King also expressed general frustration with both white moderates and certain "opposing forces in the Negro community." He wrote that white moderates, including clergymen, posed a challenge comparable to white supremacists. "Shallow understanding from people of good will is more frustrating than absolute misunderstanding from people of ill will. Lukewarm acceptance is much more bewildering than outright rejection." King said that the white church needed to take a principled stand or risk being "dismissed as an irrelevant social club."

In the closing section of the letter, King criticized the clergy's praise of the Birmingham police for maintaining order nonviolently. The recent public displays of nonviolence by the police were in stark contrast to their typical treatment of black people, and helped "to preserve the evil system of segregation." It is wrong "to use moral ends to preserve immoral ends." Instead of the police, King praised the nonviolent demonstrators in Birmingham "for their sublime courage, their willingness to suffer and their amazing discipline in the midst of great provocation. One day the South will recognize its real heroes."

Terry Newell, in his book, *Statesmanship, Character and Leadership in America*, says the Letter from the Birmingham Jail works as a vehicle for social change. On one level, the Letter is "a work of leadership artistry," blending structured reasoning, an appeal to core values, political savvy, coalition building, and forcefulness of character and expression. It defuses critics and builds allies. On a second level, the Letter is a demonstration of power without position. Sitting in jail, condemned by whites and many blacks, leading an almost bankrupt organization, politically weak, King still manages to gather power. On a third level, the Letter also

> works as a macro- and micro- level attack on racism, as a black Declaration of Independence calling for fundamental social change, and as a plea to reverse the psychological damage of two centuries in which the Declaration's promise went unfulfilled.[11]

The Letter from the Birmingham Jail was only a qualified success if one looks at its impact on conditions "on the ground" in Birmingham. The settlement on May 10 fell short of meeting the demands of the Birmingham Manifesto. Desegregation in downtown stores was to be phased in, not immediate, and the reopening of parks and pools on an integrated basis was not even in the agreement. Fair hiring was only a goal to be reached after further discussion. Charges against protesters were not dropped. The "required" biracial committee would be established but with a vague mandate and little commitment to action.

The night of May 11, over 2,500 Klansmen rallied. Shortly after the rally, there were bombings around the city. Rioting followed, state troopers intervened, and the racist effort to sabotage the settlement seemed to be working. Then, on September 15, a bomb placed by the Klan under the steps of the Sixteenth Street Baptist Church exploded, killing four young girls. Two weeks later King threatened to resume demonstrations, since progress on the provisions of the settlement were making little or no progress. But King backed down from his threats. He and the Movement had emerged in the national consciousness as oppressed, nonviolent, and moderate in demands for which they should no longer be asked to wait – and as victorious, exactly the positioning that King had wanted to achieve with the Letter.

In mid-June, President Kennedy gave a national address on civil rights, saying: "We are confronted primarily with a moral issue." He introduced civil rights legislation a week later. Plans for a March on Washington took concrete shape, concentrating on pressuring Congress to pass Kennedy's bill. On August 28, a peaceful crowd of over 200,000 heard King's "I Have a Dream" speech and demonstrated for a national television audience that blacks were neither outsiders nor extremists.

King returned to the Birmingham jail in November 1967 to serve a five-day sentence after the U.S. Supreme Court upheld his conviction for the April 12, Good Friday, 1963, march.

Notes

1 Discussion of King's Morehouse years is from Peniel E., Joseph, *The Sword and the Shield, the Revolutionary Lives of Malcolm X and Martin Luther King, Jr.* (Basic Books, The Hachette Book Group, New York, NY, 2020), pages 57–59.

2 I recall my own fascination at arriving at a university where I felt the world had opened up to me. Just reading the course catalogue each semester and having the "menu of possibilities" for courses available to me was an exhilarating feeling. As I progressed through my course work and more of my schedule did not have to be devoted to required courses, I often felt a sense of elation when I would look at the possibilities for growth in any number of directions. When I visit my alma mater, the University of Missouri, I can still be moved by the feeling of intellectual freedom I had during my studies there.

3 Ibid., Joseph, *The Sword and the Shield*, page 60.

4 Terry Newell, *Statesmanship, Character and Leadership in America* (Palgrave Macmillan, New York, NY, 2012), page 136.

5 Ibid., Joseph, *The Sword and the Shield*, page 64.

6 Newell, *Statesmanship, Character, and Leadership in America*, page 134.

7 Ibid., page 136.

8 Ibid., page 140.

9 Ibid., page 142.

10 Ibid., page 148.

11 Ibid., page 151.

Bibliography

Branch, Taylor. *The King Years: Historic Moments in the Civil Rights Movement.* New York, NY: Simon & Schuster, 2013.

Newell, Terry. *Statesmanship, Character, and Leadership in America.* New York, NY: Palgrave Macmillan, 2012.

Peniel, Joseph E. *The Sword and the Shield: The Revolutionary Lives of Malcolm X and Martin Luther King Jr.* New York, NY: Basic Books, 2021.

"Roads to Memphis: The Assassination of Martin Luther King, Jr.," directed by Sam Pollard. *PBS American Experience Series,* Insignia Films, 2010.

17

RACHEL CARSON

Mother of the Environmental Movement

DOI: 10.4324/9781003266235-19

Rachel Carson was born on May 27, 1907 in Springdale, Pennsylvania along the Allegheny River just 13 miles north of Pittsburgh, Pennsylvania. Her mother was Maria McLean and her father was Robert Warden Carson. Her mother was a key figure throughout her life, taking a keen interest in her education and living with Rachel throughout most of Rachel's life.

From her mother, Rachel developed a passion for the natural world, exploring the natural world by learning about the woods near her home on walks with her mother. Her mother also encouraged her talent for writing. In 1918, at 11 years of age, Rachel won her first prize for a story published in St. Nicholas Magazine. The two passions of her life, the natural world and writing, came together early in Rachel's life. As she aged she would become a physical scientist with literary genius, a rare and potent combination.

Rachel's Early Years and Education

Rachel was a talented and dedicated student during her time at Parnassus, Pennsylvania High School, where she graduated at the top of her class of 40 students. She won a scholarship to Pennsylvania College for Women (now Chatham University) in Pittsburgh. She had intended to major in English and become a teacher.

She attended the Pennsylvania College for Women from 1925 to 1929, and graduated Magna Cum Laude. She changed her major from English to Biology, influenced largely by biology professor Mary Scott Skinker. To stay active as a writer, she continued contributing to the school's student newspaper and literary supplement. Rachel won a summer scholarship to the Woods Hole Marine Biological Laboratory in Woods Hole, Massachusetts.

She then qualified for a scholarship from Johns Hopkins University to pursue an M.A. in Zoology. During her studies at Johns Hopkins from 1929 to 1932, financial difficulties forced her to become a part-time student, taking an assistantship with Raymond Pearl's laboratory in the Institute for Biological Research, School of Hygiene, and Public Health, where she continued her studies in zoology and genetics. After completing her dissertation project, she earned a master's degree in zoology in June 1932. She had intended to continue for a doctorate, but in 1934, she was forced to leave Hopkins to search for a full-time teaching position to help support her family during the Great Depression. In 1935, her father died suddenly, worsening the family's already tenuous financial situation and leaving Carson to care for her aging mother.

At the urging of her undergraduate biology mentor from the Pennsylvania College for Women, Mary Scott Skinker, she settled for a temporary position with the U.S. Bureau of Fisheries, writing radio copy for a series of educational broadcasts about sea life. The series of 52 seven-minute programs focused on aquatic life and was intended to generate public interest in fish biology and the bureau's work. Carson also began submitting articles on marine life in the

Chesapeake Bay to local newspapers and magazines. Carson's supervisor worked to secure her the first full-time position that became available. In 1936, she took a civil service exam and became the second woman hired by the Bureau of Fisheries for a full-time position as a junior aquatic biologist.

During her time at the Bureau of Fisheries, she continued to write a steady stream of articles for *The Baltimore Sun* and other newspapers that produced a small income supplement. But her family responsibilities increased in January 1937, when her older sister died, leaving Carson as the sole breadwinner for her mother and two nieces.

Rachel's Writing Career Flourishes

In July 1937, the *Atlantic Monthly* accepted a revised version of an essay Rachel had written originally as her first Fisheries Bureau brochure (which her supervisor had decided was too good for that purpose.) titled *Undersea*, it was a vivid narrative of a journey along the floor of the ocean. The publishing house Simon & Schuster contacted Carson to suggest that she expand it into a book. It took several years for her to write *Under the Sea-Wind*, it received excellent reviews but sold poorly. Her success as a writer continued with articles published in *Nature*, *Collier's*, and *Sun Magazine*. She first encountered the subject of Dichlorodiphenyltrichloroethane (DDT) in mid-1945 when it was lauded as a revolutionary new pesticide, sometimes called the "insect bomb" – that was only beginning to be tested for safety and ecological effects. It became one of Carson's many writing interests, but editors found the subject unappealing so she published nothing on the subject until 1962.

Carson kept rising within the ranks of the Fish and Wildlife Service (which had formed in a merger in the Department of Interior between the Bureau of Fisheries and the Wildlife Service) and she now supervised a small writing staff, becoming chief editor of publications in 1949. This position provided more opportunities for fieldwork and freedom in choosing her writing projects, but it also meant increasingly tedious administrative responsibilities.

By 1948, she was working on producing a second book and had made a conscious decision to begin a transition to becoming a full-time writer. She took on a literary agent, Marie Rodell, and they formed a close professional relationship that would span the remainder of Carson's career. Oxford University Press expressed interest in Carson's book proposal for a life history of the ocean, which motivated her to complete by early 1950 the manuscript of what would become *The Sea Around Us*. Chapters appeared in *Science Digest* and *The Yale Review*. Nine chapters were serialized in *The New Yorker*. The book was published on July 2, 1951 and remained on the New York Times Best Seller list for 86 weeks. It was abridged by *Reader's Digest*, won the 1952 National Book Award for Nonfiction and resulted in Carson being awarded two honorary doctorates. She also licensed a documentary film based on the book.[1] Finally, the success of *The Sea Around Us* led to republication of her first book *Under the Sea-Wind*, and it also became a bestseller. Her success led to financial security she had never had before, and in 1952, she was able to leave her job at the Fish and Wildlife Service.

Rachel Carson and Dorothy Freeman

With the financial stability provided by the reaction to *The Sea Around Us*, Rachel bought property on Southport Island, Maine, and built a summer house (which she called *Silverledges*). In the summer of 1953, Carson met Dorothy Freeman and her husband Sam, who were nearby neighbors and had written a letter to welcome Rachel to the area. Thus began a very close friendship that would last for the rest of Rachel's life. She and Dorothy would exchange approximately 900 letters, many of which were published in the book *Always, Rachel*, published in 1995 by Beacon Press.

One of Carson's biographers, Linda Lear, writes about her relationship with Freeman that "Carson sorely needed a devoted friend and kindred spirit who would listen to her without advising and accept her wholly, the writer as well as the woman."[2] The two women had several common interests, nature being the predominant one, and began exchanging letters regularly while apart, and would share summers for the remainder of Carson's life and meet whenever else their schedules permitted.

The expression of their love for each other seems limited to letters they sent each other, some containing very ardent statements of their commitment to each other. Freeman shared parts of her letters with her husband to help him understand the nature of their relationship, but much of their correspondence was carefully guarded. One of Carson's letters reads: "But, oh darling, I want to be with you so terribly that it hurts!" while Freeman writes in another: "I love you beyond expression … My love is as boundless as the Sea." Carson's last letter to Freeman before her death ends with: "Never forget, dear one, how deeply I have loved you for all these years."[3] Shortly before Rachel's death, she and Freeman destroyed hundreds of letters.

For most of her life, Rachel Carson devoted her emotional energies to writing, work, and her family. When she met Dorothy Freeman, she found the love of a kindred spirit, someone to whom she could unburden her heart, whose praise and affection meant more than the adoration of a demanding mother, who shared her devotion to the sea, and who was "a haven in a hostile world."

Beginning in 1953, Carson began library and field research on the ecology and organisms of the Atlantic shore. In 1955, she completed the third volume of her "sea trilogy," *The Edge of the Sea*. It focused on life in coastal ecosystems, particularly along the Eastern Seaboard. It appeared in the New Yorker in two condensed installments shortly before its October 26 book release by Houghton Mifflin. Carson's reputation for clear and poetic writing was well established, and *The Edge of the Sea* received highly favorable reviews, though not quite as enthusiastic as for *The Sea Around Us.*

Creating Silent Spring

When Rachel set out to write her next book (what Dorothy Freeman called her "poison book"), she committed herself to a crusade, driven by a sense of moral outrage. She felt that humankind was becoming more arrogant in their determination to control nature, and that human beings posed a growing threat to all life on earth, including their own. She now had a profound "anger at the senseless, brutish things that were being done." She decided to build a case against those who made wanton use of dangerous chemicals.

Coming out of World War II a consensus dominated American society. At its core lay a profound anti-communism, encouraging social and political conformity, respect for governmental and community authority, uncritical patriotism, religious faith, and a commitment to a vague notion of an American way of life defined by prosperity, material comfort, and a secure home. To come under suspicion as a subversive one had only to dissent against commonly accepted values, as Carson intended to do, to be considered disloyal. The ideal American woman of the 1950s was a suburban housewife dedicated to the career of her husband, the care of her children, and the consumption of material goods made available by benevolent corporations. Carson, on the other hand, was an unmarried career woman who headed a family for which she had always provided. The child she was to adopt was born out of wedlock, and her most intimate relationship was with another woman.

Some other lonely voices challenging the military-industrial ethos of the day were gaining a wider audience. John Kenneth Galbraith published *The Affluent Society*, criticizing the cult of private consumption, and it was a major bestseller. Galbraith argued that a "social balance" was needed between increases in the production of consumer goods in the private sector and comparable increase in the services rendered by the public sector. Galbraith also called for wider opportunity for all citizens through improved schools, a renewed commitment to public service, and a reinvigorated activist state which served its citizens by addressing pressing problems such as poverty, inadequate schools, and disease.

Another voice also questioned the consensus around technology and commercial interests – Republican President Dwight D. Eisenhower. As he came to the end of his second term in 1961, he warned in his farewell address that the nation needed to "guard against the acquisition of unwarranted influence, whether sought or unsought, by the military-industrial complex." He urged "an alert and knowledgeable citizenry" to ensure "that security and liberty may prosper together." Carson had seen a similar threat in the alliance of USDA officials, state and county agricultural agencies, the chemical corporations, and in large industrial farms now known as agribusinesses. She feared that public policy could itself become the captive of a scientific-technological elite that would need to be countered by the public receiving proper information to make informed choices. She intended to give them that information.

After completing all 16 chapters of *Silent Spring*, Rachel felt that she needed to return to the front of the book to add an introduction to make the book feel less like a technical document. So she wrote a new chapter 1, titled "A Fable for Tomorrow." It offered a dystopian scenario of what the future could look like if a balance between nature and advancing technology could not be achieved. Her book seemed to start off saying to the reader, "here is what we need to avoid." Her opening sketch said:

There was once a town in the heart of America where all life seemed to live in harmony with its surroundings. The town lay in the midst of a checker-board of prosperous farms, with fields of grain and hillsides of orchards where, in spring, white clouds of bloom drifted above the green fields. In autumn, oak and maple and birch set up a blaze of color that flamed and flickered across a backdrop of pines. The foxes barked in the hills and deer silently crossed the fields, half hidden in the mist of the fall mornings.

Along the roads, laurel, … great ferns, and wildflowers delighted the traveler's eye through much of the year. Even in winter the roadsides were places of beauty, where countless birds came to feed on the berries.

Then a strange blight crept over the area and everything began to change. Some evil spell had settled on the community: mysterious maladies swept the flocks of chickens; the cattle and sheep sickened and died. Everywhere was a shadow of death. The farmers spoke of much illness among their families. In town the doctors had become more and more puzzled by new kinds of sickness appearing among their patients. There had been several sudden and unexplained deaths, not only among adults but even among children, who would be stricken suddenly while at play and die within a few hours.

There was a strange stillness. The birds – where had they gone? Many people spoke of them, puzzled and disturbed. The feeding stations in the backyards were deserted. The few birds seen anywhere were moribund, they trembled violently and could not fly. It was a spring without voices.

The roadsides, once so attractive, were now lined with browned and withered vegetation as though swept by fire. These too were silent, deserted by all living things. … In the gutters under the eaves and between the shingles of the roofs, a white granular powder still showed a few patches; some weeks before it had fallen like snow upon the roofs and the lawns, the fields and streams.

No witchcraft, no enemy action had silenced the rebirth of new life in this stricken world. The people had done it themselves.

This town does not actually exist, but it might easily have a thousand counterparts in America or elsewhere in the world. I know of no community that has experienced all the misfortunes I describe. Yet every one of these disasters has actually happened somewhere, and many real communities have already suffered a substantial number of them. *A grim specter has crept upon us almost unnoticed, and this imagined tragedy may easily become a stark reality we all shall know. What has already silenced the voices of spring in countless towns in America? This book is an attempt to explain.* (Emphasis added)[4]

As her writing progressed during this period, Rachel continued to endure various setbacks in her personal life. The first of these was in December 1948 when her mentor and friend who had convinced her to study biology at Pennsylvania Women's College, Mary Scott Skinker, fell ill and died of cancer. In 1950, Rachel's doctor confirmed the presence of a cancerous breast tumor. He removed the tumor and suggested no further treatment. But in 1960, as her research and writing were progressing nicely, a duodenal ulcer followed by several infections kept her bedridden for weeks, delaying the completion of *Silent Spring*. As she was nearing full recovery in March (just as she was completing drafts of the two cancer chapters of the book) she discovered cysts in her left breast, one of which necessitated a mastectomy. Her doctor described the procedure as precautionary and recommended no further treatment. But by December, Rachel discovered that the tumor was malignant and had metastasized.

As Rachel's research for the "poison book" progressed, she found a significant community of scientists who were documenting the physiological and environmental effects of pesticides. She found two scientific camps regarding pesticides: those who dismissed the possible danger of pesticide spraying barring conclusive proof, and those who were open to the possibility of harm and willing to consider alternative methods, such as biological pest control.

During the research and writing of *Silent Spring*, a growing sense of alarm came from other external events, including: Japanese seamen on board the "Lucky Dragon" died from radiation exposure; fire ants in the South were sprayed by USDA with an agricultural equivalent of the atomic bomb for the "eradication of the imported fire ant"[5]; in Long Island Federal Court, alarming testimony of spraying toxic chemical pesticides in fuel oil by airplane over private land to control mosquitoes and to stop Dutch elm disease; in 1959, a controversy over radioactive fallout again makes the public wary of environmental hazards; in December 1959, cranberries sprayed with toxic chemical aminotriazole before harvesting are linked to throat cancer in rats – USDA removes cranberries from the market before Christmas; finally, Dr. Frances Oldham Kelsey at the Food and Drug Administration (FDA) blocked the drug thalidomide from the U.S. market after mounting evidence of deformities in pre-natal development in other countries. President John F. Kennedy awarded Dr. Kelsey the Distinguished Civilian Civil Service Medal for her work at the FDA.

Settling on a title for her book was not easy. "Silent Spring" was initially suggested as a title for the chapter on birds. By August 1961, Rachel finally agreed to the suggestion of her literary agent Marie Rodell: *Silent Spring* would be a metaphorical title for the entire book, suggesting a bleak future for the entire natural world. The final writing was the first chapter, *A Fable for Tomorrow*, which she intended as a gentle introduction to the sometimes technical information that followed. By mid-1962, Brooks and Carson had finished the editing and were preparing for publication.

Expecting fierce criticism of the book, Rachel and Marie Rodell amassed as many prominent supporters as possible before the book's release. In addition to many prominent scientists, Supreme Court Justice William O. Douglass, a longtime environmental advocate who had provided Rachel with some of the material included in her chapter on herbicides also spoke in support of Rachel's work. Carson attended the White House Conference on Conservation, during which proof copies were made available to many of the delegates, and the upcoming serialization in *The New Yorker* beginning on June 16, 1962 issue was publicized.

Prior to the publication on September 27, 1962 there was already strong opposition to *Silent Spring* from the chemical industry. Velsicol, the manufacturer of chlordane and heptachlor, threatened legal action against both Houghton Mifflin and *The New Yorker* unless they canceled the planned publication. Chemical companies produced many brochures and articles promoting and defending pesticide use. American Cyanamide biochemist Robert White-Stevens emerged as the industry's most aggressive critic, saying things like, "If man were to follow the teachings of Miss Carson, we would return to the Dark Ages, and the insects and disease and vermin would once again inherit the earth." He also labeled her "... a fanatic defender of the cult of the balance of nature." Eisenhower's former Secretary of Agriculture Ezra Taft Benson, in a letter to his old boss concluded that because she was unmarried despite being physically attractive, she was "probably a Communist."

Many critics asserted mistakenly that she was calling for the elimination of all pesticides. But Carson had made it clear that she was not advocating the banning or complete withdrawal of helpful pesticides but was instead encouraging responsible and carefully managed use with an awareness of the chemicals' impact on the entire ecosystem. Pesticide use became a major public issue, especially after the *CBS Reports* television special *The Silent Spring of Rachel Carson* that aired on April 3, 1963. The program included segments of Rachel reading *Silent Spring*, and interviews with several other experts including critics (such as White-Stevens.) In juxtaposition to White-Stevens who came off wild-eyed, loud-voiced, in a white lab coat, Rachel appeared anything but the hysterical alarmist that her critics portrayed.

The *CBS Reports* audiences of ten to fifteen million were overwhelmingly positive, and the program triggered a Congressional review of pesticide dangers and the public release of a pesticide report by the President's Science Advisory Committee. For one of her last public appearances, Rachel testified before the Committee, which had issued its report (called "The Use of Pesticides") on May 15, 1963 and had backed her scientific claims. She also testified before a United States Senate subcommittee to make policy recommendations. She received countless other speaking requests, but her health was declining as her cancer spread faster than the radiation therapy could arrest it. She selected some requests when she was physically able, such as a noteworthy appearance on *The Today Show*, and several dinners in her honor. By late 1963, she received the Audubon Medal, the Cullum Geographical Medal (from the American Geographical Society) and induction into the American Academy of Arts and Letters.

The Death and the Legacy of Rachel Carson

The spreading cancer and her treatment regimen weakened Rachel and she became ill with a respiratory virus in January 1964. As her condition worsened doctors determined that she had severe anemia from her radiation treatments. In March, they discovered that the cancer had reached her liver. She died of a heart attack on April 14, 1964 in her home in Silver Spring, Maryland.

The world can only be left to wonder what other environmental hazards Rachel might have warned us about and spoken up so eloquently in doing so. What might she have made of the prospect of global warming, its causes, its possible solutions, and the need for a world-wide effort to save the planet?

There was some disagreement about the funeral arrangements for Rachel. Her brother, Robert Carson, insisted that her cremated remains be buried beside their mother in Maryland. This was contrary to Rachel's wishes to be buried in Maine. A compromise was reached when an organizing committee including her agent (Marie Rodell), her editor (Paul Brooks),[6] and Dorothy Freeman carried out her wishes. In the spring of 1964, Dorothy received half of Rachel's ashes in the mail sent to her by Robert Carson. In the summer of that year, Dorothy carried out Rachel's final wishes, scattering her ashes along the rocky shores of Sheepscot Bay in Maine.

In 1965, Marie Rodell arranged for the publication of an essay Rachel had intended to expand into a book: *The Sense of Wonder*. The essay exhorts parents to help their children experience the "…lasting pleasures of contact with the natural world, available to anyone who will place himself under the influence of earth, sea, and sky and their amazing life." Rachel was encouraging parents to act as her mother had in introducing her to the natural world.

Silent Spring can still be the subject of controversy. In 2007, in honor of Rachel Carson's 100th birthday, Democratic Senator Benjamin Cardin of Maryland, along with Democratic Senator Barbara A. Mikulski of Maryland, Republican Senator Arlen Specter of Pennsylvania, and Democratic Senator Robert P. Casey of Pennsylvania introduced a resolution to commemorate Rachel Carson's work on promoting understanding and protection of the natural world, recognizing her "legacy of scientific rigor and poetic sensibility." Oklahoma Republican Senator Tom Coburn stated on his website he was blocking the resolution because he accused Carson of using "junk science" to turn public opinion against chemicals, including DDT that could have prevented the spread of insect-borne diseases such as malaria. His web statement points out that he is a doctor specializing in family medicine, obstetrics, and allergies. Coburn further stated that Carson "was the author of the now-debunked *Silent Spring*... This book was the catalyst in the deadly worldwide stigmatization against insecticides, especially DDT."[7]

Epilogue

When *Silent Spring* was published in 1962, the effects of pesticides and toxic chemicals on the environment had been documented before, but only incrementally and scattered throughout the technical literature. Environmental scientists were aware of the problem but they tended to focus only on the narrow sector of their personal expertise. Rachel Carson's achievement was to synthesize this knowledge into a single explanation that everyone, including scientists and the general public alike, could easily understand. Her writing style presented highly technical information in literary and almost poetic ways.

In the final chapter of *Silent Spring*, titled "The Other Road," Rachel Carson said:

> We stand now where two roads diverge. But unlike the roads in Robert Frost's familiar poem, they are not equally fair. The road we have long been traveling is deceptively easy, a smooth superhighway on which we progress with great speed, but at its end lies disaster. The other fork of the road – the one "less travelled by" – offers our last, our only chance to reach a destination that assures the preservation of our earth.
>
> The choice, after all, is ours to make. If having endured much, we have at last asserted our "right to know," and if knowing, we have concluded that we are being asked to take senseless and frightening risks, then we should no longer accept the counsel of those who tell us that we must fill our world with poisonous chemicals, we should look about and see what other course is open to us.[8]

Notes

1 Rachel did not insist on keeping control of the approval of the final script for this film, produced by Irwin Allen, a producer of movies and television shows that focused on fantastic tales about the sea. Rachel thought the final film was an abomination, lacking any of the educational value she had hoped to provide in the film. She never again worked with anyone to produce a film of her books.

2 Linda Lear, *Rachel Carson, Witness for Nature* (Mariner Books, Houghton Mifflin Harcourt, Boston, MA/New York, NY), 1997, page 248.

3 Mark Hamilton Lytle, *The Gentle Subversive, Rachel Carson, Silent Spring and the Rise of the Environmental Movement* (Oxford University Press, New York, NY and Oxford, 2007), page 133.

4 Rachel Carson, *Silent Spring* (Houghton Mifflin Company, Boston, MA/New York, NY, 1962), pages 1–3.

5 Paul Brooks, Rachel's editor at Houghton Mifflin, had signed Rachel to do a book about the seashore, and he became someone to whom she now turned for advice and

encouragement. She quickly sensed that he understood exactly the kind of book she wanted to produce. He became as much a part of her creative process as her agent, Marie Rodell. Brooks was able to nurture her writing and gave her freedom to discover the approach that realized the possibilities in her subject, even if it meant long delays in producing a manuscript.

6 In *Silent Spring*, Rachel Carson labeled the fire ant eradication program

> an outstanding example of an ill-conceived, badly executed, and thoroughly detrimental experiment in the mass control of insects, an experiment so expensive in dollars, in destruction of animal life, and in loss of public confidence in the Agriculture Department that it is incomprehensible that any funds should still be devoted to it.

7 The discussion of Oklahoma Senator Tom Coburn's attempts to block the resolution honoring Rachel Carson comes from David A. Fahrenthold, "Bill to Honor Rachel Carson Blocked," *Washington Post*, May 23, 2007. The article also points out that in late April 2007, a House bill to name a post office after Carson in her home town of Springdale, Pennsylvania, received 53 "nay" votes. Some of those voting "nay" cited similar concerns about Carson's impact on the decline of DDT use.

8 Carson, *Silent Spring*, pages 277–278.

Bibliography

Carson, Rachel. *Silent Spring*. Boston, MA/New York, NY: Houghton Mifflin Company, 1962.

Lear, Linda. *Rachel Carson: Witness for Nature*. Buena Vista, VA: Mariner Books, 2009.

Lytle, Mark H. *The Gentle Subversive: Rachel Carson, Silent Spring, and the Rise of the Environmental Movement*. Oxford: Oxford University Press, 2007.

"Rachel Carson," dir. by Michelle Ferrari. *PBS American Experience Series*, 42nd Parallel Films Production, 2017.

"Rachel Carson's Silent Spring." *PBS American Experience Series*, Peace River Productions, 1993.

18

ROBERT F. KENNEDY

Beacon of Hope

DOI: 10.4324/9781003266235-20

The life of Robert F. Kennedy fits the definition of odyssey: "a long wandering or voyage usually marked by many changes of fortune" or "an intellectual or spiritual wandering or quest."

Perceptions of Robert Kennedy are so varied that it seems they could not exist in the same person. There are perceptions of him as:

1. the listless and overlooked brother who moved from one boarding school to another (six in ten years) and was thought of as the "runt" of his family, the child who absorbed his mother's Catholic faith, and the undistinguished graduate of Harvard;

2. the ruthless and opportunistic enforcer of the Kennedy family's political agenda, especially during his leadership of Jack's campaigns and his contribution to Jack's presidency;

3. the aggressive lawyer on the Senate staff investigating, first, the communist presence in the American government at the right hand of Sen. Joe McCarthy, and second, the corruption of the Teamsters' Union in the person of Jimmy Hoffa;

4. the crusading Attorney General who used the power of his office to push progress on civil rights, and convince his brother, the President, to adopt civil rights as a moral issue, yet also authorizing the wiretapping of Martin Luther King, Jr.;

5. the deeply conflicted aide to President Johnson who developed a smoldering disdain bordering on hate for LBJ and later, after leaving the Johnson Administration, broke ranks with him over the war in Vietnam;

6. the initially awkward and then restless Senator from New York who used his office as a way to reach out to the forgotten, dispossessed, segments of America and become their voice; he began to find his voice during this time, becoming the "tribune of the underclass," gentle but driven, an idealistic but pragmatic politician;

7. the doting father and family patriarch who was always mindful of using his platform to stoke the "new politics" and promote the role and potential contribution of current and future generations;

8. the crusading campaigner for the presidency in the 1968 campaign, who built a coalition of working-class whites, African-Americans, Hispanics, and other minorities to win primary elections with the intent to swarm the Democratic Convention and win the nomination;

9. and suddenly ... the stricken martyr on the kitchen floor of the Ambassador Hotel in Los Angeles on the night he had finally gained the momentum needed to win the nomination of his party.

It seemed almost pre-ordained that it would all end badly for Robert Kennedy. In spite of growing up and becoming an adult in a world of affluence, the spectre of loss and tragedy were a constant presence in his life.

1. While a student at Harvard, there was a near miss with tragedy when Jack, serving in the Navy in the Pacific, was nearly killed in his PT boat, sustaining injuries that would plague him for the rest of his life.
2. Then, near the end of World War II in Europe, his oldest brother Joe Jr. volunteered for a hazardous mission and his plane loaded with explosives which were targeted at a German missile base explodes, killing him and his crewmate.
3. At the end of his first year of law school at the University of Virginia, Robert's exuberant older sister Kathleen (known as "Kick" inside the family) died in a plane crash in France at the age of 28.
4. Robert's sister Rosemary, increasingly plagued by intellectual disabilities and erratic behavior, was given a then-experimental treatment (a lobotomy) at age 23. The surgery was botched, and the lobotomy rendered her incapable of caring for herself; she was placed in a facility in the Midwest, disappeared from public view, and was seldom mentioned anymore in accounts of the family.
5. And then … the ultimate tragedy of Robert's life – Jack is assassinated on November 22, 1963 in Dallas, Texas. What follows is the darkest period of Robert's life, a dark depression and lethargy which he only shakes off after several years.

All of these experiences combined to make a man who knew what it meant to hurt and feel aggrieved. He learned to see through the eyes of America's casualties. From all of this, he developed extraordinary empathy, compassion, vision, and awareness. This all came to fruition during the 85 days of his campaign of 1968, when he showed himself as a man who could: bridge divides between races, classes, and political philosophies; inspire the youth of the nation; and make public service a noble calling.

During that campaign of 1968, America saw what a candidate for president can be, what a leader calling us to strive for our higher aspirations looks like, and what an iconic and noble public servant can offer. It was all there in Robert Kennedy. No major candidate for president has or ever will match his intensity of feeling for the poor and dispossessed, his capacity to create hope and trust, his authenticity as a human being, and his ability to be changed by his experience and grow from it. Over time he has proven to be irreplaceable.

When we heard press secretary Frank Mankiewicz announce Robert's death at age 42, it was as if he had actually announced the death of hope, and the loss of our prospects to be a great country. Robert Kennedy continues to haunt our imagination. We continue to mourn the loss of our best opportunity to achieve the America our forefathers had envisioned.

Bibliography

MacAfee, Norman. *The Gospel According to RFK: Why it Matters Now.* New York, NY: Basic Books, 2008.

Newfield, Jack. *RFK: A Memoir.* New York, NY: Bold Type Books, 2003.

"RFK," directed by David Grubin. *PBS American Experience Series,* David Grubin Films, 2004.

Schlesinger, Arthur. *Robert Kennedy: His Life and Times.* Boston, MA: Harcourt Mifflin Publishing, 1980.

Thomas, Evan. *Robert Kennedy: His Life.* New York, NY: Simon & Schuster, 2000.

Tye, Larry. *Bobby Kennedy: The Making of a Liberal Icon.* New York, NY: Random House Publishing, 2017.

19

SERGIO VIEIRA DE MELLO

Diplomat in Harm's Way

DOI: 10.4324/9781003266235-21

Sergio Vieira de Mello was born in Rio de Janeiro, Brazil, on March 15, 1948. After he graduated from a Franco-Brazilian high school in Rio, and a short stint at the University of Rio, he moved to Europe, where he studied philosophy at the University of Fribourg and then at the Sorbonne in Paris, France. In May 1968, students and workers staged mass demonstrations in Paris, where he was badly beaten.

Sergio's father, Arnaldo was forced to retire from the Brazilian foreign service. Because of his father's postings in Argentina; Genoa, Milan, Rome, and Naples, Italy; Beirut; and Brazil (twice); Sergio had lived in many parts of the world, in effect becoming a "citizen of the world." After graduating from the Sorbonne, Sergio joined the office of the U. N. High Commissioner for Refugees (UNHCR) in Geneva, Switzerland, becoming an assistant editor at the agency's headquarters. While working at UNHCR, Sergio completed his doctorate in philosophy at the Sorbonne.

Vieira de Mello took his first field assignment in 1971–1972, where he served as a UNHCR project officer in Dhaka, East Pakistan/Bangladesh. His early assignments were operational rather than political; he was organizing and distributing food aid, and arranging shelter and other types of aid to refugees. He continued in the field, with a posting to Mozambique to assist refugees fleeing white rule and civil war in Zimbabwe (then still known as Rhodesia) where he was deputy head of the office.

On June 2, 1973, Sergio married Annie Personazz near her parent's home in France. Annie was a French staff member at UNHCR Headquarters in Geneva. They had two sons, Laurent and Adrien, and they made their home in the French village of Massongy, very near Geneva. Only 10 days later after their marriage, Sergio's father Arnaldo Vieira de Mello died suddenly in Rio de Janeiro.

Through a succession of assignments with the U.N. in trouble spots– from Sudan to Lebanon to Cambodia to Bosnia to Congo to Kosovo to East Timor to Iraq –

> he learned to tailor his tactics to the troubles around him and tried to enlist the powerful. He brought a gritty pragmatism to negotiations, yet no amount of exposure to brutality seemed to dislodge his ideals. Usually, he managed simultaneously to perform high-stakes peacemaking and nation-building tasks *and* to reflect critically on them.[1]

Though his career was already well-established, Vieira de Mello also took the time to continue his education, completing an MA in moral philosophy and a PhD by correspondence from the Sorbonne. His doctorate thesis in 1974 was entitled *The Role of Philosophy in Contemporary Society.* In 1985, he submitted a second "state" doctorate, the highest degree in the French education system. Also, he was a fluent speaker of many languages, including his native Portuguese, English, Spanish, Italian, and French, as well as conversational Arabic.

He then spent three years in charge of UNHCR operations in Mozambique during the civil war that followed its independence from Portugal in 1975, and three more years in Peru. Vieira de Mello then served as Special Envoy for the UNHCR for Cambodia. He was the first and only UN Representative to hold talks with the Khmer Rouge. He became a senior political adviser to the United Nations Interim Force in Lebanon between 1981 and 1983. In 1985, he returned to Latin America to serve as the head of the Argentina office in Buenos Aires.

Much of the 1990s for Vieira de Mello involved the clearing of land mines in Cambodia, and then in Yugoslavia. Then, after working on the refugee problem in central Africa, he was appointed Assistant High Commissioner for Humanitarian Affairs and Emergency Relief Coordinator two years later. He would hold this position simultaneously with others until January 2001. He was also a special UN envoy in Kosovo after the UN took control over his Serbian province in 1999.

The pattern of Vieira de Mello's career was that he was sent by the UN anywhere that trouble broke out. This was explained, in part, by Sergio's adherence to three principles. First, his career choices were guided by his belief that *he had the most to contribute to situations in the field*, rather than remaining in headquarters' operations fighting bureaucratic wars. When he was in the field, he was guided by the principle that *the UN should never surrender its impartiality, its greatest asset*. The third principle that guided Sergio was to *always keep open communication lines with all parties in a dispute, even opponents and rivals*. These principles served him well through all of his many endeavors at the UN.

Before becoming the UN High Commissioner for Human Rights in 2002, he was the UN Transitional Administrator in East Timor from December 1999 to May 2002, guiding the former Portuguese colony occupied by Indonesia to independence.

Guiding East Timor to Independence

UN Secretary-General Kofi Annan reached out to Vieira de Mello to lead the UN Transitional Administration in East Timor (UNTAET). Sergio was the UN official best suited to performing tasks as varied as overseeing the drafting of a constitution, planning elections, and facilitating the return of Timorese refugees. However, Vieira de Mello already had a job as an under-secretary-general for humanitarian affairs. But Annan asked Vieira de Mello to take a leave from UN headquarters to become Special Representative of the Secretary-General in East Timor. Vieira de Mello accepted eagerly, having found himself bristling at his desk job in New York. He lured others who had worked with him on previous missions to join him for what he described as "six months max … we will be back in New York in time for the summer."[2] But the mission in East Timor would last for two and a half years. Before going to East Timor, he flew to Geneva to see Annie and his sons. East Timor was a very inaccessible place and Vieira de Mello knew that he would see his family even less than while he had been working at Headquarters.

He had been appointed what he called "a benevolent despot," in a country he had never even visited. Neither the Timorese nor any international organizations had been given a say in how the country was to be built or run. Nothing like this had ever been tried before, and although the preferred outcome was clear – an independent state – he would have to create his own path to that goal. He would often say that he did not have "an instruction manual." Although the UN Resolution creating UNTAET was very detailed it lacked a plan for sharing power with the Timorese and for providing them with day-to-day economic and physical security. These gaps presented a challenge that made the mission more complex and take much longer than anyone had initially thought.

On the other hand, East Timor had certain advantages over other situations where Vieira de Mello had worked for the UN. It was ethnically homogeneous, 90 percent Catholic, so he would not have to worry about calming sectarian or ethnic strife of the kind he had seen in Kosovo. The people were united in their goal of achieving independence. Most of the militiamen and voters who had favored remaining part of Indonesia had fled to West Timor. Many of the existing leaders preached reconciliation and patience. Vieira de Mello noted the absence of the "mortal hatred" he had observed in the Balkans. In addition, all of the countries on the Security Council were united behind the aims of the UN mission, supporting East Timor's march to independence. Rich countries seemed prepared to give generously to assist the birth of the new country.

As the UN Administrator, he would be facing many decisions in a matter of days or weeks. Airports and ports had to be opened, clean water procured, health care provided, schools resuscitated, a currency created, relations with Indonesia normalized, a constitution drafted, an official language adopted, and tax, customs, and banking systems devised. Policies and procedures normally evolved over decades would have to be decided within months of his arrival.

Vieira de Mello's top priority on his arrival in East Timor was to build governing structures. He knew his success in East Timor would hinge on his relationship with Xanana Gusmao, who was both the rebel commander and the unquestioned political leader. Upon landing in Dili after traveling 24 hours, he announced that he would visit Gusmao the next day to pay his respects to him. The two hour-drive to Aileu, where Gusmao was encamped was grueling, along steep, unpaved mountain roads, and it gave him his first look at the country he now ruled. Gusmao welcomed the gesture. On December 2, 1999, Vieira de Mello set up the National Consultative Council (NCC), an advisory council that he hoped would be a vehicle for involving the Timorese in deciding their future. The NCC had three UN officials, in addition to Vieira de Mello, seven members from Gusmao's party, three members of other political groups, and one member of the Timorese Catholic Church. It did not take long for the Timorese to feel that they were just a rubber stamp for Vieira de Mello's decrees and regulations so the UN could claim to be consulting. As an administrator, Vieira de Mello had to find a way simultaneously to take immediate short-term actions and to build the Timorese capacity to govern themselves in the long term. He repeatedly stressed that the UN was not there to rule, but to prepare the Timorese to do so. In the meantime, the UN mission would have to ensure that tax revenue was collected, the garbage was picked up, the schools were refurbished and reopened, and a local civil service was recruited and trained while the UN provided basic services in the interim. He also pointed out that the UN Security Council had tasked UNTAET to work itself out of existence.

Vieira de Mello complained repeatedly that he could hire political officers and administrators but he could not find the road engineers, waste managers, tax policy experts, and electrical engineers he needed to make the nation run. The UN was formally responsible for everything and yet had zero capacity for anything. Jonathan Prentice, who served as Vieira de Mello's special assistant described the situation: "…we had all these people sent in from New York who could write diplomatic cables, but nobody who could lay electrical cable."[3]

Vieira de Mello never imagined that he would stay in East Timor as long as he did. Most of his colleagues assumed that he would be appointed to the job of UN High Commissioner for Refugees. Vieira de Mello had drafted more repatriation agreements, negotiated with more government officials, and led more field missions than any other candidate. Everyone around him assumed that he would serve his time in East Timor, return to Geneva to take the refugee position, and then someday ascend to the secretary-general position. But that was not to be for two reasons. First, Annan liked to fill his senior positions with individuals from countries that donated significant funds. Second, the very qualities that made Vieira de Mello a good candidate for the high commissioner's job made Annan reluctant to let him leave East Timor. Richard Holbrooke, President Clinton's ambassador to the UN, believed that the East Timor mission had given the UN a chance to redeem itself from the "triple failure" of Somalia, Bosnia, and Rwanda. When Vieira de Mello's name began circulating for the high commissioner job, he called Annan and told him to keep his "ultimate go-to guy" in East Timor. Annan recalled, "I did not need any persuading …I knew Sergio was too valuable to bring home early." Holbrooke called Vieira de Mello and said he was sorry to do this to him but he was recommending to Annan that he keep him in East Timor. The high commissioner job went to Ruud Lubbers, the former prime minister of the Netherlands, the third-largest source of funding for UNHCR. Though disappointed in not being selected, he was particularly stung by the way the news of the appointment was imparted – he learned about it from the news media and thought he at least warranted a phone call to be told about it. Thus, at a crucial juncture of his UN career, he was not promoted because he was too successful in his current job.[4]

Vieira de Mello needed to begin a power-sharing arrangement with the Timorese, as it was time to move them into more responsible governing roles to facilitate the eventual transition to their own government. He proposed a "co-government" relationship, in which he would create a mixed cabinet divided evenly between four Timorese and four internationals. The plan was in defiance of UN rules and he needed to talk Headquarters through what he had in mind. So he set up a conference call with Headquarters and invited his Timorese associates who would serve on the cabinet to participate in the call. Sergio wanted to put Headquarters officials in the awkward position of explaining directly to the Timorese why they should not be allowed to serve in the formation of the government. UN officials in New York muted their concerns, allowing Vieira de Mello on July 15, 2000 to swear in a new mixed cabinet. UN officials would keep control of the police and emergency services, and the political affairs, justice, and financial portfolios. Timorese would be responsible for ministries for internal administration, infrastructure, economic affairs, and social affairs.

The plan would result in high-paid foreigners working under Timorese managers. There was a strong negative reaction among the staff at the mission who felt that their contracts stipulated that they were to work for the UN Secretary-General. Vieira de Mello assembled the entire UN staff of the mission – 700 people – along with four new Timorese cabinet ministers, in the auditorium of the parliament building. When someone pointed out to Vieira de Mello that there was nothing in the Security Council Resolution that authorized UNTAET to have the UN staff work for the East Timorese, Vieira de Mello was defiant: "I assume full responsibility. You can either obey, or you can leave."[5]

Vieira de Mello next laid out a political road map in January 2001. An 88 member constituent assembly would be elected in August, and this assembly would draft and adopt a constitution within ninety days, decide upon the date for presidential elections, and choose the date on which East Timor would become independent. The assembly, duly elected, decided to sign the constitution in March 2002, hold presidential elections in April, and receive full independence in late May. By mid-September, Vieira de Mello had formed a new cabinet composed only of Timorese.

Vieira de Mello led a very solitary life during his time in East Timor. He attended all the parties and other functions that his position required, but he grew tired of "being on" as his stature demanded. He realized that he had become very lonely and was asking himself "What is all this for?" In late 2000, he met Carolina Larriera, a 27-year-old Argentinian who had gone to University in New York and had a staff job as a public information office in UN Headquarters. Her first field posting was in East Timor, where she helped dispense World Bank microcredit grants to Timorese businesses. She had steered clear of Vieira de Mello during her posting but in October 2000, she briefed him on the microcredit program in advance of a donors' conference he was to attend.

A month later she attended a small dinner party at which Vieira de Mello approached her, and they drifted into easy conversation. They became romantically involved in January 2001 and conducted their relationship privately. Vieira de Mello was not sure he could carry on a serious relationship with someone he worked around, and they paused their relationship, staying in touch but not escalating the situation. Then, in October 2001, he invited her over to his house and they decided to start again, this time with equally serious intent. He seemed to want what others around him had, a serious partner with whom he would be romantically involved. Realizing he was in love with Carolina he decided to file for divorce from Annie in December 2001. Though he had lived apart from Annie since 1996, she took the news hard. However distant they had grown, she never expected him to leave the marriage, but he was determined to go ahead. He was also determined, as he wrote to friends during that time "to make the most of what remains of my life instead of wasting the few years that are left."[6]

He also told friends that with only six months left in his posting in East Timor, he planned to take three months off to do many of the things he had dreamed of doing and delayed his whole life. At Christmastime he had done something he had never done with any of his girlfriends – he brought her home to Brazil to meet his mother. Larriera, in turn, took him to Buenos Aires. When they returned to East Timor, she moved into his house and they started a quiet domestic life together. At a dinner in his honor one week before the scheduled independence ceremony, his toast included these words about Larriera:

> East Timor is special to me for many reasons, but none more than because this is where I met Carolina. For two years we worked together in the same building in New York and never met. We had to travel to this small island ten thousand miles away in order to find one another.[7]

His close friends were stunned by his transformation, and all seemed to agree that Larriera brought out the relaxed side of him that they had not seen in such abundance before.

As he prepared to leave East Timor, he could reflect on the accomplishments of his tenure. The UN had spent $2.2 billion. It had renovated 700 schools, restored 17 rural power stations, trained thousands of teachers, recruited more than 14,000 civil servants for 15,000 jobs, established two army battalions, and trained and readied more than 1,500 police officers. A constitution had been developed and ratified, an assembly had been formed, and elections held. He had learned a valuable lesson about legitimacy: it was performance-based. People wanted results and the UN needed to show why they were beneficial to people on the ground, and they need to show that quickly.

They arrived at the airport to board their plane to leave East Timor. There was no celebration or tributes planned for his departure. Inside the plane, he rested his head on the window and was filled with melancholy. He pressed his hand up to the glass as if waving goodbye. As the plane lifted off, he turned away from the window, buried his head in Larriera's lap, and sobbed.

Sergio Vieira de Mello's Final Assignment

Still not sure of his next posting, Vieira de Mello drew on 30 years of accumulated earned leave and went traveling with Larriera for several months. This was probably the first time in his adult life that he felt truly suspended in time and space. He took Larriera to Bali, West Papua, Myanmar, Thailand, Laos, Cambodia, Vietnam, Macau, and Hong Kong. While in Thailand, they went to the Foreign Correspondents Club which had a wall-to-wall television where they watched Brazil defeat Germany in the World Cup finals.

The couple finally returned to New York in late July, Larriera returning to the public information job she held before taking her East Timor posting and preparing to take the GRE exams to apply to graduate programs in public policy. Annan finally decided to offer Vieira de Mello the job of UN High Commissioner for Human Rights, based in Geneva. Vieira de Mello did not wish to go back to a field job yet, so he accepted the offer. The position was one that called for someone to criticize governments for human rights transgressions, which was not a role that Vieira de Mello relished, since his strength was more in negotiating with governments to secure consensus. Some observers in the human rights field were skeptical of Vieira de Mello's willingness to criticize offending governments, as his predecessor (Mary Robinson, the former Irish president) had done to the United States over its treatment of prisoners at its Guantanamo Bay prison. Over this and other matters, the United States refused to support her bid for a second term in the position. After Robinson, Annan felt that Vieira de Mello might be a good bet to smooth out relations with the United States.

Vieira de Mello and Larriera spent the summer living in her studio flat in New York. He was determined not to let his new job get in the way of his personal life, which was now a priority. One potential benefit of moving back to Geneva was his proximity to his sons. His divorce was dragging on, and he had been advised by friends to do nothing to hasten or disrupt the process.

On October 12, 2002, several bombs exploded in and near a popular nightclub on the Indonesian island of Bali. More than 200 people were killed, many Australian youths. The Al Jazeera network broadcast a statement from Osama bin Laden, in which he said he had warned Australia not to send troops to join the UN's "despicable effort to separate East Timor" from Indonesia, and this bombing was in response to the Australian participation in East Timor. This was the second speech in which bin Laden had used East Timor's liberation from Indonesia as a rallying cry. He saw the liberation as an effort to divide Indonesia, "the most populous country in the Islamic world."

The Secretary General had a new assignment for his "go-to guy" before sending him to the High Commissioner post in Geneva. He needed him to serve as the UN representative in Iraq. It would be Sergio's last mission.

August 19, 2003

Vieira de Mello had a 4 p.m. meeting scheduled with Gil Loescher and Arthur Helton, American refugee experts. Loescher, 58, was a researcher from Oxford University, and Helton, 34, was based at the Council of Foreign Relations in New York. They were there to do a two-week "field assessment" of the situation on the ground in Iraq. Vieira de Mello was always skeptical of these assessments since their recommendations were often ill-advised and did not have much impact on actual operations. They had come from an hour-long briefing in the Green Zone with Paul Bremer, the head of the coalition provisional authority, who told them there were few security issues and that everything was under control.

But a flatbed truck was driving along Canal Road, a multilane highway separated by a canal. The flatbed looked similar to many commercial trucks, and at 4:26 p.m. the driver made a right turn onto the narrow unguarded access road that ran along the back of the Canal Hotel complex. Nobody paid much attention to the truck, since they mostly carried building supplies used to fortify the wall around U.N. headquarters or to renovate offices in nearby buildings. All that was visible on the bed of this truck was a metal casing that looked like the shell of an air conditioning unit. Underneath the casing, however, was a cone-shaped bomb the size of a large man. About 1,000 pounds of explosives were heading to the Canal Hotel. When the driver reached the hotel he turned toward a spot two stories beneath the occupants of Vieira de Mello's office.

Vieira de Mello began the meeting sitting directly across from Loescher and Helton. It was 4:27 p.m. Loescher remembers the blast as a bright and sudden glare of "a million flashbulbs."

Larriera was sitting in her small third-floor office at the top of the staircase. She had recently asked for Sergio's help in moving her desk against a wall in her office, and the move had just saved her life. Larriera had been spared any injury, so she walked down the hall in the direction of Vieira de Mello's office. The dust had filled the hallways so she could not see, but she thought Sergio would be worried about her and be trying to find her. She called out "Sergio, I'm here … Are you there?" As she continued to walk down the hallway toward a side door to Sergio's office, she saw light coming from the end of the corridor. But then she realized that the light she was seeing was the natural light from the afternoon sunshine, and she determined that the light she was seeing was because the corridor ended abruptly. Where there had once been a floor and a ceiling, now she could only see clouds and sunshine. She then tried to enter Sergio's office through the small office of his secretaries. There she got her first glimpse of the casualties from the blast, and the scale of the devastation finally struck her. She began screaming

"SERGIO." The passage in front of her was blocked by the beams and rubble piled high. He did not respond to her calls. She turned around, went back to the corridor, trying to find Sergio. This time, at the end of the corridor, she looked more carefully into the pit of rubble below, where she saw movement below. She considered jumping into the pit, but realized she might not survive the fall and might disturb more beams and other material in the still-settling building.

The floors and beams of Sergio's office had exploded upward and then crashed down. His third-floor office had effectively become the first floor. The ceiling of his office and the roof of the Canal had collapsed diagonally. Moving to the outside of the building, Larriera found a UN staffer who told her that Sergio had been found alive but trapped in a pile of rubble. Some of Vieira de Mello's staff had gone to the rear of the building to where they thought their boss's office might have settled amidst the rubble. They pulled away a concrete slab and created a slight hole which they looked into and shouted. Miraculously, Vieira de Mello answered, saying clearly "Jeff, my legs." They could not see him but they could hear him, and he was lucid, but while he knew his legs were injured, he could not describe the rest of his predicament. Pinned beneath the rubble he could neither feel nor see his legs. They also determined that a man nearby in the rubble was Gil Loescher, who had been meeting with Vieira de Mello. They went to find help and grabbed a U.S. soldier, William von Zehle, a Connecticut fireman who was assisting another part of the rescue operation. They went around to the opening where they had made contact with Loescher and Vieira de Mello. Von Zehle felt he could likely save Loescher, but realized that Vieira de Mello would need a separate rescue effort. He quickly went to the front of the building to get access to the shaft from the third floor and began working to get Loescher free.

When von Zehle had ventured 15 feet into the shaft he could see Loescher and another man to his right. He shouted to the man to ask if he was okay and the reply was that he was alive, von Zehle introduced himself as Bill and the man introduced himself as Sergio. Sergio asked, "I'm not going to get out of here, am I?" Bill reassured him, "You have my word. We'll get you both out." At the top of the shaft, three men appeared and von Zehle asked if any of them had any rescue training. One was a firefighter paramedic from New York City and von Zehle went to the top of the shaft to meet him and discuss the situation they were facing. His name was Andre Valentine and they spent the next few hours trying to extricate Gil and Sergio from the shaft.

Meanwhile, members of Bremer's staff were on-site trying unsuccessfully to get the appropriate equipment and materials to help with the rescue effort. Von Zehle and Valentine began the slow process of clearing enough debris to get Loescher free and then get access to Vieira de Mello. They had only a large women's purse and a curtain cord to ferry debris out to the opening above. The overall rescue operation was poorly coordinated and badly managed. Much of the confusion stemmed from "multiple dueling command structures and improper planning that gave rise to insufficient capacity."[8] In brief interactions with Vieira de Mello, Valentine tried to get him to pray with him. Vieira de Mello would have none of it, and he became angry toward Valentine. From the time of the blast at 4:28 p.m. to the time the rescue effort was stopped after dark, the most powerful military in the history of mankind was forced to rely for rescue on brute force, a curtain rope, and a woman's handbag.

As the minutes ticked by Vieira de Mello was growing less responsive. Valentine kept urging Sergio to stay awake and work with him to get rescued. Sergio asked, "I'm going to die, aren't I?" Valentine tried to urge him to have faith. By 7 p.m. Sergio stopped initiating conversation but would still respond lucidly when spoken to. His breathing became more labored around 7:30, and he seemed to be going into shock.

Valentine and von Zehle amputated both of Loescher's lower legs, wrestled him free and placed him on a makeshift stretcher, as men at the top of the shaft pulled him out. He was lucid enough to say thank you as he was put on a helicopter and taken to a hospital. Larriera had spent the first hour after the bombing scrambling between the third floor and the rear of the building. She had managed to talk briefly to Sergio through a gap in the rubble, but now was being kept away and did not have any current information about Sergio's condition. She implored a U.S. soldier to go to the rescuers and find out more for her. When the soldier returned he told her that Sergio had just been loaded on a helicopter and taken to a hospital. He said they had to amputate his legs but that he was alive.

She breathed a sigh of relief, but then had the feeling that the soldier was not credible. He assured her that the rescuers had told him that was Sergio on the helicopter. By 9 p.m. Larriera was still at the Canal Hotel awaiting news about Sergio. About 15 minutes after her conversation with the soldier, she overheard someone on Sergio's staff say that he was dead. She was informed at 11 p.m. that his body had already been taken to the American morgue. She was taken to a private home rented by some UN officials and given a sedative. Early the next morning friends helped her get to the morgue, "His body was there, but Sergio was gone." He was wearing his gold engagement ring. From his first day in Iraq he had kept on his nightstand an email that Larriera had sent him: "While Iraq is a deviation from our goal of permanently establishing ourselves and our life, nothing will separate us again. We are one, and we will walk this road of life together." She placed the email in his pocket. She sobbed as she left him, saying "I will always love you, Sergio."

Of all the blows the world has suffered from the many terrorist attacks of the past 30 years, perhaps the most impactful was the attack on the Canal Hotel which killed Sergio Vieira de Mello. Thought of by some as a cross between James Bond and Robert Kennedy, he blended many of the necessary features of the leaders that the world will need going forward, if we are to conquer the problems of the future – income inequality, climate change, public health challenges, persistent forms of racism. In the person of Sergio Vieira de Mello we had built a world statesman, and there have been few like him in world history, and we can only hope that on the horizon some will step forward.

Notes

1 Samantha Power, *Chasing the Flame, Sergio Vieira de Mello and the Fight to Save the World* (Penguin Press, New York, NY, 2008), page 10. Note the presence of earlier themes from this book in Power's description of how Sergio operated in these assignments: using a "gritty **pragmatism**"; not allowing his **ideals** to be dislodged; and having the ability to **reflect** critically on the tasks before him.
2 *Power, Chasing the Flame*, page 301.
3 Ibid., page 309.
4 Ibid., page 320.
5 Ibid., page 330.
6 Ibid., page 339.
7 Ibid., page 340.
8 Ibid., page 480.

Bibliography

Power, Samantha. *Chasing the Flame: One Man's Fight to Save the World.* London: Penguin Books, 2008.

EPILOGUE TO PART II

Lessons Learned from the Public Service Heroes

The profiles of public service heroes presented in this book are of two types: full-life portraits which cover childhood beginnings to the death of the subject (e.g., Harry Truman, Frances Perkins); and significant segments in which the subject accomplished something especially noteworthy (e.g., Abraham Lincoln and his Second Inaugural Address, Martin Luther King, Jr., and the Letter from the Birmingham Jail) accompanied by some useful context about their life.

Each of the dozen individuals profiled in this book was chosen for the instructive value of their lives and accomplishments. They are a diverse group:

> five white males (Lincoln, Sinclair, Truman, Marshall, and Robert Kennedy);
> one Hispanic male (Vieira De Mello);
> two African American males (Douglass, King);
> three white females (Paul, Perkins, Carson);
> and one African-American female (Wells).

The heroes hail from diverse backgrounds also in terms of economic status:

> many were from working-class families (e.g., Lincoln, Sinclair, Truman, Marshall, Wells, Carson, Paul, Perkins);
> one was a former slave (Douglass);
> one grew up in a clergyman's family (King);
> and two grew up in relative affluence (Kennedy, Vieira De Mello).

Many of the heroes were very skilled communicators, either as: *writers* (Sinclair, who had a career as a novelist, Wells, who was a newspaper reporter and publisher, Lincoln, who as a writer of masterful speeches, Carson, who wrote nature books and educated the world about the science of ecology, and Douglass, who wrote bestselling autobiographies), or as: *orators* (King, in his "I Have a Dream," speech, Kennedy, in his Day of Affirmation speech in South Africa, Douglass in many speeches during his lifetime, and Lincoln in his Gettysburg Address and the Second Inaugural Address).

Other heroes showed *leadership abilities* early in their careers: (King, as a pastor and civil rights leader; Kennedy, as U.S. Attorney General and a 1968 presidential candidate; Truman, as a captain in World War I, as a county judge, Senator, and President; Marshall, as a rising officer in the U.S. Army; and Vieira De Mello as a diplomat assigned to increasingly responsible and difficult posts by the United Nations).

Several themes that have dominated American history run through these profiles. The *quest for rights "guaranteed" by the Constitution* is the subject of six of the profiles. The stain of slavery and racism and the denial of woman's suffrage are persistent themes of several profiles, as several of the public service heroes (Lincoln, Douglass, Wells, Paul, King, and Kennedy) respond to slavery, civil rights, and suffrage battles in various ways. These battles continue to this day in their more modern forms, showing up as voter suppression efforts, instances of police and criminal justice system misconduct, and persistent racist behavior.

Three of the profiles show the importance of international relations. The premier example of the importance of attending to relationships with allies and other nations is in the George Marshall profile, in which he devises a plan to restore Europe after World War II by assembling a cooperative group of western European countries to determine how best to use American aid to fix their economies. These developments also had the important ancillary benefit of allowing the western European countries to resist the Communist pressures and enticements to join their sphere. In the example of Sergio Vieira de Mello, we can see the importance of keeping open communication lines with rivals and opponents to reach settlements to ensure peace and bring stability to troubled regions. In the profile of President Truman, we see an American president perform adroitly on the international stage to bring about peaceful arrangements, though he has little knowledge and even less experience dealing with the likes of Stalin and Churchill. His decisiveness in ending the war with Japan has been debated, but he likely saved thousands of American lives in bringing the war in the Pacific to an end. In an attempt to rally support and build pressure in America, Frederick Douglass and Ida Wells toured Europe for months at a time to lecture about racism (including lynching and slavery) in America.

In other profiles, we see public service heroes addressing troubling domestic issues such as environmental degradation, workplace safety, and food safety. Rachel Carson, a scientist with a flair for writing, acquaints the nation with the interdependence of all living things to warn us that when man tries to alter the balance of nature there are often difficult and unforeseen consequences for humans. Upton Sinclair, a writer and a socialist who became one of the nation's foremost "muckrakers," published his account of work practices and unsanitary conditions in the meatpacking industry and alerted Americans to dangers in the workplace, the unhealthy condition of their food, and the political power of the meatpacking industry.

The heroes discussed in this book contribute in many ways, but many of them are instrumental in getting significant social problems in front of the public and getting the problems on the agenda for public action.[1] They play a role in spotting an injustice and bringing it to the public's attention, or helping the public get a more precise sense of particular aspects of the problem. They can present the problem in memorable ways (e.g., King's letter from the Birmingham jail, or his "I Have a Dream Speech," Sinclair's book *The Jungle*, Ida Wells's newspaper accounts and reports about lynchings), they can engage legislators and policy-makers to develop options for addressing the issue, and even work with implementing agencies to develop the policies and mechanisms for delivering services and addressing particular aspects of the issue.

Mark Moore's conception of *creating public value* described in Chapter 3 also helps characterize the work of the heroes profiled in this book. Though he talks primarily about people who are managers in public sector organizations, much of what he says about creating public value pertains to anyone who is engaged in public service because he describes them as **explorers who, with others, seek to discover, define, and produce public value**. Many of the profiled heroes are engaged in defining what issues and problems need the attention of the public, and in what ways the public needs to be active on the issues. The work of discovering, defining, and producing public value is done with others. Many of the heroes speak up about issues in an attempt to reach out to the public and urge particular changes that they need to pursue. The term "*explorers*" fits the heroes in this book. They are seekers of positive, meaningful outcomes to produce value for the public. They are summoning others to join them in their quest to help the nation live up to the aspirations set forth in the founding documents.

This quest to be an explorer for creating public value is a perpetual one. It will continue as long as there are conditions to address, improvements to make, injustices to stop, ideals to pursue and achieve, and people willing to summon themselves and put their energy into making our nation better. It is for these people that this book was written.

Note

1 See Chapter 3 of this book, "A Philosophy for Reflective Practitioners: Creating Public Value and Solving Public Problems," and Chapter 4 of this book, "Implementing Public Policy and Using Networks," for discussions of how public issues get advanced onto the agenda for public actions such as legislation, rulemaking, or other initiatives. The discussion in Chapter 3 about how public issues emerge from the interaction of "three

streams" (problems, politics, and policies) and how they merge to open a window for change, describes how policy advocates and entrepreneurs promote a set of ideas and look for opportunities to move them forward. The discussion in Chapter 4 about the sets of actors that are important in various phases of the policy implementation process, describes the roles of actors in defining a public issue. Issues can be discovered, analyzed, and publicized by the media, academia, interest groups and advocates, legislators, and executive branch managers.

APPENDIX

Ripples of Hope

Sustaining Quotations for Public Servants

In Chapter 1, I cited Robert F. Kennedy, in his June 1966 speech at the Day of Affirmation celebration at the University of Cape Town in South Africa. In that speech, he said

> each time a man stands up for an ideal, or acts to improve the lot of others, he sends forth a tiny ripple of hope ... that can build a current that can sweep down the mightiest walls of oppressions and resistance.

This quotation, and others like it, can be beneficial to public servants to impart useful ideas in efficient and powerful ways. At many points in my own career, it was helpful to look to the words of authors, leaders, and public figures throughout history as a source of inspiration and uplift.

In Chapter 2 of this book, I pointed out the practice of Thomas Jefferson to keep a "commonplacing" book of notable quotations and passages of literature in a volume so he could consult them as needed. The quotations in this appendix constitute a portion of my commonplacing book assembled over 40 years of public service, offered to the current and coming generations of public servants. These quotations helped me at various points in my career, and I am sure they can inspire others.

The quotations are organized into elements needed by public servants described in Chapter 2, "The Attitude of a Public Servant." For each of these elements – idealism, altruism, pragmatism, moral courage, perseverance, and resilience – the quotations are listed in alphabetical order by the author's last name. In addition, a number of quotations appear under a category called "legacy" since so many of the quotes speak to creating a record of lasting accomplishments.

Idealism

Ideals offer a standard of perfection or excellence that can serve as the ultimate aim or objective of an endeavor. Ideals are often aspirational, and are sometimes viewed as impractical and beyond our reach. But ideals have value in developing and implementing public policy because they can serve as important benchmarks for achievement of public goals and outcomes.

> Citizen service is the very American idea that we meet our challenges not as isolated individual but as members of a true community, with all of us working together. Our mission is nothing less than to spark a renewed sense of obligation, a new sense of duty, a new season of service.
>
> *William Clinton*

In Chapter 7, I said that current and future public servants need certain qualities to be successful, including being "stewards of the public interest" both during and after their careers in public service. In this quote, the former president reinforces the need for citizens to work collectively to serve the public interest. From Marc Holzer, *A Call to Serve, Quotes on Public Service* (American Society for Public Administration/Suffolk University, Institute for Public Service), page 9.

> Lord make me an instrument of Thy Peace, where there is hatred let me sow love; where there is injury, pardon; where there is doubt, faith; where there is despair, hope; where there is sadness, joy. O Divine Master, grant that I may not so much seek to be consoled, as to console; to be understood as to understand; to be loved, as to love; for it is in giving that we receive, it is in pardoning that we are pardoned, and it is in dying that we are born to eternal life.
>
> *St. Francis of Assisi*

This famous passage, with which I became familiar from the funeral of my father-in-law James R. Pontius on 11/3/20 during the time I was writing this book, can be seen as a personal code that suggests behaviors that are commendable for public servants, and perhaps part of being a "reflective practitioner," as urged in Chapter 7.

> The moral test of a society is how that society treats those who are in the dawn of life, the children; those who are in the twilight of life, the

elderly; and those who are in the shadow of life, the sick, the needy, and the handicapped.

Hubert Humphrey

As mayor of Minneapolis, Senator from Minnesota, and as Vice President, Hubert Humphrey sponsored and passed many civil rights and social welfare laws during his storied career. Here he provides a way of assessing whether a society is meeting the needs of its most vulnerable. From Holzer, *ibid.*, page 20.

For I can assure you that we love our country, not for what it was, though it has always been great ... not for what it is, though of this we are deeply proud ... but for what it can someday can, and, through the efforts of us all, will someday be.

John F. Kennedy

President Kennedy, and his speechwriter/counselor Theodore Sorenson, authored much of the most moving and idealistic language about public service. Here, Kennedy states some of his best thoughts about the ideals for which he became known. From *Quotations of John F. Kennedy* (Applewood Books, Inc., Bedford, MA, 2008), page 32.

Few will have the greatness to bend history itself. But each of us can work to change a small portion of events, and in the total of all those acts will be written the history of this generation. It is from numberless diverse acts of courage and belief that human history is shaped. Each time a man stands up for an ideal, or acts to improve the lot of others, he sends forth a tiny ripple of hope. And crossing each other from a million different centers of energy and daring, those ripples can bring down the mightiest walls of oppression and resistance.

Robert F. Kennedy

This is an excerpt from Robert Kennedy's speech on the Day of Affirmation celebration at the University of South Africa in June, 1966. I think this quote stands as a kind of creed for public servants, inspiring them to use their energy to send forth "ripples of hope," in the face of oppression and resistance. This was displayed on the wall of every office I occupied throughout my career as a public servant. From MacAfee. Norman, *The Gospel According to RFK, Why It Matters Now* (Basic Books, New York, NY, 2008), page 178.

The future does not belong to those who are content with today, apathetic toward common problems and their fellow man alike, timid and fearful in the face of new ideas and bold projects. Rather it will belong to those who can blend vision, reason, and courage in a personal commitment to the ideals and great enterprises of American Society. Our future may lie beyond our vision, but it is not completely beyond our control. It is the shaping impulse of America that neither fate nor nature nor the irresistible tides of history, but the work of our own hands, matched to reason and principle, that will determine our destiny.

Robert F. Kennedy

This is also from the Day of Affirmation speech in South Africa. It tells current and future public servants they will need to blend vision, reason, and courage in a commitment to ideals, reinforcing the importance of idealism discussed in Chapter 2. From MacAfee, Norman, *ibid.*, page 179.

Never doubt that a small group of thoughtful committed citizens can change the world; indeed it is the only thing that ever has.

Margaret Mead

Endorsing the idea that change can be generated by any committed group of persons, and that public service is something that can be performed by a diverse group of people inside and outside of government, as mentioned in Chapter 1's "Elements of the New Public Service," Margaret Mead urges "thoughtful, committed citizens" to try their hand at changing the world. From Holzer, Marc, *ibid.*, page 5.

Public managers are explorers who, with the help of others, seek to discover, define, and produce public value.

Mark H. Moore

Moore is an academician who speaks very effectively to the practitioners of public service. Here he offers a succinct job description for people who lead government programs. Practitioners who seek and explore all opportunities to focus on creating public value will find many ways to produce value with the assets entrusted to them. From Moore, Mark H., *Creating Public Value, Strategic Management in Government* (Harvard University Press, Cambridge, MA, 1995), page 20.

Some men see things as they are and ask why. Other men see things that never were and ask why not?

George Bernard Shaw

Robert Kennedy used this as the final line of his daily stump speech in his 1968 presidential campaign. That campaign was full of Kennedy's idealistic rhetoric that raised the hopes of many Americans, and those hopes were dashed with his assassination in June, 1968, just weeks after the assassination of Rev. Martin Luther King, Jr. in April, 1968. Ted Kennedy also used this Shaw quote as the final line of his very moving eulogy for Robert Kennedy on June 8, 1968. From *Robert*

F. Kennedy: Promises to Keep, Memorable Writings and Statements (Hallmark Cards, Inc., Kansas City, MO, 1969), page 60.

> Do your little bit of good where you are, it is those little bits of good put together that overwhelm the world.
>
> *Desmond Tutu*

Similar to Robert Kennedy's "ripple[s] of hope that sweep down the mightiest walls of oppression and resistance," Tutu urges that we create improvements in our respective spheres of influence so they can accumulate and "overwhelm the world."

Altruism

Altruism is the principle and moral practice of concern for the welfare and happiness of other human beings. Altruists exhibit an unselfish regard for or devotion to the welfare of others. Altruism can be thought of as a primary motivator of those seeking careers in public service, a way of giving expression to their sense of compassion or empathy.

> I shall pass through this world but once. Any good therefore that I can do, or any kindness I can show to any human being, let me do it now. Let me not defer it or neglect it, for I shall not pass this way again.
>
> *Mahatma Gandhi*

Gandhi's famous entreaty about the urgency of doing good for others in the present moment stands out as an eloquent call for altruism. Public servants can be spurred by these words to use the resources and the authority entrusted to them to help citizens at every opportunity. From Holzer, Marc, *ibid.*, page 7.

> You can be filled with bitterness, with hatred, and a desire for revenge. Or we can make an effort, as Martin Luther King did, to understand, and to comprehend, and to replace that violence, that stain of bloodshed that has spread across our land, with an effort to understand with compassion and love.
>
> What we need in the United States is love and wisdom and compassion toward one another, and a feeling of justice toward those who still suffer within our own country, whether they be white or whether they be black. Aeschylus wrote: "In our sleep, pain that falls drop by drop upon the heart and in our own despair, against our will, comes wisdom through the awful grace of God." Let us dedicate ourselves to what the Greeks wrote so many years ago; to tame the savageness of men and make gentle the life of the

world. Let us dedicate ourselves to that, and say a prayer for our country and for our people.

Robert F. Kennedy

Robert Kennedy had only a few minutes to prepare to speak to a crowd of African-Americans in the Indianapolis ghetto who had not been told of the death of the Rev. Martin Luther King, Jr. earlier in the evening. The Indianapolis police told Kennedy he should not go into the scheduled location of the speech, because they could not guarantee his safety. Kennedy went anyway, and he begins his remarks by informing the crowd of King's murder, and empathizes with the crowd by pointing out that he had had a brother killed (the first time he had ever spoken publicly about the death of John Kennedy). He closes his speech with the words of Aeschylus urging them to learn from their pain, and offering a plea to "make gentle the life of the world." From McAfee, Norman, *ibid.*, page 98.

With malice toward none, with charity for all, with firmness in the right as God gives us to see the right, let us strive on to finish the work we are in: to bind up the hate and wounds; to care for him who shall have borne the battle, and for the widow and his orphan – to do all which may achieve and cherish a just, and a lasting peace, among ourselves, and with all nations.

Abraham Lincoln

In this book's profile of Abraham Lincoln, I focus on his second inaugural speech, considered to be his best speech in his long career of writing exceptional speeches, and many consider it the best speech ever by an American president. The speech occurred at a time when the Civil War was moving toward a conclusion, and Lincoln could have used the speech to update the nation about progress toward winning the war, or plans for reuniting the Union in the coming months. Instead, he urges individuals to find compassion for those they had just confronted on the battlefield, prescribing an approach for individuals to take to understand how to heal, and to work together to achieve a "just and lasting peace." From White, Ronald C., *Lincoln's Greatest Speech, the Second Inaugural* (Simon & Schuster, New York, NY, 2002), page 19.

There is no higher religion than human service. To work for the common good is the greatest creed.

Albert Schweitzer

Schweitzer, a philosopher and humanitarian, characterizes working for the common good and performing human service by saying there is no "higher religion." This is one of many quotes in this appendix that places serving the public and working for the common good as a noble way to spend a lifetime's work. From Holzer, Marc, *ibid.*, page 11.

Pragmatism

Public servants need an attitude that is grounded in practical possibilities. While they should never lose sight of the idealistic and altruistic possibilities or options that might be available to them, they need to be aware of: (1) the limits of the organization's fiscal and human resources; (2) the authority available to address a public problem; and (3) the capacity of their organization to engage a particular problem.

> Public managers have a bundle of assets entrusted to their stewardship. The task of public managers is to judge in what particular ways the assets entrusted can be redeployed to increase the value of the enterprises for which they are responsible.
> *From Mark H. Moore,* Creating Public Value, Strategic Management in Government, *pages 16, 39, see below*

> Operational managers should seek, find, and exploit opportunities to create public value. Greater public value can be produced by: 1) increasing the quantity or quality of public activities per resources expended; 2) making public organizations better able to identify and respond to citizens aspirations; 3) enhancing the fairness with which public sector organizations operate; 4) increasing their continuing capacity to respond and innovate.
> *From Mark H. Moore,* Creating Public Value, Strategic Management in Government, *page 211, see below*

> Those who would lead public organizations need an appropriate managerial temperament – a cool inner concentration which combines the psychological strength and energy that come from being committed to a cause coupled with a capacity for diagnosis, reflection, and objectivity.
> *From Moore, Mark H.* Creating Public Value, Strategic Management in Government *(Harvard University Press, Cambridge, MA, 1995), page 308, see below*

In these three quotations, Moore gives pragmatic advice to practitioners about what it takes to excel in public service and in managing government programs, and he specifies ways in which greater public value can be produced. He also supplies a set of behaviors to guide public managers, "a cool inner concentration that combines the strength and energy that comes from being committed to a cause coupled with a capacity for diagnosis, reflection, and objectivity." I used this quote to occasionally ask if my own behavior was consistent with this standard.

Moral Courage

Moral courage involves the bravery to take action for moral reasons despite the risk of adverse consequences. Courage is required to take action when one has doubts or fears about the consequences, and moral courage, therefore, requires deliberation and careful thought.

> Few are willing to brave the disapproval of their fellows, the censure of their colleagues, the wrath of society. Moral courage is a rarer commodity than bravery in battle or great intelligence. Yet it is the one essential vital quality for those who seek to change a world that yields most painfully to change.
>
> *Robert F. Kennedy*

The speeches and writings of John and Robert Kennedy are replete with references to courage, which they clearly valued very highly. Robert Kennedy particularly revered moral courage, calling it "the one essential vital quality for those who seek to change [the] world..." Part II of this book, "Examples for Effective Service," contains many examples of people serving the public and showing moral courage to take a stand on issues that would have personal consequences.

Perseverance

During a public service career there can be many instances when obstacles block efforts to improve the performance of individuals or organizations. Public servants need to be aware of these obstacles, understand their causes, adapt and learn to work with them, overcome them, or to move them so they no longer obstruct progress.

> Not everything that is faced can be changed. But nothing can be changed until it is faced.
>
> *James Baldwin*

Baldwin describes the first step in perseverance, turning to face the present challenge. Only when a person decides to confront and address the problem can it be resolved. From Holzer, Marc, *ibid.*, page 15.

> A disposition to persevere, and an ability to improve, taken together, would be my standard of a statesman.
>
> *Edmund Burke*

Burke offers a concise, two-ingredient formula for his standard of a statesman. Finding perseverance and the ability to improve as the indispensable elements of a statesman, which always struck me as the qualities truly necessary for any public servant. The ability to bounce back after setbacks or obstacles and the capacity to improve from the experience, will lead to much success as a public servant. From Holzer, Marc, *ibid.*, page 59.

> Every day you make progress. Every step may be fruitful. Yet there will stretch out before you an ever-lengthening, ever ascending, ever-improving path. You know you never get to the end of the journey. But this, so far from discouraging, only adds to the joy and glory of the climb.
>
> *Winston Churchill*

This is Churchill's version of the idea that the "journey means more than the destination." Indeed, Churchill asserts that "you never get to the end of the journey, [and it] only adds to the joy and glory of the climb." In Chapter 2, "The Attitude of a Public Servant," I discuss the ability of public servants to resolutely persist in spite of obstacles, and that persistence can even help buy time for incremental progress toward larger goals.

> In the end the great truth will have been learned, that the quest is greater than what is sought, the effort finer than the prize, the victory cheap and hollow were it not for the rigor of the game.
>
> *Supreme Court Justice Benjamin Cardozo*

Another in the family of quotations about the journey being more important than the destination, Cardozo's idea helps us see the value of a long-term outlook ("the quest is greater that the prize") toward our careers in public service.

> Everything can be taken from a man but one thing: the last of the human freedoms, to choose one's own attitude in any given set of circumstances, to choose one's own way. ... Between stimulus and response there is a space. In that space is our power to choose our own response. In our response lies our growth and freedom.
>
> *Viktor Frankl*

The practical value of Frankl's idea about the last of the human freedoms (i.e., to choose one's own way in any given set of circumstances), and the space between stimulus and response should not be overlooked. Being aware of that space in day-to-day discourse with colleagues, can help lead to conversations that are more focused and productive in solving problems or managing relationships. From Frankl, Viktor, *Man's Search for Meaning* (Beacon Press, Boston, MA, 2006 edition), page 66.

Those things that are hard, instruct.

Benjamin Franklin

Franklin reminds us things we do that are difficult almost always have instructive value. Part of being a reflective practitioner, as discussed in Chapter 3, is the ability to reflect on one's actions so as to engage in a process of continuous learning. This concept of the "instructive value" of situations and episodes in day-to-day activities became increasingly more important as I reached the management and executive portions of my career. I would ask myself and others, "What does this episode/ situation/ interaction teach us as we go forward toward fulfilling an objective?"

Encourage all your virtuous dispositions, and exercise them whenever an opportunity arises; being assured that they will gain strength by exercise, as a limb of the body does, and that exercise will make them habitual.

Thomas Jefferson

Jefferson urges that we practice using our "virtuous dispositions" to make sure that they are always strong and effective when called upon. The more we exercise the virtuous dispositions, the stronger they will be, just like a muscle that is strengthened by exercise. From Holzer, Marc, *ibid.*, page 42.

What really counts is not the immediate act of courage or valor, but those who bear the struggle day in and day out – not the sunshine patriots, but those who are willing to stand for a long period of time.

John F. Kennedy

Kennedy echoes others in crediting those who "are willing to stand for a long period of time." As I accumulated a long record of public service (as one of those who was "bear[ing] the struggle day in and day out"), this quotation became more important to me. It pays tribute to those who remain in public service, sometimes in the same organization, and contribute in a variety of ways to the public good. From *Quotations of John F. Kennedy* (Applewood Books, Bedford, MA, 2008), page 15.

The dogmas of the quiet past are inadequate to the stormy present. The occasion is piled high with difficulty, and we must rise with the occasion. As our case is new, so we must think anew and act anew. We must disenthrall ourselves, and then we shall save our country.

Abraham Lincoln

Lincoln's suggestion that we must "think anew and act anew," to face our current situation struck me as appropriate advice at many points in my public service career when a new challenge emerged and demanded attention. From *Quotations of Abraham Lincoln* (Applewood Books, Carlisle, MA, 2003), page 17.

> You gain strength, courage, and confidence by every experience in which you really stop to look fear in the face. You must do the thing you think you cannot do.
>
> *Eleanor Roosevelt*

Eleanor Roosevelt had her own public service career separate from her husband the president, becoming an icon for humanitarian causes and a much-followed columnist and thought leader. In this quotation, she counsels that you gain strength by engaging causes and issues that make you stop and look fear in the face, doing things that you did not think you could do. From Binker, Mary Jo, editor, *What Are We For? The Words and Ideals of Eleanor Roosevelt* (Harper Collins Publishers, New York, NY, 2019).

> It is not the critic who counts, not the man who points out how the strong man stumbles or where the doer of deeds could have done better. The credit belongs to the man who is actually in the arena, whose face is marred by dust and sweat and blood, who strives valiantly, who errs and comes up short again and again. Because there is no effort without error or short-coming, but he who knows the great enthusiasms, the great devotions, who spends himself for a worthy cause, at the best knows, in the end, the triumph of high achievement, and who, at the worst, if he fails, at least he fails while daring greatly, so that his place shall never be with those cold and timid souls who know neither victory nor defeat.
>
> *Theodore Roosevelt*

This "man in the arena" quotation has been used (and misused) countless times to describe various heroes (and faux heroes) in the world of public affairs, since it was first uttered by Theodore Roosevelt. The quote describes instances when great toil ("spends himself for a worthy cause") is used to accomplish something significant, and it is also used to discredit those who stand on the sidelines and heckle the "doer of deeds." From Holzer, Marc, *ibid.*, page 53.

Resilience

Resilience is the ability to bounce back, though different fields use the term to mean slightly different things. In engineering, resilience refers to the degree to which a structure or building can return to a baseline state after being disturbed. In ecology, it connotes an ecosystem's ability to resist being irrevocably degraded. In psychology, it signifies the capacity of an individual to deal effectively with trauma.

In business, it is used to mean putting in place backups to ensure continuous operations in the face of disaster. These definitions have two essential aspects: continuity and recovery in the face of change.

> Most of the important things in the world have been accomplished by people who have kept on trying when there seemed to be no hope at all.
>
> *Dale Carnegie*

People who are resilient are capable of functioning with a sense of core purpose, meaning, and forward momentum in the face of trauma. Public servants need a capacity to overcome, steer through or bounce back from adversity.

> Human beings are not born once and for all on the day their mothers give birth to them, but life obliges them over and over again to give birth to themselves.
>
> *Gabriel Garcia Marquez*

One of my favorite authors, Gabriel Garcia Marquez drops sharp insights into the flow of his stories, and this one from his greatest novel is an eloquent description of resilience. In Chapter 2 of this book, "The Attitude of a Public Servant" the definitions of resilience used by various fields cannot rival Marquez's definition utilizing birth and rebirth. From Marquez, Gabriel Garcia, *Love in the Time of Cholera* (Penguin Books, New York, NY, 1988), page 165.

Legacy

Many of the leaders whose quotes appear in this appendix offer ideas about having an impact and creating a set of accomplishments that will be felt for many years. Most public servants will not assume positions and responsibilities that will allow them to "bend the arc of history," but they can be conscientious about the sphere of events they influence, and they can use their service to create a record of accomplishments.

> The tragedy is not to die. The tragedy is to die with commitments undefined, convictions unexpressed, and with service unfulfilled.
>
> *Former U.S. Senator Bill Bradley (D-NJ)*

Former Senator Bill Bradley of New Jersey, former two-time champion professional basketball player with the New York Knickerbockers, NCAA All-American basketball star at Princeton University, Olympic gold medalist, Rhodes scholar, and native of my home state of Missouri, was a figure I admired during his entire career in public service. He expresses here that dying with commitments undefined, convictions unexpressed, and service unfulfilled – i.e., with contributions still to make – is the true tragedy. He is urging, in the parlance of the professional basketball player, to "leave it all on the court" by the end of the game, to make the maximum effort with the life you are given.

> Perhaps we can bring the day when children will learn from their earliest days that being fully man and fully woman means to give one's life to the liberation of the brother who suffers.
>
> *Cesar Chavez*

Chavez here suggests making your contribution through service to "the brother who suffers." This comports with the element of altruism that this book urges all public servants to utilize in their careers. From Holzer, Marc, *ibid.*, page 24.

> What is the use of living, if it is not to strive for noble causes, and make the muddled world a better place for those who will live in it after we have gone.
>
> *Winston Churchill*
> *see below*

> We must always be ready to make sacrifices for the great causes; only in that way shall we live to keep our souls alive.
>
> *Winston Churchill*

Churchill asserts that our involvement in the great and noble causes of the day is a way to keep our souls alive and make the world a better place for those who follow. For all his gruff manners and blunt demeanor, Churchill is clearly an idealist and an altruist at heart and recommends it as a way of living.

> Try not to be a man of success, but rather a man of value.
>
> *Albert Einstein*
> *see below*

> Only a life lived for others is a life worthwhile.
>
> *Albert Einstein*

Einstein, through these quotes and his lifetime of actions, proves that he, like Churchill, is also an idealist and altruist. These elements often travel together in the same person, and in many public servants.

> If you would not be forgotten as soon as you are dead and rotten, either write things worth reading, or do things worth writing.
>
> *Benjamin Franklin*

Here Franklin urges, in rather graphic terms, to spend your life doing things worth reading or writing about.

> I think as life is action and passion, it is required of a man that he should share the passion and the action of his time, at peril of being judged not to have lived.
>
> *Oliver Wendell Holmes*

This was the political slogan of the State Senator I worked for in my three years working in the Missouri State Senate. By making this part of his political persona, I believe he was signaling his intention to be an aspirational leader. Many of the people profiled in Part II of this book were in the ranks of aspirational leaders.

> Thus it is our task in our time and in our generation to hand down undiminished to those who come after us, as was handed down to us by those who went before, the natural wealth and beauty which is ours.
>
> *John F. Kennedy*
> *see below*

> For in the final analysis, our most basic common link, is that we all inhabit this small planet, we all breathe the same air, we all cherish our children's future, and we are all mortal.
>
> *John F. Kennedy*
> *see below*

> I am certain that after the dust of centuries has passed over our cities, we, too, will be remembered not for victories or defeats in battle or politics, but for our contributions to the human spirit.
>
> *John F. Kennedy*

John Kennedy summons us to act in the interests of future generations, assert a higher calling for leadership (our contributions to "the human spirit") and he calls on us so that we will truly be remembered for our highest aspirations. From *Quotations of John F. Kennedy* (Applewood Books, Bedford, MA, 2008), pages 15, 25.

> My brother need not be idealized or enlarged in death beyond what he was in life.
>
> He should be remembered simply as a good and decent man, who saw wrong and tried to right it, saw suffering and tried to heal it, saw war and tried to stop it.

Those of us who loved him and who take him to his rest today pray that what he was to us, and what he wished for others, will someday come to pass for all the world.

As he said many times, in many parts of this nation to those he touched and those who sought to touch him:

Some men see things as they are and say, why. I dream things that never were and say, why not.

Edward M. Kennedy

These are the final few paragraphs in Edward Kennedy's moving eulogy for Robert Kennedy. It stands as an eloquent tribute to the man who was hitting his stride as a national leader when he was cut down by the attack of an assassin. In Part II of this book, "Examples for Effective Public Service," Robert Kennedy stands as a beacon of hope at a critical time for America, amid the tumult of 1968 with its protests over war, civil rights strife, and general feeling that things were coming apart. From Kennedy, Robert F., *Promises to Keep* (Hallmark Books, Kansas City, MO, 1969), page 60.

The time is always right to do what is right.

Rev. Martin Luther King, Jr.

Rev. King urges public servants and others never to hesitate to do what is right, as the time to do so is always right. Public servants should utilize this heightened sense of urgency in pursuing large and small objectives. From Holzer, Marc, *ibid.*, page 27.

I learned that courage was not the absence of fear, but the triumph over it … The brave man is the one who does not feel afraid, but he who conquers that fear.

Nelson Mandela

Nelson Mandela knew what it was like to live with fear, and here he advises others to learn to manage that fear in order to conquer it, and triumph over it. Mandela was an exemplar of the element of "moral courage" described in Chapter 2, "The Attitude of a Public Servant." From Holzer, Marc, *ibid.*, page 79.

Progress occurs when courageous, skillful leaders seize the opportunity to change things for the better.

Harry S. Truman

In simple, direct prose, Truman describes the main task of leaders – i.e., to change things for the better. From a brochure of the Truman Library Institute.

> Keep working on a plan. Make no little plans. Make the biggest plan you can think of, and spend the rest of your life carrying it out.
>
> *Harry S. Truman*

Truman, who presided over a period when events came rushing at him, advises others to "make no little plans." From Keyes, Ralph, *The Wit & Wisdom of Harry Truman, a Treasury of Quotations, Anecdotes, and Observations* (Gramercy Books, New York, NY, 1995), page 44.

> I would much rather be an honorable public servant and known as such than to be the richest man in the world.
>
> *Harry S. Truman*

When the University of Missouri established the Harry S. Truman School of Public Affairs, they adopted this quotation as a kind of slogan. Throughout his life, accumulating money for himself and his family did not matter much to Harry Truman. Instead, doing his duty and finishing the tasks before him were his focus. After leaving office, he returned home to Independence, where he turned down opportunities to serve for money on various boards, never trading on his good name. From Keyes, Ralph, *ibid.*, page 52.

> I have tried my best to give the nation everything I had in me ... I always quote one epitaph which is on a tombstone in the cemetery in Tombstone, Arizona. It says, "Here lies Jack Williams. He done his damndest." I think that is the greatest epitaph that a man can have.
>
> *Harry S. Truman*

The straightforward nature of this epitaph would, of course, appeal to Harry Truman. Being able to say, simply, he did "his damndest," succinctly described what he set out to do as President. It seemed as if Truman understood well the bargain that is at the heart of this book: you take the oath and receive the opportunity to serve the public, doing your damndest to carry out your duties to the best of your abilities. From Keyes, Ralph, *ibid.*, page 61.

AUTHOR'S NOTE

The idea for this book started in a hospital bed at the Pauley Heart Institute, at the Virginia Commonwealth University Medical Center in Richmond, Virginia, in 2014. I had received a heart transplant two days earlier, and having assured myself I was now going to survive and come through this experience, I began to think about how I was going to use the "new time" I had been granted. After considering such things as where I wanted to travel or what other experiences I wanted to have, I began to think about larger purposes I wanted to serve.

Having spent my career in public service, and knowing I was going to end my career in government service not long after emerging from the hospital, I began to think about how I would fill the void in my life after retiring about six short months later. I still wanted to teach about public service or public affairs, and there could still be opportunities to do that.

But then I thought back to one of my frustrations about my master's degree program at the University of Missouri some 30 years earlier, and my experience as an adjunct faculty member at George Mason University over the previous 20 years. I could rarely find a book that spoke to practitioners of public service. With only about three exceptions, I only was able to find books by public affairs academicians that were written for other academicians, leaving practitioners without a literature that spoke to the "how" of public service. Nothing seemed to contain information that would be immediately useful for practitioners to know, and that could help them be effective in their jobs as analysts, implementers, managers, and executives in public service.

Perhaps I could fill that void by using some of my "new time" to write that book, a combination of useful ideas for practitioners and examples of people who have contributed something important to the public good. That is the book you now have in your hands.

I considered drafting an epilogue section about "public service in the time of Donald Trump." I would focus on his dysfunctional handling of the Covid-19 pandemic and his insistence on spreading the Big Lie about his election defeat. There were certainly many sources to draw from about these failures. But when I finished drafting this section, it seemed completely out of place in a book written to encourage students and young practitioners to give themselves to a life in public service. Although the Trump years became a major motivation to write this book, I have chosen not to dwell on his disastrous tenure in office in a book designed to encourage the view of public service as a noble calling. Frankly, after some of the comments I received from reviewers about the negative tone the Trump section added to the book, I decided he is not worthy of having a place in this book.

One of the people I have most admired throughout my life is Bill Bradley, the former Democratic senator from New Jersey, former basketball great for the New York Knicks and Princeton University, and a native of my home state of Missouri. He excelled at two things I loved in my life – basketball and public service. One of the most meaningful quotes I have ever read came from him, and it sums up what it means to live a life devoted to serving others: **"The tragedy is not to die. The tragedy is to die with commitments undefined, convictions unexpressed, and with service unfulfilled."**

With the publication of this book, I have defined a commitment (to those who serve the public), expressed many convictions I hold (about the best ways to serve the public), and fulfilled my service (to the public and those who serve it).

Thank you for reading my book.

ACKNOWLEDGMENTS

By the time a book manuscript is ready to be submitted to the publisher (in my case, Routledge/Taylor and Francis Group), an author has many people to thank for assistance in writing and producing the book. This effort was greatly aided by many people who helped during the journey to publication.

First and foremost, my wife Ann Pontius served as proofreader, editor, sounding board, and chief supporter during this effort. In addition to all these contributions, her patience with my writing routine, was much appreciated. I was pinned down for many days when we would otherwise have been exploring the area we have retired to in Virginia's Shenandoah Valley or enjoying the many pleasures of our new hometown of Staunton, Virginia.

A panel of former colleagues, friends, and others were particularly helpful during the early stages of writing. My former colleagues from the U.S. Environmental Protection Agency, some of whom have retired, others who are still working there, were crucial in affirming early in the writing that I had ideas that were worth expressing. In this group, I include and thank, Marion Herz, Robert Tolpa, Robbi Farrell, and Betsy Smidinger. Also in this panel were two of my closest friends, Luiz Guimaraes, my "brother from another mother" who I met on an EPA recruiting trip to my alma mater, the University of Missouri, many years ago and who has been a life-long friend since, and Steve Narrow, who I met many years ago on the basketball courts of St. Louis County and with whom we renewed our friendship many years later. Their reactions and suggestions at various points in the text made me consider ideas that needed more thought and clarity.

Two newer friends in my life, who I have gotten to know since retiring and moving to Staunton, Virginia in 2015, also contributed to this book. Retired U.S. Marine Colonel Michael Cathey was an inspiration, sounding board, and adviser during the writing of the book. Michael is as well-read as anyone I have met, approachable, and full of useful ideas and insights. On several short road trips during the course of this project, I spoke at length with Michael about this book, and he was always a willing participant in these discussions, getting me to examine my purposes about what I wanted to contribute to the public affairs literature. Also, Ed Piper, of Staunton, who I met through the Osher Lifelong Learning Institute (OLLI) at the University of Virginia, where I took some of the courses that Ed has taught for OLLI, has been a useful confidante and supporter of this project. Ed is a former professor, former education administrator at the university level, and an ordained minister – he has far-ranging expertise in many subjects. Following Ed's example, I have taught several OLLI courses (one on the events of 1968, one on the life of Robert Kennedy, and a third on profiles in public leadership which I taught with Ed) to cover subjects I was unable to cover during my 20 years teaching at George Mason University.

I also want to mention two other folks from Staunton. Each year, Staunton hosts the Heifetz International Music Institute and its Festival of Concerts, for which they select promising students from all over the world to perform 60 classical music concerts during the months of July and August. The Institute's CEO Ben Roe and its Artistic Director Nicholas Kitchen (of the Borromeo Quartet) are the two most responsible for selecting students, selecting the music they will perform, and getting faculty to coach the students and perform at the festival. They have brought classical music into my life these last few years. In 2019, one concert included the Mendelson Octet in E flat major, op.20, which my wife Ann and I loved. I listened to it each morning as I began to write for that day. It became part of my routine to propel my writing, filling me with the right feelings and emotions to start my day.

I would also like to thank the surgeons, cardiologists, other attending physicians, nurses, and staff at the Pauley Heart Center of the Medical Center of Virginia Commonwealth University, who brought me through two major surgeries; first, to implant an artificial heart (on June 18, 2013) which served to keep me alive and gave me a one-year bridge to a heart transplant; second, they worked with the United Network for Organ Sharing to find a donor heart one year later and they implanted a new heart (on June 25, 2014) donated by a family that still remains anonymous to me eight years later. I literally would not be here without any of these folks, and that team includes my wife Ann, who has managed my care during the artificial heart period and after the transplant. The skill and caring of all these people has brought me to this day.

Finally, I would like to thank Guy Adams, Professor Emeritus at the Harry S. Truman School of Government and Public Affairs at the University of Missouri in Columbia, Missouri. After struggling to find the right publisher, he and his co-author Danny Balfour at Grand Valley State University (together they authored *Unmasking Administrative Evil* in 2004) opened the door for me to meet Laura Varley at the Routledge/Taylor and Francis Group. Laura's patience explaining and overseeing the publishing process, and her encouragement about the book I wanted to write came to me at a time when I was beginning to question whether I could finish this project. During the preparations for submitting this manuscript, I was assisted by Joshua Henson of Mary Baldwin University, in Staunton, Virginia, who brought the needed energy to help put the manuscript submission to Routledge across the finish line.

INDEX